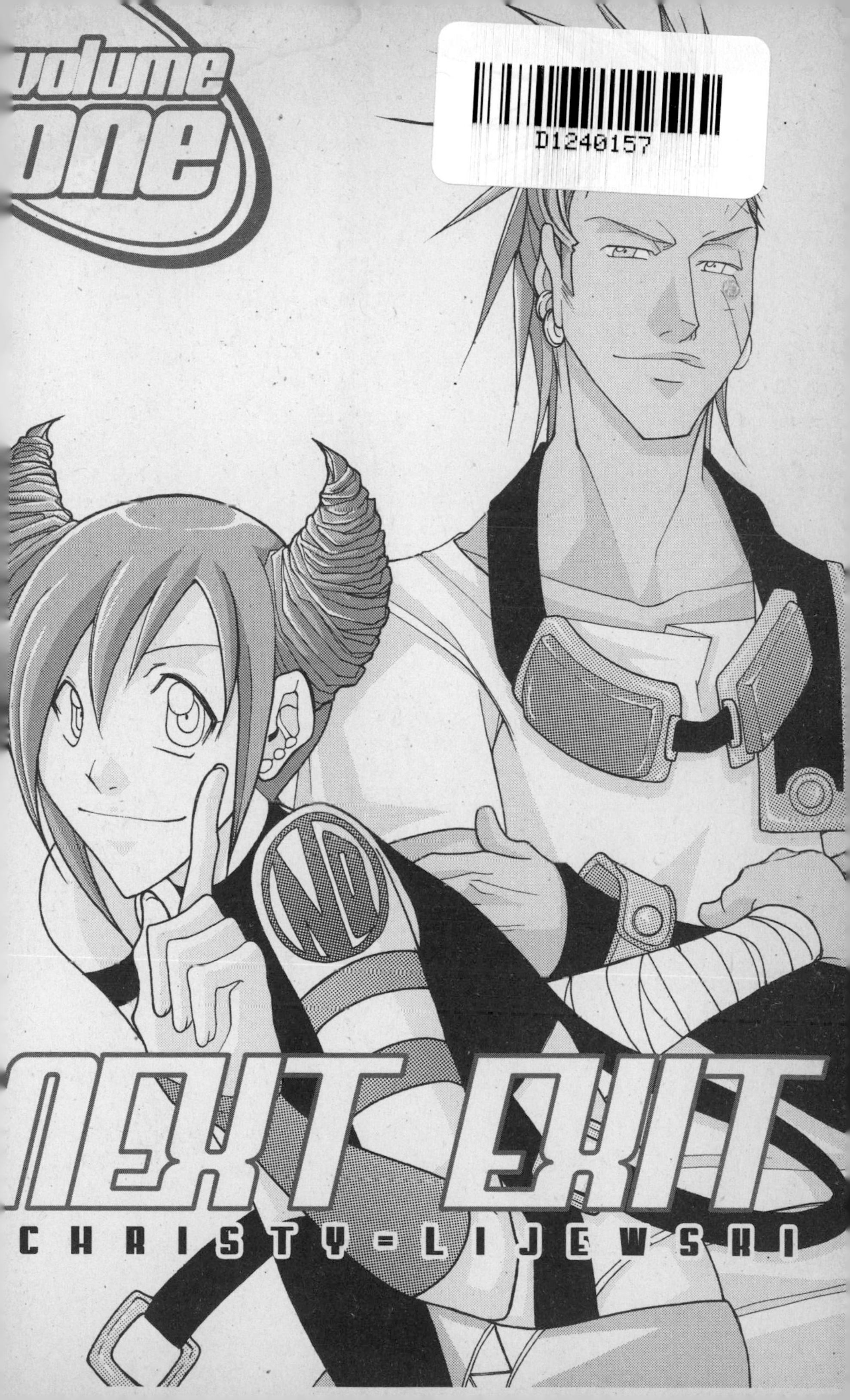
volume one
NEXT EXIT
CHRISTY=LIJEWSKI

WRITTEN AND ILLUSTRATED BY
Christy Lijewski

TONE ASSIST BY
Catarina Sarmento

Published by SLG Publishing
Dan Vado, President and Publisher
Jennifer de Guzman, Editor-in-Chief
Deb Moskyok, Director of Sales

P.O. Box 26427
San Jose, CA 95113

WWW.SLAVELABOR.COM

Next Exit Volume 1 collects issue
1–6 of *Next Exit.*

Second Printing: July 2006
ISBN 1-59362-037-3

Next Exit Volume 1

BY CHRISTY LIJEWSKI

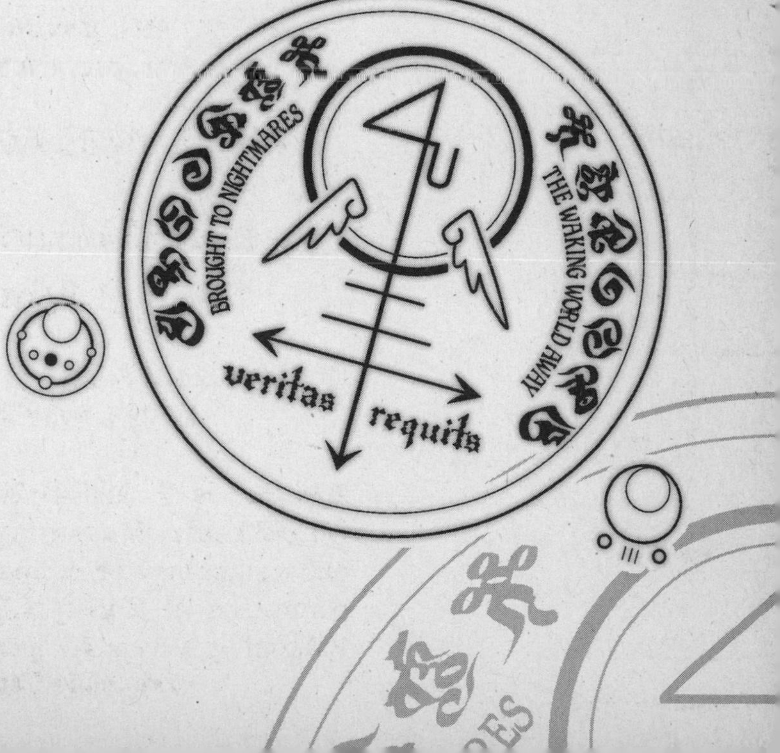

BROUGHT TO NIGHTMARES
THE WAKING WORLD AWAY
veritas
requits

Table of Contents

Chapter 1: Checkmate Start

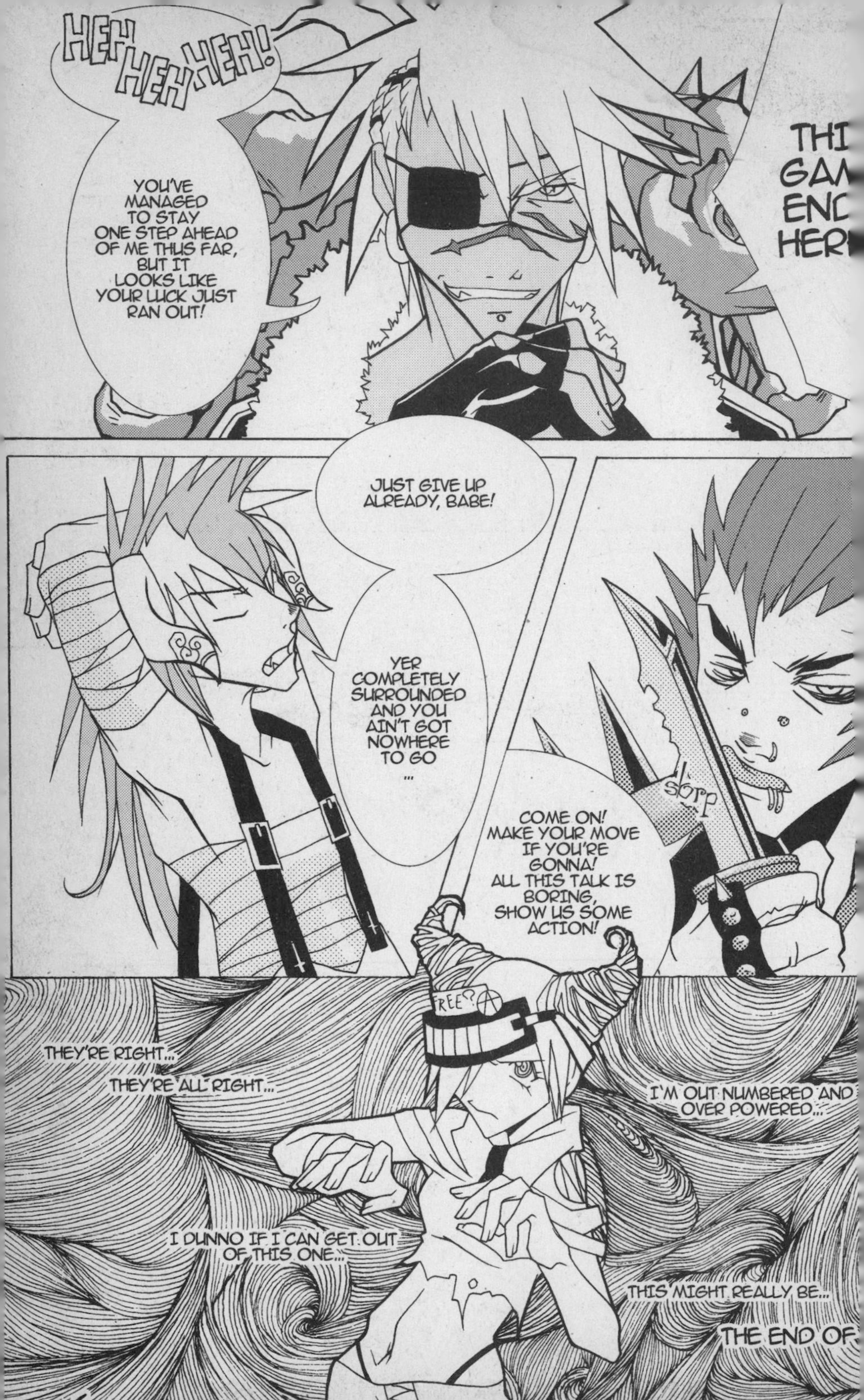
HEH HEH HEH!
YOU'VE MANAGED TO STAY ONE STEP AHEAD OF ME THUS FAR, BUT IT LOOKS LIKE YOUR LUCK JUST RAN OUT!
THI
GAM
END
HER
JUST GIVE UP ALREADY, BABE!
YER COMPLETELY SURROUNDED AND YOU AIN'T GOT NOWHERE TO GO ...
COME ON! MAKE YOUR MOVE IF YOU'RE GONNA! ALL THIS TALK IS BORING, SHOW US SOME ACTION!
slorp
FREE?
THEY'RE RIGHT...
THEY'RE ALL RIGHT...
I'M OUT NUMBERED AND OVER POWERED...
I DUNNO IF I CAN GET OUT OF THIS ONE...
THIS MIGHT REALLY BE...
THE END OF

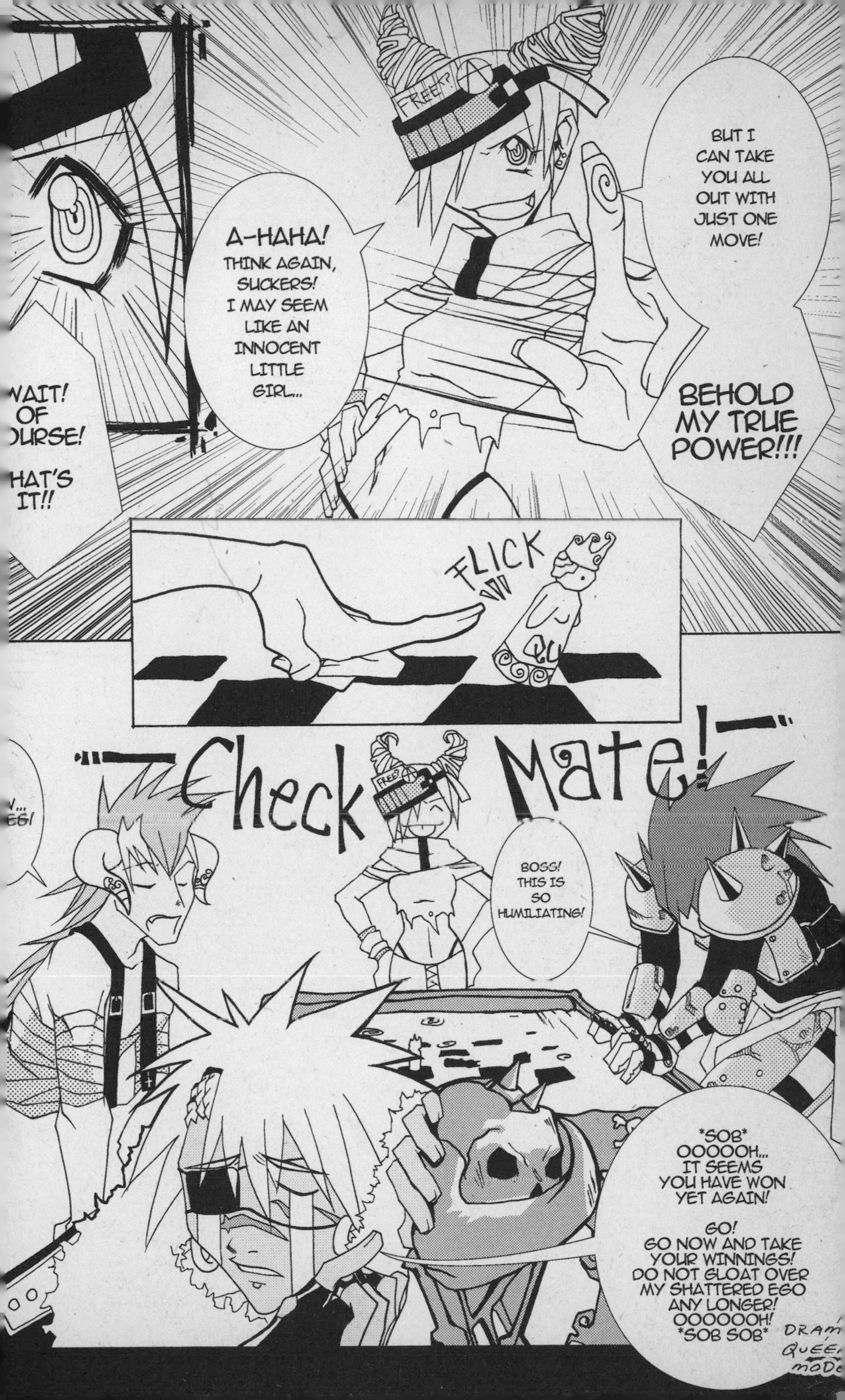

BUT I CAN TAKE YOU ALL OUT WITH JUST ONE MOVE!
A-HAHA! THINK AGAIN, SUCKERS! I MAY SEEM LIKE AN INNOCENT LITTLE GIRL...
WAIT! OF OURSE! HAT'S IT!!
BEHOLD MY TRUE POWER!!!
FLICK
FREE?
"Check Mate!"
BOSS! THIS IS SO HUMILIATING!
SOB OOOOOH... IT SEEMS YOU HAVE WON YET AGAIN!
GO! GO NOW AND TAKE YOUR WINNINGS! DO NOT GLOAT OVER MY SHATTERED EGO ANY LONGER! OOOOOOH! *SOB SOB*
DRAM QUEEN MODE

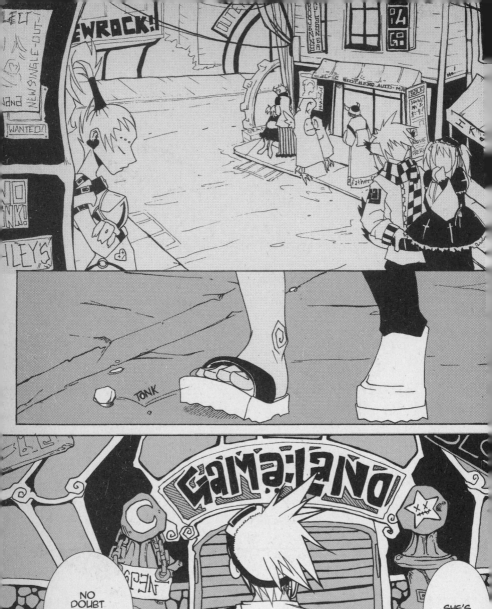

NO DOUBT ABOUT IT...

SHE'S HERE.

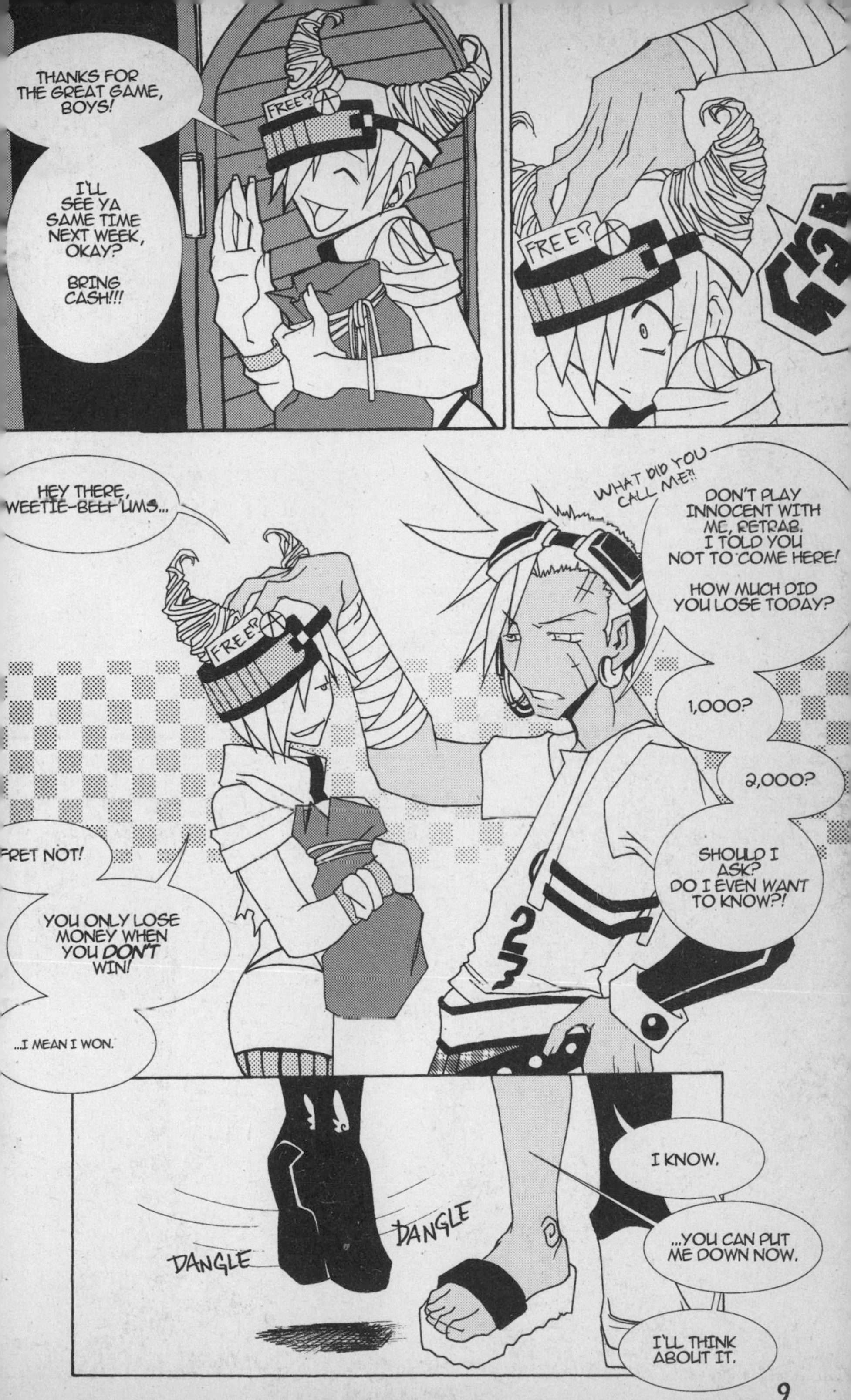
THANKS FOR THE GREAT GAME, BOYS!
I'LL SEE YA SAME TIME NEXT WEEK, OKAY?
BRING CASH!!!
HEY THERE, WEETIE-BEET'UMS...
WHAT DID YOU CALL ME?!
DON'T PLAY INNOCENT WITH ME, RETRAB. I TOLD YOU NOT TO COME HERE!
HOW MUCH DID YOU LOSE TODAY?
1,000?
2,000?
SHOULD I ASK? DO I EVEN WANT TO KNOW?!
FRET NOT!
YOU ONLY LOSE MONEY WHEN YOU *DON'T* WIN!
...I MEAN I WON.
I KNOW.
DANGLE
DANGLE
...YOU CAN PUT ME DOWN NOW.
I'LL THINK ABOUT IT.

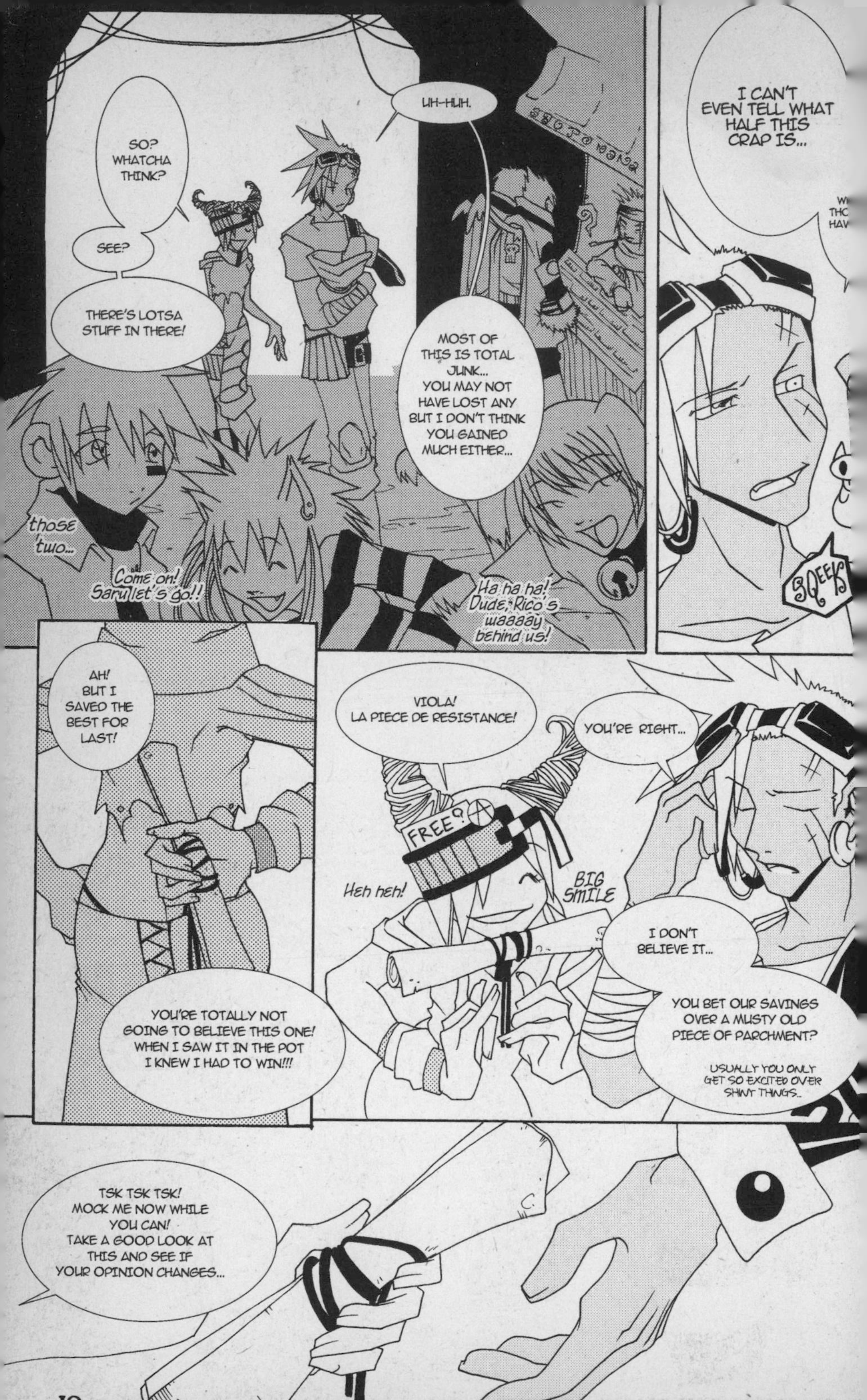
SO?
WHATCHA
THINK?
SEE?
THERE'S LOTSA
STUFF IN THERE!
UH-HUH.
MOST OF
THIS IS TOTAL
JUNK...
YOU MAY NOT
HAVE LOST ANY
BUT I DON'T THINK
YOU GAINED
MUCH EITHER...
those
two...
Come on!
Saru let's go!!
Ha ha ha!
Dude, Rico's
waaaay
behind us!
I CAN'T
EVEN TELL WHAT
HALF THIS
CRAP IS...
AH!
BUT I
SAVED THE
BEST FOR
LAST!
YOU'RE TOTALLY NOT
GOING TO BELIEVE THIS ONE!
WHEN I SAW IT IN THE POT
I KNEW I HAD TO WIN!!!
VIOLA!
LA PIECE DE RESISTANCE!
FREE
Heh heh!
BIG
SMILE
YOU'RE RIGHT...
I DON'T
BELIEVE IT...
YOU BET OUR SAVINGS
OVER A MUSTY OLD
PIECE OF PARCHMENT?
USUALLY YOU ONLY
GET SO EXCITED OVER
SHINY THINGS...
TSK TSK TSK!
MOCK ME NOW WHILE
YOU CAN!
TAKE A GOOD LOOK AT
THIS AND SEE IF
YOUR OPINION CHANGES...

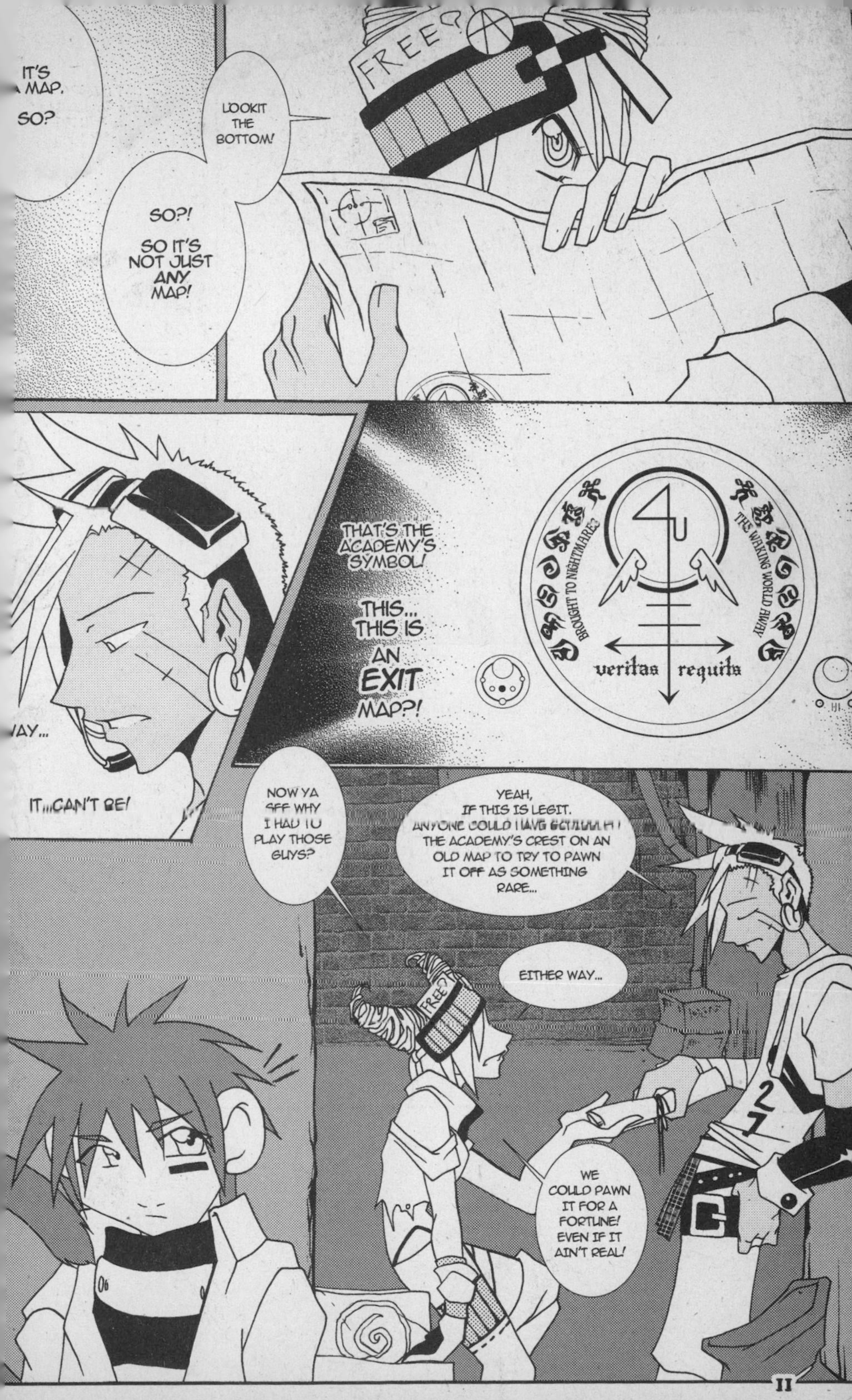
IT'S A MAP.
SO?
LOOKIT THE BOTTOM!
SO?! SO IT'S NOT JUST ANY MAP!
FREE?
THAT'S THE ACADEMY'S SYMBOL!
THIS... THIS IS AN EXIT MAP?!
BROUGHT TO NIGHTMARES
THE WAKING WORLD AWAY
veritas requita
IT...CAN'T BE!
NOW YA SEE WHY I HAD TO PLAY THOSE GUYS?
YEAH, IF THIS IS LEGIT, ANYONE COULD HAVE
THE ACADEMY'S CREST ON AN OLD MAP TO TRY TO PAWN IT OFF AS SOMETHING RARE...
EITHER WAY...
WE COULD PAWN IT FOR A FORTUNE! EVEN IF IT AIN'T REAL!

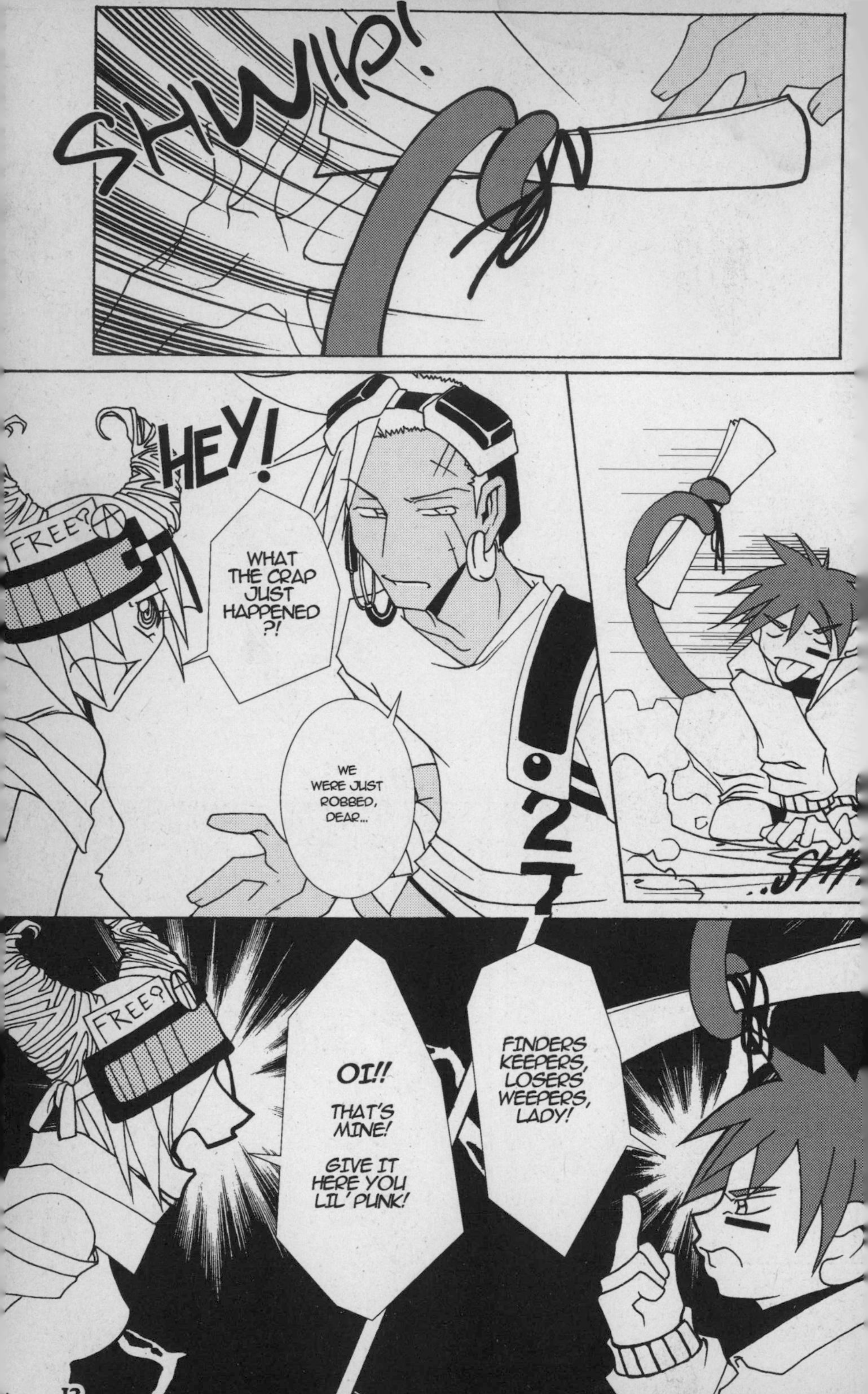
SHWIP!
...SHP
HEY!
WHAT THE CRAP JUST HAPPENED ?!
WE WERE JUST ROBBED, DEAR...
FREE?
FINDERS KEEPERS, LOSERS WEEPERS, LADY!
OI!! THAT'S MINE! GIVE IT HERE YOU LIL' PUNK!

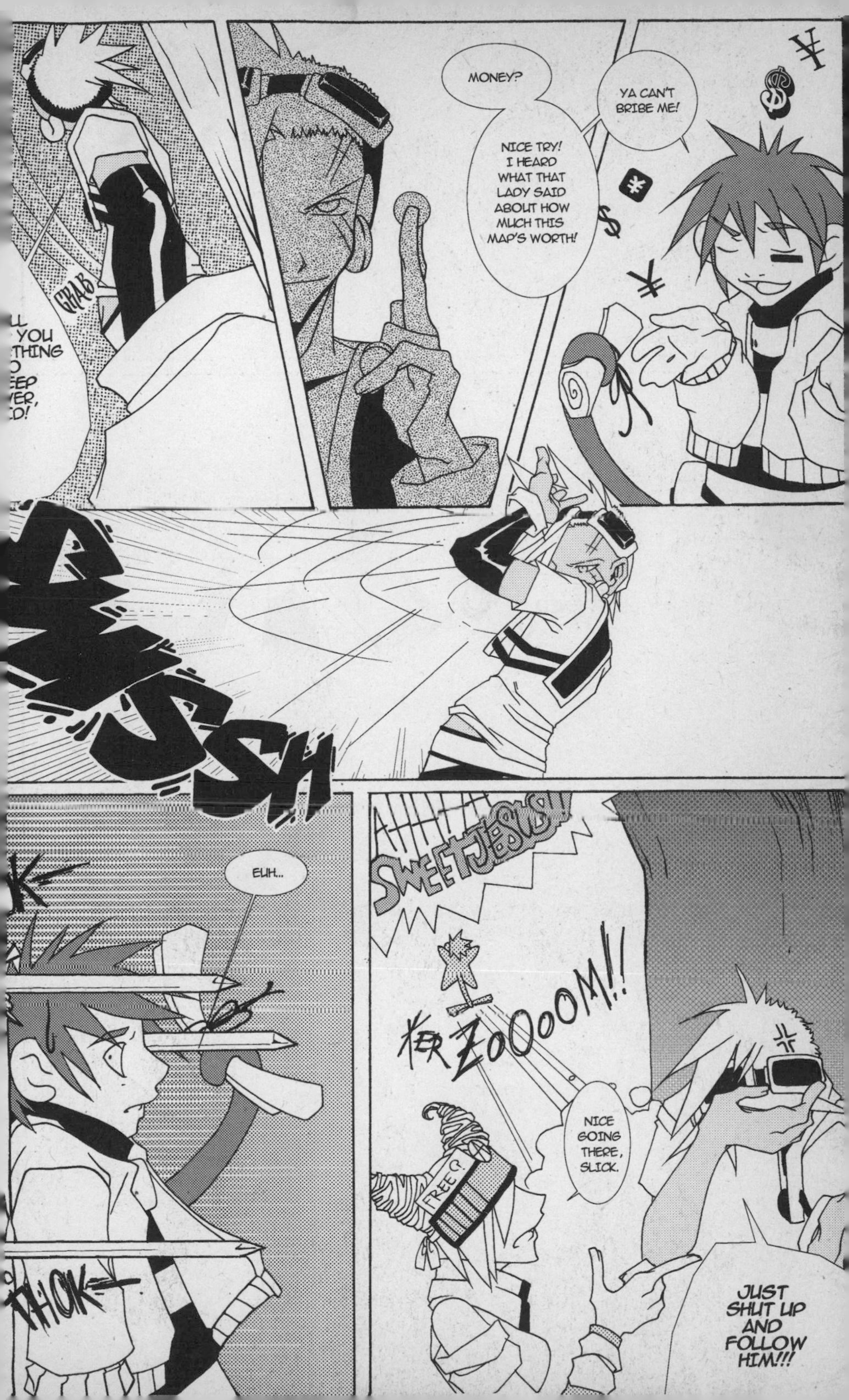

GRAB
MONEY?
NICE TRY! I HEARD WHAT THAT LADY SAID ABOUT HOW MUCH THIS MAP'S WORTH!
YA CAN'T BRIBE ME!
EUH...
THOK
SWEETJESUS!!
KERZOOOOM!!
NICE GOING THERE, SLICK.
FREE
JUST SHUT UP AND FOLLOW HIM!!!

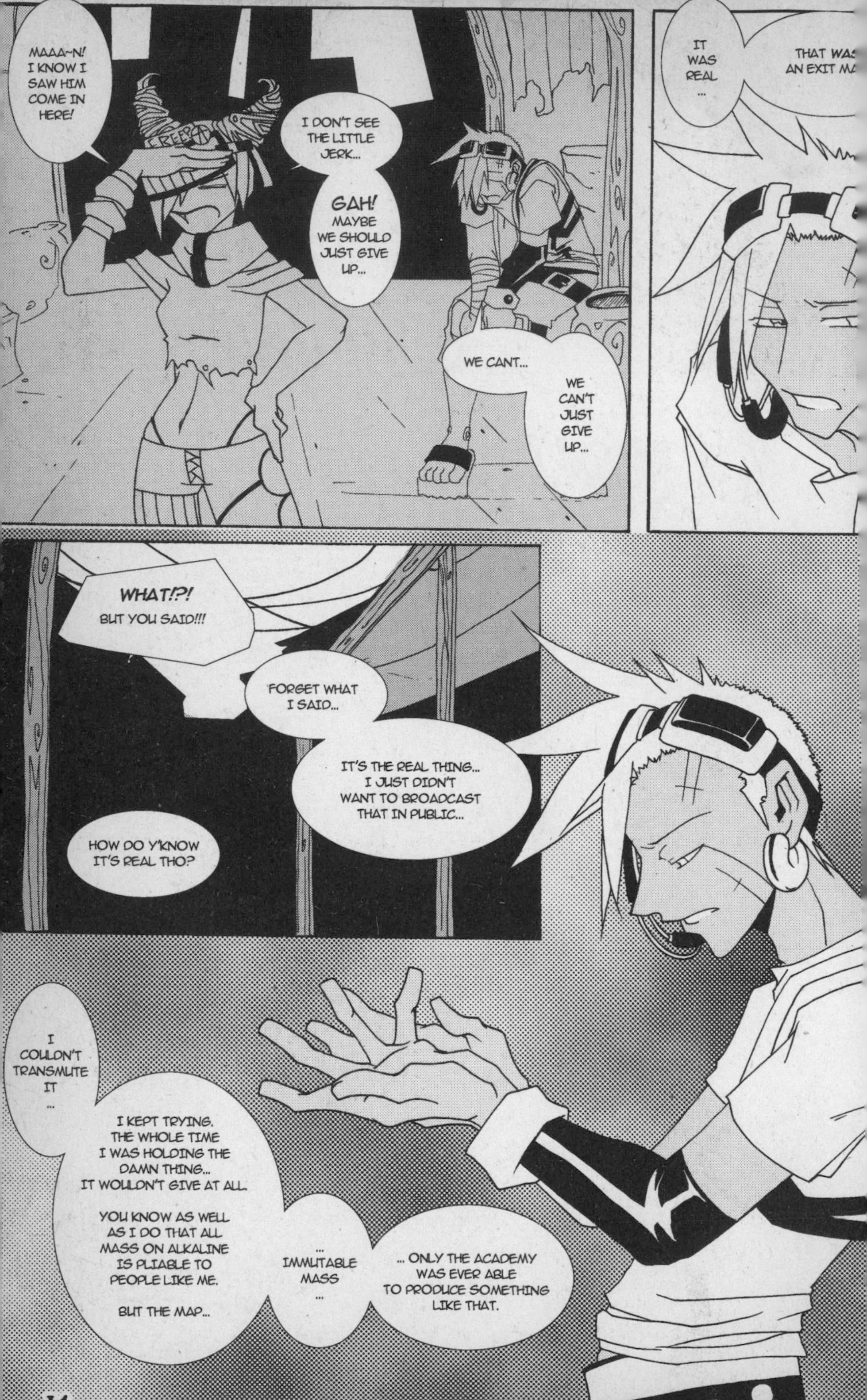
MAAA~N! I KNOW I SAW HIM COME IN HERE!
I DON'T SEE THE LITTLE JERK...
GAH! MAYBE WE SHOULD JUST GIVE UP...
WE CANT...
WE CAN'T JUST GIVE UP...
IT WAS REAL ...
THAT WAS AN EXIT MA
WHAT!?! BUT YOU SAID!!!
FORGET WHAT I SAID...
IT'S THE REAL THING... I JUST DIDN'T WANT TO BROADCAST THAT IN PUBLIC...
HOW DO Y'KNOW IT'S REAL THO?
I COULDN'T TRANSMUTE IT ...
I KEPT TRYING. THE WHOLE TIME I WAS HOLDING THE DAMN THING... IT WOULDN'T GIVE AT ALL.
YOU KNOW AS WELL AS I DO THAT ALL MASS ON ALKALINE IS PLIABLE TO PEOPLE LIKE ME.
BUT THE MAP...
... IMMUTABLE MASS ...
... ONLY THE ACADEMY WAS EVER ABLE TO PRODUCE SOMETHING LIKE THAT.

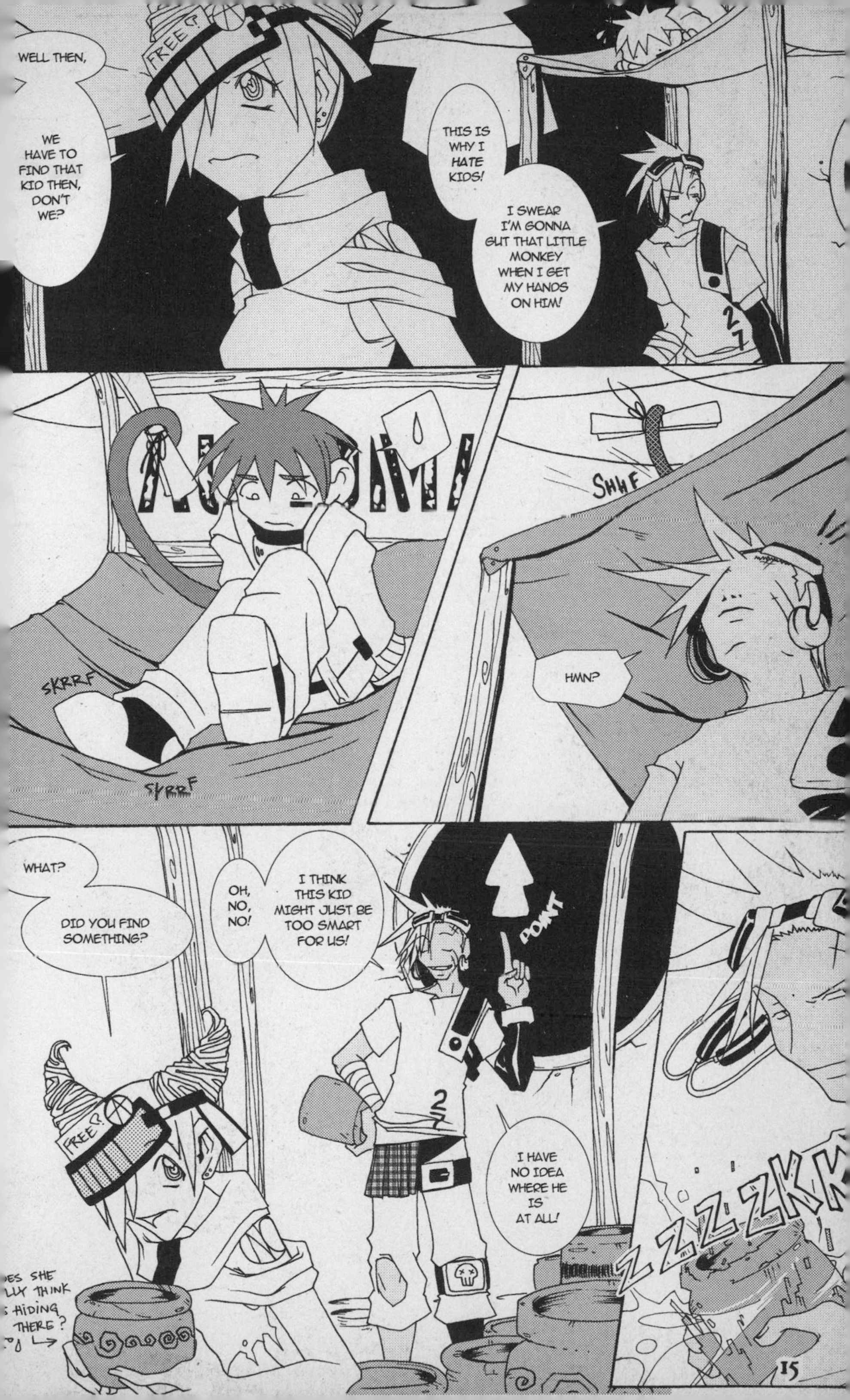
WELL THEN,
WE HAVE TO FIND THAT KID THEN, DON'T WE?
THIS IS WHY I HATE KIDS!
I SWEAR I'M GONNA GUT THAT LITTLE MONKEY WHEN I GET MY HANDS ON HIM!
SKRRF
SKRRF
SHHF
HMN?
WHAT?
DID YOU FIND SOMETHING?
OH, NO, NO!
I THINK THIS KID MIGHT JUST BE TOO SMART FOR US!
POINT
I HAVE NO IDEA WHERE HE IS AT ALL!

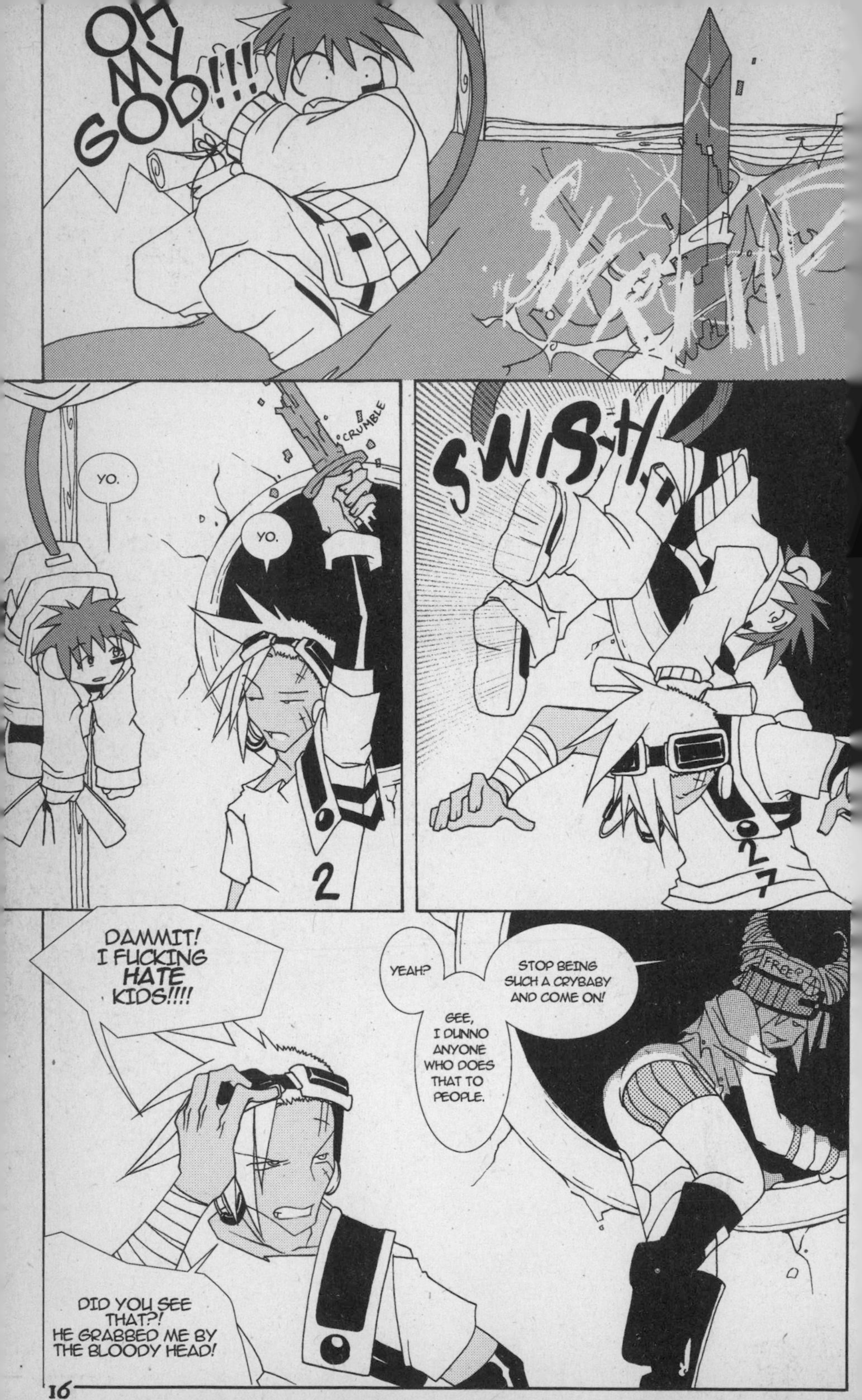
OH MY GOD!!!!
SHRRUP
CRUMBLE
YO.
YO.
SWISH
DAMMIT! I FUCKING HATE KIDS!!!!
DID YOU SEE THAT?! HE GRABBED ME BY THE BLOODY HEAD!
YEAH?
GEE, I DUNNO ANYONE WHO DOES THAT TO PEOPLE.
STOP BEING SUCH A CRYBABY AND COME ON!

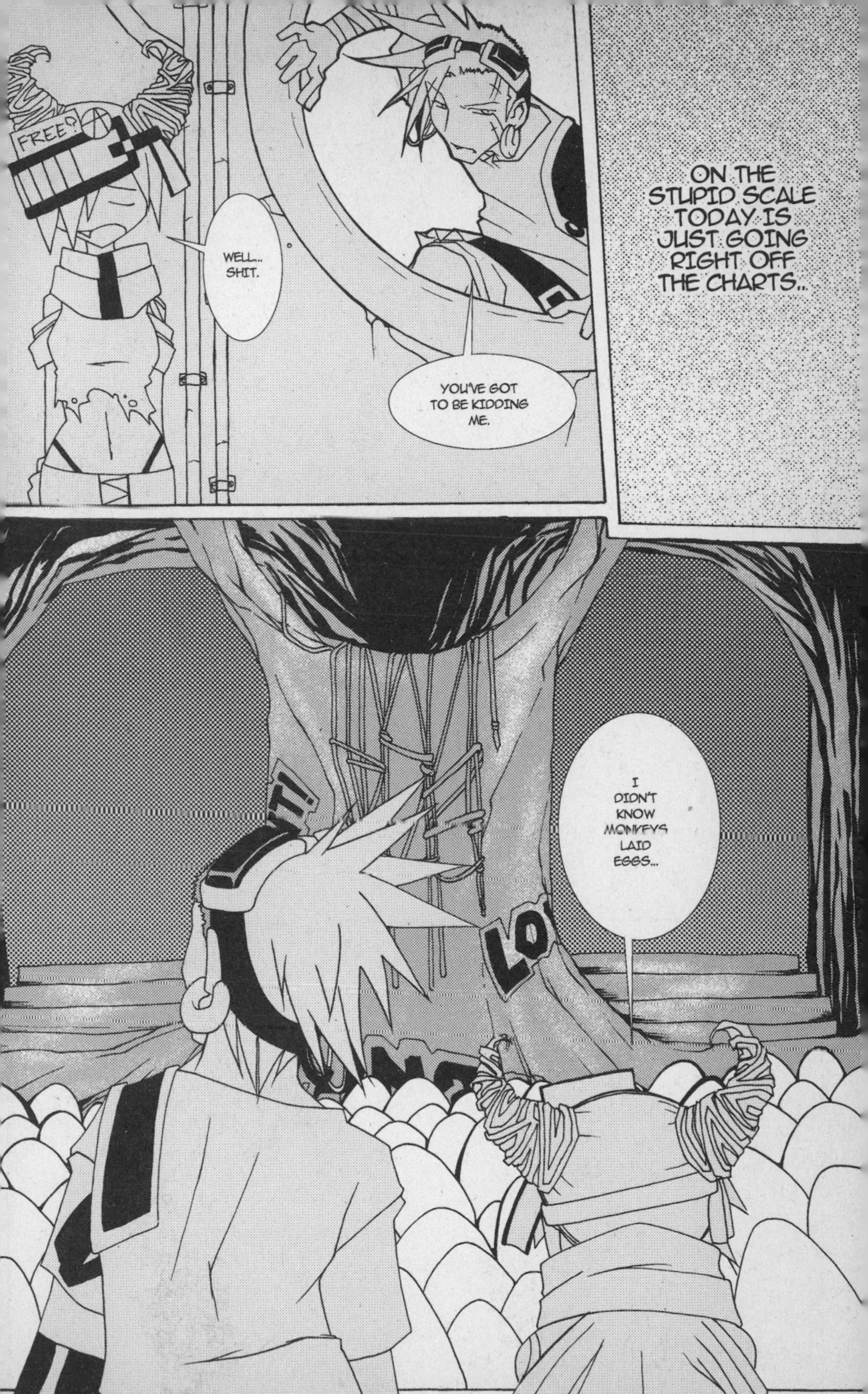
FREE?
WELL... SHIT.
YOU'VE GOT TO BE KIDDING ME.
ON THE STUPID SCALE TODAY IS JUST GOING RIGHT OFF THE CHARTS..
I DIDN'T KNOW MONKEYS LAID EGGS...

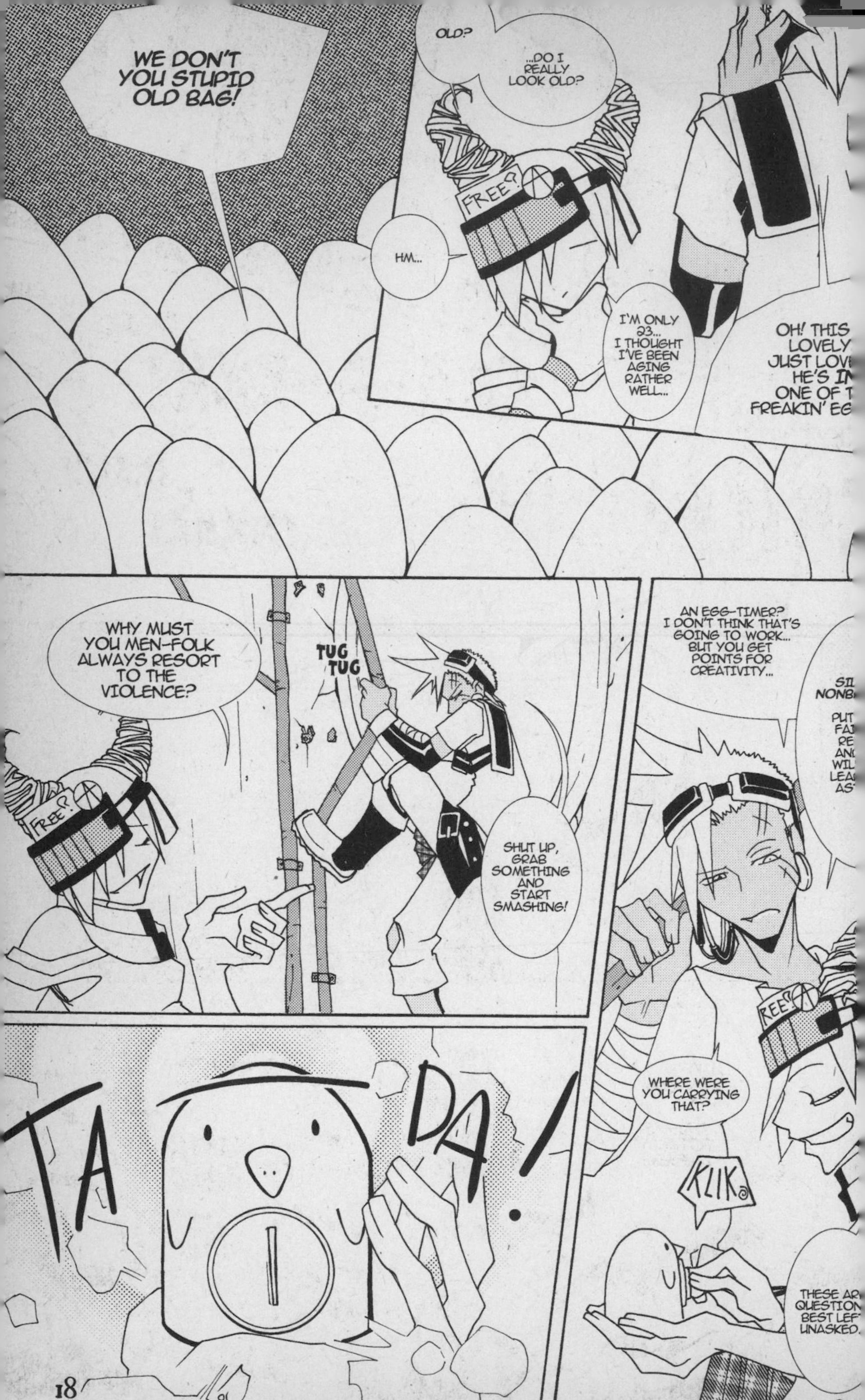
WE DON'T YOU STUPID OLD BAG!
OLD?
...DO I REALLY LOOK OLD?
HM...
I'M ONLY 23... I THOUGHT I'VE BEEN AGING RATHER WELL...
OH! THIS
WHY MUST YOU MEN-FOLK ALWAYS RESORT TO THE VIOLENCE?
TUG TUG
SHUT UP, GRAB SOMETHING AND START SMASHING!
AN EGG-TIMER? I DON'T THINK THAT'S GOING TO WORK... BUT YOU GET POINTS FOR CREATIVITY...
TA DA!
WHERE WERE YOU CARRYING THAT?
KLIK
UNASKED.

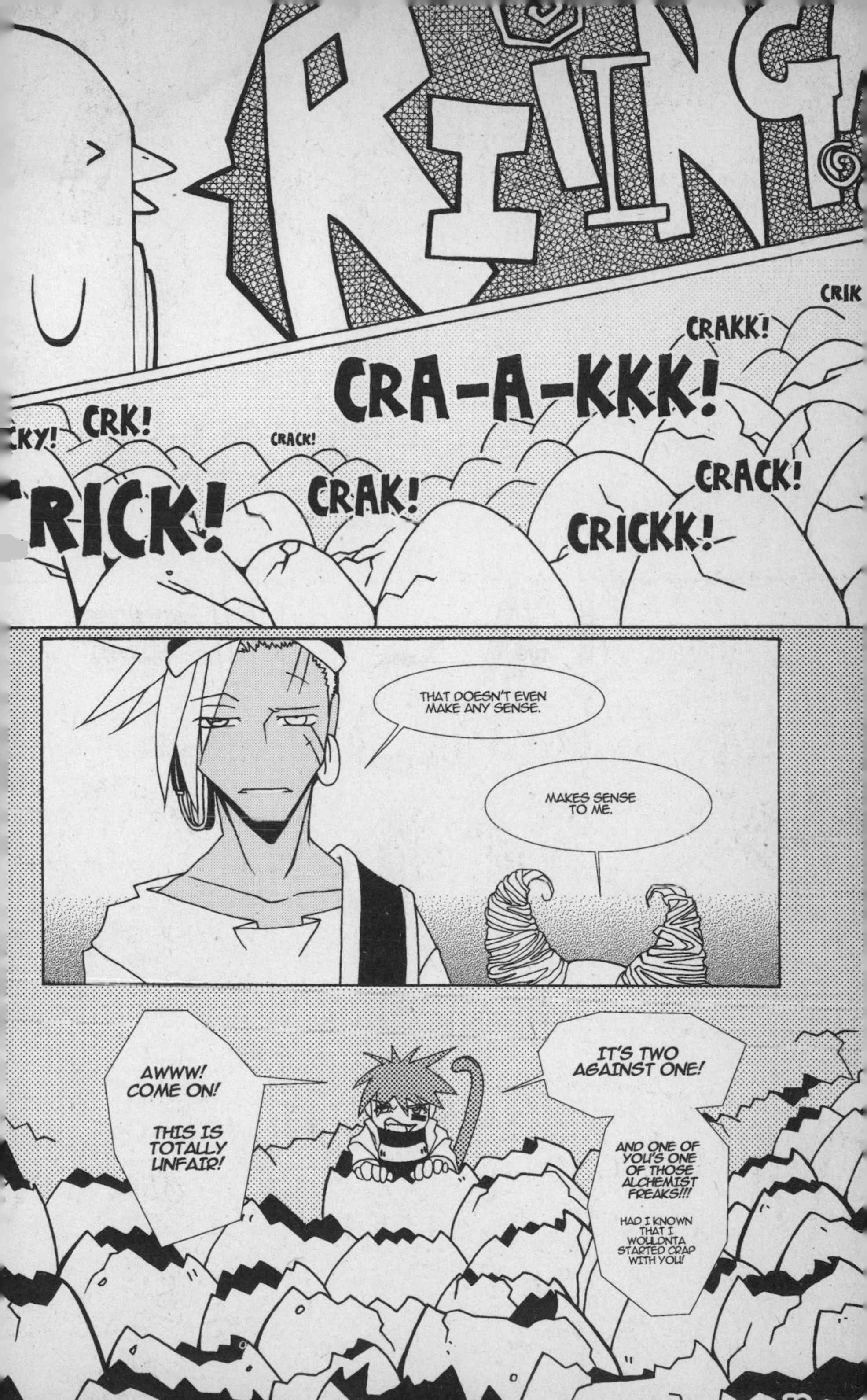
RING
CRIK
CRAKK!
CRA-A-KKK!
CKY!
CRK!
CRACK!
RICK!
CRAK!
CRACK!
CRICKK!
THAT DOESN'T EVEN MAKE ANY SENSE.
MAKES SENSE TO ME.
AWWW! COME ON!
THIS IS TOTALLY UNFAIR!
IT'S TWO AGAINST ONE!
AND ONE OF YOU'S ONE OF THOSE ALCHEMIST FREAKS!!!
HAD I KNOWN THAT I WOULDNTA STARTED CRAP WITH YOU!

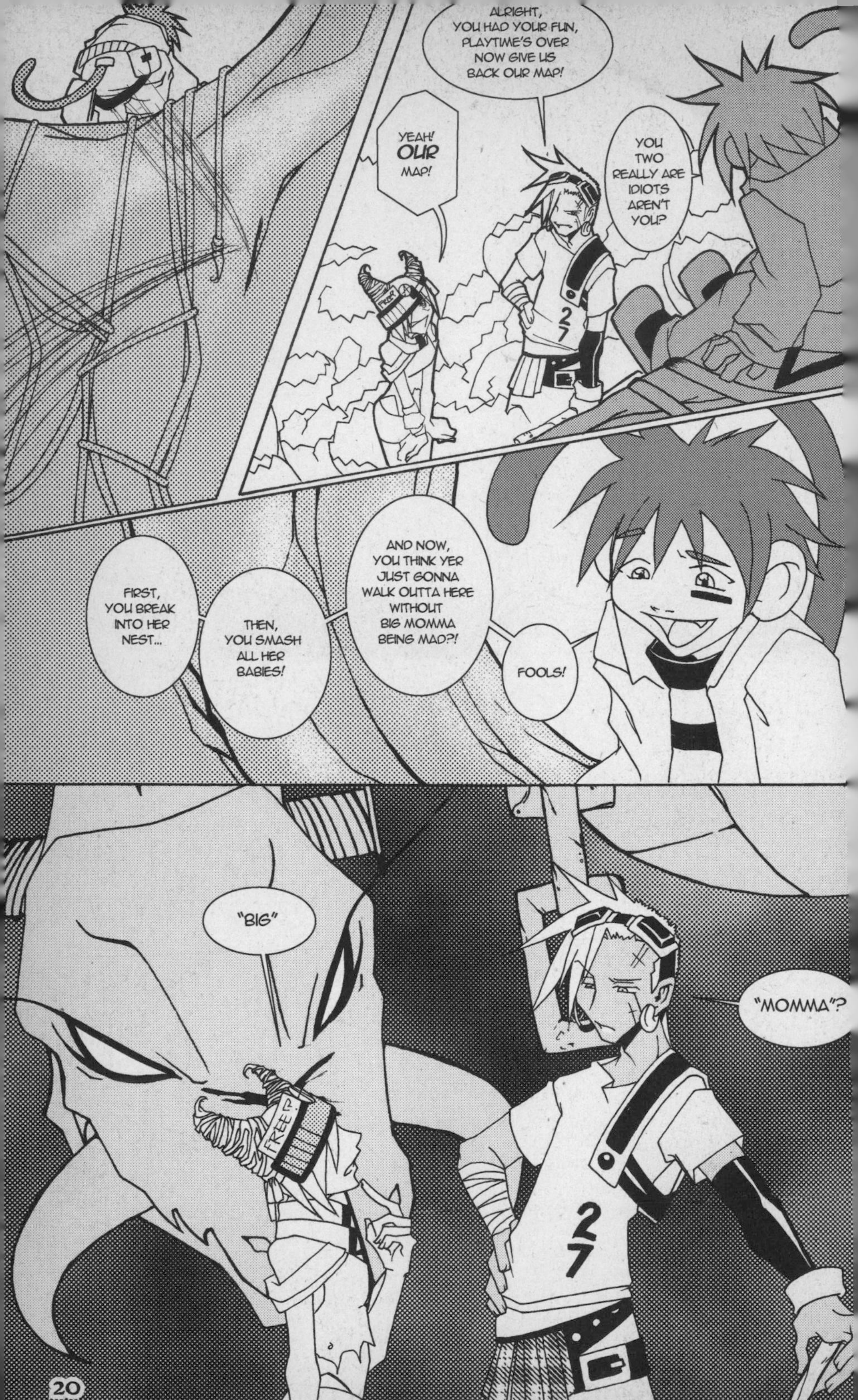
ALRIGHT, YOU HAD YOUR FUN, PLAYTIME'S OVER NOW GIVE US BACK OUR MAP!
YEAH! OUR MAP!
YOU TWO REALLY ARE IDIOTS AREN'T YOU?
FIRST, YOU BREAK INTO HER NEST...
THEN, YOU SMASH ALL HER BABIES!
AND NOW, YOU THINK YER JUST GONNA WALK OUTTA HERE WITHOUT BIG MOMMA BEING MAD?!
FOOLS!
"BIG"
"MOMMA"?

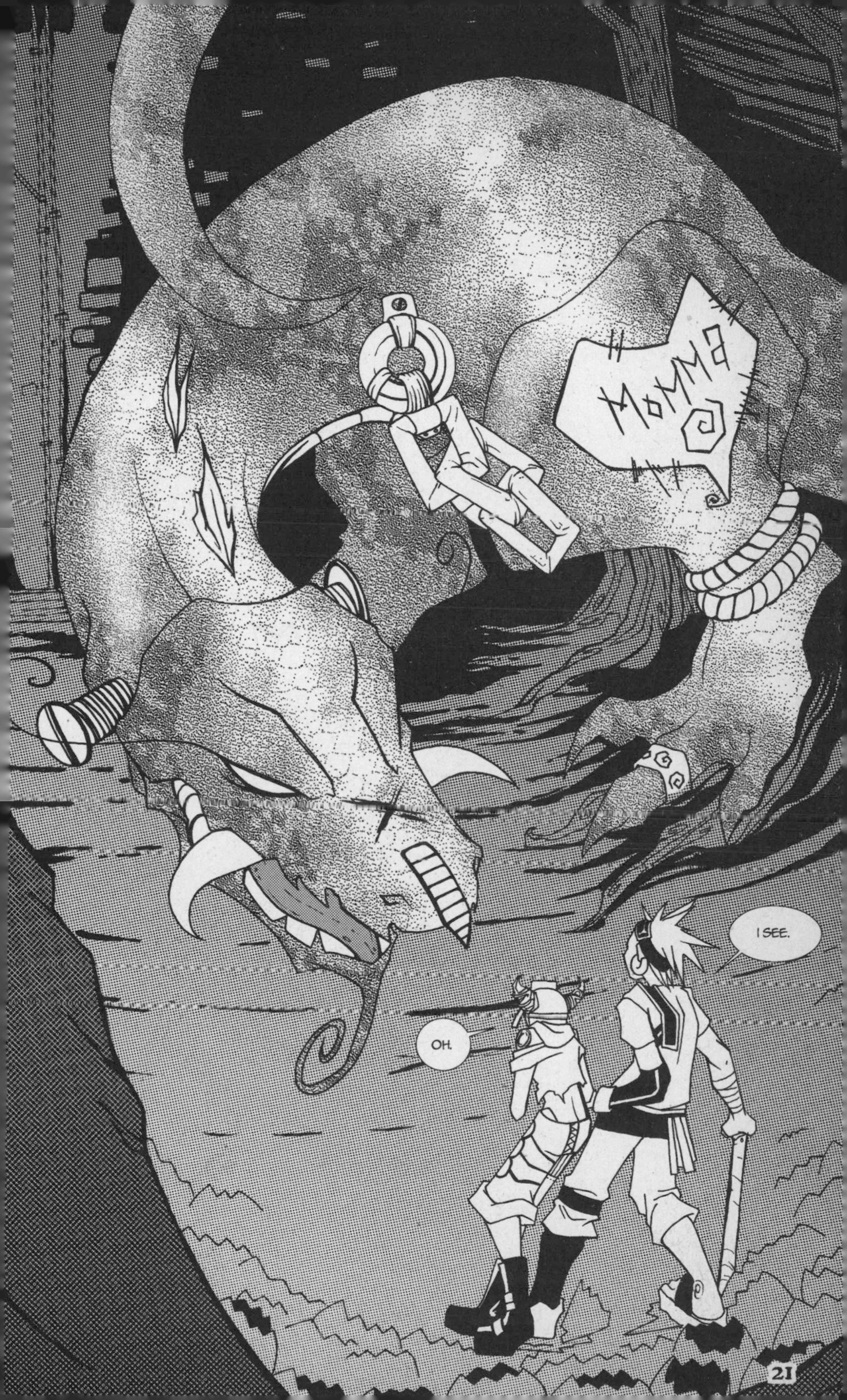
MOMMA
I SEE.
OH.

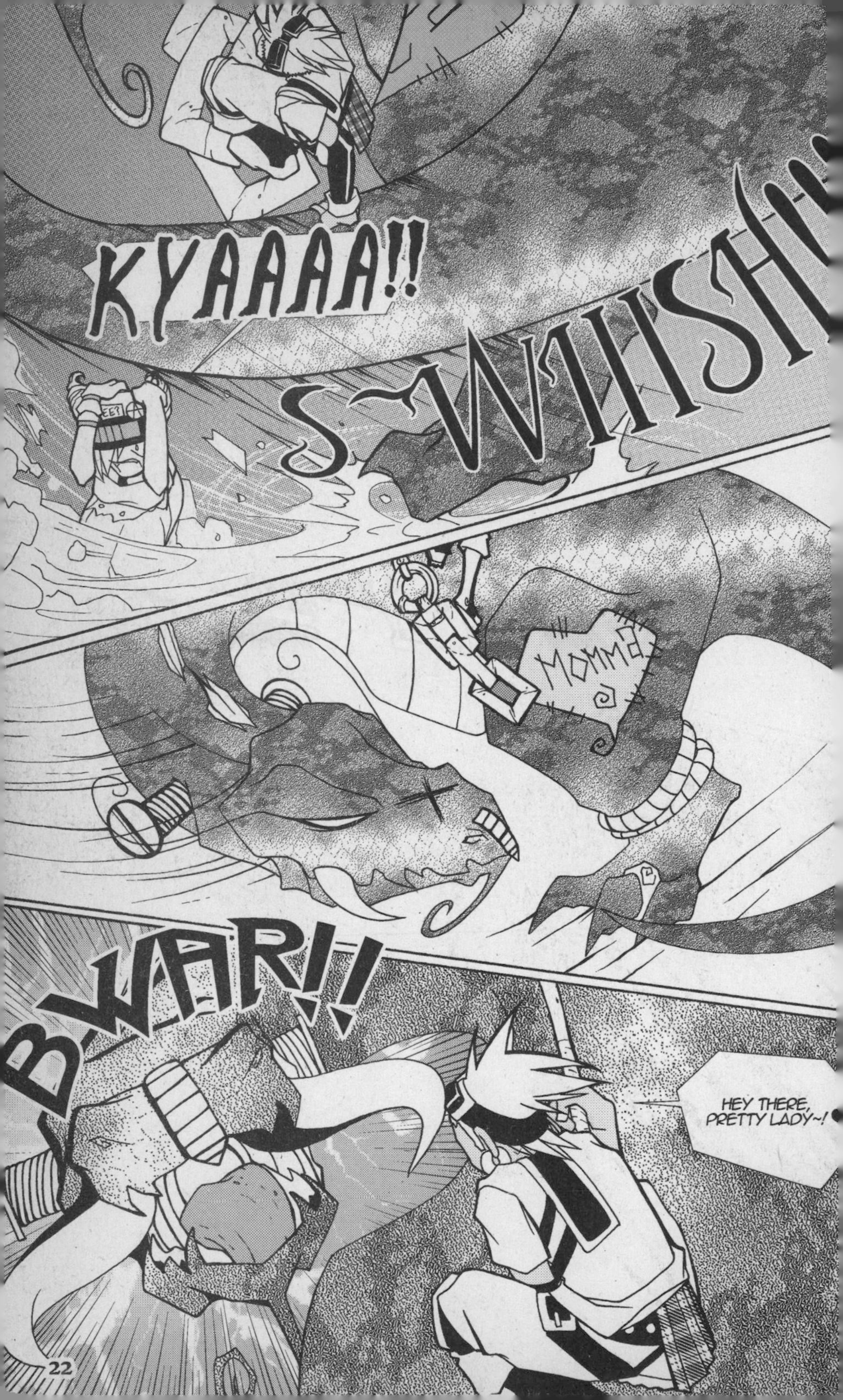
KYAAAA!!
SWIISH!!
MOMMA
BWAR!!
HEY THERE, PRETTY LADY~!

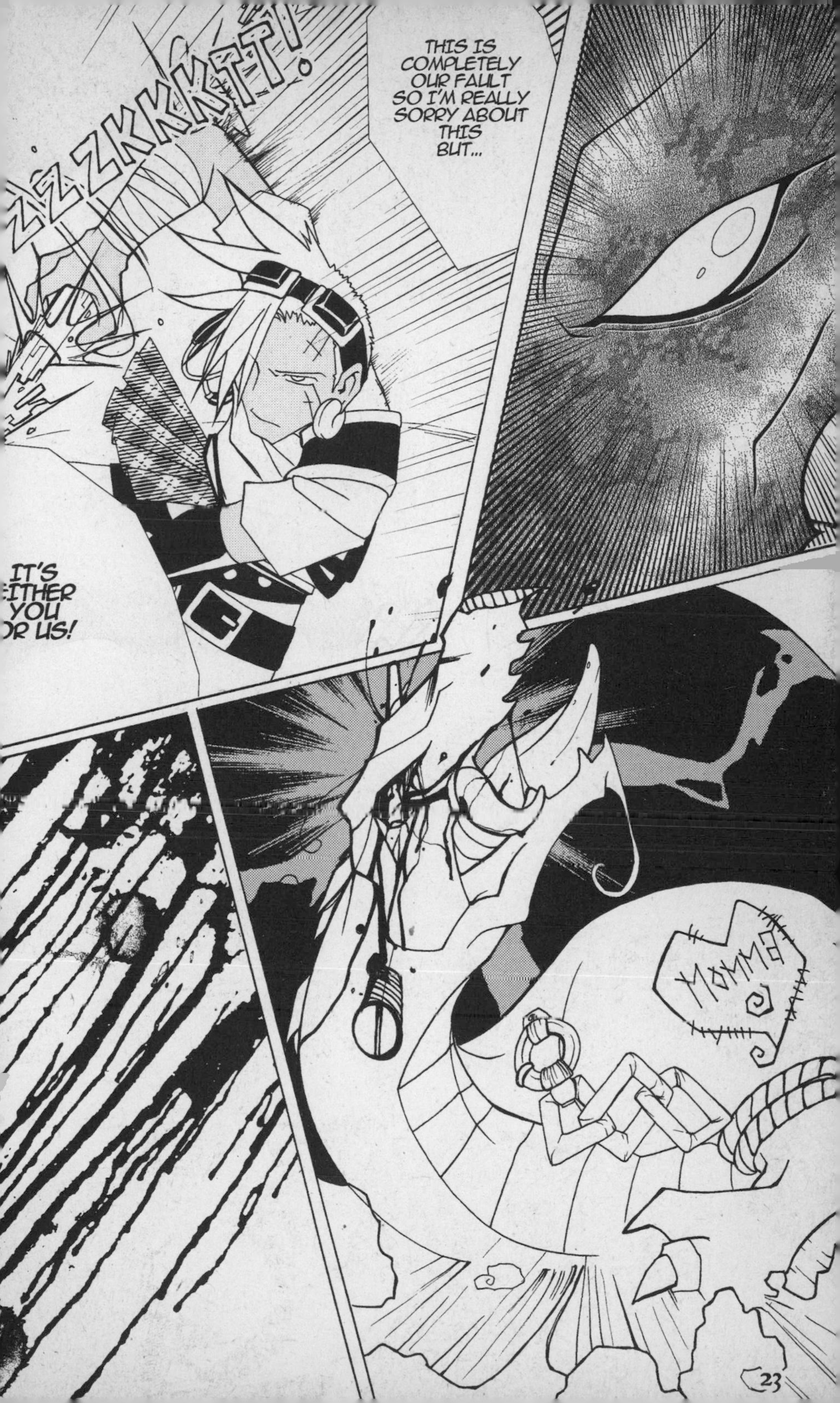
ZZZZKKKKTTT!
THIS IS COMPLETELY OUR FAULT SO I'M REALLY SORRY ABOUT THIS BUT...
IT'S EITHER YOU OR US!
MOMMA

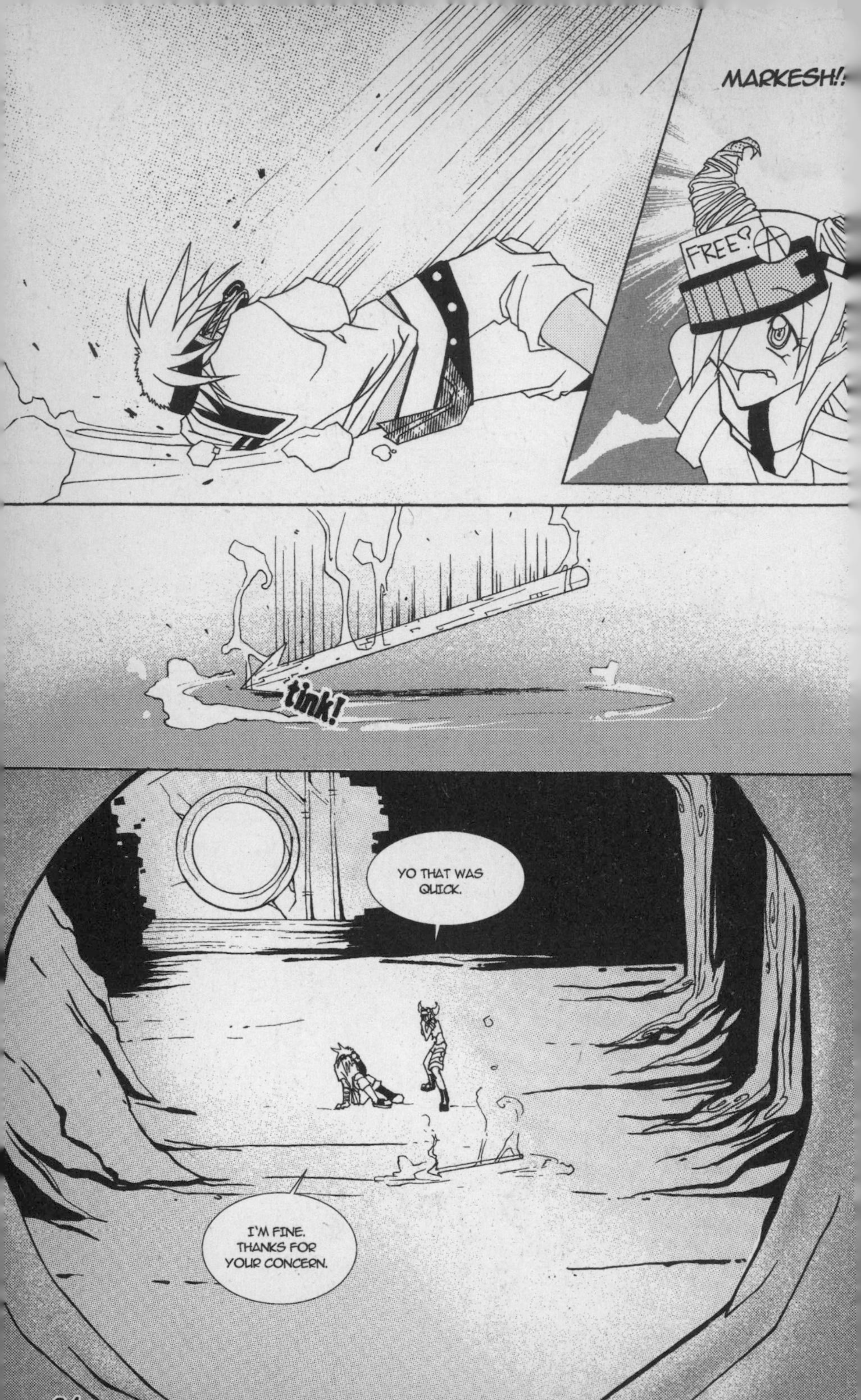
MARKESH!!
FREE?
tink!
YO THAT WAS QUICK.
I'M FINE. THANKS FOR YOUR CONCERN.

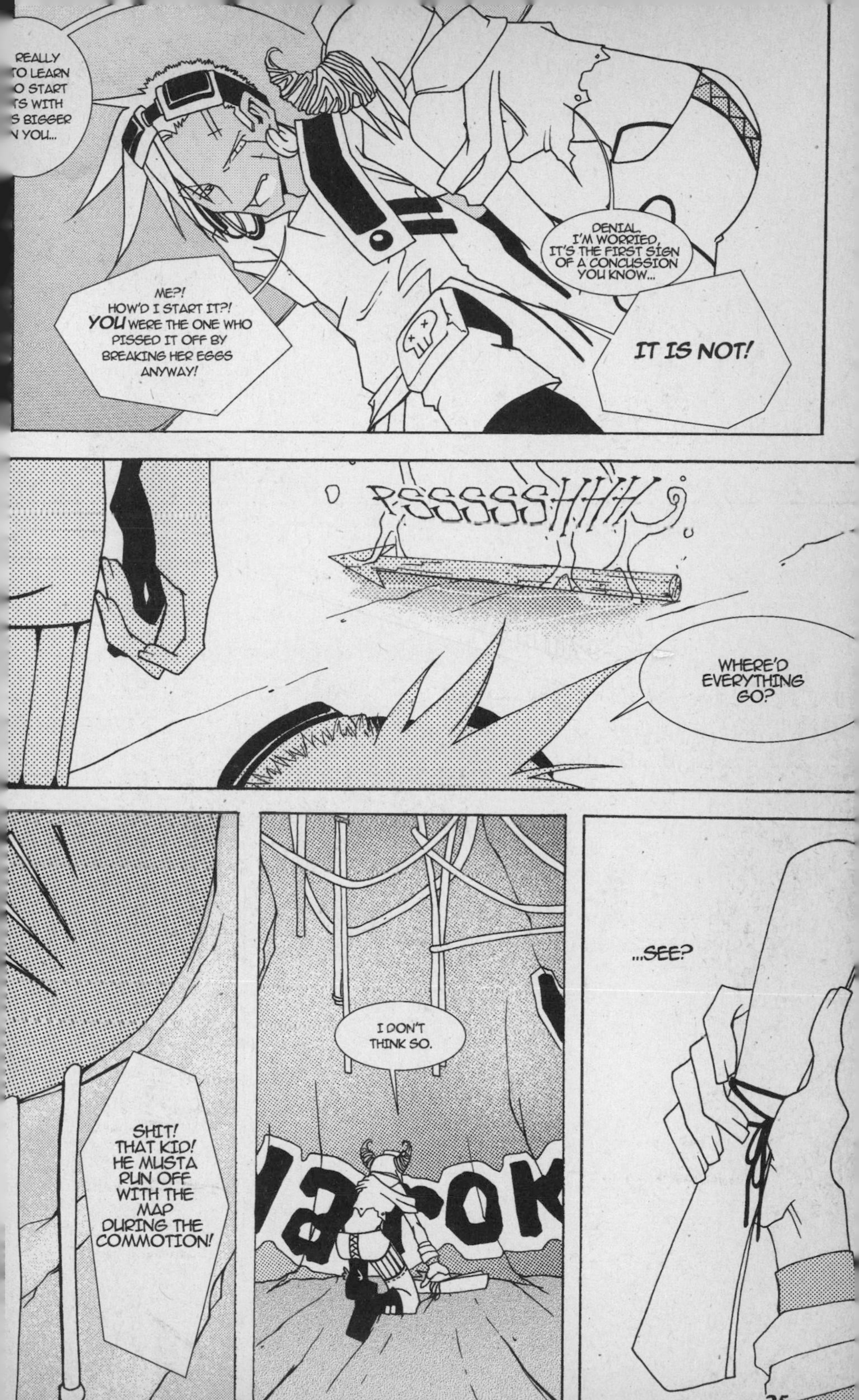

REALLY
TO LEARN
O START
TS WITH
S BIGGER
N YOU...
DENIAL.
I'M WORRIED,
IT'S THE FIRST SIGN
OF A CONCUSSION
YOU KNOW...
ME?!
HOW'D I START IT?!
YOU WERE THE ONE WHO
PISSED IT OFF BY
BREAKING HER EGGS
ANYWAY!
IT IS NOT!
PSSSSSSHHH
WHERE'D
EVERYTHING
GO?
...SEE?
I DON'T
THINK SO.
SHIT!
THAT KID!
HE MUSTA
RUN OFF
WITH THE
MAP
DURING THE
COMMOTION!

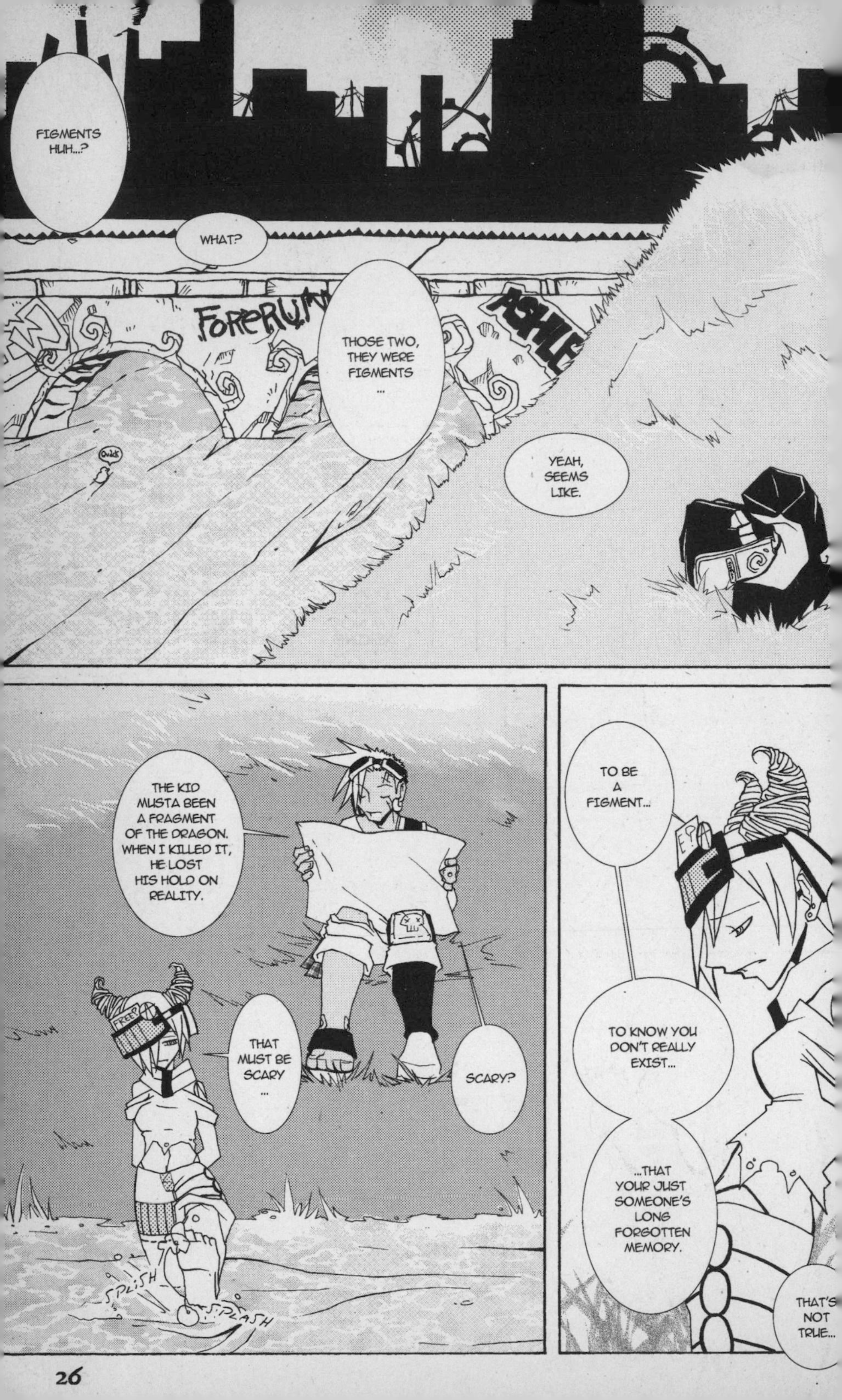
FIGMENTS HUH...?
WHAT?
FORERU.N
ASHLE
THOSE TWO, THEY WERE FIGMENTS ...
QUICK
YEAH, SEEMS LIKE.
THE KID MUSTA BEEN A FRAGMENT OF THE DRAGON. WHEN I KILLED IT, HE LOST HIS HOLD ON REALITY.
THAT MUST BE SCARY ...
SCARY?
SPLISH
SPLASH
TO BE A FIGMENT...
TO KNOW YOU DON'T REALLY EXIST...
...THAT YOUR JUST SOMEONE'S LONG FORGOTTEN MEMORY.
THAT'S NOT TRUE...

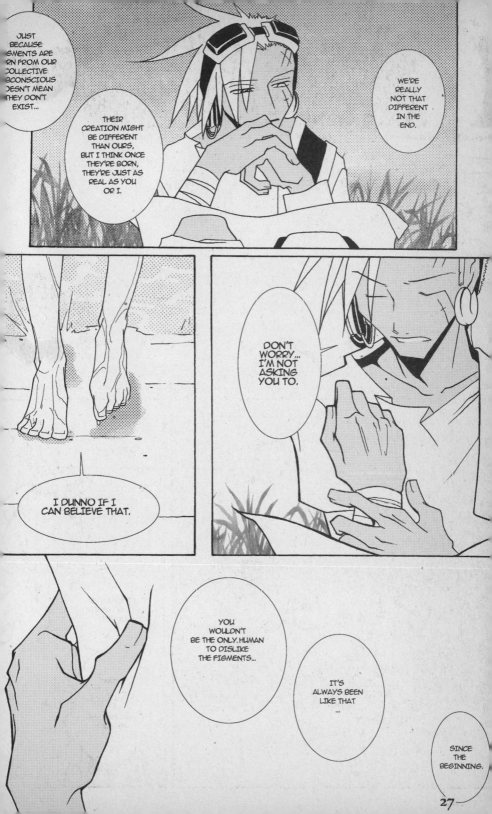

JUST BECAUSE SMENTS ARE RN FROM OUR COLLECTIVE SCONSCIOUS DESN'T MEAN THEY DON'T EXIST...

THEIR CREATION MIGHT BE DIFFERENT THAN OURS, BUT I THINK ONCE THEY'RE BORN, THEY'RE JUST AS REAL AS YOU OR I.

WE'RE REALLY NOT THAT DIFFERENT IN THE END.

I DUNNO IF I CAN BELIEVE THAT.

DON'T WORRY... I'M NOT ASKING YOU TO.

YOU WOULDN'T BE THE ONLY HUMAN TO DISLIKE THE FIGMENTS...

IT'S ALWAYS BEEN LIKE THAT ...

SINCE THE BEGINNING.

27

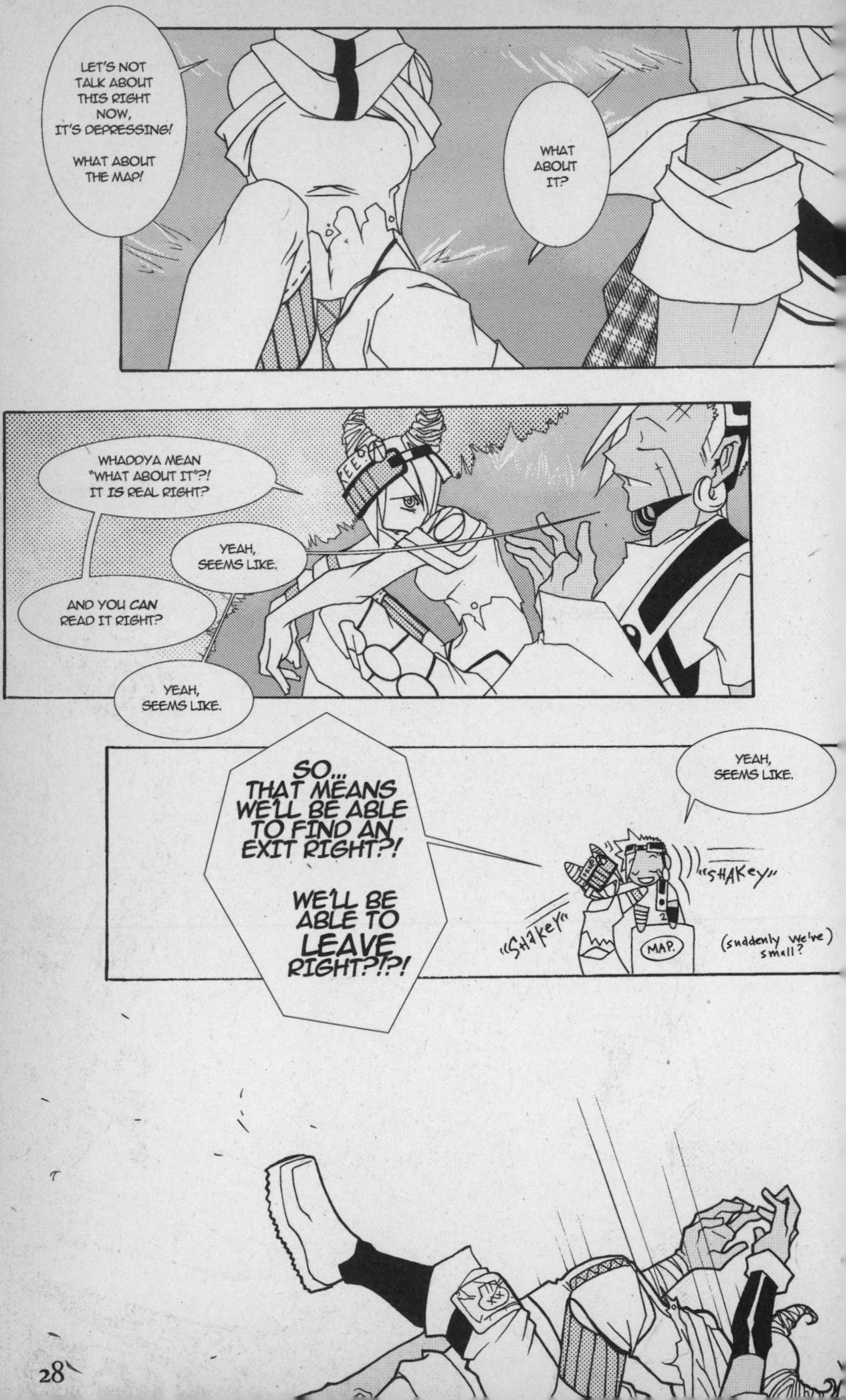
LET'S NOT TALK ABOUT THIS RIGHT NOW, IT'S DEPRESSING!
WHAT ABOUT THE MAP!
WHAT ABOUT IT?
WHADDYA MEAN "WHAT ABOUT IT"?! IT IS REAL RIGHT?
YEAH, SEEMS LIKE.
AND YOU CAN READ IT RIGHT?
YEAH, SEEMS LIKE.
SO... THAT MEANS WE'LL BE ABLE TO FIND AN EXIT RIGHT?!
WE'LL BE ABLE TO LEAVE RIGHT?!?!
YEAH, SEEMS LIKE.
"SHAKEY"
"SHAKEY"
MAP.
(suddenly we're) small?

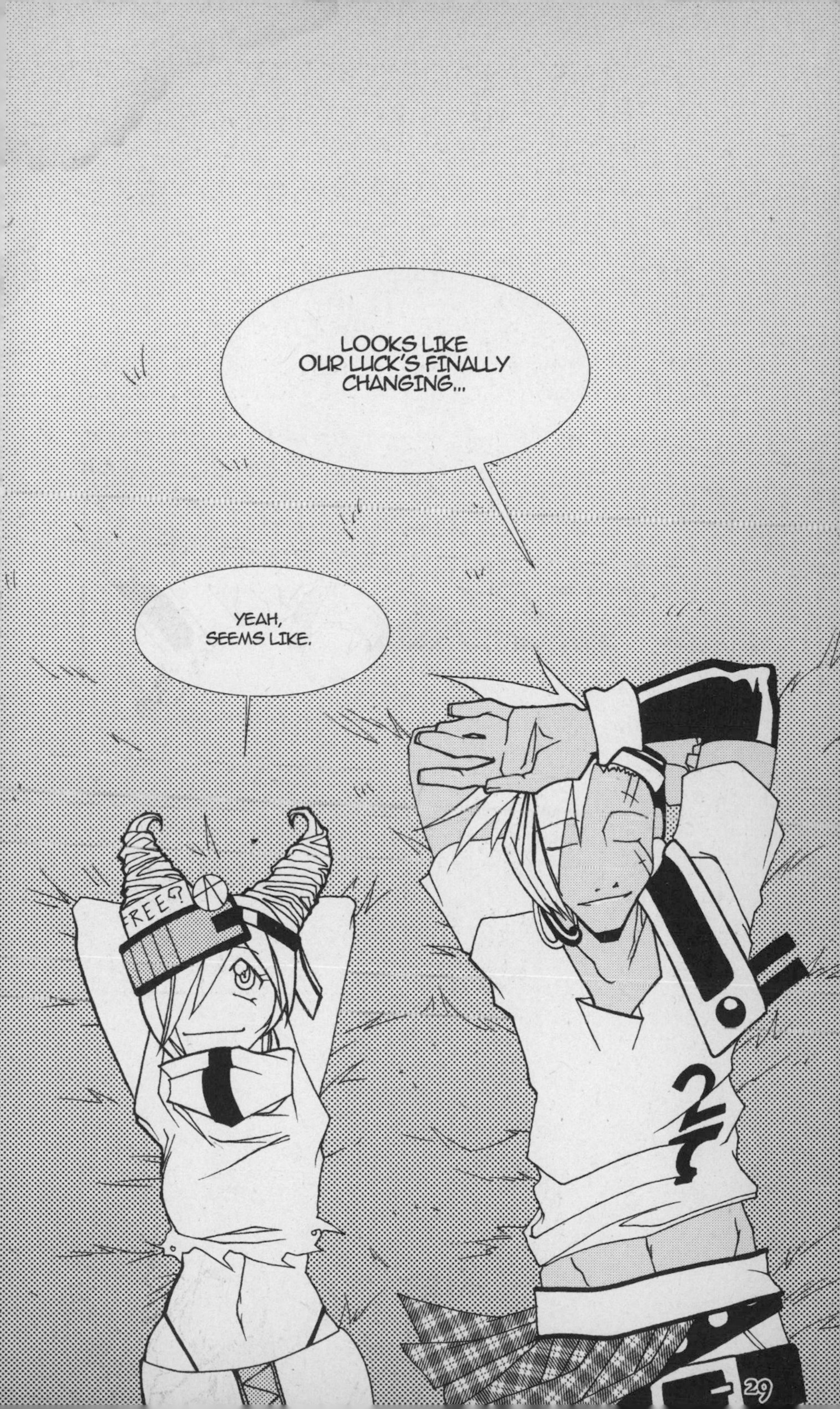
LOOKS LIKE OUR LUCK'S FINALLY CHANGING...
YEAH, SEEMS LIKE.
FREE?

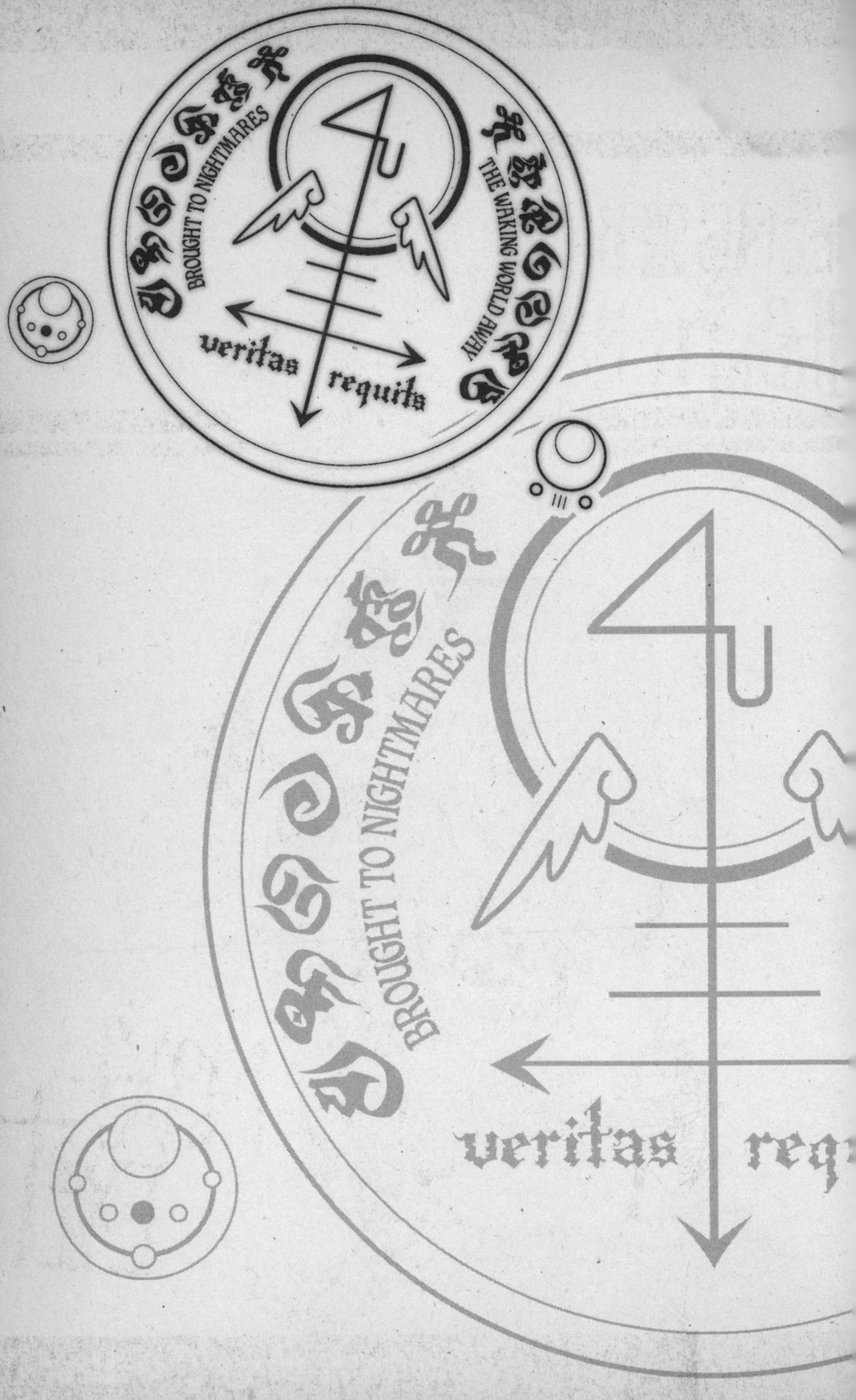
BROUGHT TO NIGHTMARES
THE WAKING WORLD AWAY
veritas
requits
BROUGHT TO NIGHTMARES
veritas

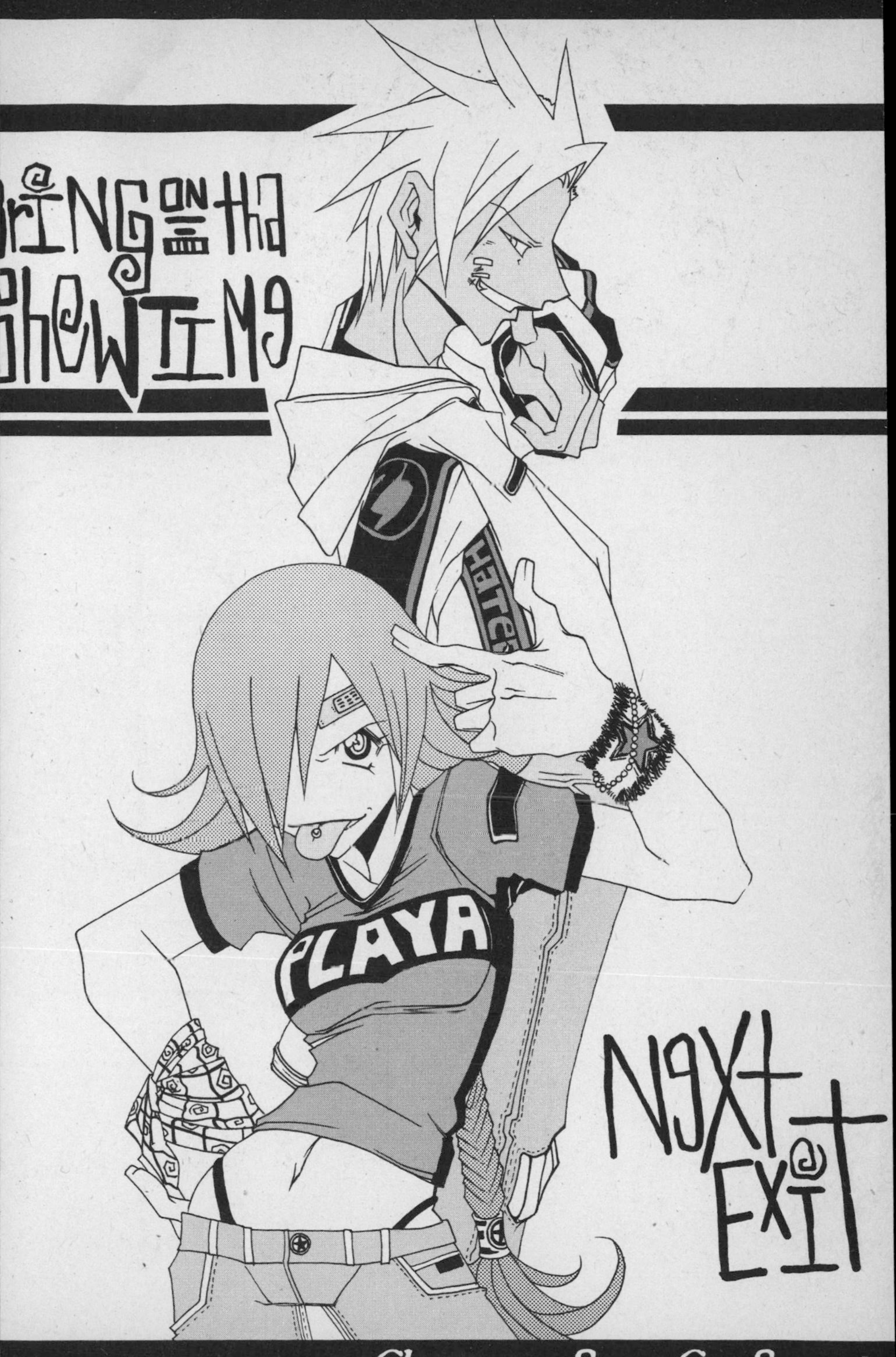
Bring on tha Showtime
Hater
PLAYA
Next Exit

Chapter 2: Stray Cat Strut

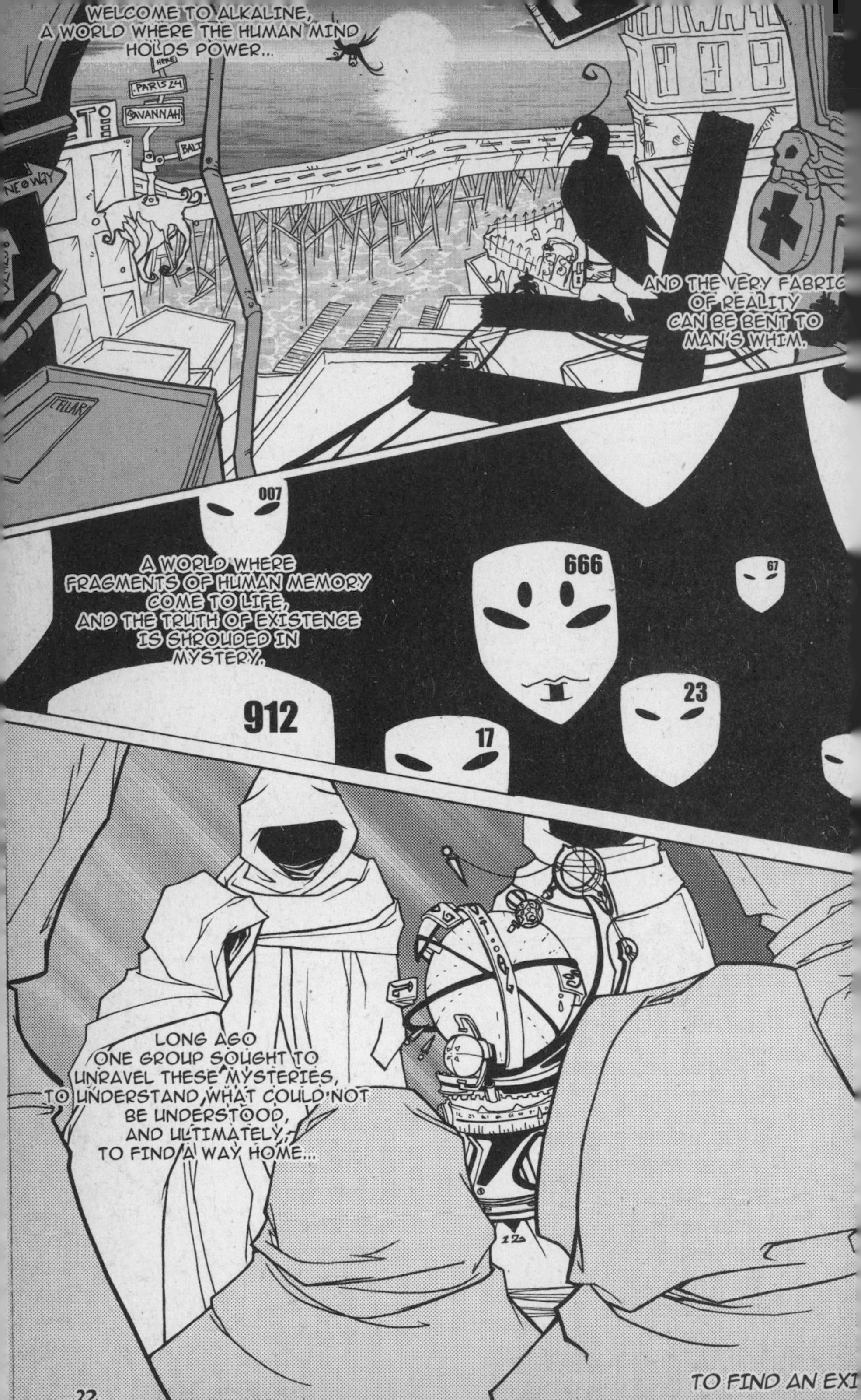
WELCOME TO ALKALINE, A WORLD WHERE THE HUMAN MIND HOLDS POWER...
HERE
PARIS 24
SAVANNAH
AND THE VERY FABRIC OF REALITY CAN BE BENT TO MAN'S WHIM.
007
A WORLD WHERE FRAGMENTS OF HUMAN MEMORY COME TO LIFE, AND THE TRUTH OF EXISTENCE IS SHROUDED IN MYSTERY.
666
67
912
17
23
LONG AGO ONE GROUP SOUGHT TO UNRAVEL THESE MYSTERIES, TO UNDERSTAND WHAT COULD NOT BE UNDERSTOOD, AND ULTIMATELY, TO FIND A WAY HOME...
TO FIND AN EXI

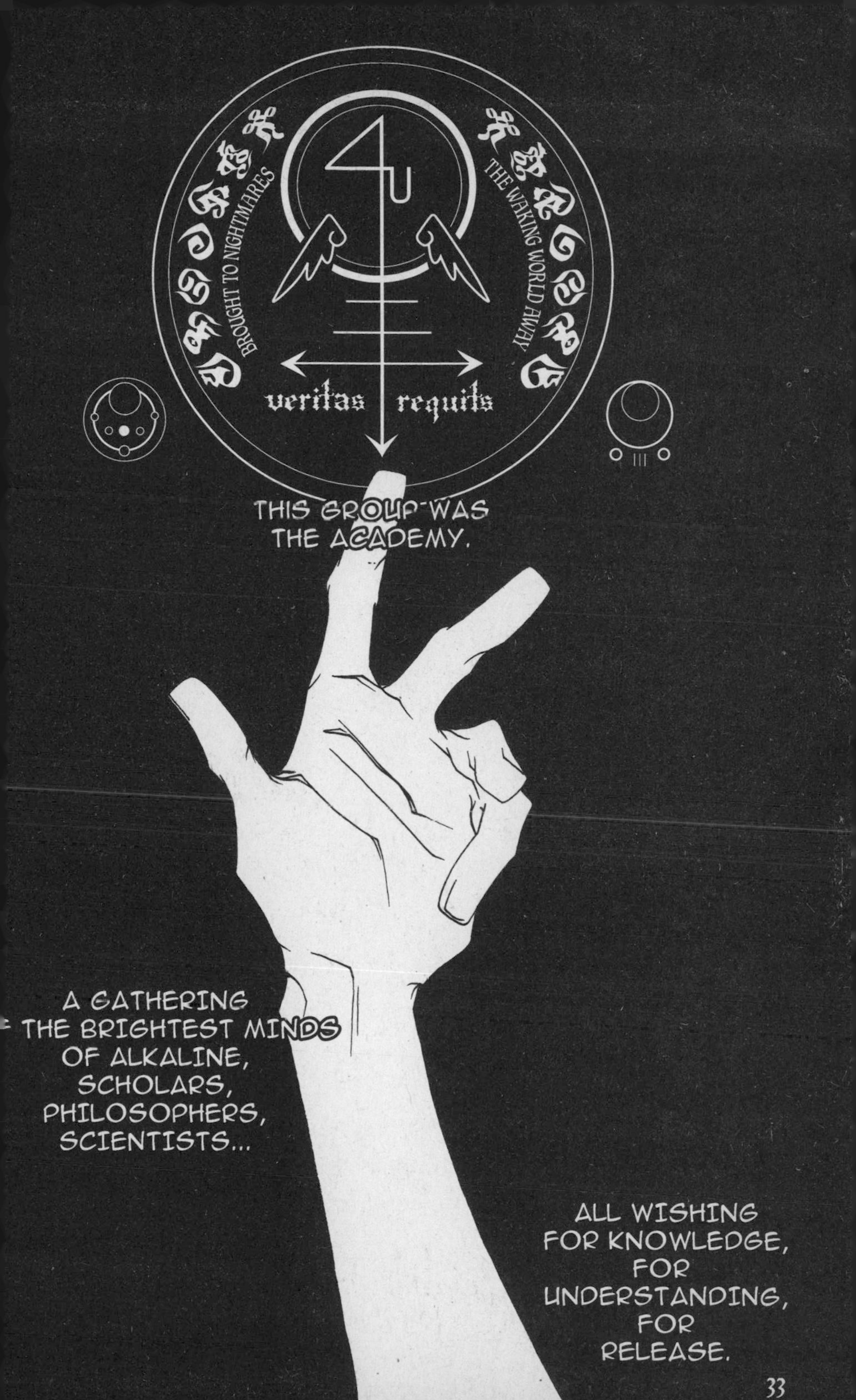
BROUGHT TO NIGHTMARES
THE WAKING WORLD AWAY
veritas
requits
THIS GROUP WAS THE ACADEMY.
A GATHERING
THE BRIGHTEST MINDS
OF ALKALINE,
SCHOLARS,
PHILOSOPHERS,
SCIENTISTS...
ALL WISHING FOR KNOWLEDGE, FOR UNDERSTANDING, FOR RELEASE.

FOR MANY YEARS
THESE MEN SOUGHT
AFTER THEIR
GOAL...

AS TIME WENT ON
THEIR KNOWLEDGE GREW,
AND WITH IT...

...THEIR INFLUENCE.

THIS TROUBLED
THE POWERS THAT BE...

THEY WEREN'T ABOUT TO
LET THEIR HOLD ON ALKALINE
NOT FOR ANYTHING, OR ANY

THUS THE DECISION WAS MADE,
AND THE ORDERS GIVEN...

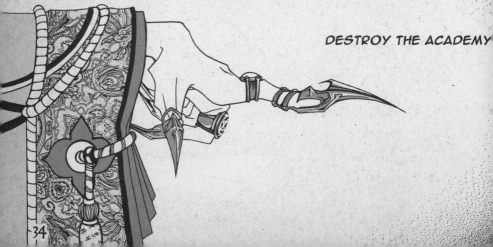

DESTROY THE ACADEMY

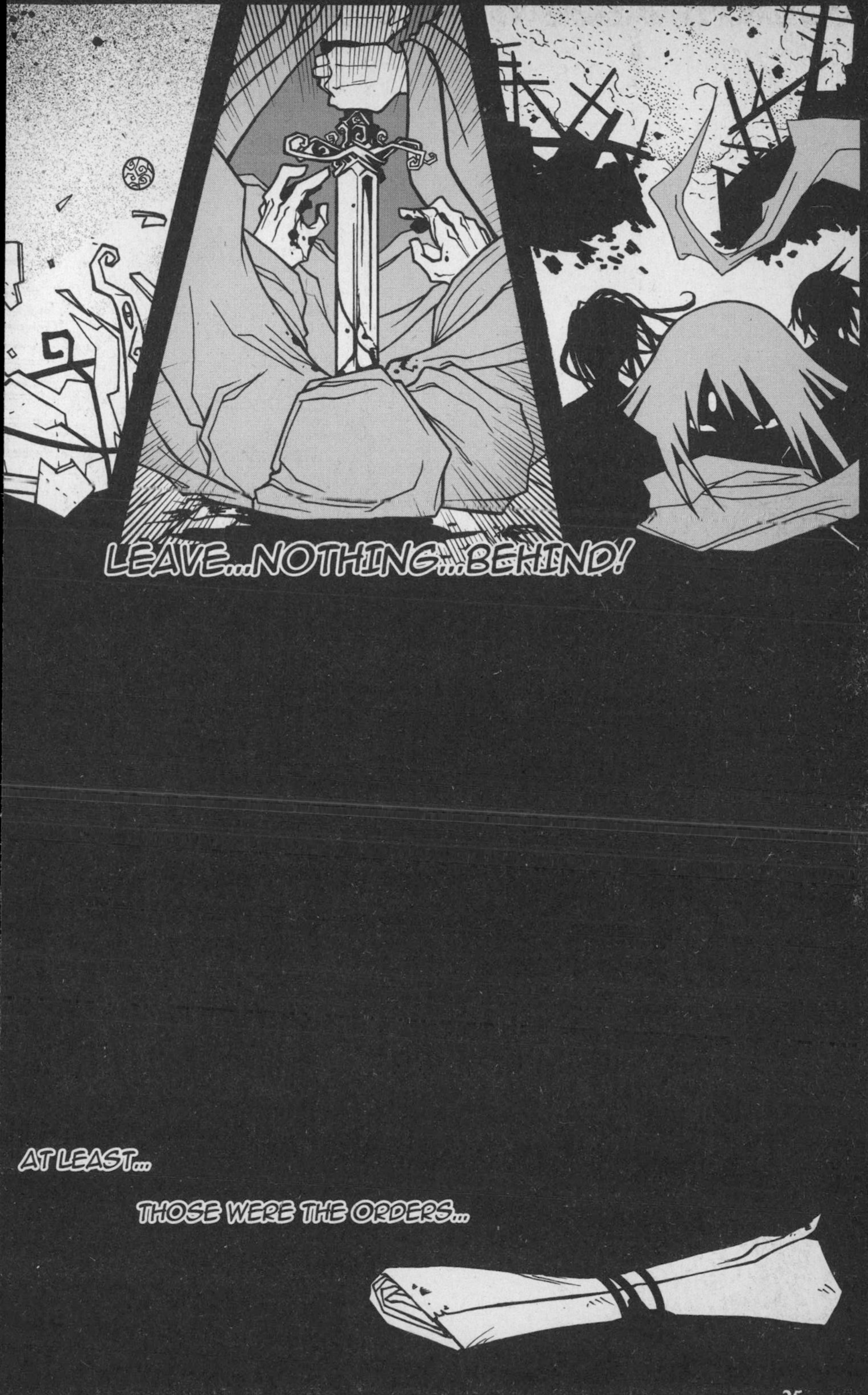
LEAVE...NOTHING...BEHIND!
AT LEAST...
THOSE WERE THE ORDERS...

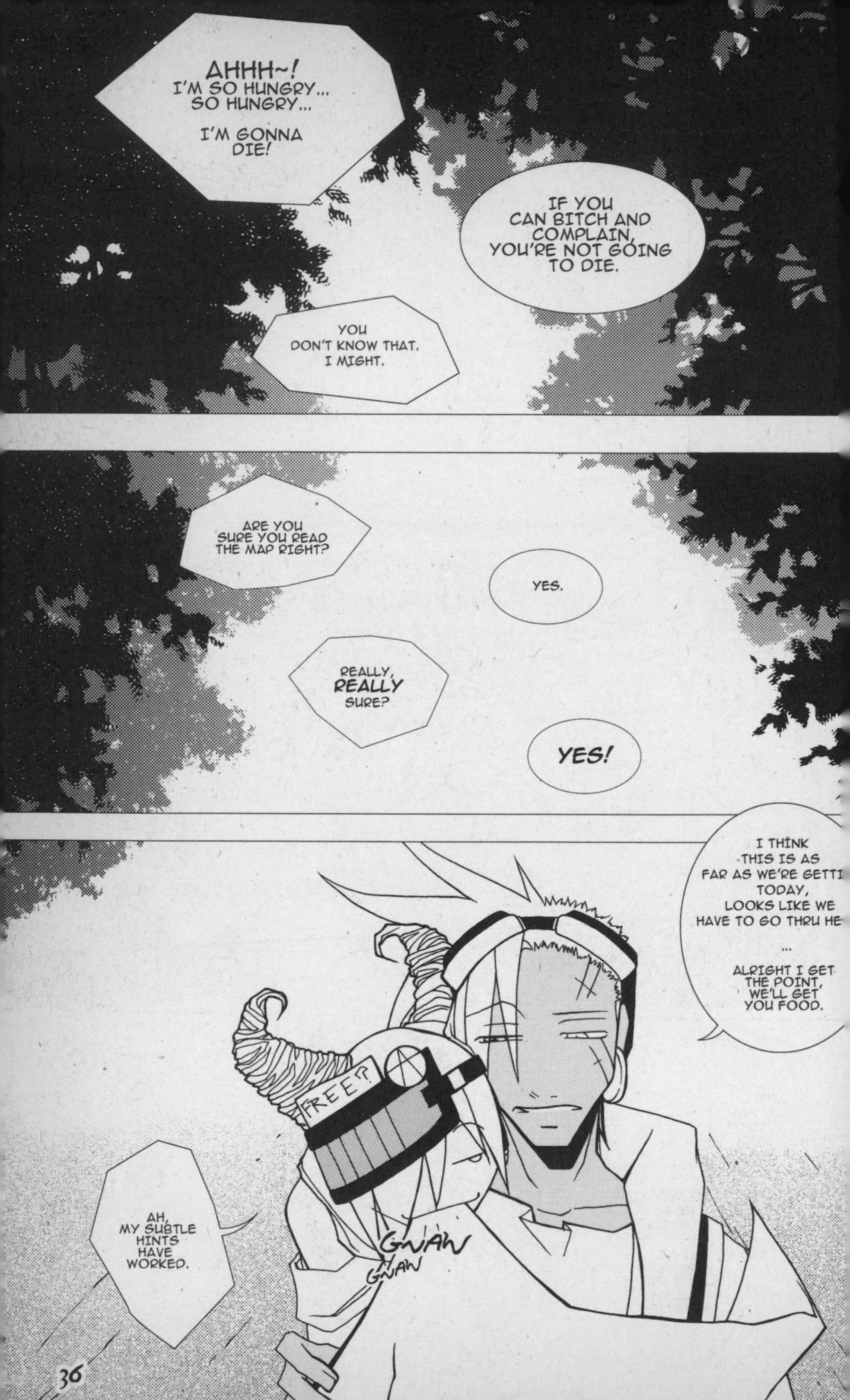

AHHH~! I'M SO HUNGRY... SO HUNGRY... I'M GONNA DIE!
IF YOU CAN BITCH AND COMPLAIN, YOU'RE NOT GOING TO DIE.
YOU DON'T KNOW THAT. I MIGHT.
ARE YOU SURE YOU READ THE MAP RIGHT?
YES.
REALLY, REALLY SURE?
YES!
I THINK THIS IS AS FAR AS WE'RE GETTI TODAY, LOOKS LIKE WE HAVE TO GO THRU HE ... ALRIGHT I GET THE POINT, WE'LL GET YOU FOOD.
FREE?
AH, MY SUBTLE HINTS HAVE WORKED.
GNAW GNAW

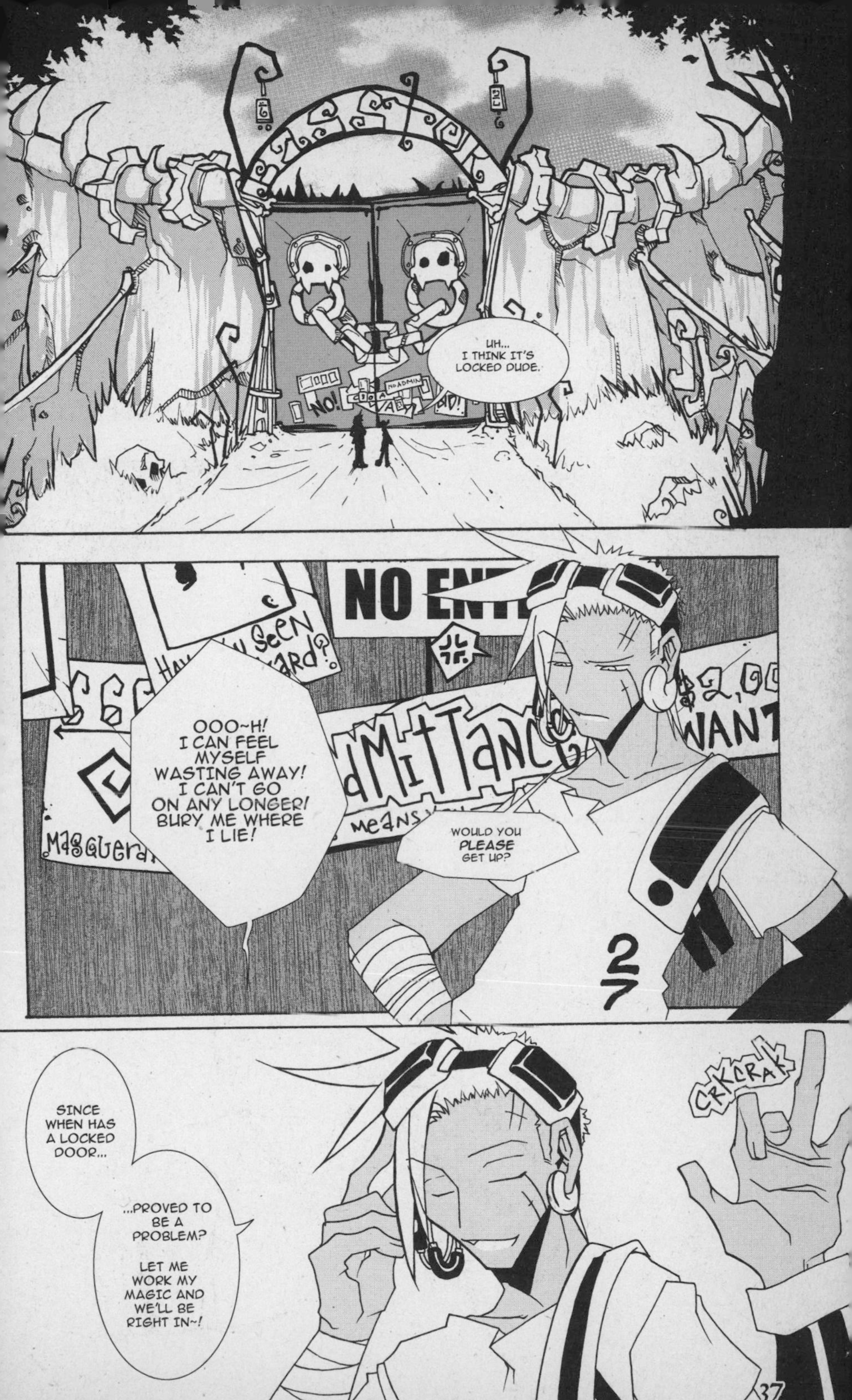
UH... I THINK IT'S LOCKED DUDE.
OOO~H! I CAN FEEL MYSELF WASTING AWAY! I CAN'T GO ON ANY LONGER! BURY ME WHERE I LIE!
WOULD YOU PLEASE GET UP?
SINCE WHEN HAS A LOCKED DOOR...
...PROVED TO BE A PROBLEM?
LET ME WORK MY MAGIC AND WE'LL BE RIGHT IN~!
CRKCRAK

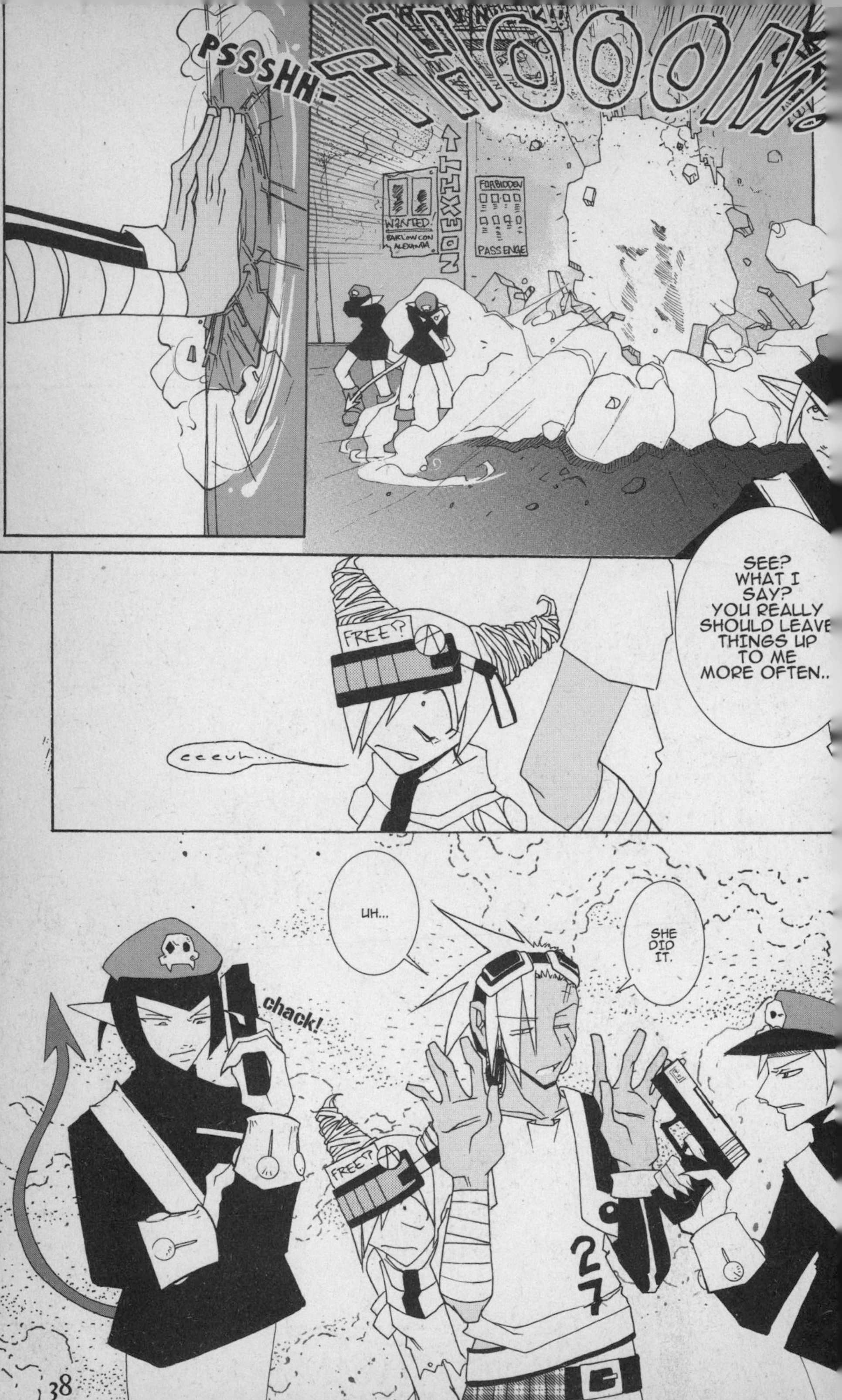
PSSSHH-
THOOOM
NEXT ON
WANTED
FORBIDDEN
PASSENGE
SEE? WHAT I SAY? YOU REALLY SHOULD LEAVE THINGS UP TO ME MORE OFTEN..
eeeuh...
FREE?
UH...
SHE DID IT.
chack!
FREE?
27

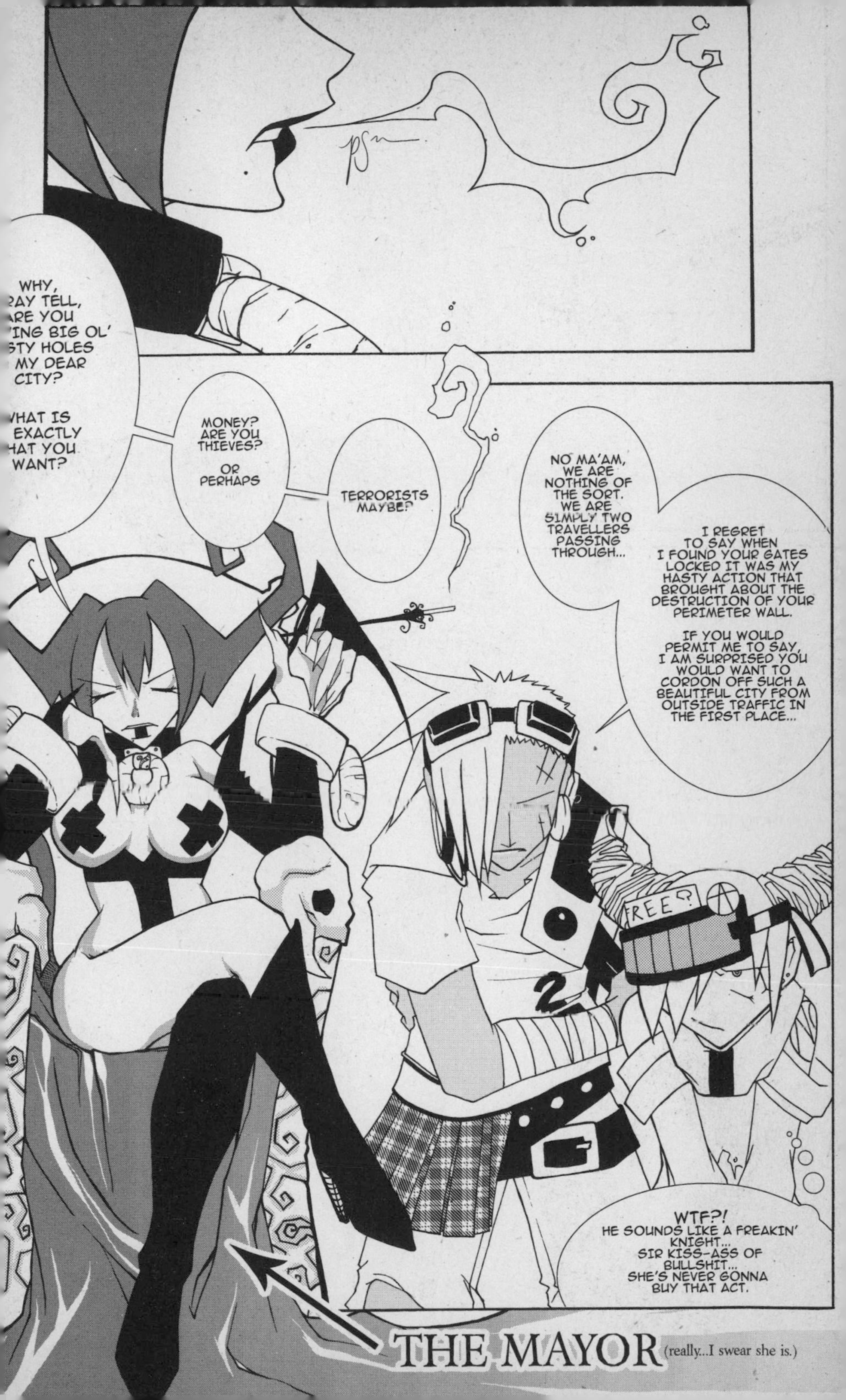

PS~
WHY, RAY TELL, ARE YOU 'ING BIG OL' STY HOLES MY DEAR CITY?
WHAT IS EXACTLY HAT YOU WANT?
MONEY? ARE YOU THIEVES? OR PERHAPS
TERRORISTS MAYBE?
NO MA'AM, WE ARE NOTHING OF THE SORT. WE ARE SIMPLY TWO TRAVELLERS PASSING THROUGH...
I REGRET TO SAY WHEN I FOUND YOUR GATES LOCKED IT WAS MY HASTY ACTION THAT BROUGHT ABOUT THE DESTRUCTION OF YOUR PERIMETER WALL.
IF YOU WOULD PERMIT ME TO SAY, I AM SURPRISED YOU WOULD WANT TO CORDON OFF SUCH A BEAUTIFUL CITY FROM OUTSIDE TRAFFIC IN THE FIRST PLACE...
FREE?
WTF?! HE SOUNDS LIKE A FREAKIN' KNIGHT... SIR KISS-ASS OF BULLSHIT... SHE'S NEVER GONNA BUY THAT ACT.
THE MAYOR (really...I swear she is.)

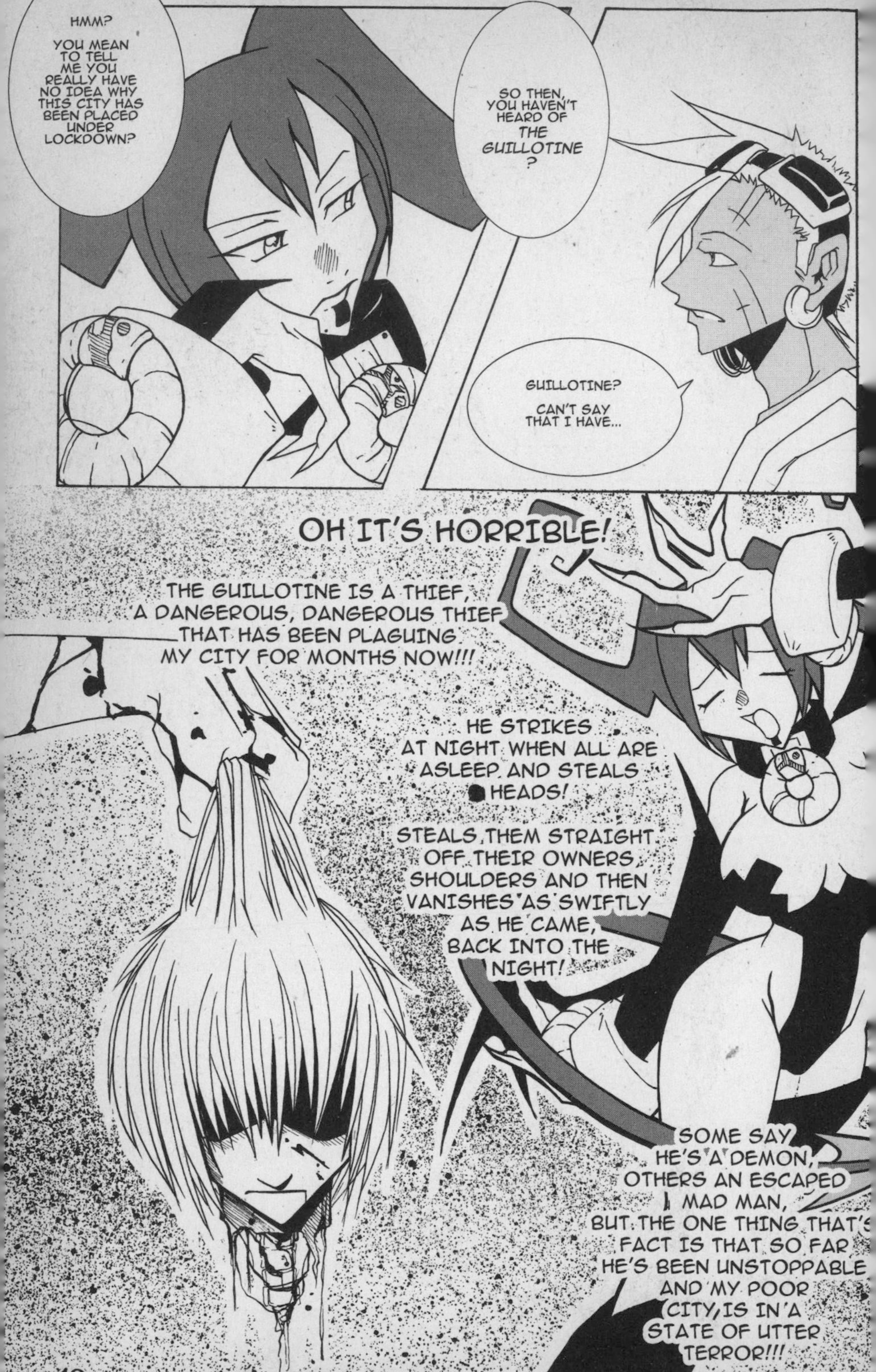
HMM? YOU MEAN TO TELL ME YOU REALLY HAVE NO IDEA WHY THIS CITY HAS BEEN PLACED UNDER LOCKDOWN?
SO THEN, YOU HAVEN'T HEARD OF THE GUILLOTINE ?
GUILLOTINE? CAN'T SAY THAT I HAVE...
OH IT'S HORRIBLE!
THE GUILLOTINE IS A THIEF, A DANGEROUS, DANGEROUS THIEF THAT HAS BEEN PLAGUING MY CITY FOR MONTHS NOW!!!
HE STRIKES AT NIGHT WHEN ALL ARE ASLEEP AND STEALS HEADS!
STEALS THEM STRAIGHT OFF THEIR OWNERS SHOULDERS AND THEN VANISHES AS SWIFTLY AS HE CAME, BACK INTO THE NIGHT!
SOME SAY HE'S A DEMON, OTHERS AN ESCAPED MAD MAN, BUT THE ONE THING THAT'S FACT IS THAT SO FAR HE'S BEEN UNSTOPPABLE AND MY POOR CITY IS IN A STATE OF UTTER TERROR!!!

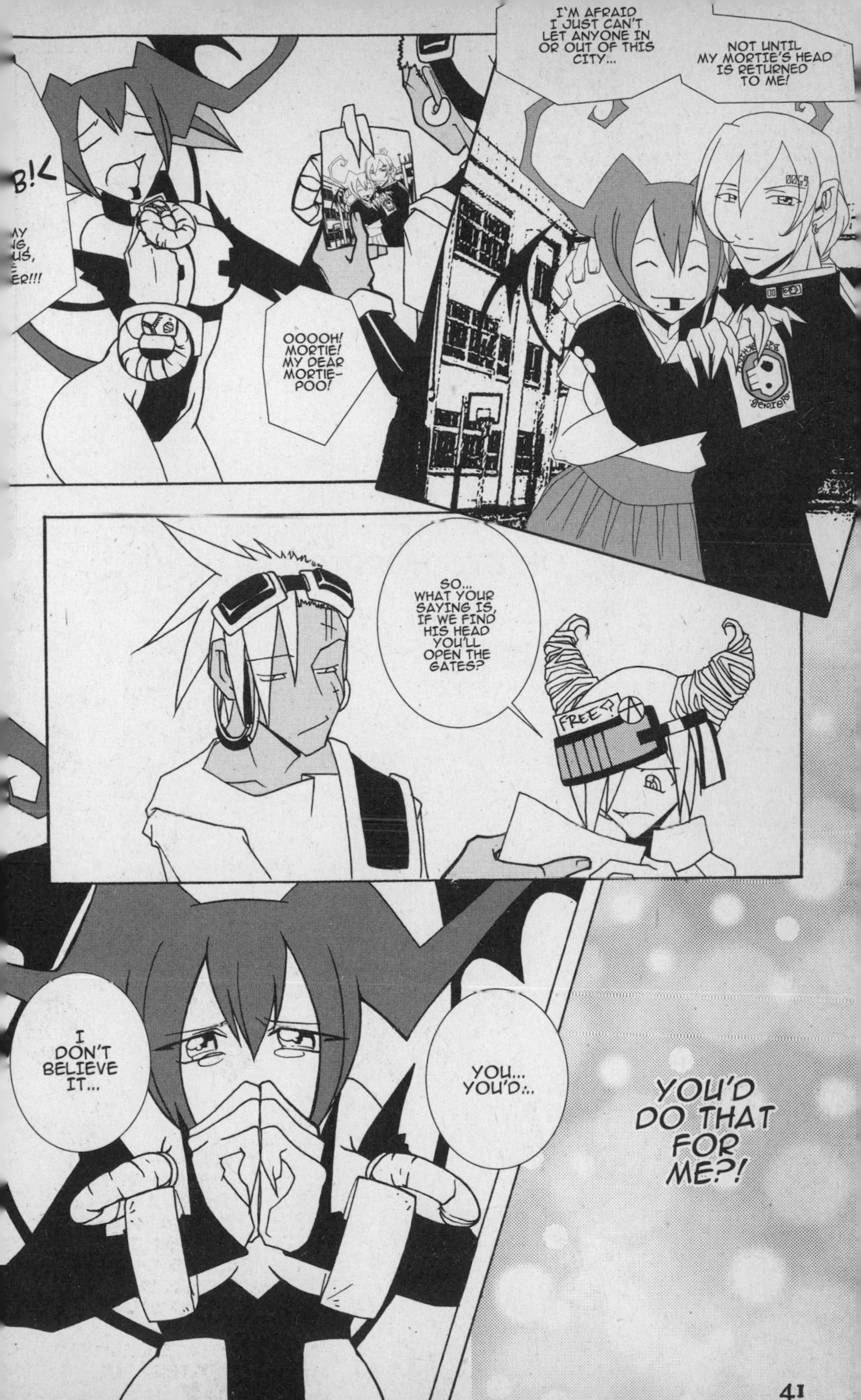
OOOOH! MORTIE! MY DEAR MORTIE-POO!
I'M AFRAID I JUST CAN'T LET ANYONE IN OR OUT OF THIS CITY...
NOT UNTIL MY MORTIE'S HEAD IS RETURNED TO ME!
SO... WHAT YOUR SAYING IS, IF WE FIND HIS HEAD YOU'LL OPEN THE GATES?
FREE?
I DON'T BELIEVE IT...
YOU... YOU'D...
YOU'D DO THAT FOR ME?!

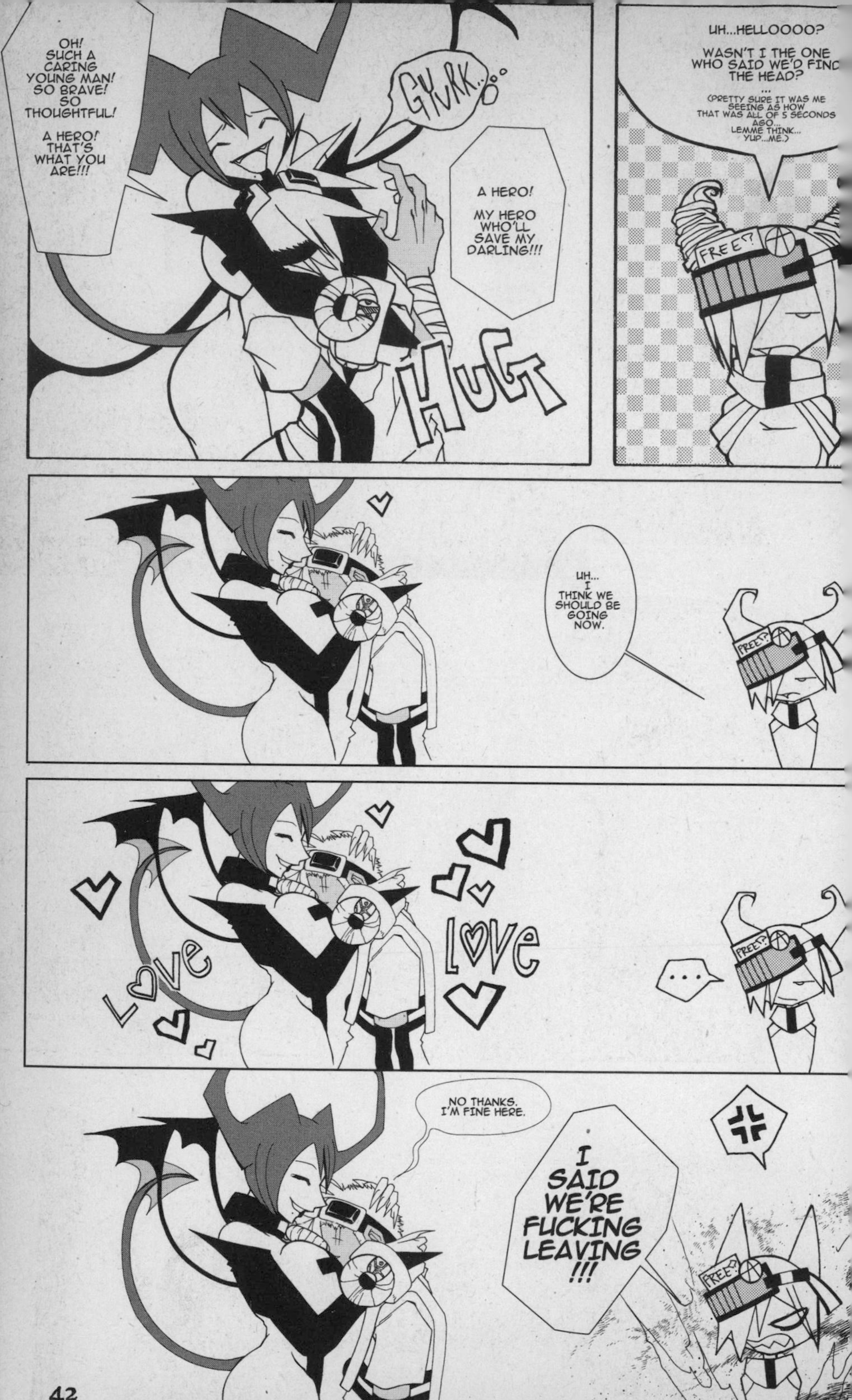
OH! SUCH A CARING YOUNG MAN! SO BRAVE! SO THOUGHTFUL!
A HERO! THAT'S WHAT YOU ARE!!!
GYURK...
A HERO! MY HERO WHO'LL SAVE MY DARLING!!!
HUG
UH...HELLOOOO?
WASN'T I THE ONE WHO SAID WE'D FIND THE HEAD?
...
(PRETTY SURE IT WAS ME SEEING AS HOW THAT WAS ALL OF 5 SECONDS AGO... LEMME THINK... YUP...ME.)
FREE?
UH... I THINK WE SHOULD BE GOING NOW.
FREE?
LOVE
LOVE
FREE?
...
NO THANKS. I'M FINE HERE.
I SAID WE'RE FUCKING LEAVING!!!
FREE?

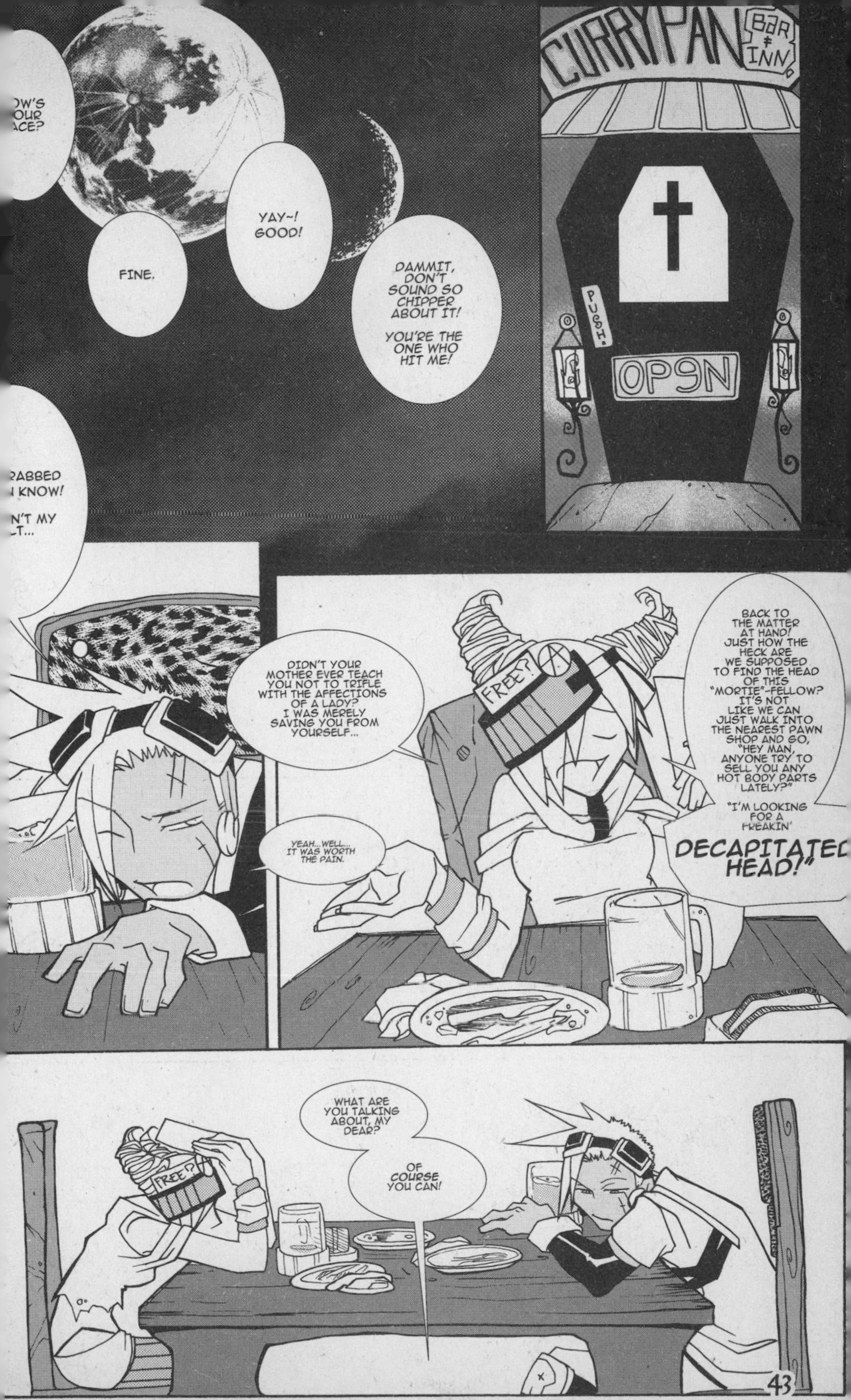

OW'S
OUR
ACE?
FINE.
YAY~! GOOD!
DAMMIT, DON'T SOUND SO CHIPPER ABOUT IT!
YOU'RE THE ONE WHO HIT ME!
CURRY PAN
BAR & INN
PUSH.
OP9N
RABBED
N KNOW!
N'T MY
T...
DIDN'T YOUR MOTHER EVER TEACH YOU NOT TO TRIFLE WITH THE AFFECTIONS OF A LADY? I WAS MERELY SAVING YOU FROM YOURSELF...
YEAH...WELL... IT WAS WORTH THE PAIN.
FREE?
BACK TO THE MATTER AT HAND! JUST HOW THE HECK ARE WE SUPPOSED TO FIND THE HEAD OF THIS "MORTIE"-FELLOW? IT'S NOT LIKE WE CAN JUST WALK INTO THE NEAREST PAWN SHOP AND GO, "HEY MAN, ANYONE TRY TO SELL YOU ANY HOT BODY PARTS LATELY?"
"I'M LOOKING FOR A FREAKIN'
DECAPITATED HEAD!"
WHAT ARE YOU TALKING ABOUT, MY DEAR?
OF COURSE YOU CAN!
FREE?

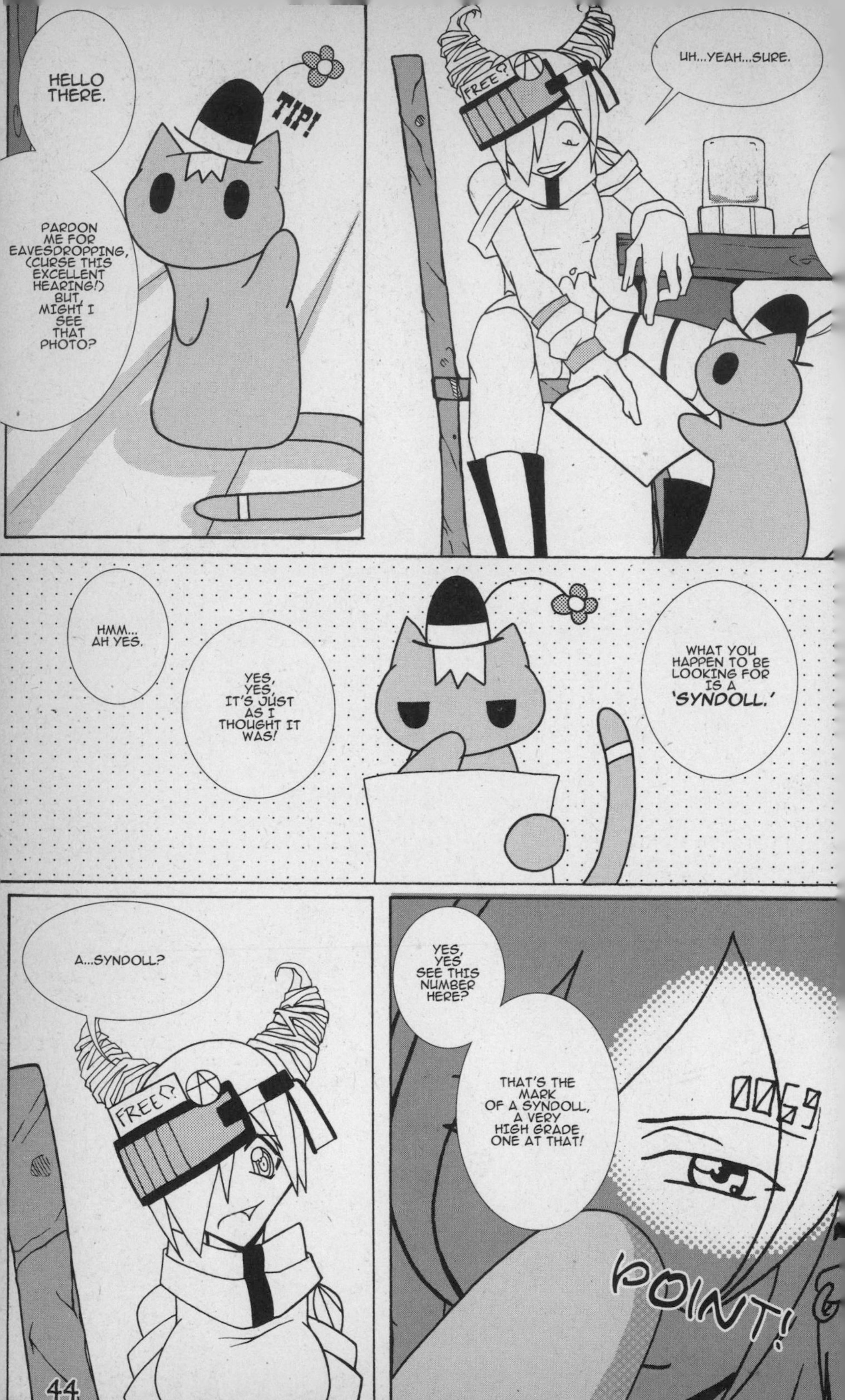
HELLO THERE.
TIP!
PARDON ME FOR EAVESDROPPING, (CURSE THIS EXCELLENT HEARING!) BUT, MIGHT I SEE THAT PHOTO?
FREE?
UH...YEAH...SURE.
HMM... AH YES.
YES, YES, IT'S JUST AS I THOUGHT IT WAS!
WHAT YOU HAPPEN TO BE LOOKING FOR IS A 'SYNDOLL.'
A...SYNDOLL?
FREE?
YES, YES' SEE THIS NUMBER HERE?
THAT'S THE MARK OF A SYNDOLL, A VERY HIGH GRADE ONE AT THAT!
0069
POINT!

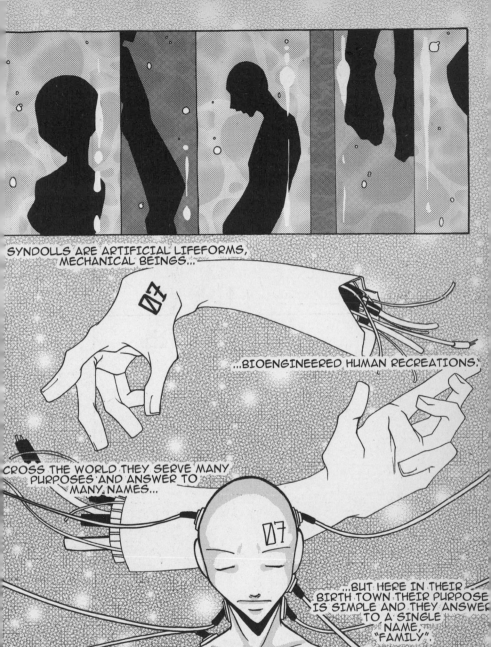

SYNDOLLS ARE ARTIFICIAL LIFEFORMS, MECHANICAL BEINGS...

...BIOENGINEERED HUMAN RECREATIONS.

CROSS THE WORLD THEY SERVE MANY PURPOSES AND ANSWER TO MANY NAMES...

...BUT HERE IN THEIR BIRTH TOWN THEIR PURPOSE IS SIMPLE AND THEY ANSWER TO A SINGLE NAME, "FAMILY".

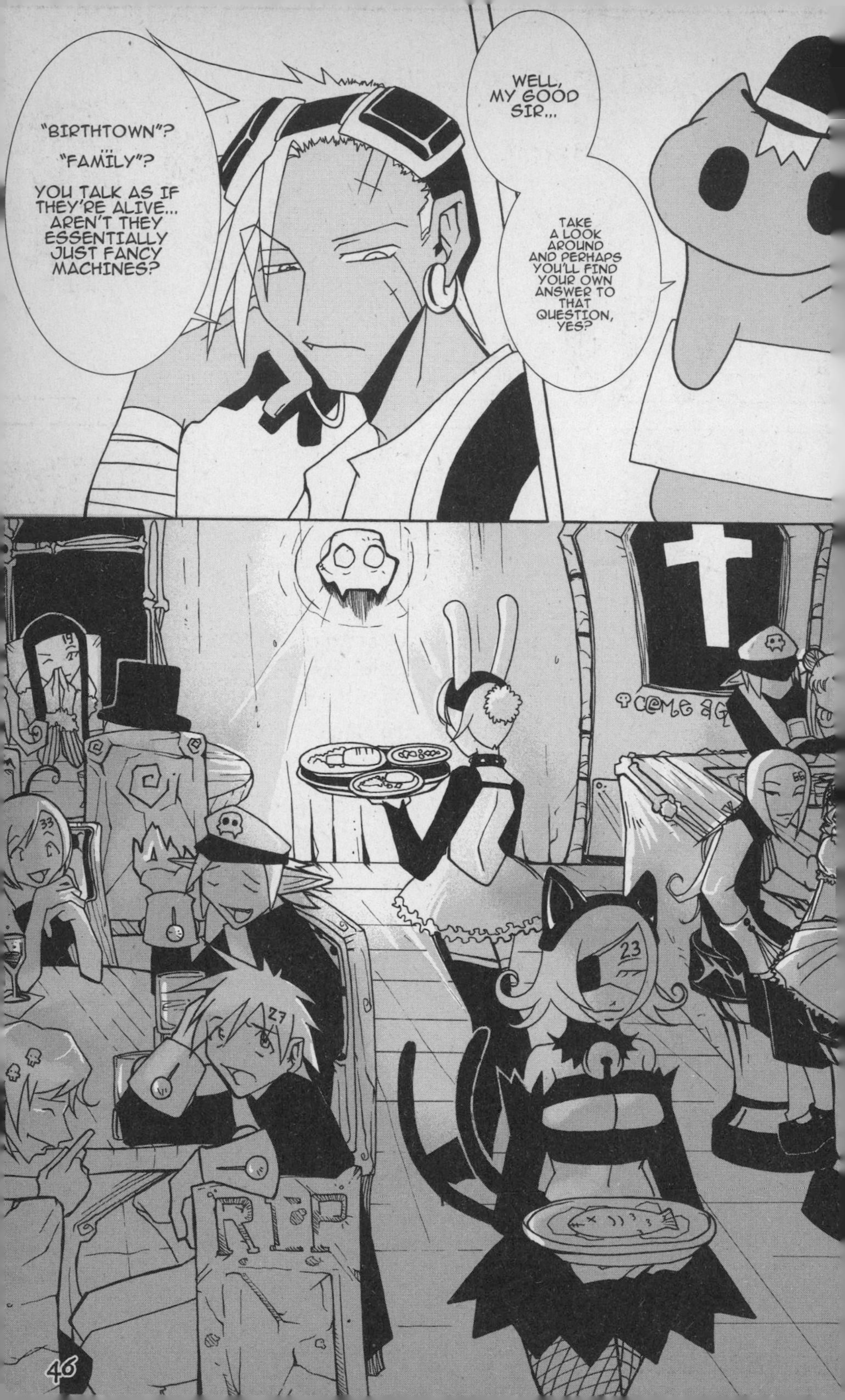
"BIRTHTOWN"? ... "FAMILY"? YOU TALK AS IF THEY'RE ALIVE... AREN'T THEY ESSENTIALLY JUST FANCY MACHINES?
WELL, MY GOOD SIR...
TAKE A LOOK AROUND AND PERHAPS YOU'LL FIND YOUR OWN ANSWER TO THAT QUESTION, YES?
RIP

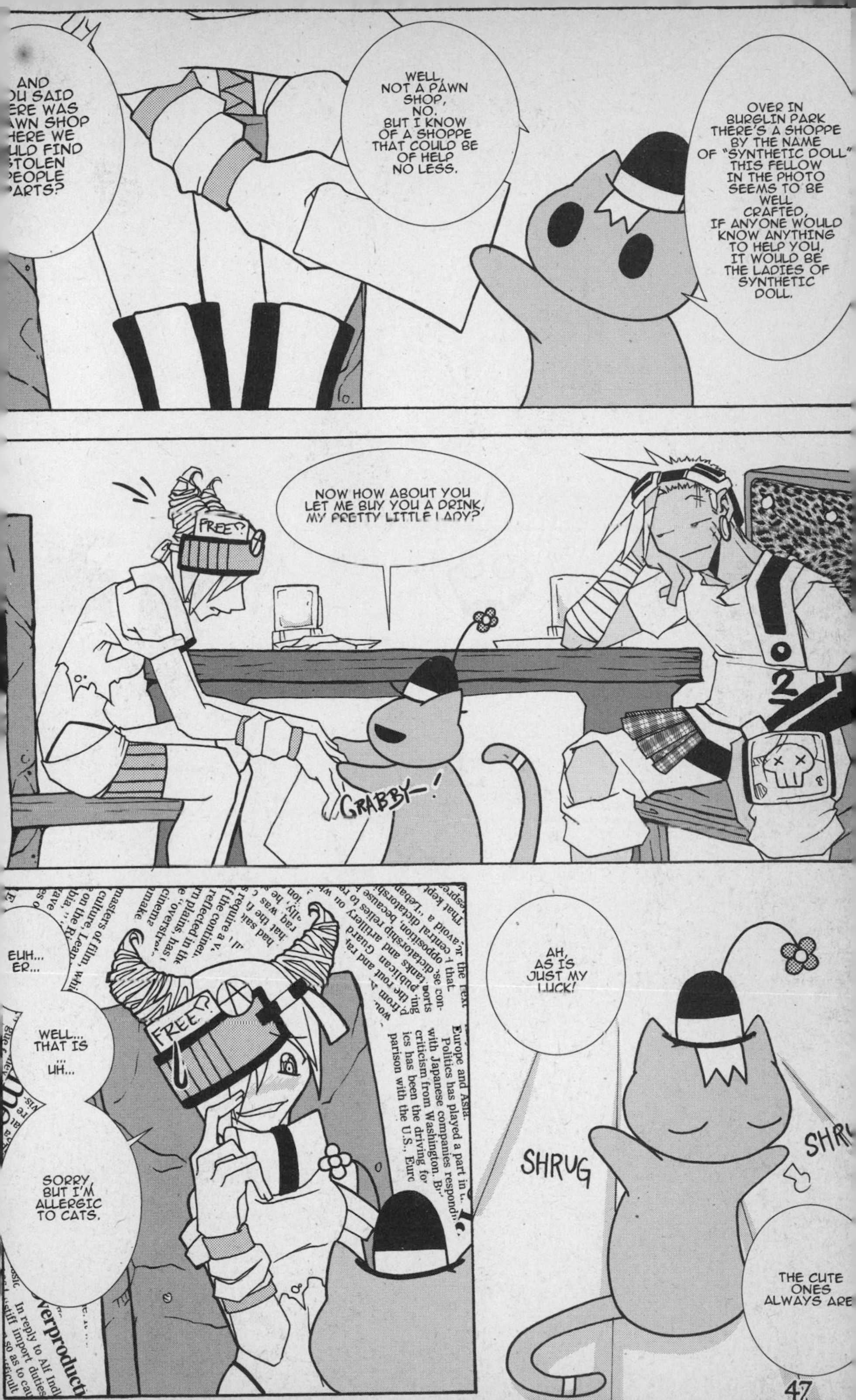
AND OU SAID ERE WAS AWN SHOP HERE WE ULD FIND STOLEN PEOPLE PARTS?
WELL, NOT A PAWN SHOP, NO. BUT I KNOW OF A SHOPPE THAT COULD BE OF HELP NO LESS.
OVER IN BURGLIN PARK THERE'S A SHOPPE BY THE NAME OF "SYNTHETIC DOLL" THIS FELLOW IN THE PHOTO SEEMS TO BE WELL CRAFTED, IF ANYONE WOULD KNOW ANYTHING TO HELP YOU, IT WOULD BE THE LADIES OF SYNTHETIC DOLL.
FREE?
NOW HOW ABOUT YOU LET ME BUY YOU A DRINK, MY PRETTY LITTLE LADY?
GRABBY—!
EUH... ER...
WELL... THAT IS ... UH...
SORRY, BUT I'M ALLERGIC TO CATS.
FREE?
AH, AS IS JUST MY LUCK!
SHRUG
SHRU
THE CUTE ONES ALWAYS ARE

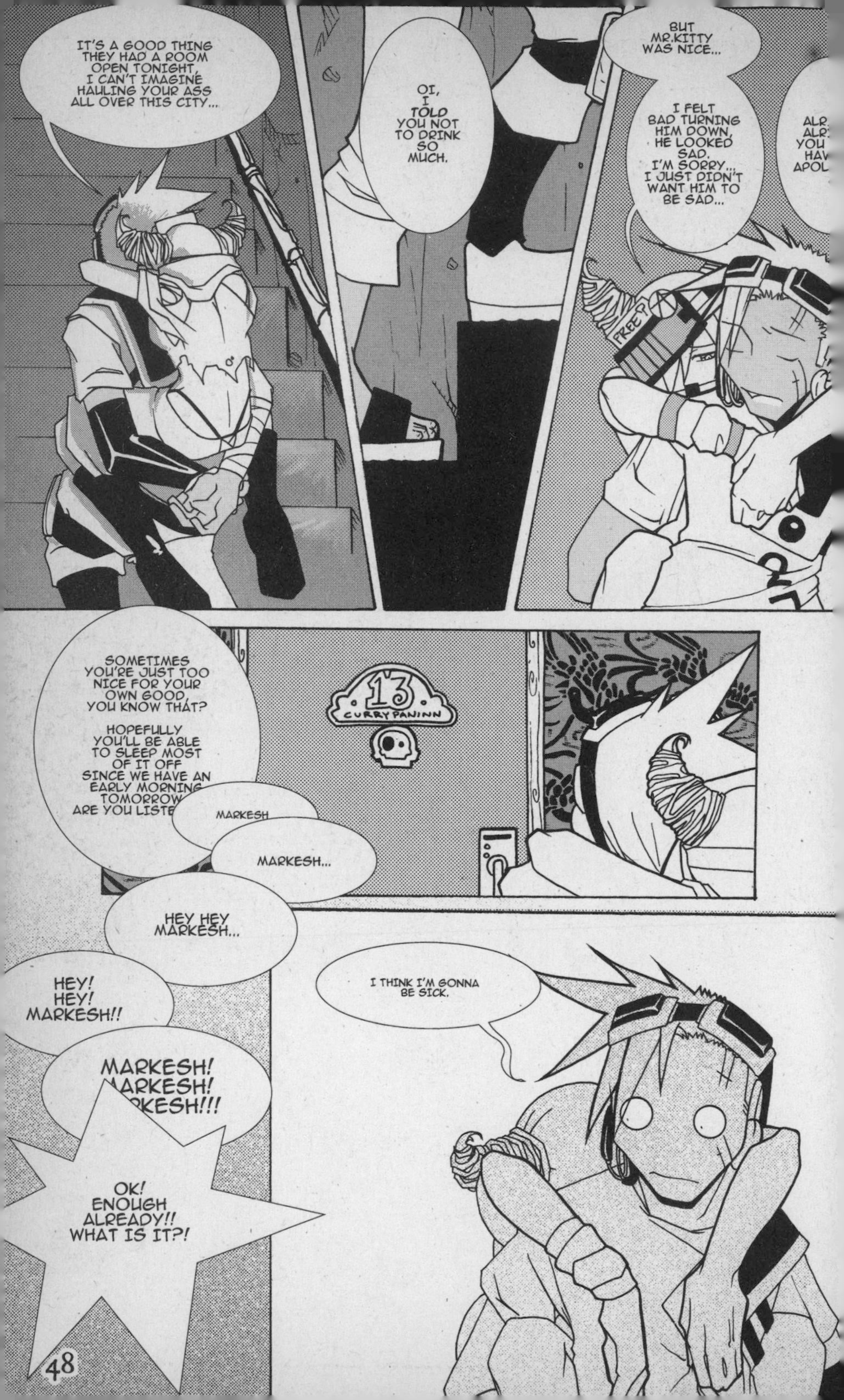

IT'S A GOOD THING THEY HAD A ROOM OPEN TONIGHT, I CAN'T IMAGINE HAULING YOUR ASS ALL OVER THIS CITY...
OI, I TOLD YOU NOT TO DRINK SO MUCH.
BUT MR.KITTY WAS NICE...
I FELT BAD TURNING HIM DOWN, HE LOOKED SAD. I'M SORRY... I JUST DIDN'T WANT HIM TO BE SAD...
FREE?
SOMETIMES YOU'RE JUST TOO NICE FOR YOUR OWN GOOD, YOU KNOW THAT? HOPEFULLY YOU'LL BE ABLE TO SLEEP MOST OF IT OFF SINCE WE HAVE AN EARLY MORNING TOMORROW. ARE YOU LISTE
13
CURRY PAN INN
MARKESH
MARKESH...
HEY HEY MARKESH...
HEY! HEY! MARKESH!!
I THINK I'M GONNA BE SICK.
MARKESH!
OK! ENOUGH ALREADY!! WHAT IS IT?!

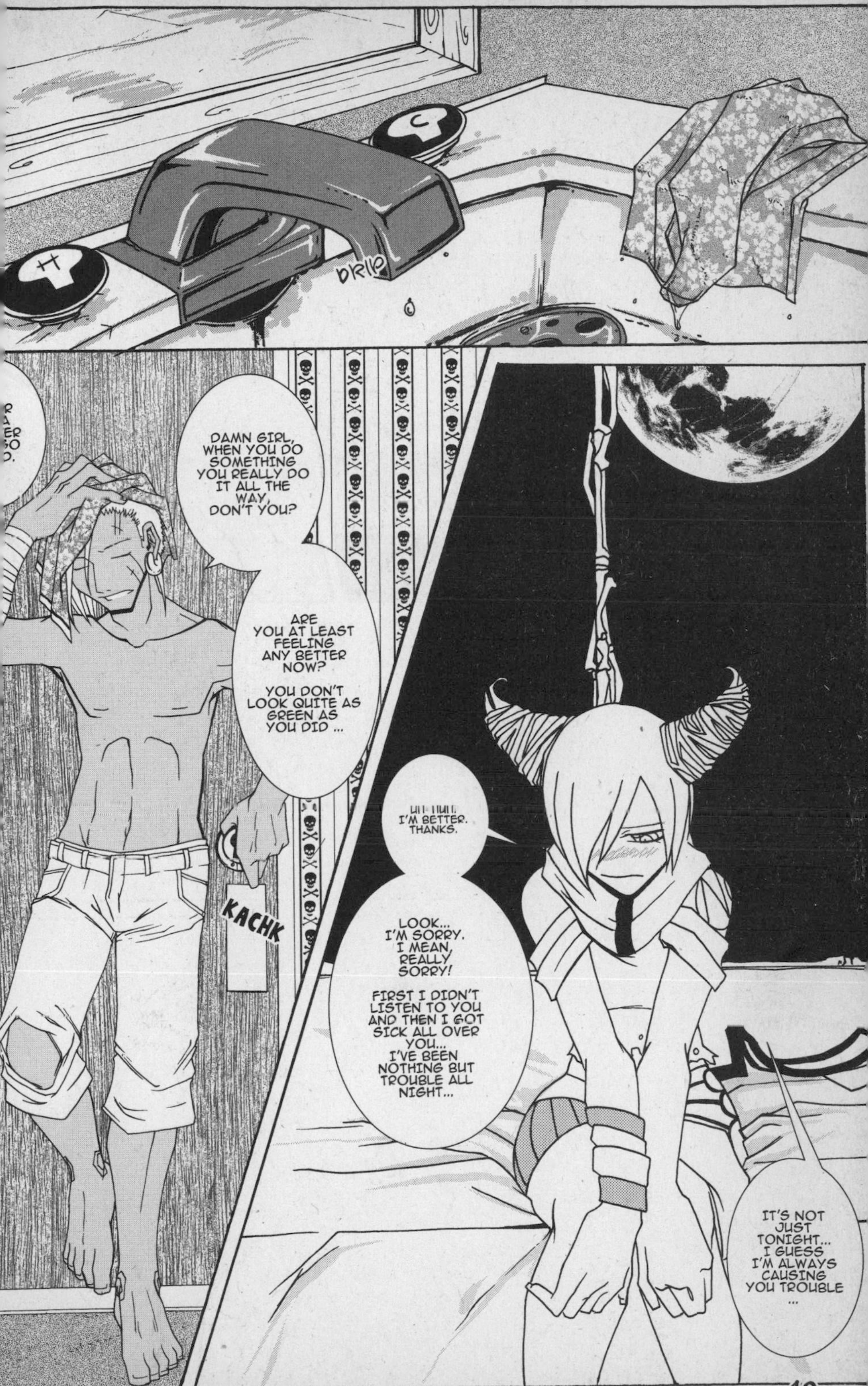
DRIP
DAMN GIRL, WHEN YOU DO SOMETHING YOU REALLY DO IT ALL THE WAY, DON'T YOU?
ARE YOU AT LEAST FEELING ANY BETTER NOW?
YOU DON'T LOOK QUITE AS GREEN AS YOU DID ...
KACHK
I'M BETTER. THANKS.
LOOK... I'M SORRY. I MEAN, REALLY SORRY!
FIRST I DIDN'T LISTEN TO YOU AND THEN I GOT SICK ALL OVER YOU... I'VE BEEN NOTHING BUT TROUBLE ALL NIGHT...
IT'S NOT JUST TONIGHT... I GUESS I'M ALWAYS CAUSING YOU TROUBLE ...

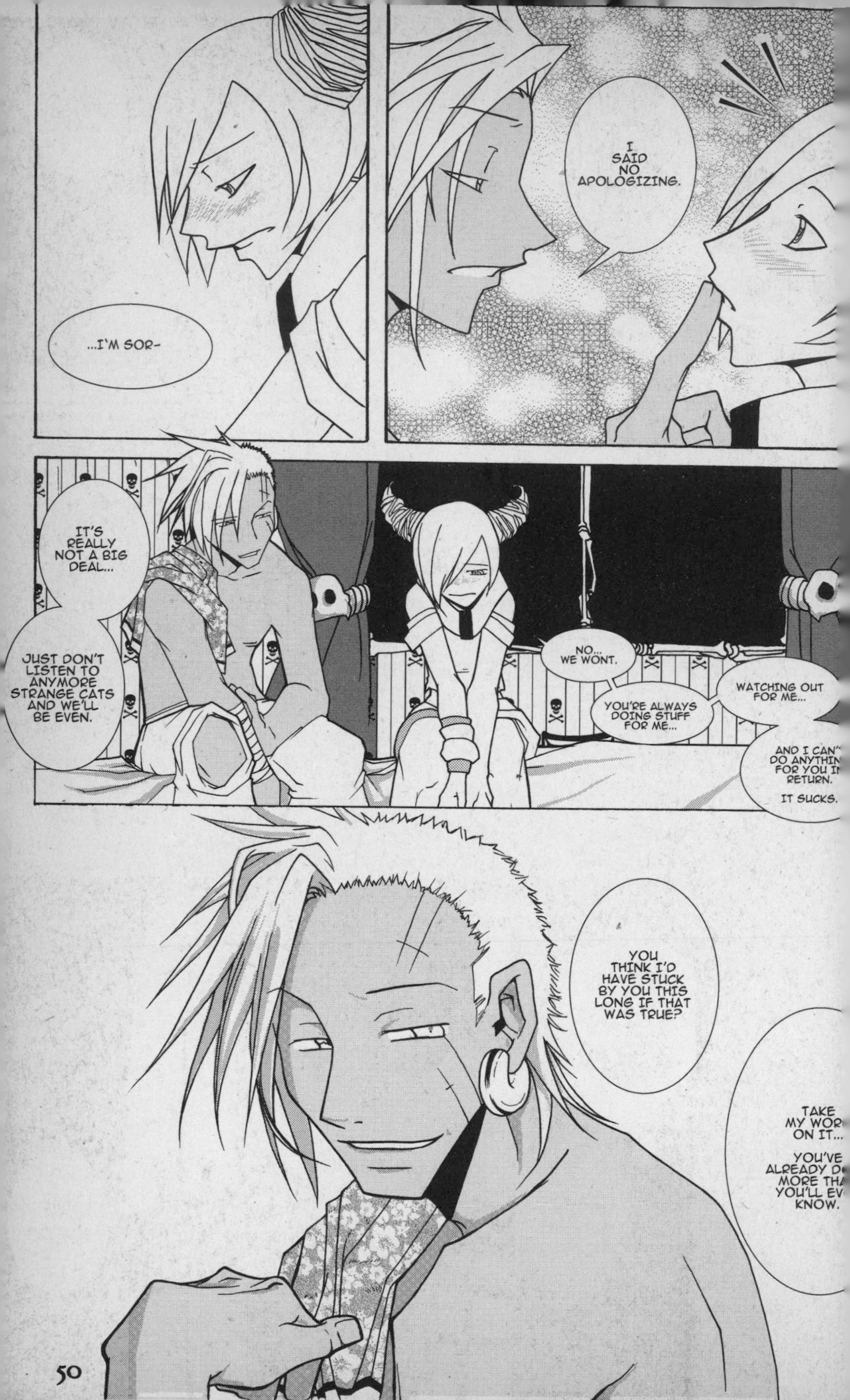
...I'M SOR-
I SAID NO APOLOGIZING.
IT'S REALLY NOT A BIG DEAL...
JUST DON'T LISTEN TO ANYMORE STRANGE CATS AND WE'LL BE EVEN.
NO... WE WONT.
YOU'RE ALWAYS DOING STUFF FOR ME...
WATCHING OUT FOR ME...
AND I CAN' DO ANYTHIN FOR YOU I RETURN.
IT SUCKS.
YOU THINK I'D HAVE STUCK BY YOU THIS LONG IF THAT WAS TRUE?
TAKE MY WOR ON IT...
YOU'VE ALREADY D MORE THA YOU'LL EV KNOW.

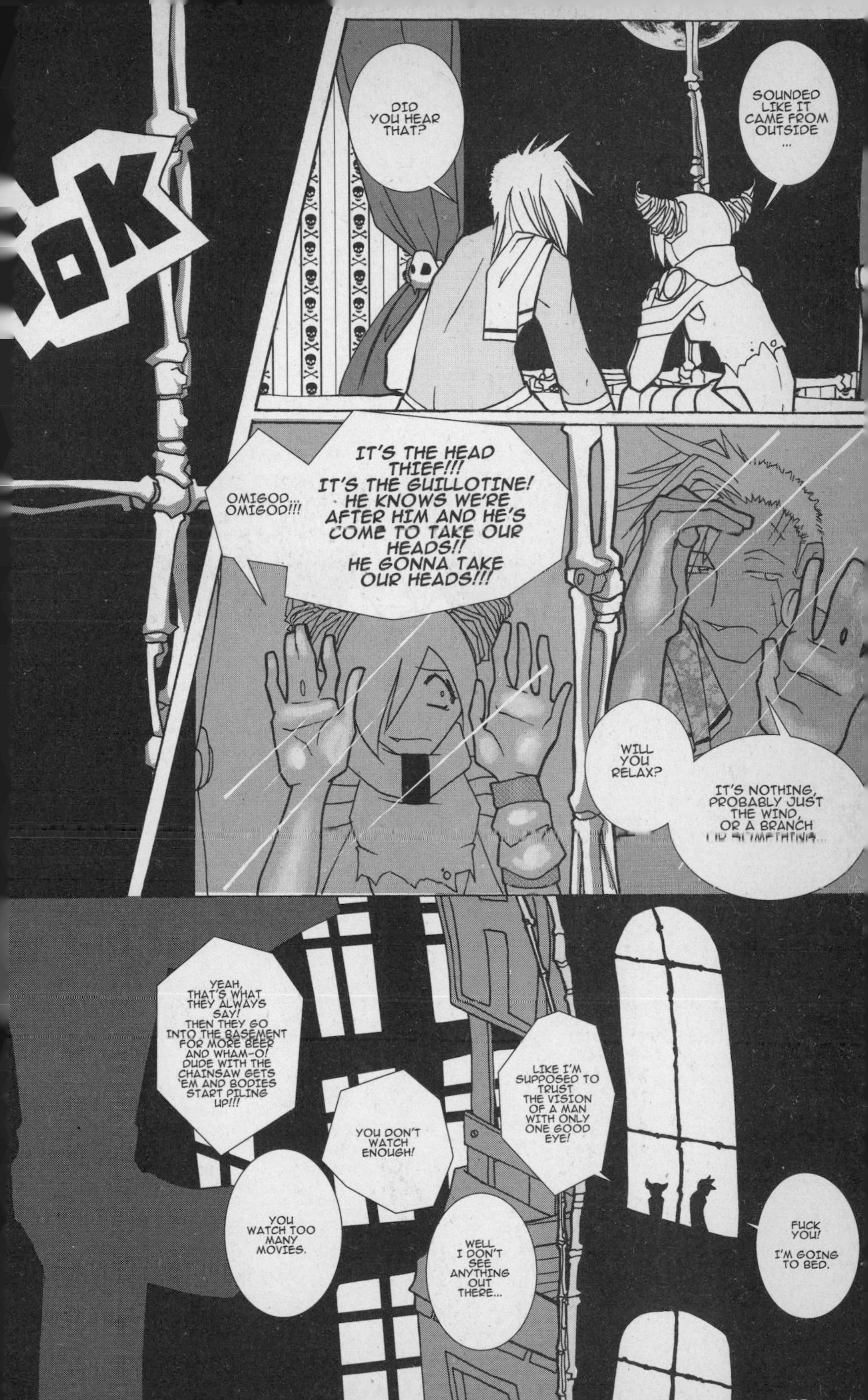
OK
DID YOU HEAR THAT?
SOUNDED LIKE IT CAME FROM OUTSIDE ...
OMIGOD... OMIGOD!!!
IT'S THE HEAD THIEF!!! IT'S THE GUILLOTINE! HE KNOWS WE'RE AFTER HIM AND HE'S COME TO TAKE OUR HEADS!! HE GONNA TAKE OUR HEADS!!!
WILL YOU RELAX?
IT'S NOTHING, PROBABLY JUST THE WIND, OR A BRANCH
YEAH, THAT'S WHAT THEY ALWAYS SAY! THEN THEY GO INTO THE BASEMENT FOR MORE BEER AND WHAM-O! DUDE WITH THE CHAINSAW GETS 'EM AND BODIES START PILING UP!!!
YOU DON'T WATCH ENOUGH!
LIKE I'M SUPPOSED TO TRUST THE VISION OF A MAN WITH ONLY ONE GOOD EYE!
YOU WATCH TOO MANY MOVIES.
WELL I DON'T SEE ANYTHING OUT THERE...
FUCK YOU!
I'M GOING TO BED.

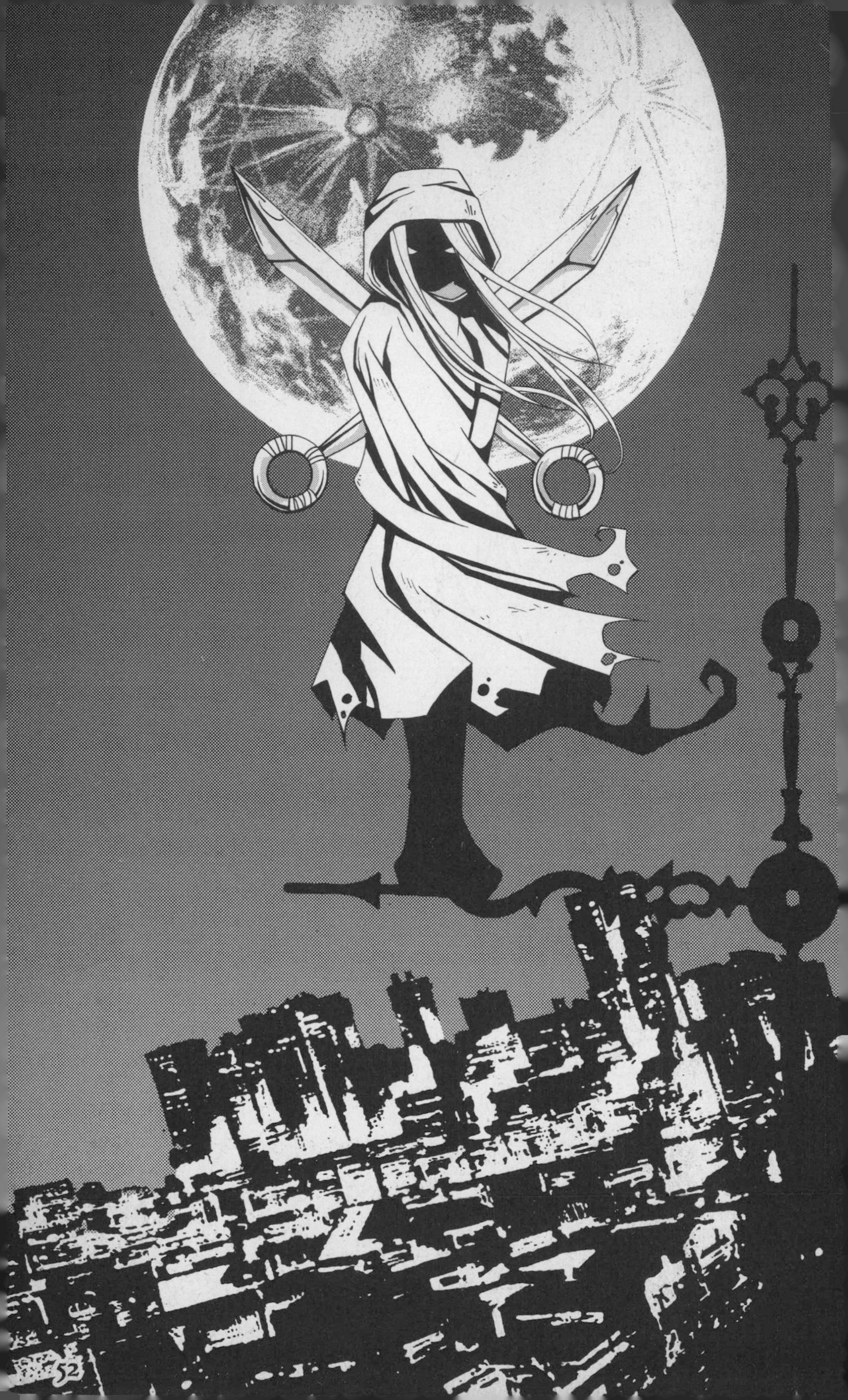

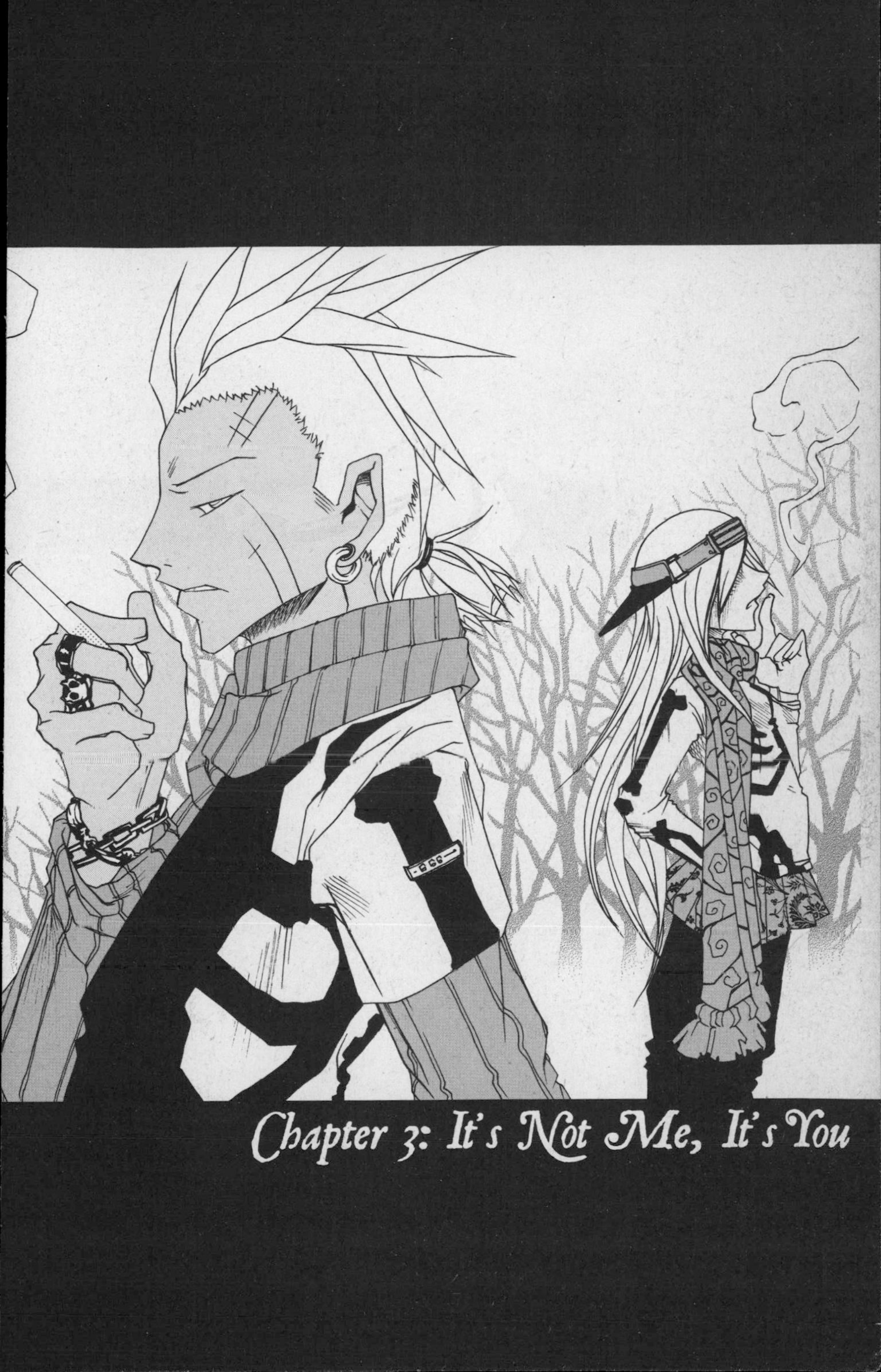

Chapter 3: It's Not Me, It's You

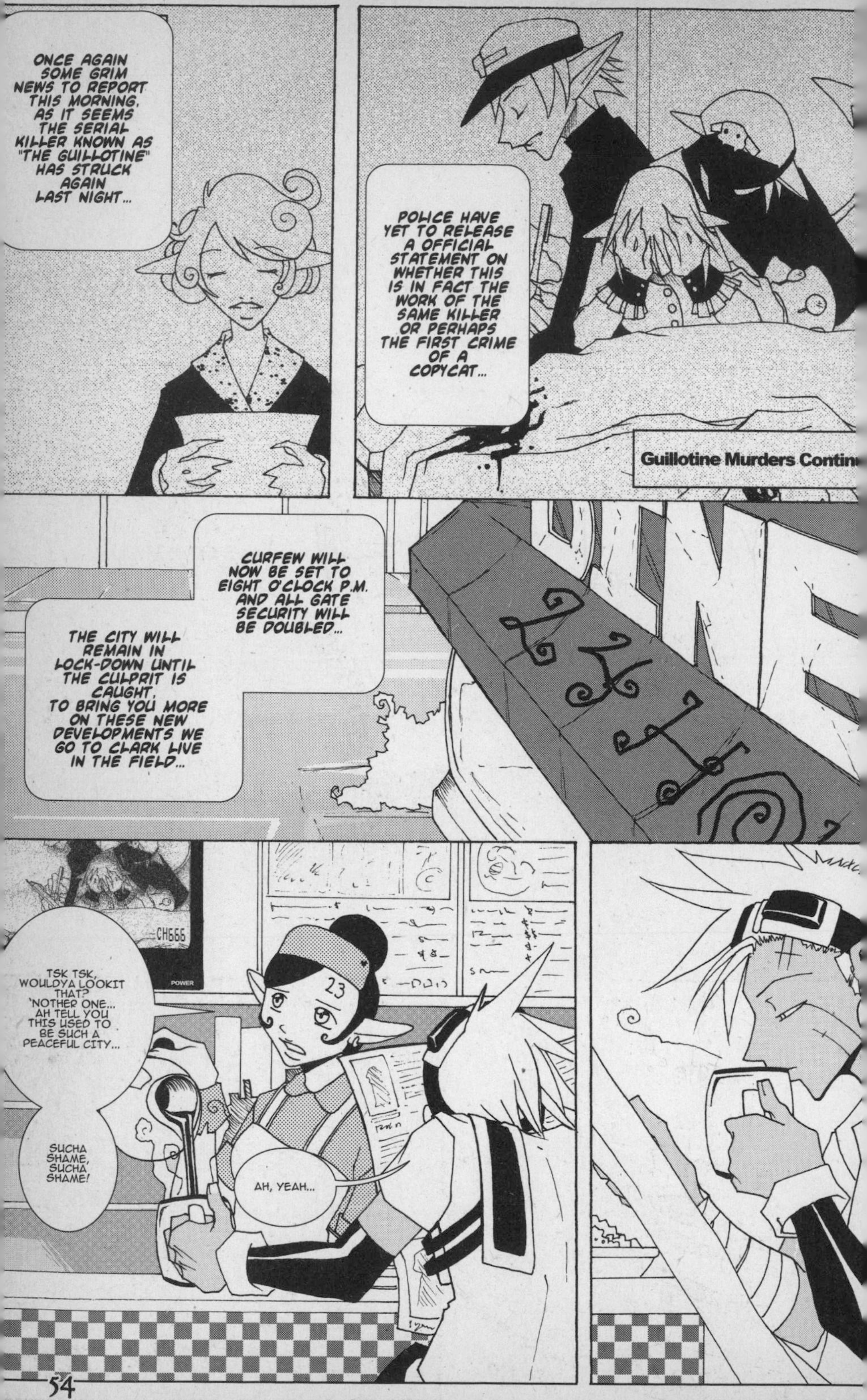
ONCE AGAIN SOME GRIM NEWS TO REPORT THIS MORNING, AS IT SEEMS THE SERIAL KILLER KNOWN AS "THE GUILLOTINE" HAS STRUCK AGAIN LAST NIGHT...
POLICE HAVE YET TO RELEASE A OFFICIAL STATEMENT ON WHETHER THIS IS IN FACT THE WORK OF THE SAME KILLER OR PERHAPS THE FIRST CRIME OF A COPYCAT...
Guillotine Murders Contin
CURFEW WILL NOW BE SET TO EIGHT O'CLOCK P.M. AND ALL GATE SECURITY WILL BE DOUBLED...
THE CITY WILL REMAIN IN LOCK-DOWN UNTIL THE CULPRIT IS CAUGHT, TO BRING YOU MORE ON THESE NEW DEVELOPMENTS WE GO TO CLARK LIVE IN THE FIELD...
CH666
POWER
TSK TSK, WOULDYA LO'OKIT THAT? 'NOTHER ONE... AH TELL YOU THIS USED TO BE SUCH A PEACEFUL CITY...
SUCHA SHAME, SUCHA SHAME!
AH, YEAH...

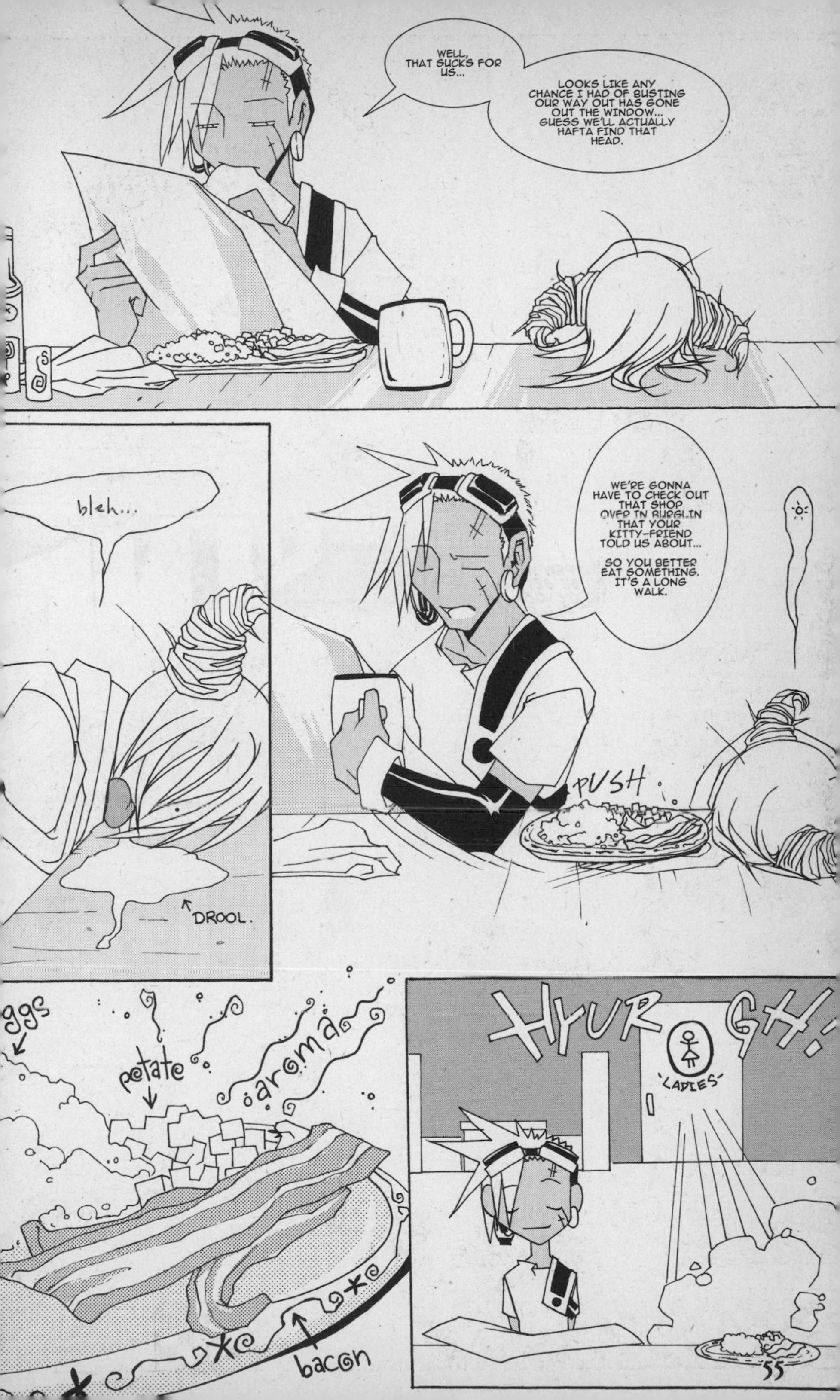
WELL, THAT SUCKS FOR US...
LOOKS LIKE ANY CHANCE I HAD OF BUSTING OUR WAY OUT THE WINDOW HAS GONE OUT THE WINDOW... GUESS WE'LL ACTUALLY HAFTA FIND THAT HEAD.
bleh...
DROOL.
WE'RE GONNA HAVE TO CHECK OUT THAT SHOP OVER IN BURGLIN THAT YOUR KITTY-FRIEND TOLD US ABOUT...
SO YOU BETTER EAT SOMETHING. IT'S A LONG WALK.
PUSH
ggs
potate
aroma
bacon
HYURGH!
LADIES

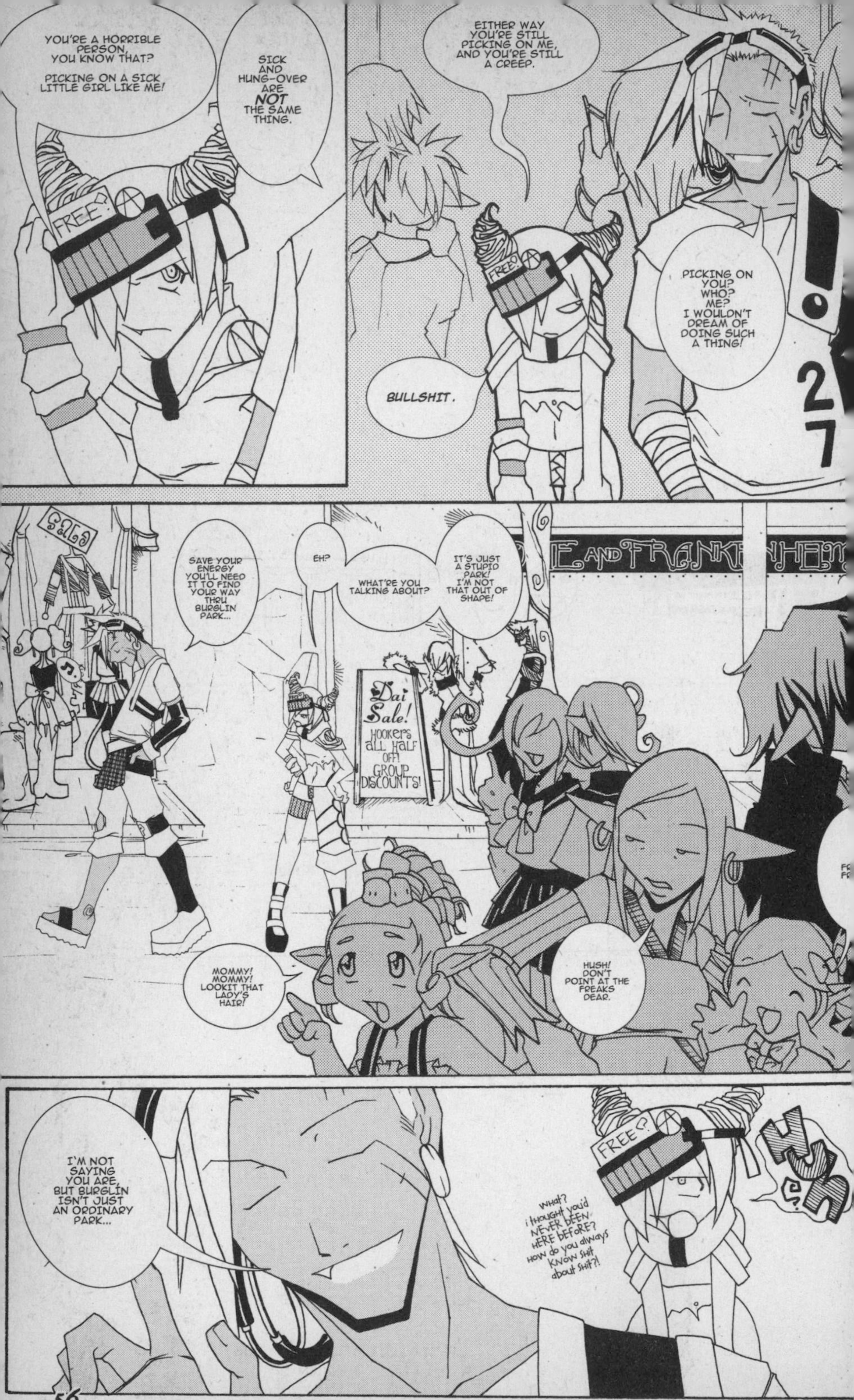

YOU'RE A HORRIBLE PERSON, YOU KNOW THAT?
PICKING ON A SICK LITTLE GIRL LIKE ME!
SICK AND HUNG-OVER ARE ***NOT*** THE SAME THING.
EITHER WAY YOU'RE STILL PICKING ON ME, AND YOU'RE STILL A CREEP.
PICKING ON YOU? WHO? ME? I WOULDN'T DREAM OF DOING SUCH A THING!
BULLSHIT.
SAVE YOUR ENERGY YOU'LL NEED IT TO FIND YOUR WAY THRU BURGLIN PARK...
EH?
WHAT'RE YOU TALKING ABOUT?
IT'S JUST A STUPID PARK! I'M NOT THAT OUT OF SHAPE!
Dai Sale! HOOKERS ALL HALF OFF! GROUP DISCOUNTS!
MOMMY! MOMMY! LOOKIT THAT LADY'S HAIR!
HUSH! DON'T POINT AT THE FREAKS DEAR.
I'M NOT SAYING YOU ARE, BUT BURGLIN ISN'T JUST AN ORDINARY PARK...
what? i thought you'd NEVER BEEN HERE BEFORE? How do you always KNOW shit about shit?!
HUH

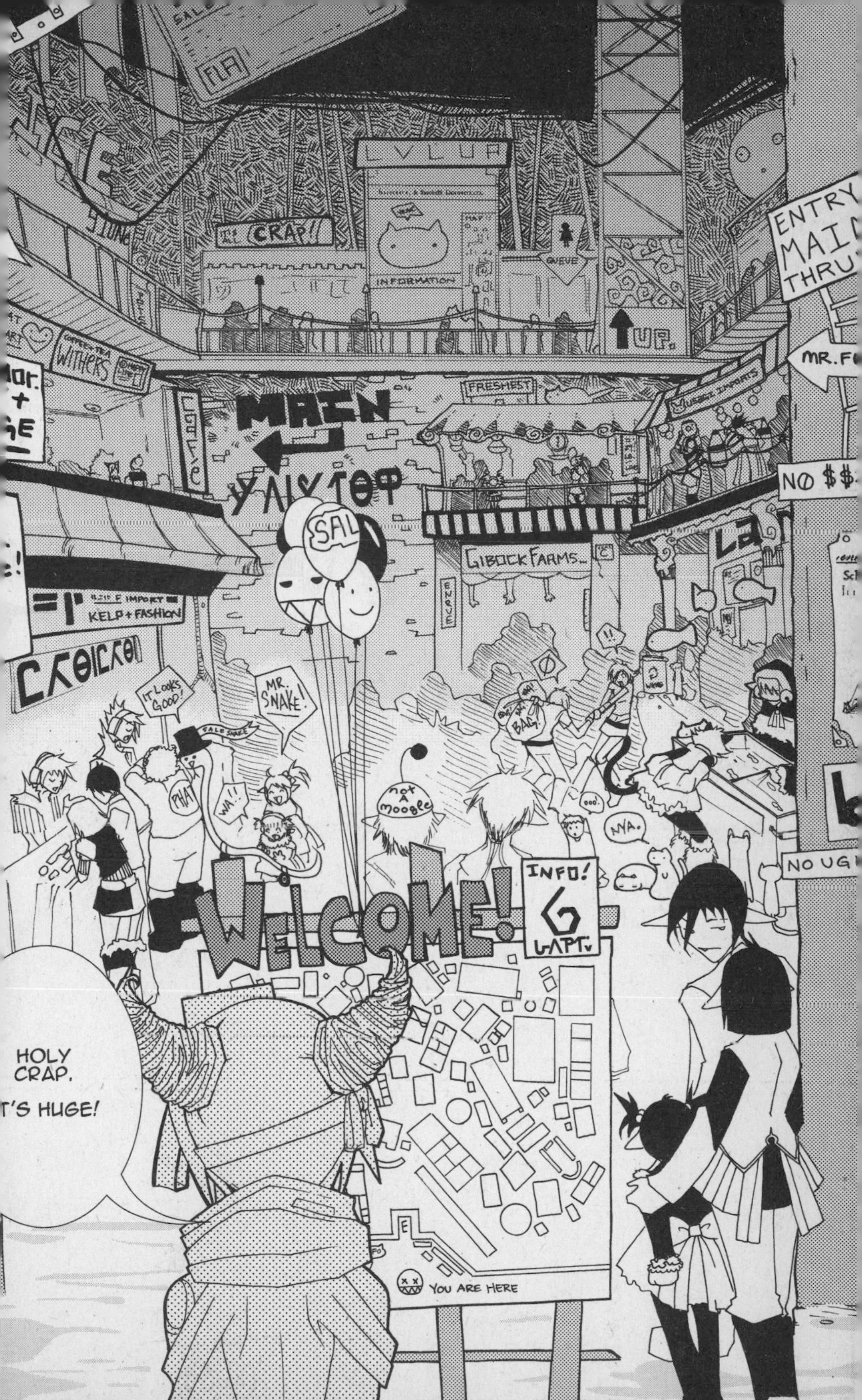

HOLY CRAP.
T'S HUGE!
WELCOME!
INFO!
YOU ARE HERE
MAIN
ENTRY
MAI
THRU
MR. F
NO $$
NO UG
GIBOCK FARMS
FRESHEST
INFORMATION
CRAP!
QUEUE
UP
WITHERS
KELP + FASHION
IT LOOKS GOOD!
MR. SNAKE!
SALE SNAKE
PHAT
WA!!
not a moogle
NYA.
BAG
SAL

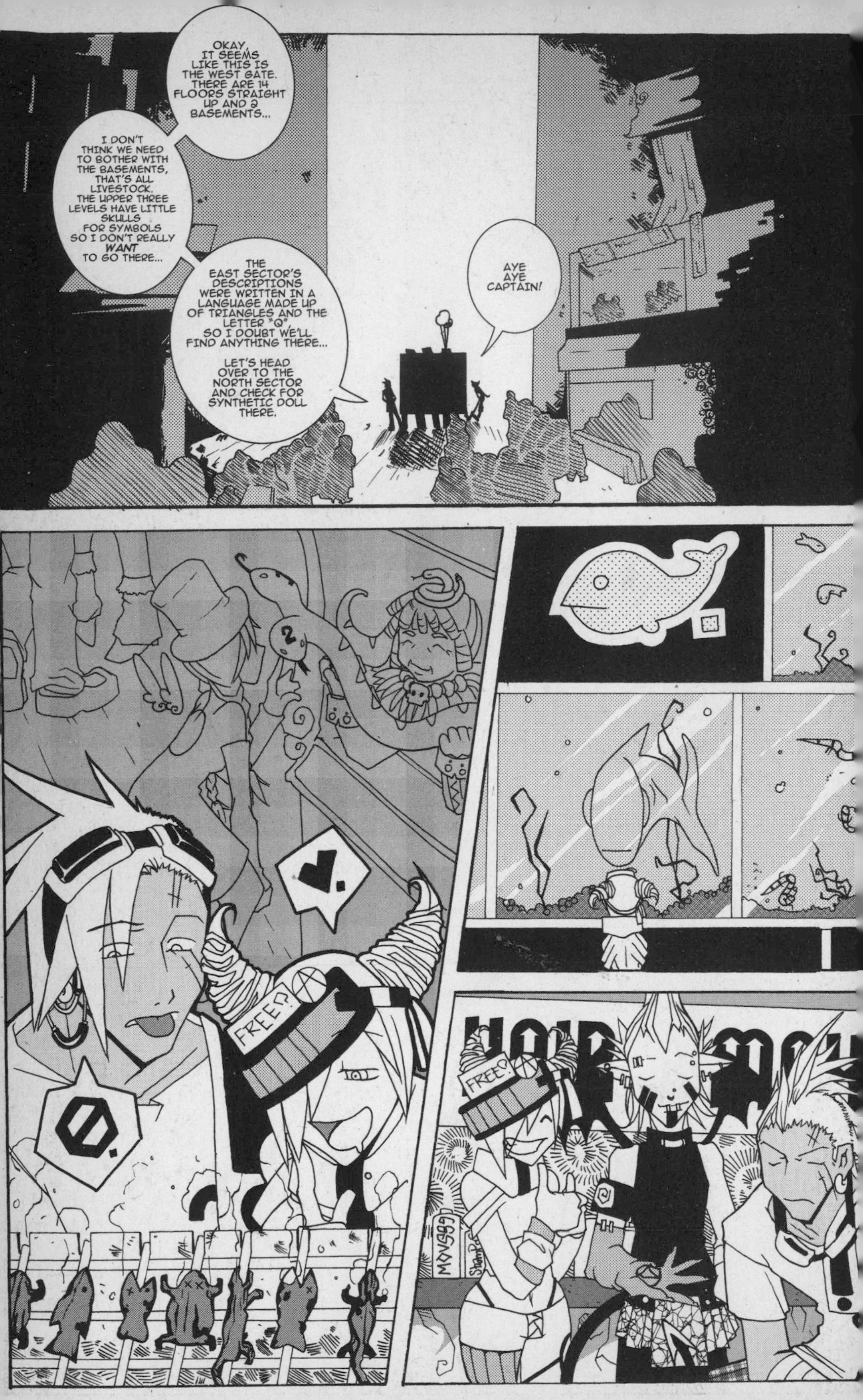
OKAY, IT SEEMS LIKE THIS IS THE WEST GATE. THERE ARE 14 FLOORS STRAIGHT UP AND 2 BASEMENTS...
I DON'T THINK WE NEED TO BOTHER WITH THE BASEMENTS, THAT'S ALL LIVESTOCK. THE UPPER THREE LEVELS HAVE LITTLE SKULLS FOR SYMBOLS SO I DON'T REALLY *WANT* TO GO THERE...
THE EAST SECTOR'S DESCRIPTIONS WERE WRITTEN IN A LANGUAGE MADE UP OF TRIANGLES AND THE LETTER "Q", SO I DOUBT WE'LL FIND ANYTHING THERE... LET'S HEAD OVER TO THE NORTH SECTOR AND CHECK FOR SYNTHETIC DOLL THERE.
AYE AYE CAPTAIN!
FREE?
FREE?

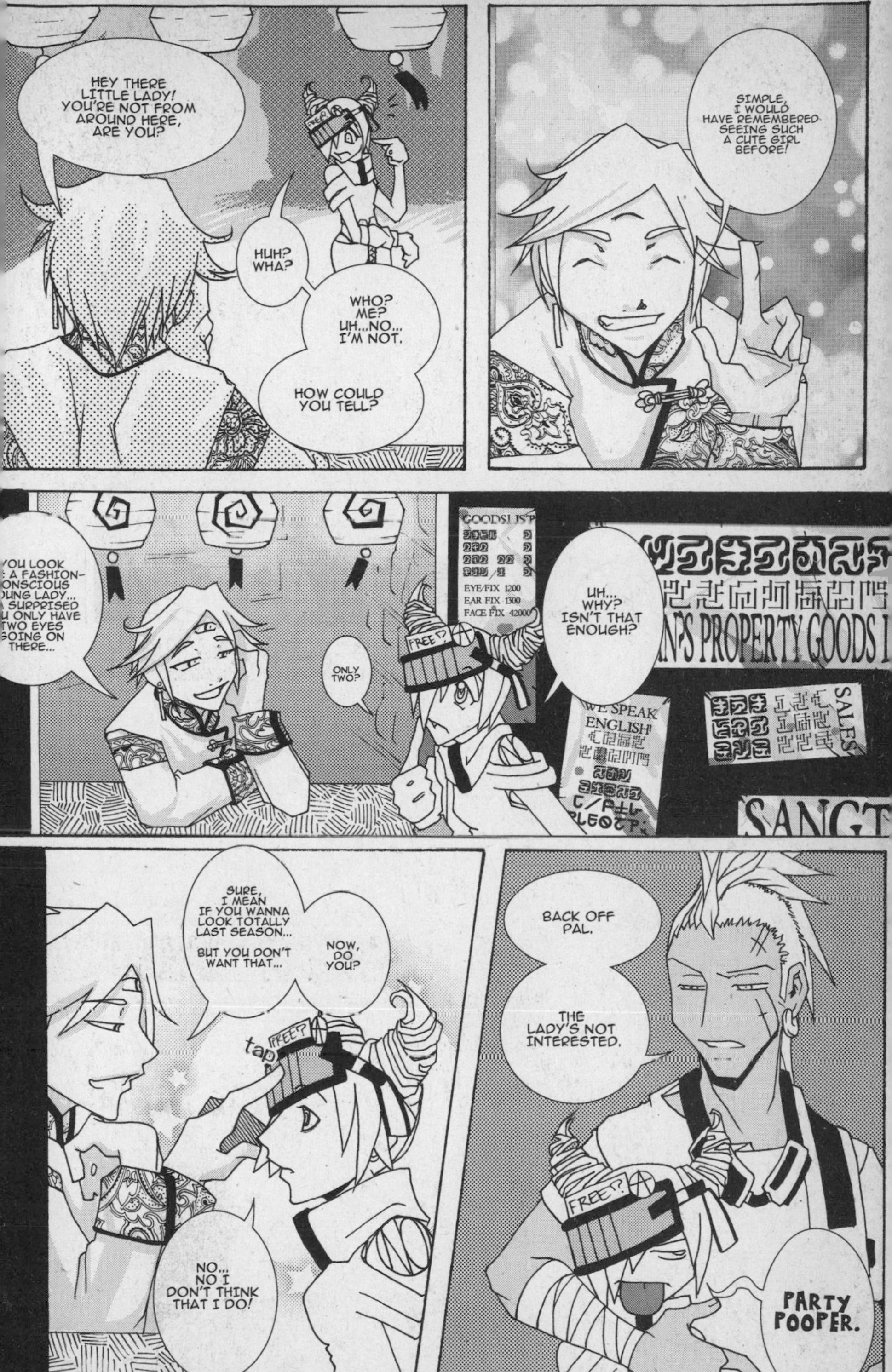
HEY THERE LITTLE LADY! YOU'RE NOT FROM AROUND HERE, ARE YOU?
HUH? WHA?
WHO? ME? UH...NO... I'M NOT.
HOW COULD YOU TELL?
SIMPLE, I WOULD HAVE REMEMBERED SEEING SUCH A CUTE GIRL BEFORE!
YOU LOOK E A FASHION- ONSCIOUS OUNG LADY... SURPRISED U ONLY HAVE TWO EYES GOING ON THERE...
ONLY TWO?
FREE?
GOODS LIST
EYE/FIX 1200
EAR FIX 1300
FACE FIX 42000
UH... WHY? ISN'T THAT ENOUGH?
AN'S PROPERTY GOODS
WE SPEAK ENGLISH!
SALES
SANGT
SURE, I MEAN IF YOU WANNA LOOK TOTALLY LAST SEASON...
BUT YOU DON'T WANT THAT...
NOW, DO YOU?
tap
FREE?
NO... NO I DON'T THINK THAT I DO!
BACK OFF PAL.
THE LADY'S NOT INTERESTED.
FREE?
PARTY POOPER.

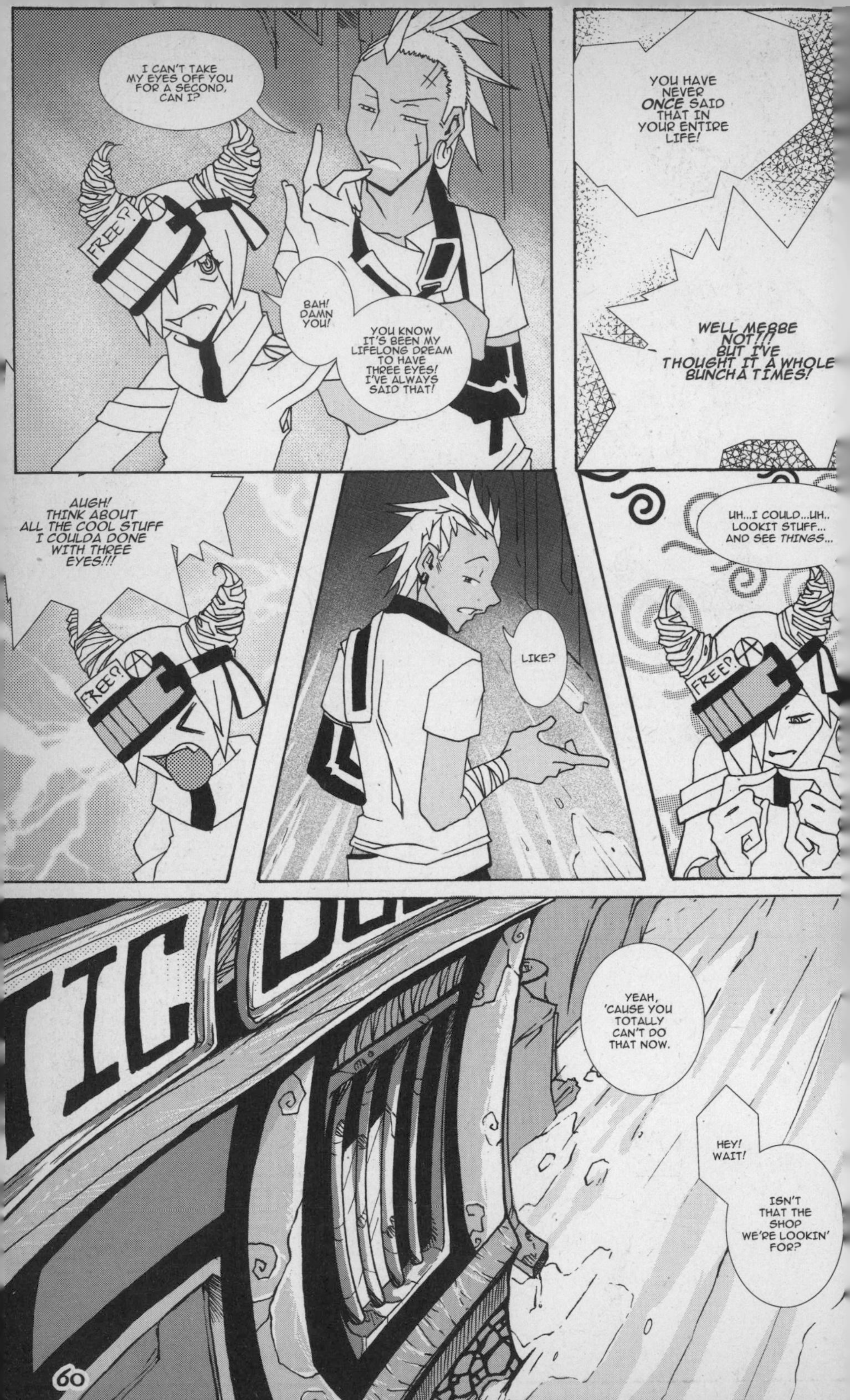
I CAN'T TAKE MY EYES OFF YOU FOR A SECOND, CAN I?
BAH! DAMN YOU!
YOU KNOW IT'S BEEN MY LIFELONG DREAM TO HAVE THREE EYES! I'VE ALWAYS SAID THAT!
FREE?
YOU HAVE NEVER ONCE SAID THAT IN YOUR ENTIRE LIFE!
WELL MEBBE NOT!!! BUT I'VE THOUGHT IT A WHOLE BUNCHA TIMES!
AUGH! THINK ABOUT ALL THE COOL STUFF I COULDA DONE WITH THREE EYES!!!
FREE?
LIKE?
UH...I COULD...UH.. LOOKIT STUFF... AND SEE THINGS...
FREE?
YEAH, 'CAUSE YOU TOTALLY CAN'T DO THAT NOW.
HEY! WAIT!
ISN'T THAT THE SHOP WE'RE LOOKIN' FOR?

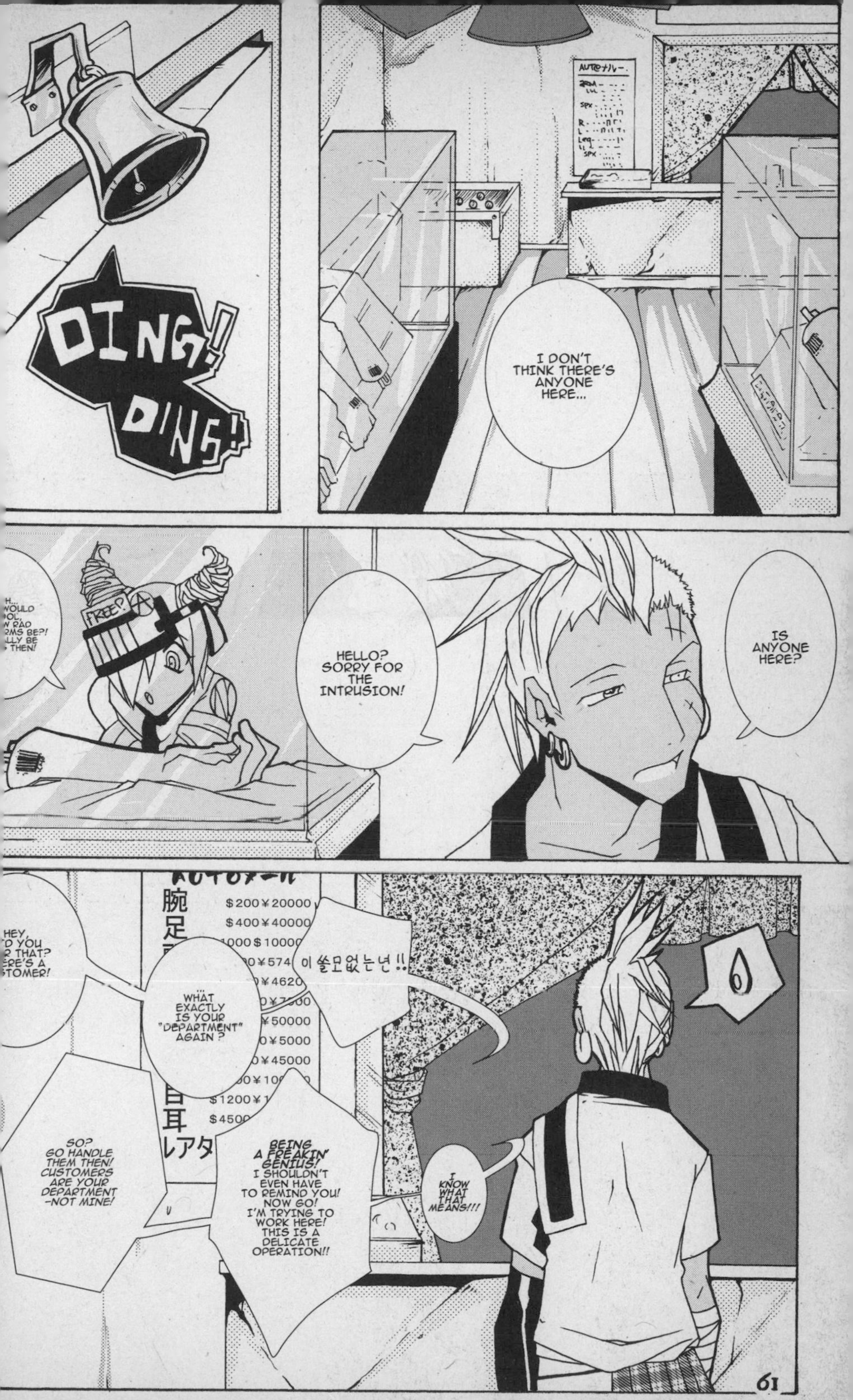

I DON'T THINK THERE'S ANYONE HERE...
DING! DING!
IS ANYONE HERE?
HELLO? SORRY FOR THE INTRUSION!
腕 $200 ¥20000
足 $400 ¥40000
이 쓸모없는 년!!
...WHAT EXACTLY IS YOUR "DEPARTMENT" AGAIN?
BEING A FREAKIN' GENIUS! I SHOULDN'T EVEN HAVE TO REMIND YOU! NOW GO! I'M TRYING TO WORK HERE! THIS IS A DELICATE OPERATION!!
I KNOW WHAT THAT MEANS!!!
SO? GO HANDLE THEM THEN! CUSTOMERS ARE YOUR DEPARTMENT -NOT MINE!

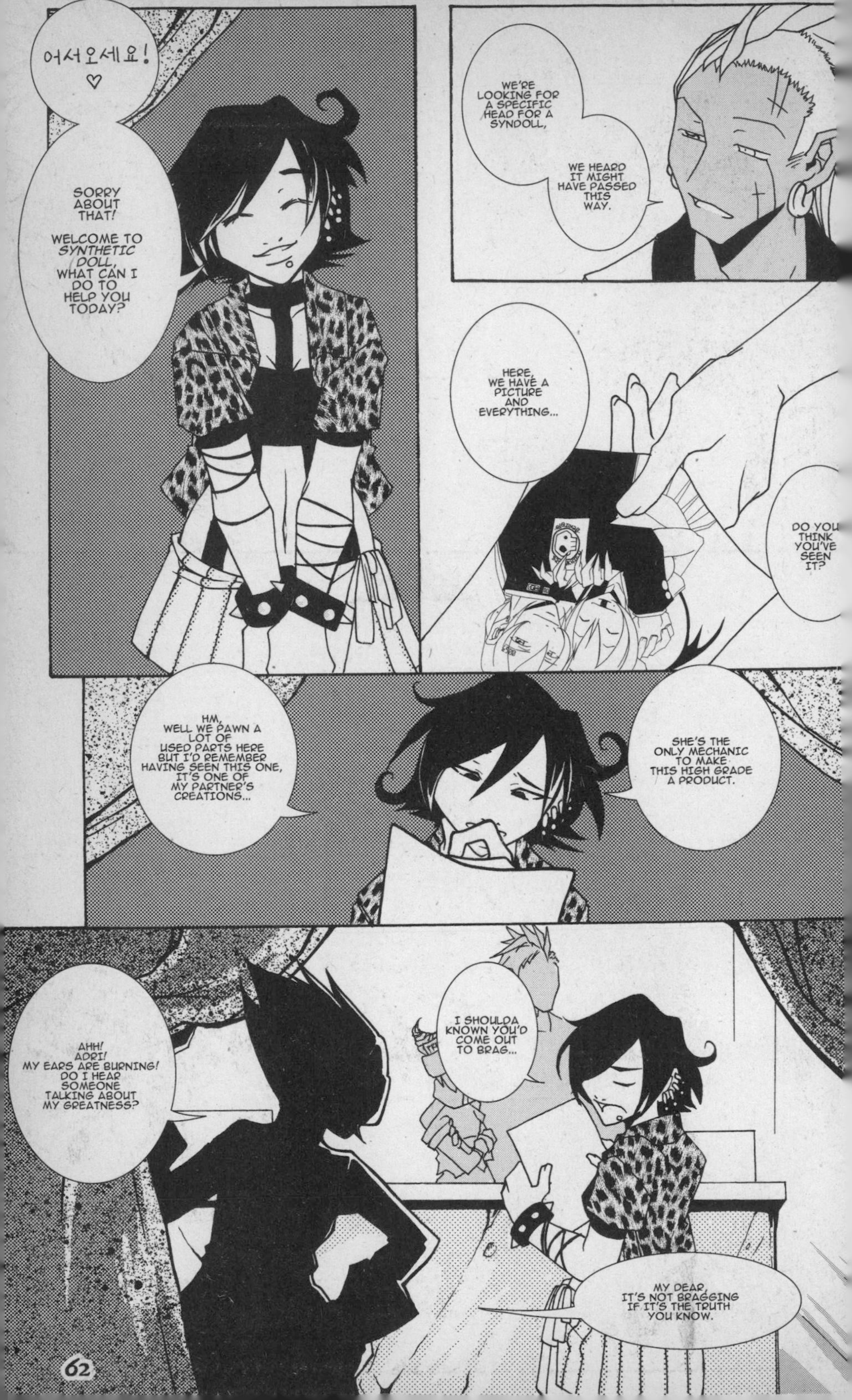

어서오세요! ♡
SORRY ABOUT THAT! WELCOME TO *SYNTHETIC DOLL*, WHAT CAN I DO TO HELP YOU TODAY?
WE'RE LOOKING FOR A SPECIFIC HEAD FOR A SYNDOLL,
WE HEARD IT MIGHT HAVE PASSED THIS WAY.
HERE, WE HAVE A PICTURE AND EVERYTHING...
DO YOU THINK YOU'VE SEEN IT?
HM, WELL WE PAWN A LOT OF USED PARTS HERE BUT I'D REMEMBER HAVING SEEN THIS ONE, IT'S ONE OF MY PARTNER'S CREATIONS...
SHE'S THE ONLY MECHANIC TO MAKE THIS HIGH GRADE A PRODUCT.
AHH! ADRI! MY EARS ARE BURNING! DO I HEAR SOMEONE TALKING ABOUT MY GREATNESS?
I SHOULDA KNOWN YOU'D COME OUT TO BRAG...
MY DEAR, IT'S NOT BRAGGING IF IT'S THE TRUTH YOU KNOW.

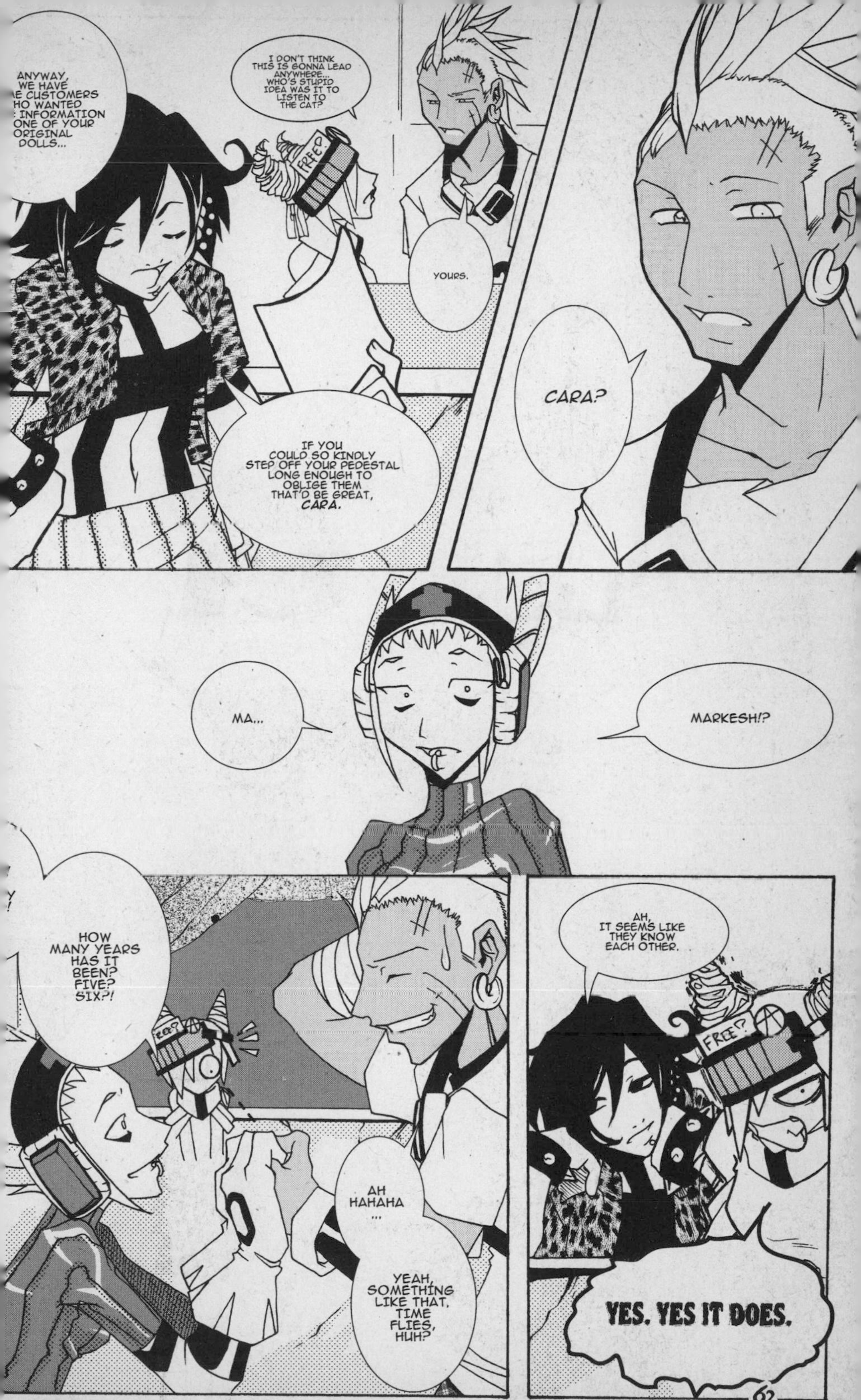
ANYWAY, WE HAVE E CUSTOMERS HO WANTED INFORMATION ONE OF YOUR ORIGINAL DOLLS...
I DON'T THINK THIS IS GONNA LEAD ANYWHERE... WHO'S STUPID IDEA WAS IT TO LISTEN TO THE CAT?
FREE?
YOURS.
IF YOU COULD SO KINDLY STEP OFF YOUR PEDESTAL LONG ENOUGH TO OBLIGE THEM THAT'D BE GREAT, CARA.
CARA?
MA...
MARKESH!?
HOW MANY YEARS HAS IT BEEN? FIVE? SIX?!
AH HAHAHA ...
YEAH, SOMETHING LIKE THAT, TIME FLIES, HUH?
AH, IT SEEMS LIKE THEY KNOW EACH OTHER.
FREE?
YES. YES IT DOES.

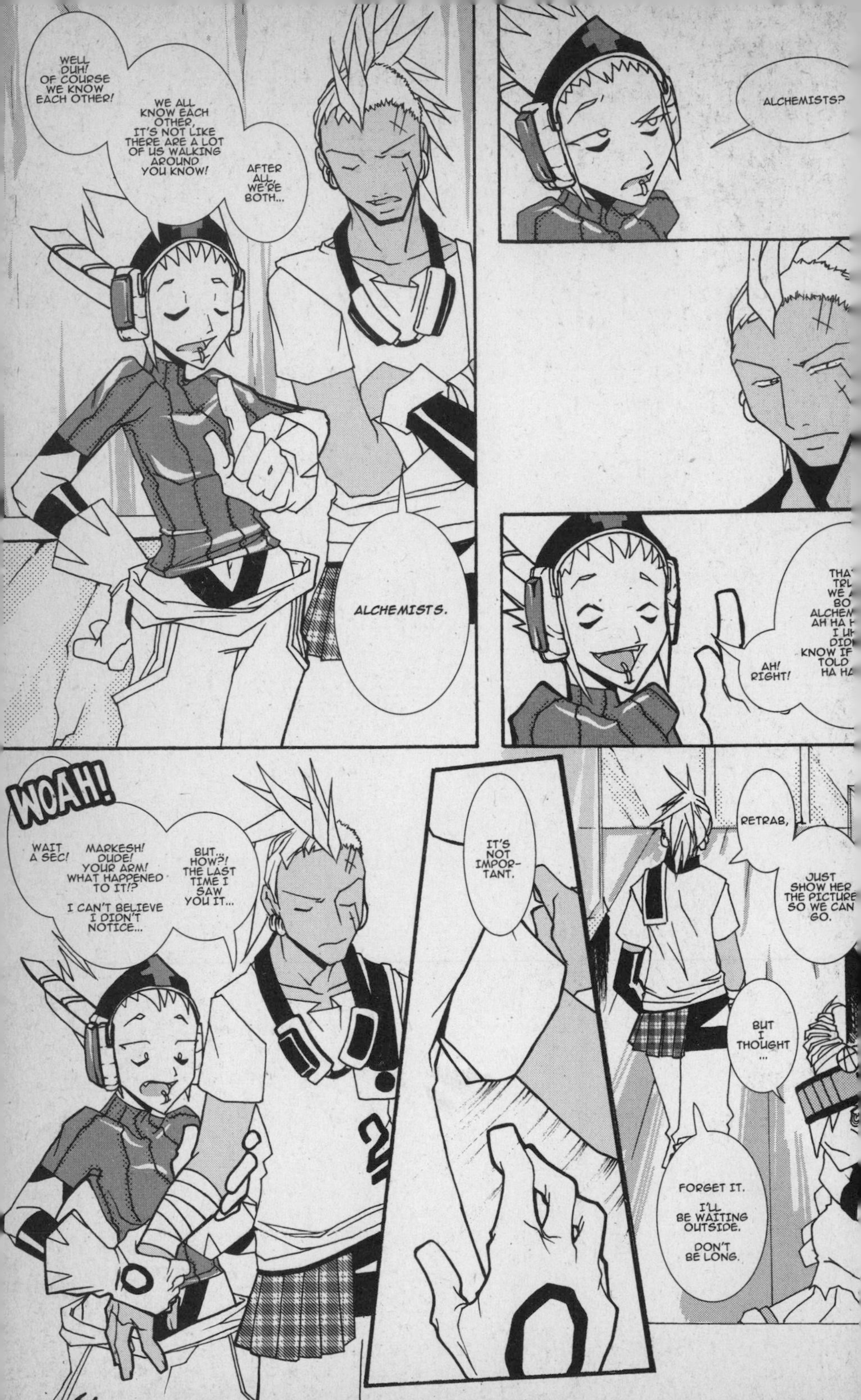
WELL DUH! OF COURSE WE KNOW EACH OTHER!
WE ALL KNOW EACH OTHER, IT'S NOT LIKE THERE ARE A LOT OF US WALKING AROUND YOU KNOW!
AFTER ALL, WE'RE BOTH...
ALCHEMISTS.
ALCHEMISTS?
AH! RIGHT!
THA TRU WE A BO ALCHEM AH HA H I UH DIDN KNOW IF TOLD HA HA
WOAH!
WAIT A SEC!
MARKESH! DUDE! YOUR ARM! WHAT HAPPENED TO IT!? I CAN'T BELIEVE I DIDN'T NOTICE...
BUT... HOW?! THE LAST TIME I SAW YOU IT...
IT'S NOT IMPORTANT.
RETRAB,
JUST SHOW HER THE PICTURE SO WE CAN GO.
BUT I THOUGHT ...
FORGET IT. I'LL BE WAITING OUTSIDE. DON'T BE LONG.

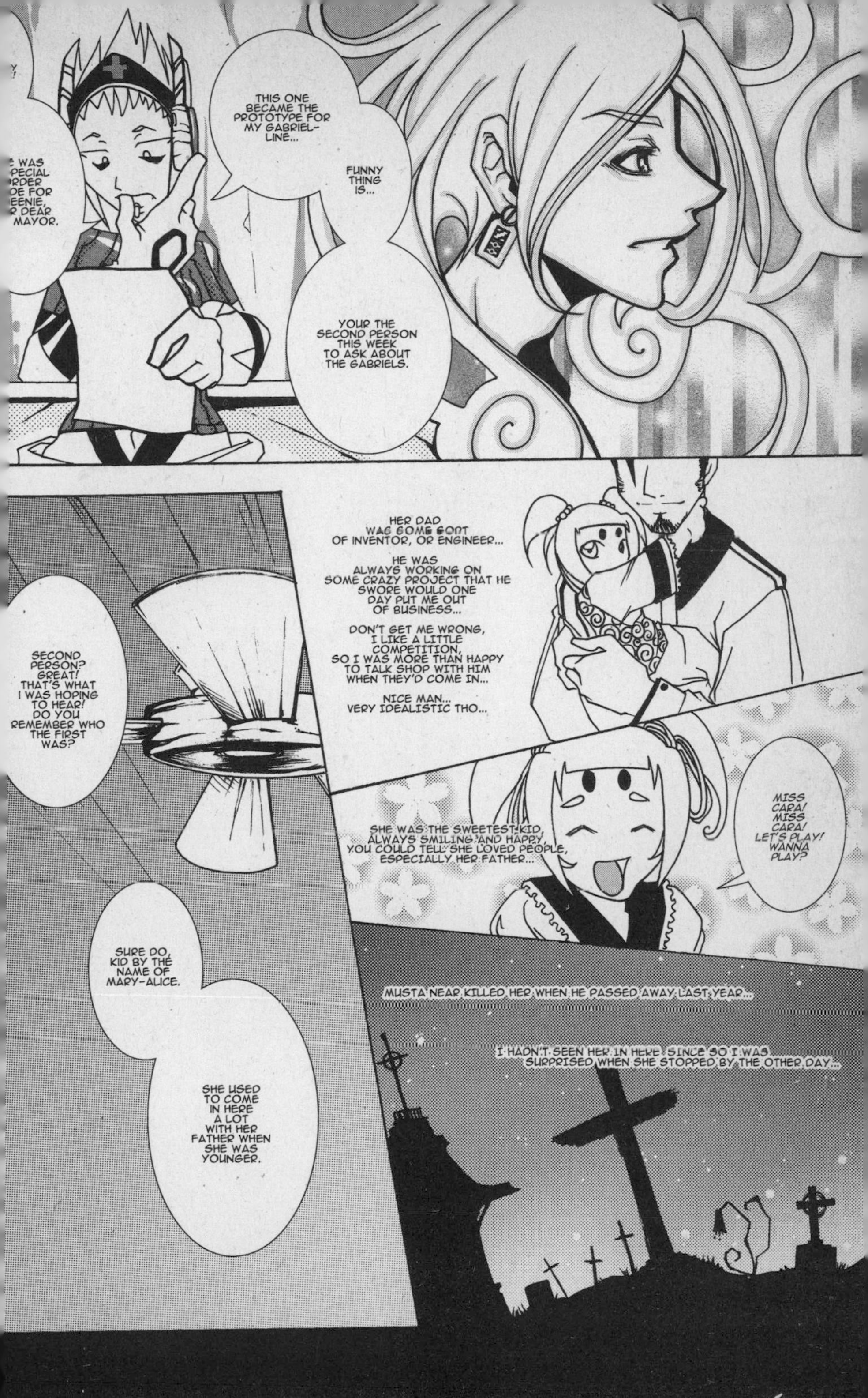
E WAS PECIAL ORDER DE FOR EENIE, R DEAR MAYOR.
THIS ONE BECAME THE PROTOTYPE FOR MY GABRIEL-LINE...
FUNNY THING IS...
YOUR THE SECOND PERSON THIS WEEK TO ASK ABOUT THE GABRIELS.
SECOND PERSON? GREAT! THAT'S WHAT I WAS HOPING TO HEAR! DO YOU REMEMBER WHO THE FIRST WAS?
SURE DO, KID BY THE NAME OF MARY-ALICE.
SHE USED TO COME IN HERE A LOT WITH HER FATHER WHEN SHE WAS YOUNGER.
HER DAD WAS SOME SORT OF INVENTOR, OR ENGINEER...
HE WAS ALWAYS WORKING ON SOME CRAZY PROJECT THAT HE SWORE WOULD ONE DAY PUT ME OUT OF BUSINESS...
DON'T GET ME WRONG, I LIKE A LITTLE COMPETITION, SO I WAS MORE THAN HAPPY TO TALK SHOP WITH HIM WHEN THEY'D COME IN...
NICE MAN... VERY IDEALISTIC THO...
MISS CARA! MISS CARA! LET'S PLAY! WANNA PLAY?
SHE WAS THE SWEETEST KID, ALWAYS SMILING AND HAPPY, YOU COULD TELL SHE LOVED PEOPLE, ESPECIALLY HER FATHER...
MUSTA NEAR KILLED HER WHEN HE PASSED AWAY LAST YEAR...
I HADN'T SEEN HER IN HERE SINCE SO I WAS SURPRISED WHEN SHE STOPPED BY THE OTHER DAY...

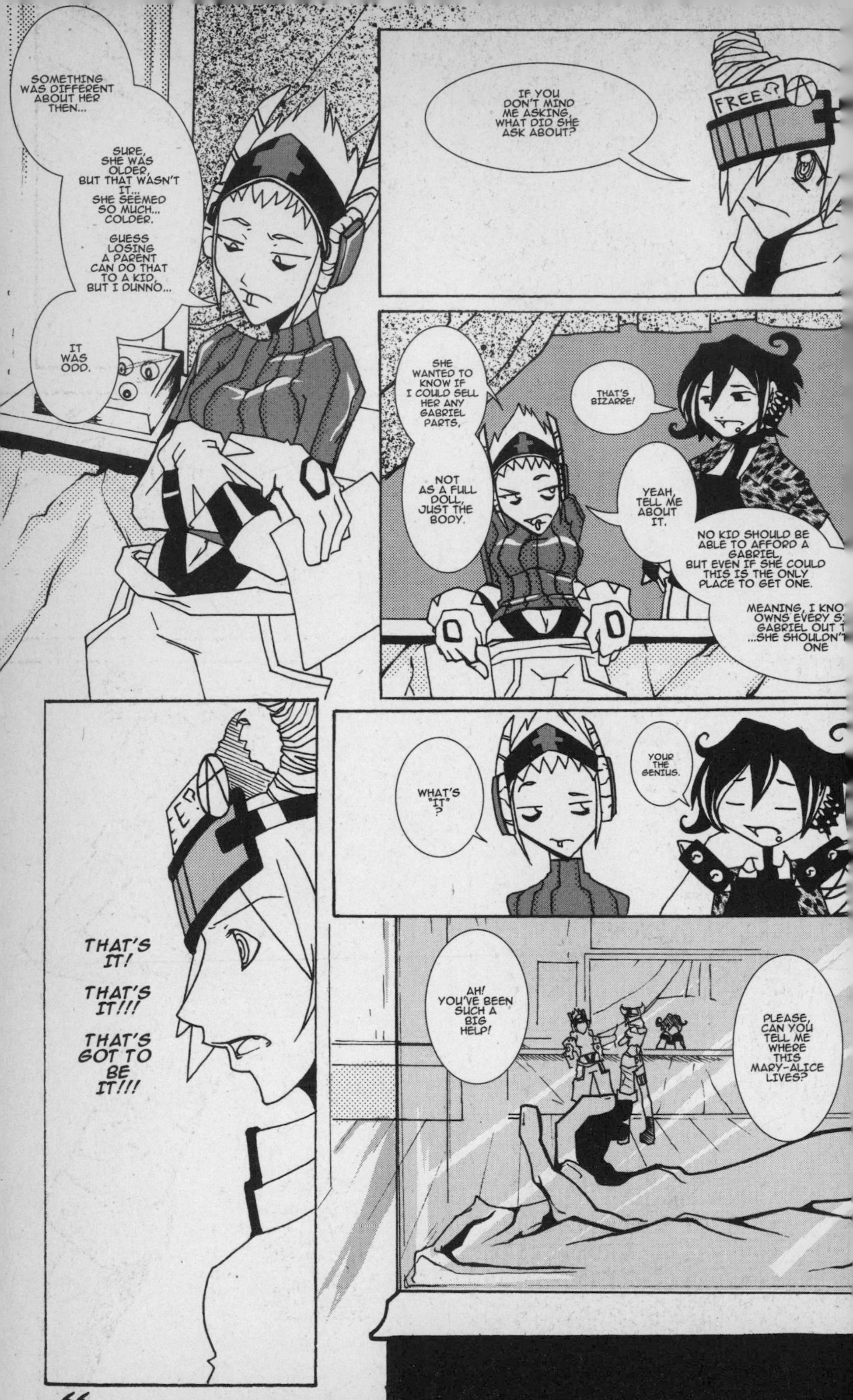

SOMETHING WAS DIFFERENT ABOUT HER THEN...
SURE, SHE WAS OLDER, BUT THAT WASN'T IT... SHE SEEMED SO MUCH... COLDER.
GUESS LOSING A PARENT CAN DO THAT TO A KID, BUT I DUNNO...
IT WAS ODD.
IF YOU DON'T MIND ME ASKING, WHAT DID SHE ASK ABOUT?
SHE WANTED TO KNOW IF I COULD SELL HER ANY GABRIEL PARTS,
NOT AS A FULL DOLL, JUST THE BODY.
THAT'S BIZARRE!
YEAH, TELL ME ABOUT IT.
NO KID SHOULD BE ABLE TO AFFORD A GABRIEL, BUT EVEN IF SHE COULD THIS IS THE ONLY PLACE TO GET ONE.
MEANING, I KNO
OWNS EVERY S
GABRIEL OUT T
...SHE SHOULDN'T
ONE
WHAT'S "IT"?
YOUR THE GENIUS.
THAT'S IT!
THAT'S IT!!!
THAT'S GOT TO BE IT!!!
AH! YOU'VE BEEN SUCH A BIG HELP!
PLEASE, CAN YOU TELL ME WHERE THIS MARY-ALICE LIVES?

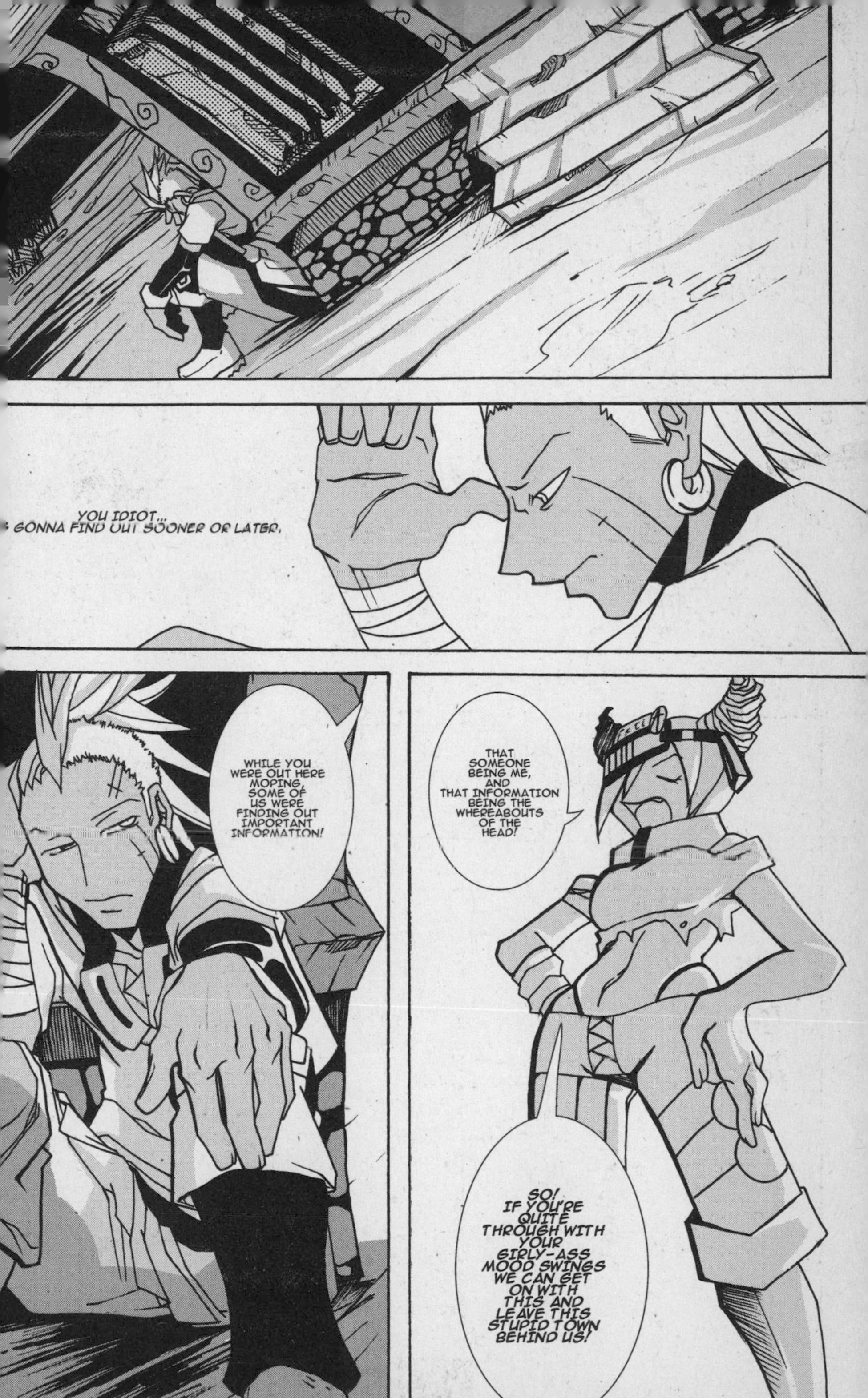
YOU IDIOT...
S GONNA FIND OUT SOONER OR LATER.
WHILE YOU WERE OUT HERE MOPING, SOME OF US WERE FINDING OUT IMPORTANT INFORMATION!
THAT SOMEONE BEING ME, AND THAT INFORMATION BEING THE WHEREABOUTS OF THE HEAD!
SO! IF YOU'RE QUITE THROUGH WITH YOUR GIRLY-ASS MOOD SWINGS WE CAN GET ON WITH THIS AND LEAVE THIS STUPID TOWN BEHIND US!

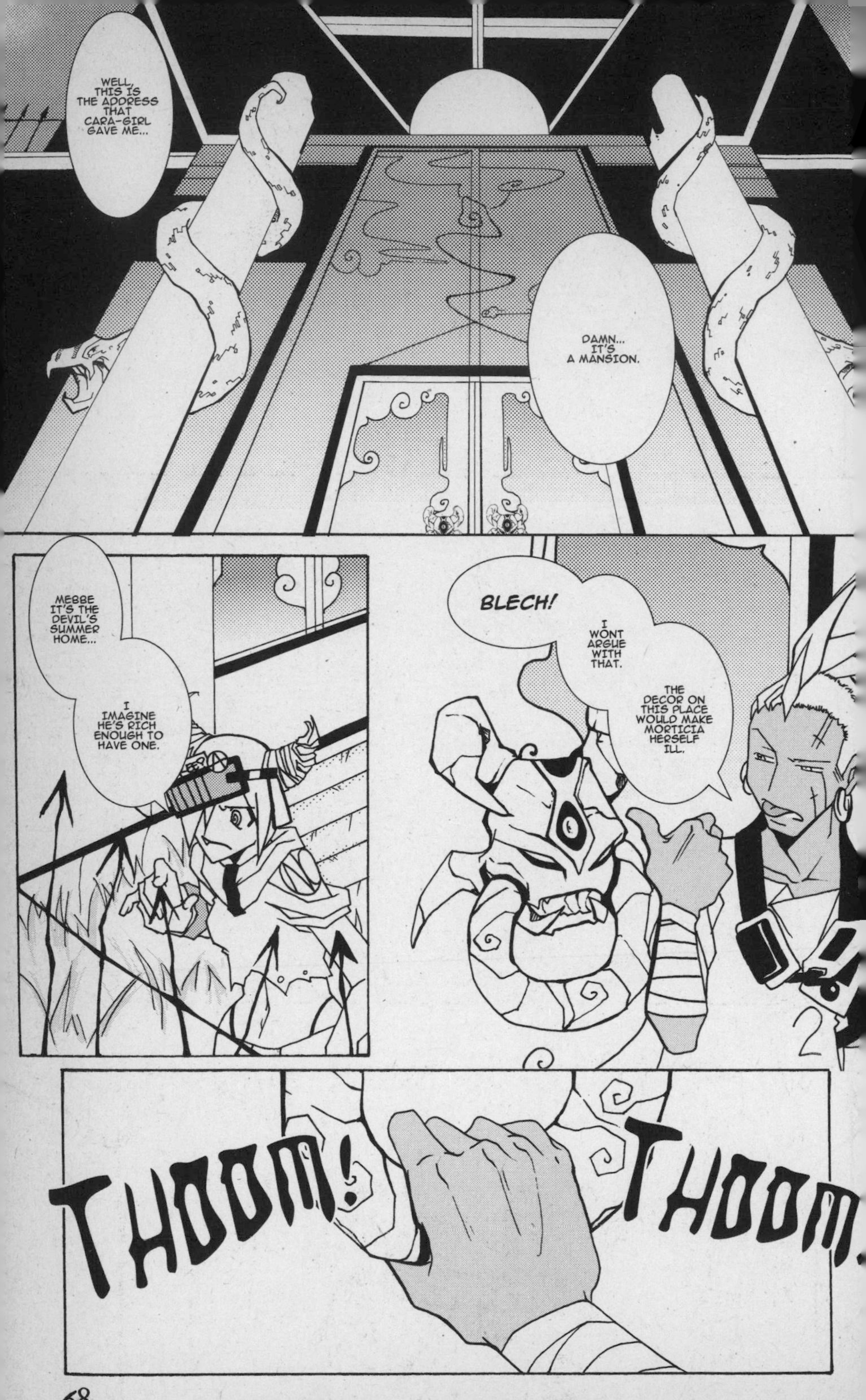
WELL, THIS IS THE ADDRESS THAT CARA-GIRL GAVE ME...
DAMN... IT'S A MANSION.
MEBBE IT'S THE DEVIL'S SUMMER HOME...
I IMAGINE HE'S RICH ENOUGH TO HAVE ONE.
BLECH!
I WONT ARGUE WITH THAT.
THE DECOR ON THIS PLACE WOULD MAKE MORTICIA HERSELF ILL.
THOOM! THOOM.

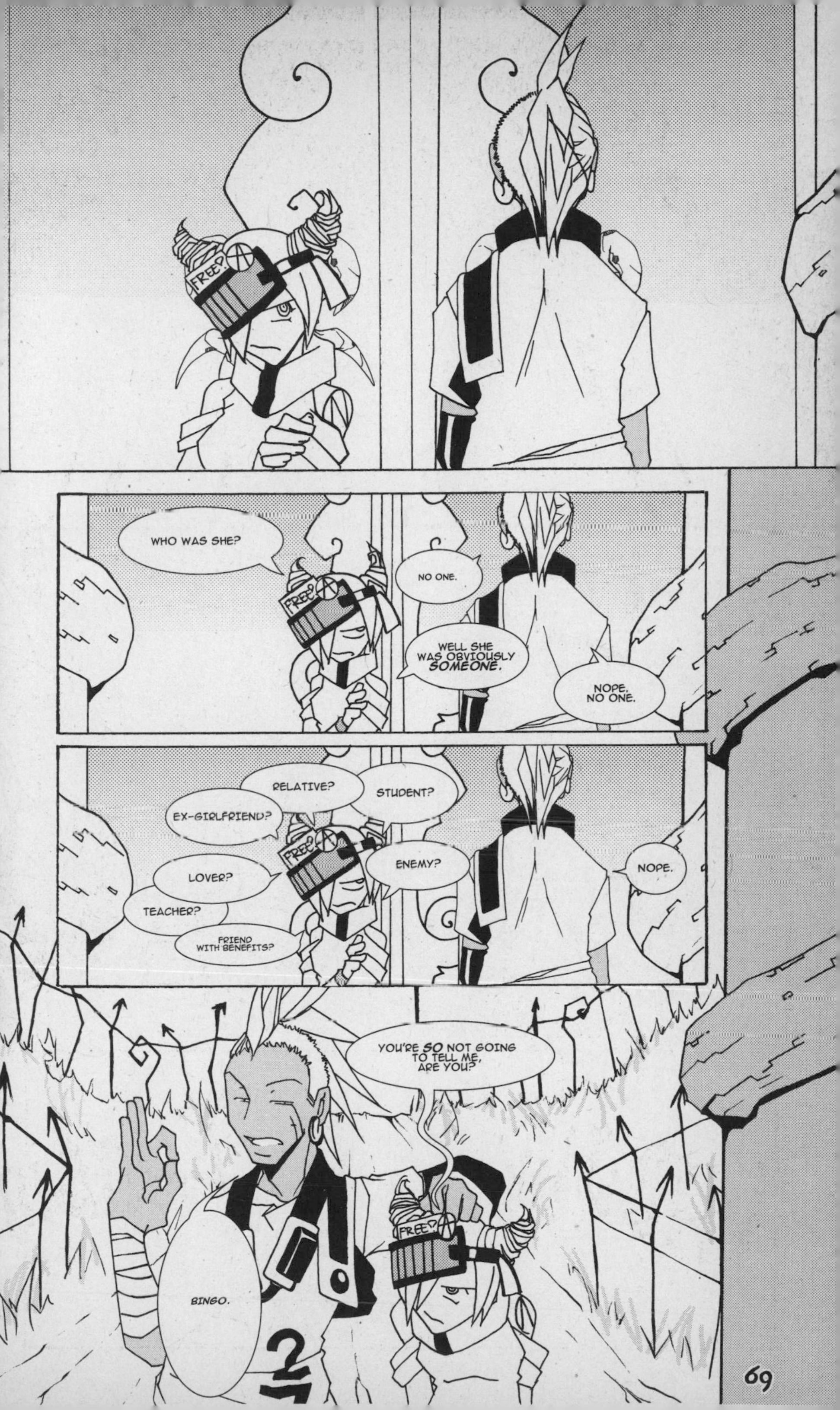
WHO WAS SHE?
NO ONE.
WELL SHE WAS OBVIOUSLY *SOMEONE.*
NOPE. NO ONE.
RELATIVE?
STUDENT?
EX-GIRLFRIEND?
ENEMY?
LOVER?
TEACHER?
FRIEND WITH BENEFITS?
NOPE.
YOU'RE *SO* NOT GOING TO TELL ME, ARE YOU?
BINGO.

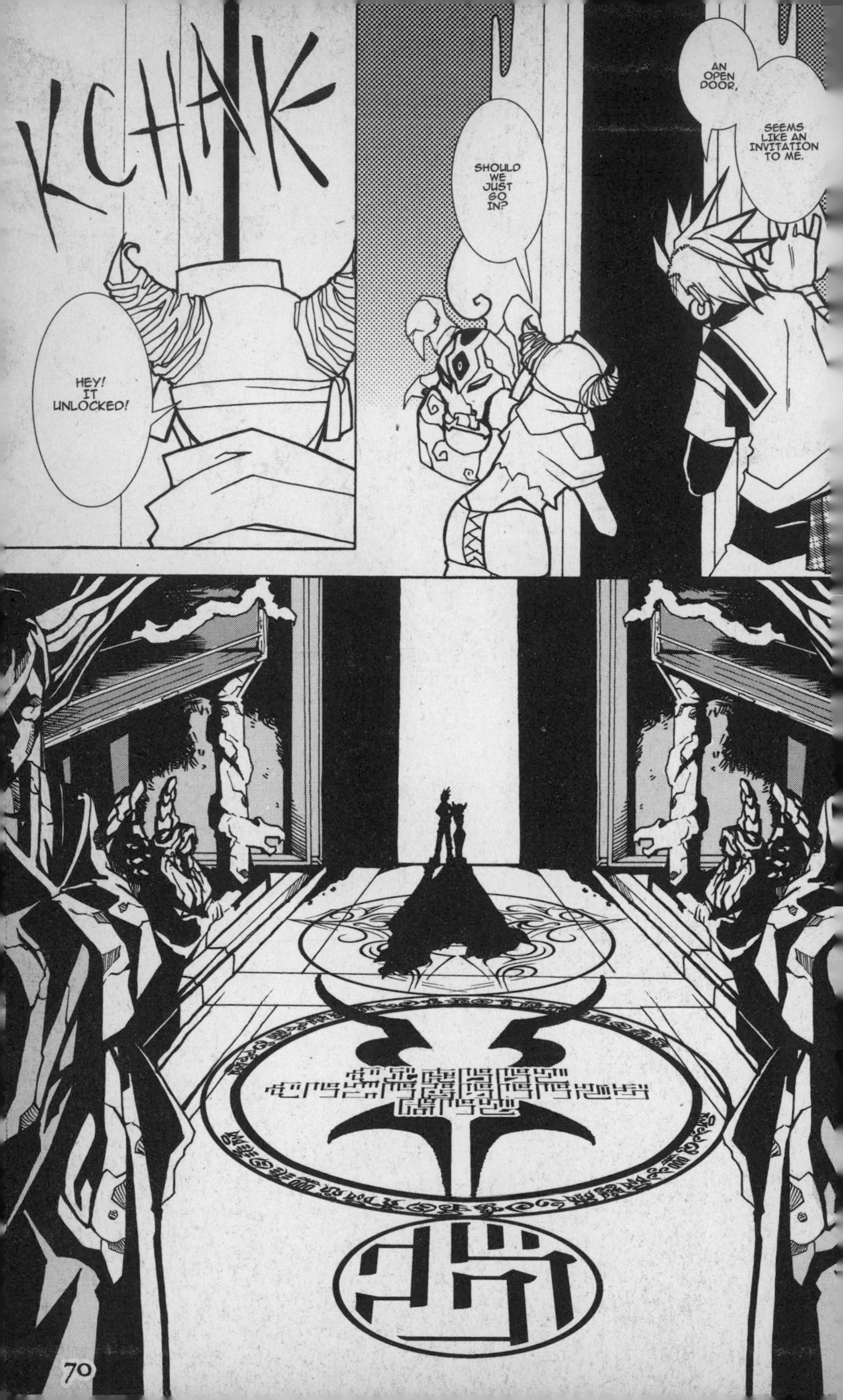
KCHAK
HEY! IT UNLOCKED!
SHOULD WE JUST GO IN?
AN OPEN DOOR,
SEEMS LIKE AN INVITATION TO ME.

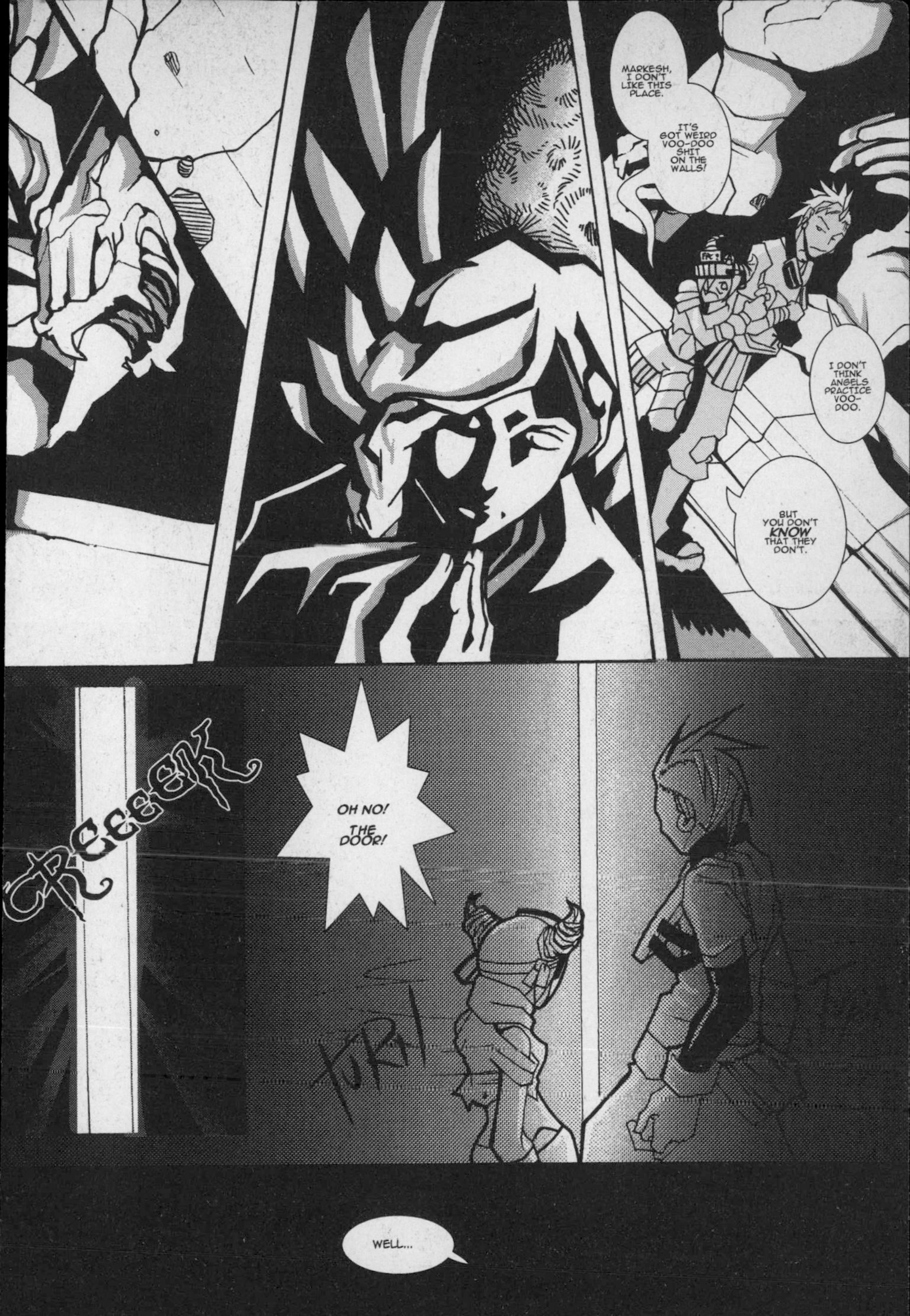
MARKESH, I DON'T LIKE THIS PLACE.
IT'S GOT WEIRD VOO-DOO SHIT ON THE WALLS!
I DON'T THINK ANGELS PRACTICE VOO-DOO.
BUT YOU DON'T KNOW THAT THEY DON'T.
CREEEEK
OH NO! THE DOOR!
TURN
WELL...

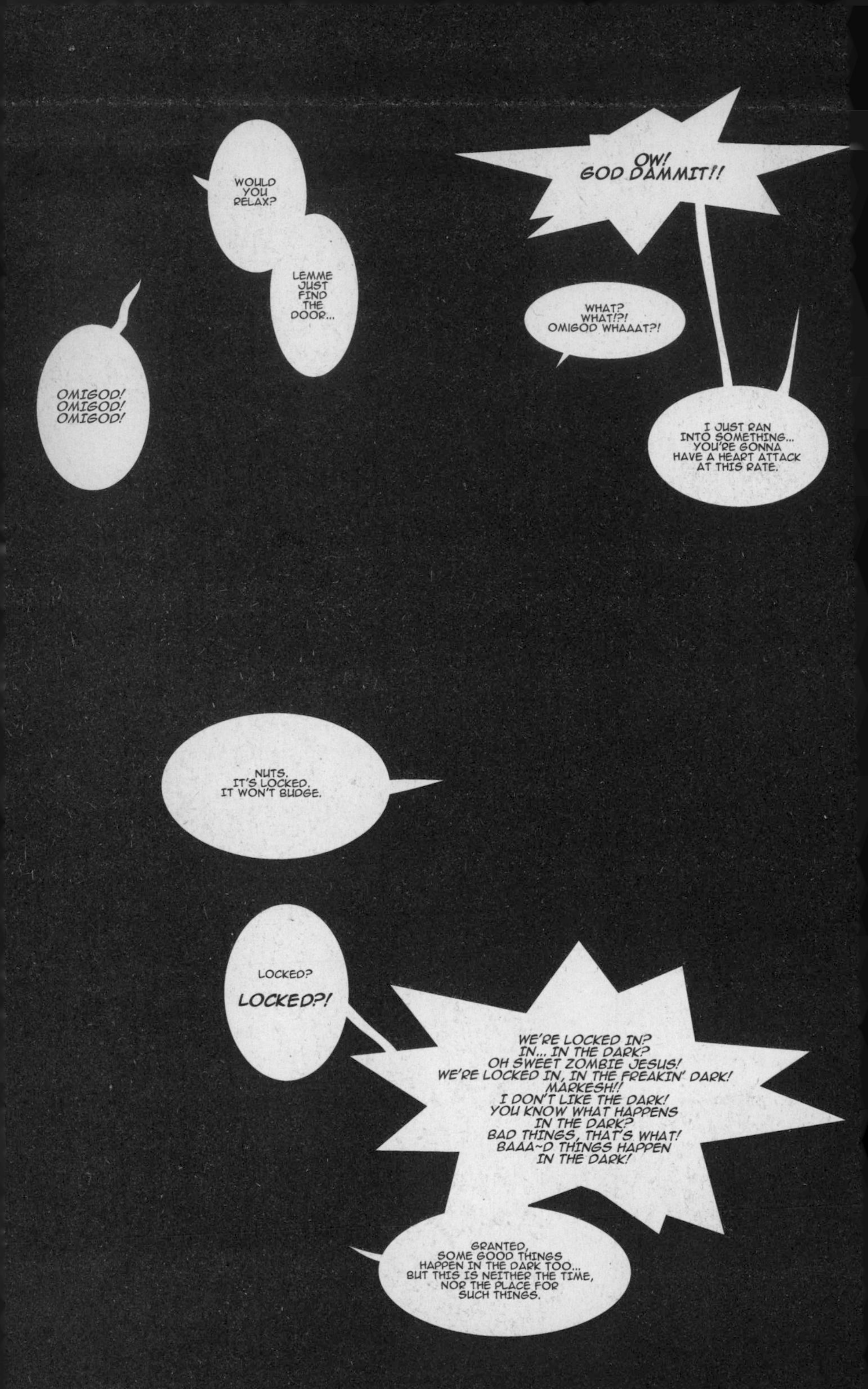
OMIGOD! OMIGOD! OMIGOD!
WOULD YOU RELAX?
LEMME JUST FIND THE DOOR...
OW! GOD DAMMIT!!
WHAT? WHAT!?! OMIGOD WHAAAT?!
I JUST RAN INTO SOMETHING... YOU'RE GONNA HAVE A HEART ATTACK AT THIS RATE.
NUTS. IT'S LOCKED. IT WON'T BUDGE.
LOCKED? LOCKED?!
WE'RE LOCKED IN? IN... IN THE DARK? OH SWEET ZOMBIE JESUS! WE'RE LOCKED IN, IN THE FREAKIN' DARK! MARKESH!! I DON'T LIKE THE DARK! YOU KNOW WHAT HAPPENS IN THE DARK? BAD THINGS, THAT'S WHAT! BAAA~D THINGS HAPPEN IN THE DARK!
GRANTED, SOME GOOD THINGS HAPPEN IN THE DARK TOO... BUT THIS IS NEITHER THE TIME, NOR THE PLACE FOR SUCH THINGS.

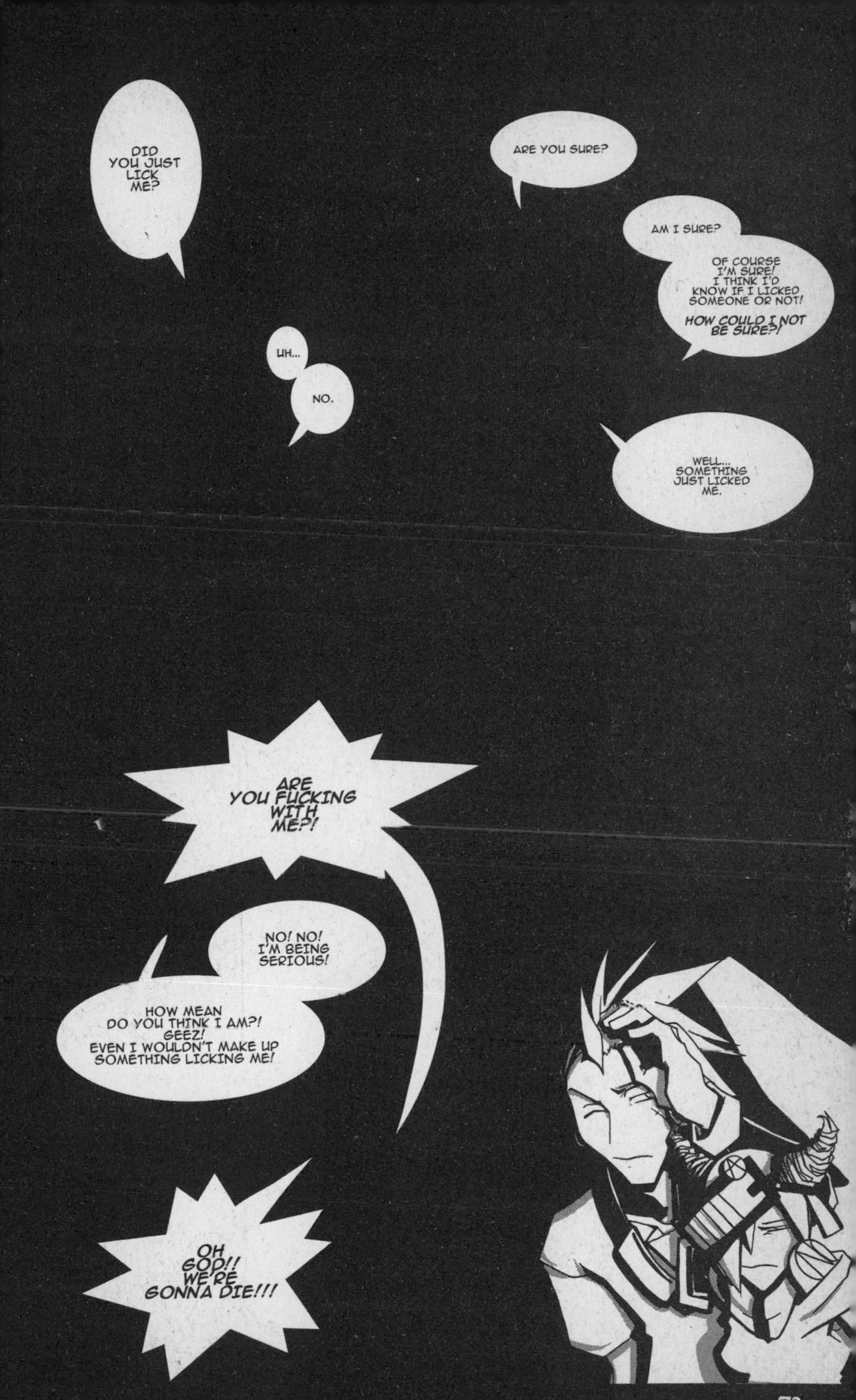
DID YOU JUST LICK ME?
ARE YOU SURE?
AM I SURE?
OF COURSE I'M SURE! I THINK I'D KNOW IF I LICKED SOMEONE OR NOT!
HOW COULD I NOT BE SURE?!
UH...
NO.
WELL... SOMETHING JUST LICKED ME.
ARE YOU FUCKING WITH ME?!
NO! NO! I'M BEING SERIOUS!
HOW MEAN DO YOU THINK I AM?! GEEZ! EVEN I WOULDN'T MAKE UP SOMETHING LICKING ME!
OH GOD!! WE'RE GONNA DIE!!!

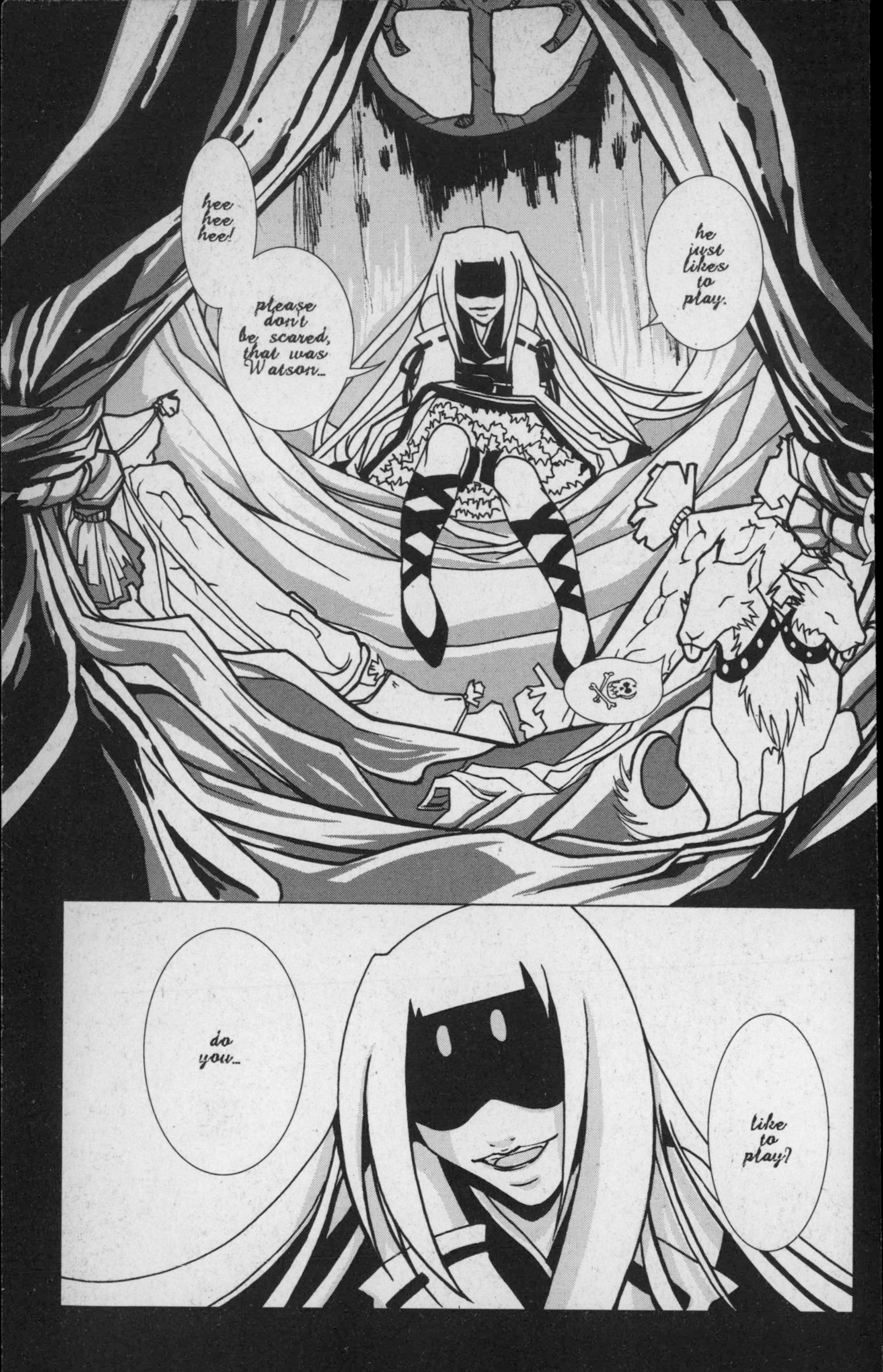
hee hee hee!
please don't be scared, that was Watson...
he just likes to play.
do you...
like to play?

Chapter 4: Sherlock Rock

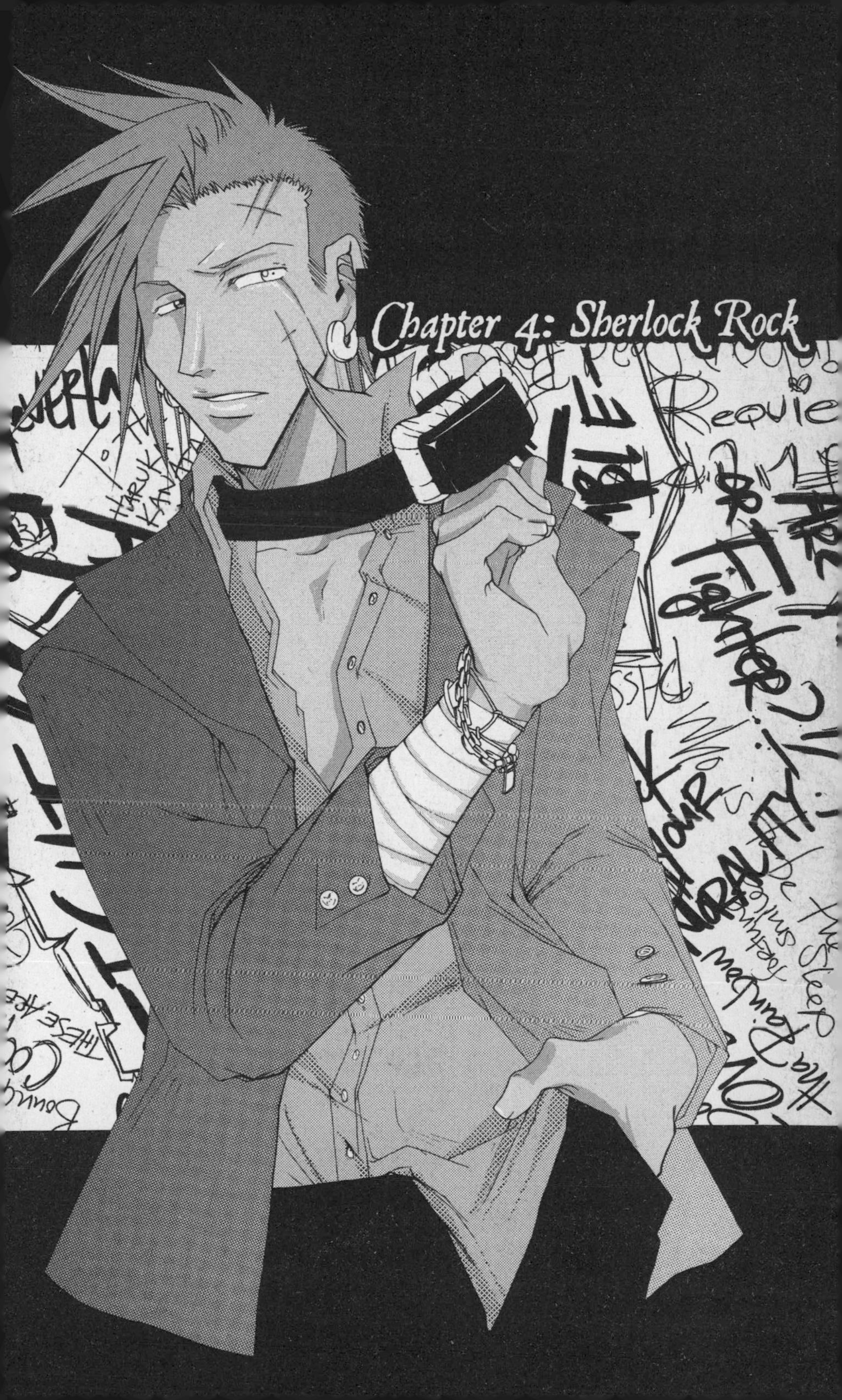

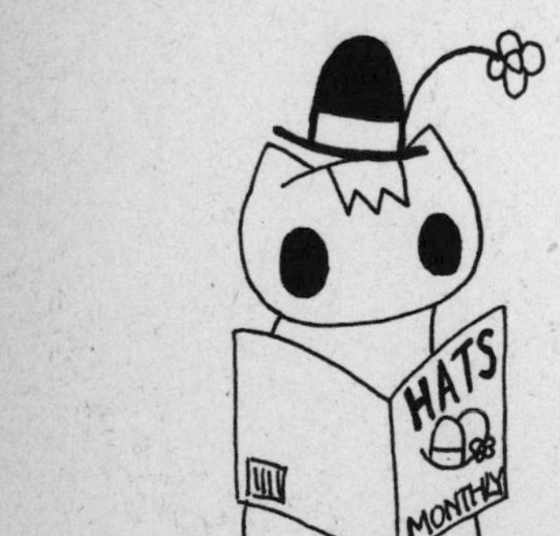
HATS
MONTHLY

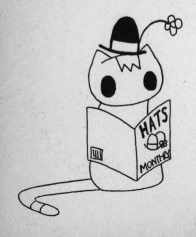

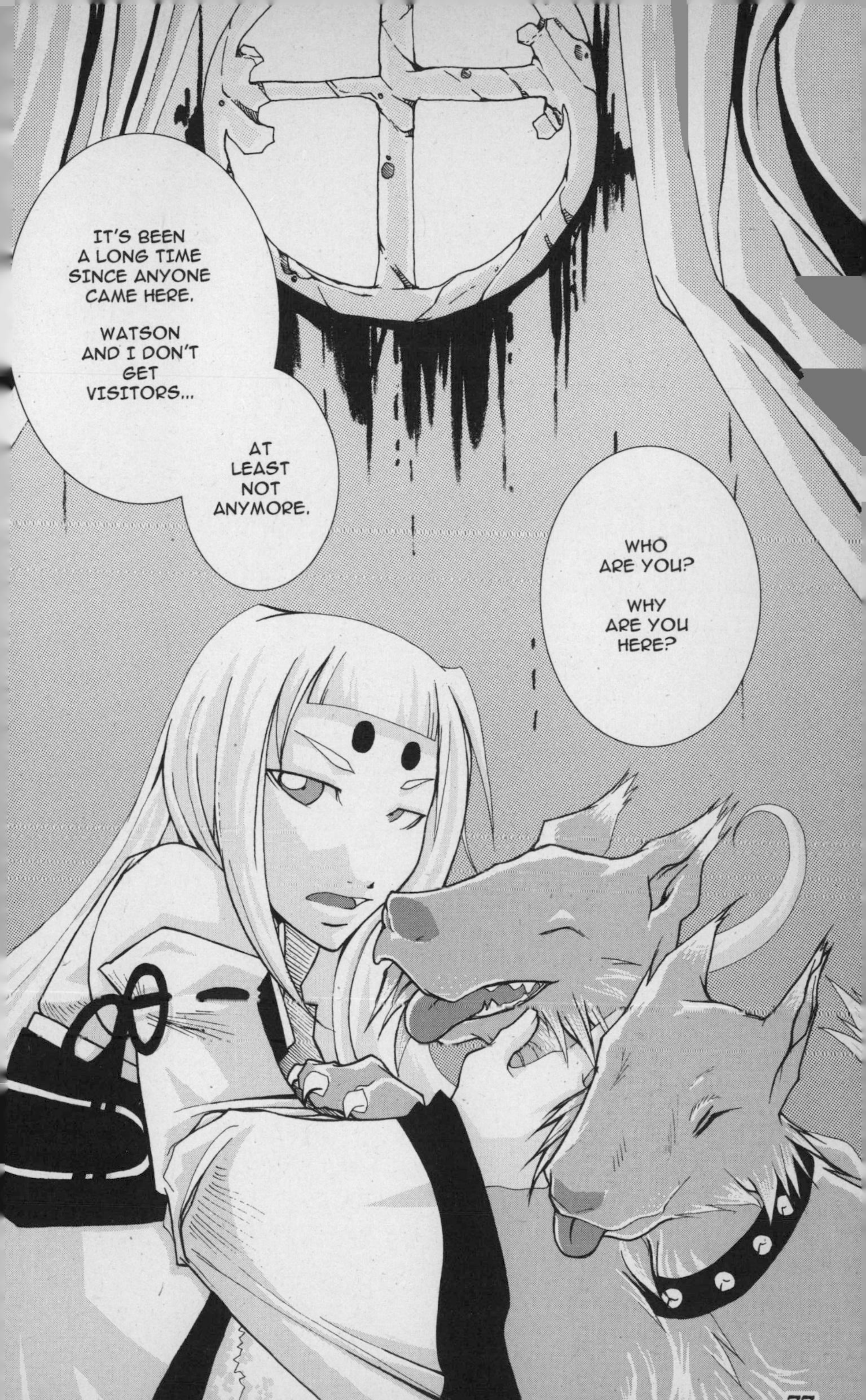

IT'S BEEN A LONG TIME SINCE ANYONE CAME HERE.
WATSON AND I DON'T GET VISITORS...
AT LEAST NOT ANYMORE.
WHO ARE YOU?
WHY ARE YOU HERE?

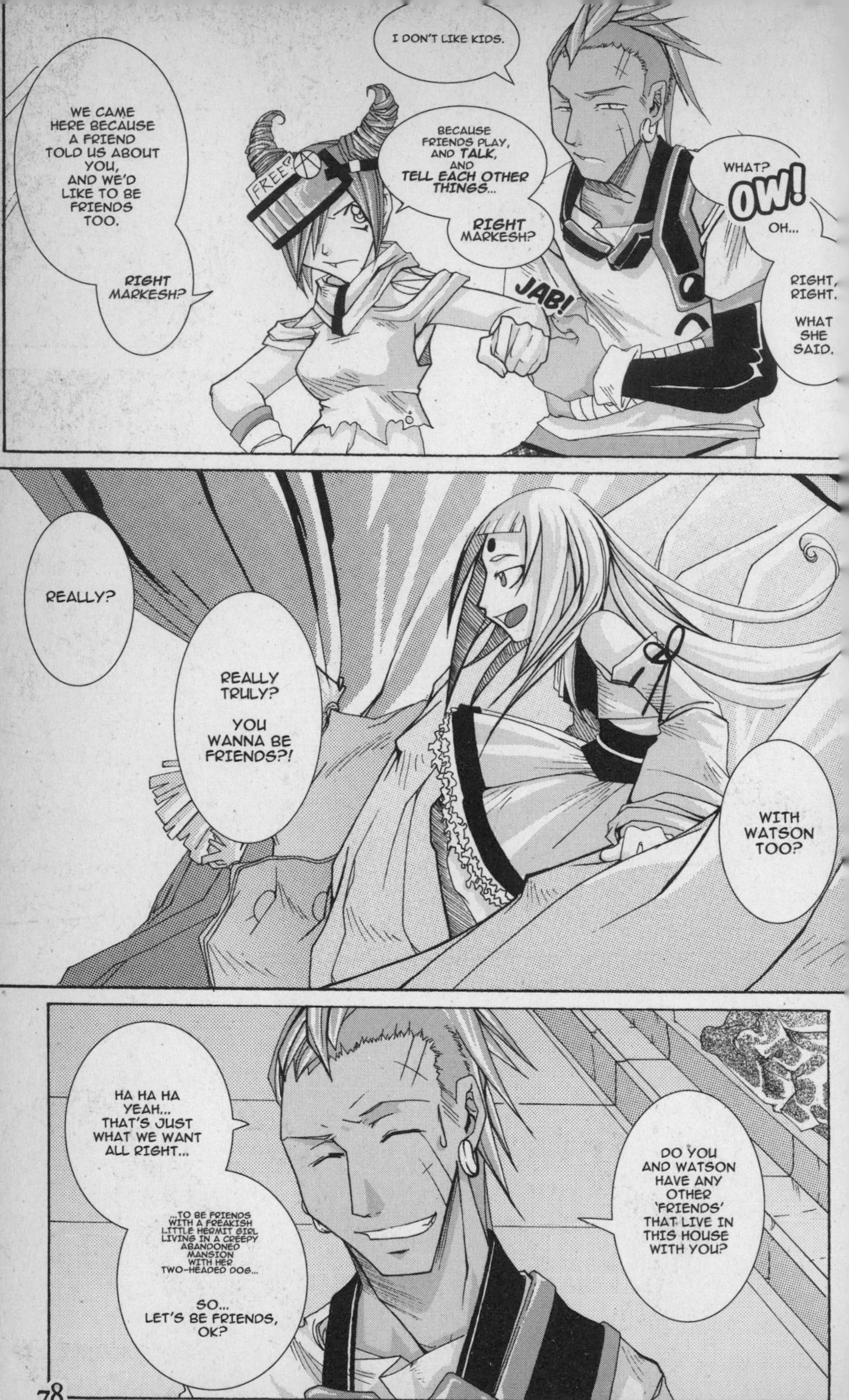
I DON'T LIKE KIDS.
WE CAME HERE BECAUSE A FRIEND TOLD US ABOUT YOU, AND WE'D LIKE TO BE FRIENDS TOO.
RIGHT MARKESH?
FREE?
BECAUSE FRIENDS PLAY, AND TALK, AND TELL EACH OTHER THINGS...
RIGHT MARKESH?
JAB!
WHAT?
OW!
OH...
RIGHT, RIGHT.
WHAT SHE SAID.
REALLY?
REALLY TRULY?
YOU WANNA BE FRIENDS?!
WITH WATSON TOO?
HA HA HA YEAH... THAT'S JUST WHAT WE WANT ALL RIGHT...
...TO BE FRIENDS WITH A FREAKISH LITTLE HERMIT GIRL LIVING IN A CREEPY ABANDONED MANSION WITH HER TWO-HEADED DOG...
SO... LET'S BE FRIENDS, OK?
DO YOU AND WATSON HAVE ANY OTHER 'FRIENDS' THAT LIVE IN THIS HOUSE WITH YOU?

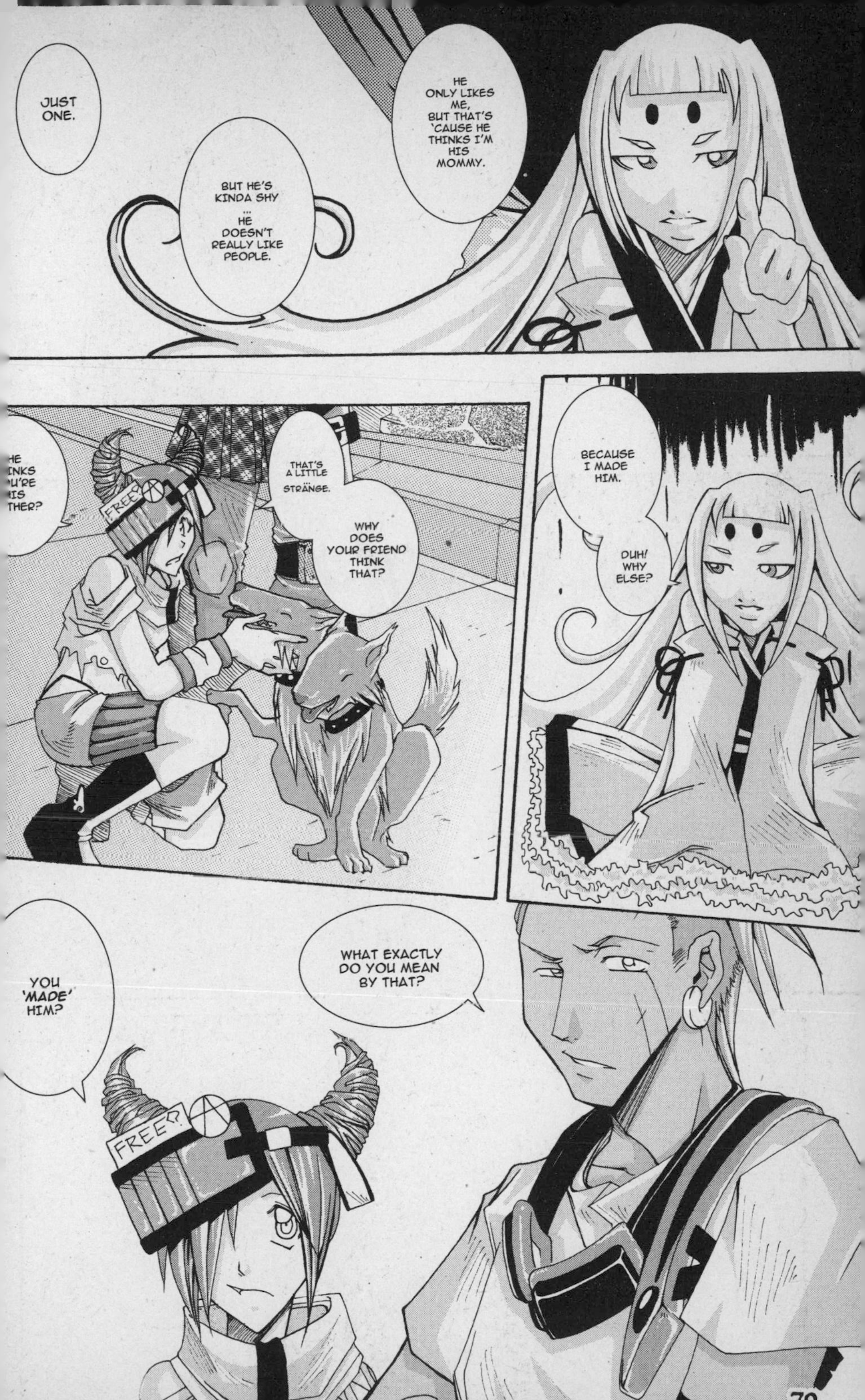
JUST ONE.
BUT HE'S KINDA SHY ... HE DOESN'T REALLY LIKE PEOPLE.
HE ONLY LIKES ME, BUT THAT'S 'CAUSE HE THINKS I'M HIS MOMMY.
HE INKS U'RE IS THER?
FREE
THAT'S A LITTLE STRÄNGE.
WHY DOES YOUR FRIEND THINK THAT?
BECAUSE I MADE HIM.
DUH! WHY ELSE?
YOU 'MADE' HIM?
WHAT EXACTLY DO YOU MEAN BY THAT?
FREE?

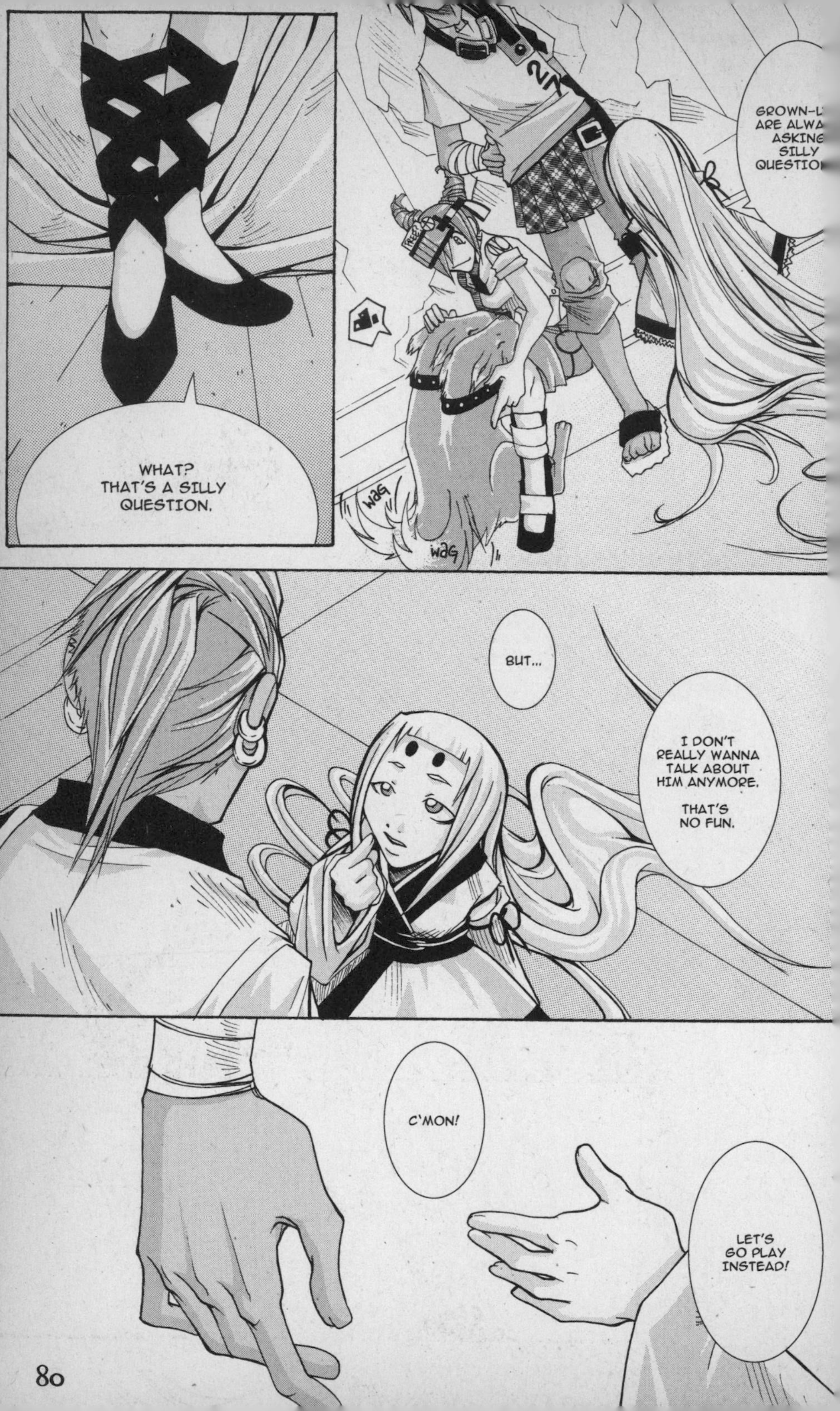
WHAT? THAT'S A SILLY QUESTION.
GROWN-U ARE ALWA ASKING SILLY QUESTIO
WAG
WAG
BUT...
I DON'T REALLY WANNA TALK ABOUT HIM ANYMORE.
THAT'S NO FUN.
C'MON!
LET'S GO PLAY INSTEAD!

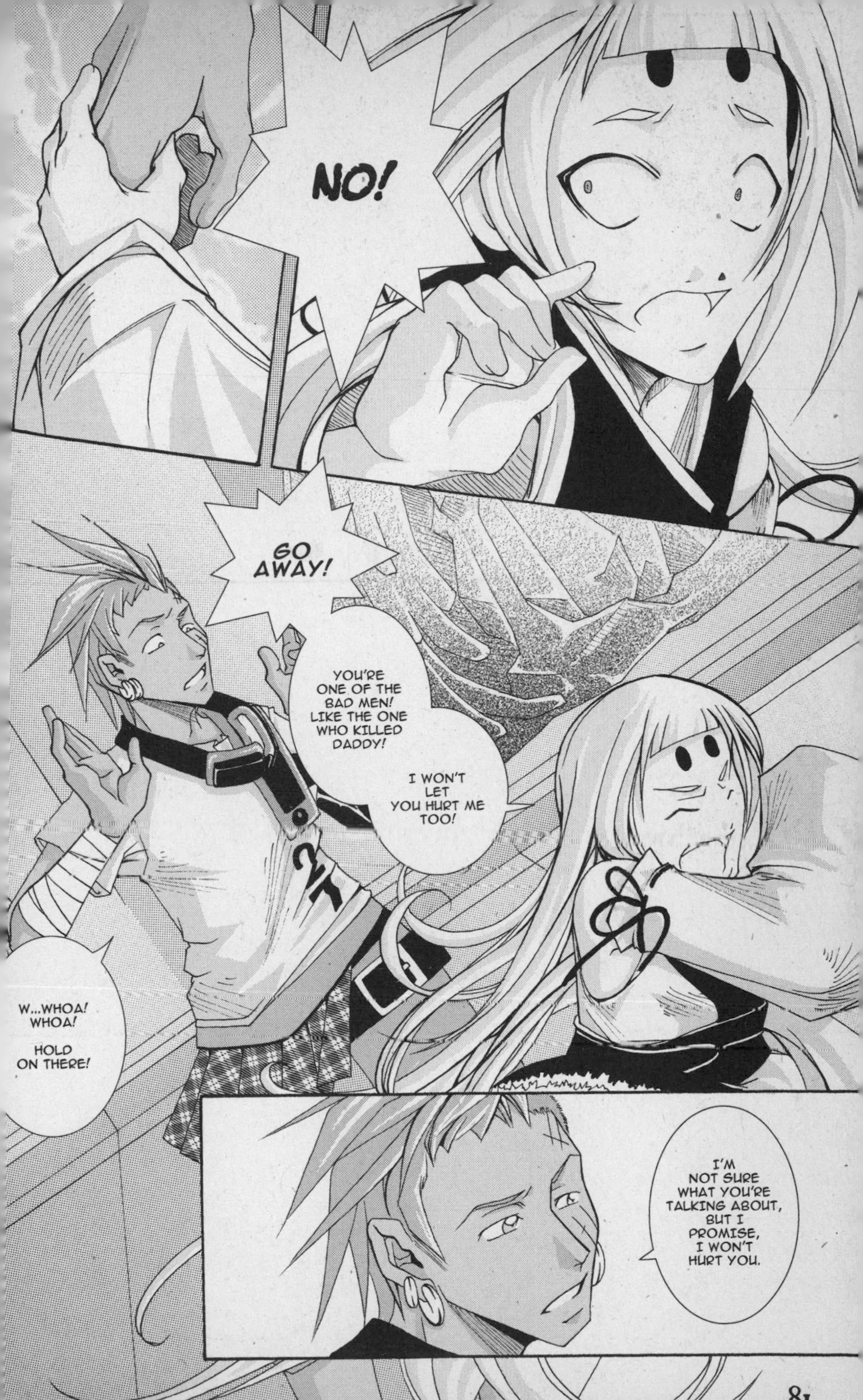
NO!
GO AWAY!
YOU'RE ONE OF THE BAD MEN! LIKE THE ONE WHO KILLED DADDY!
I WON'T LET YOU HURT ME TOO!
W...WHOA! WHOA! HOLD ON THERE!
I'M NOT SURE WHAT YOU'RE TALKING ABOUT, BUT I PROMISE, I WON'T HURT YOU.

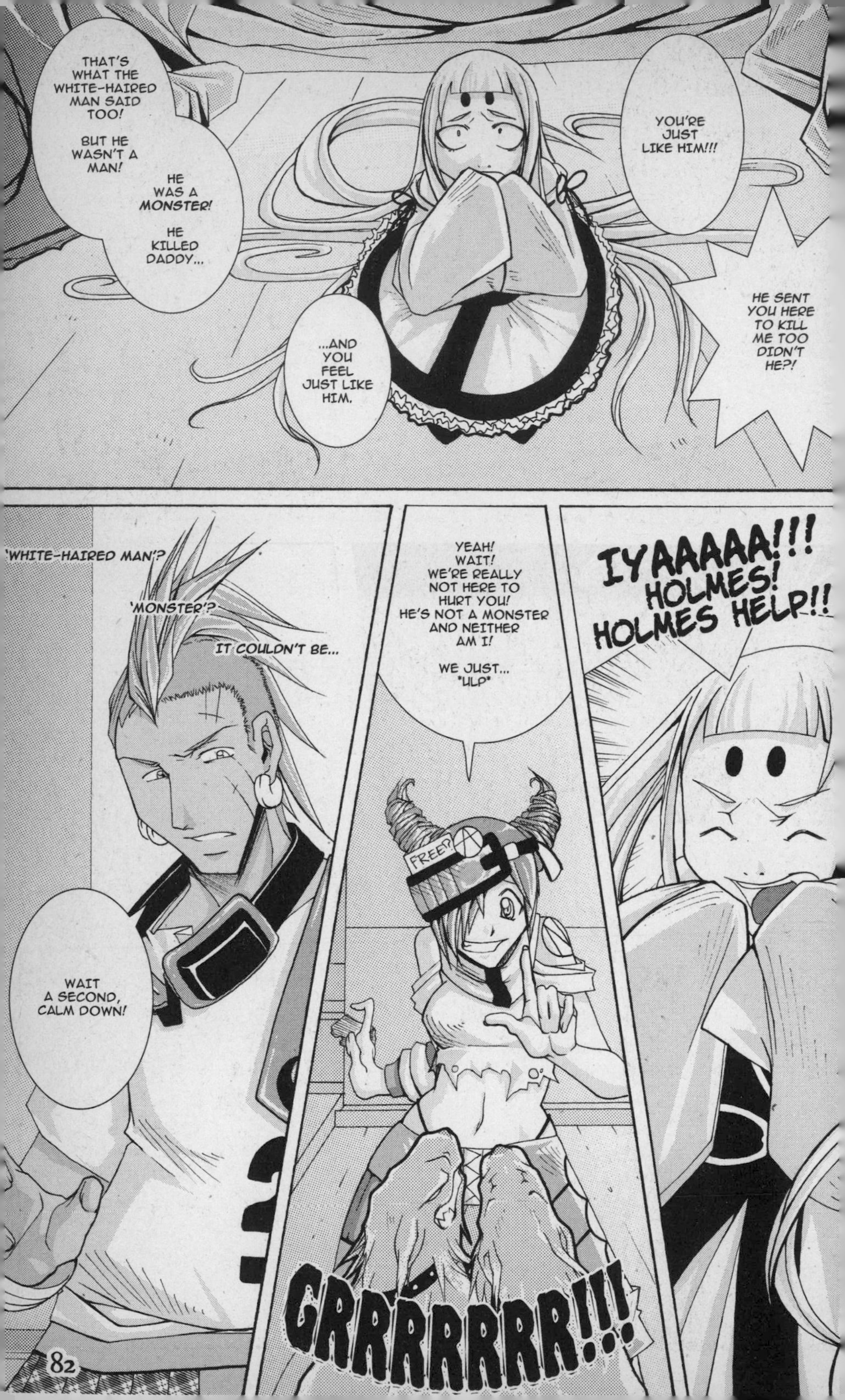

THAT'S WHAT THE WHITE-HAIRED MAN SAID TOO!
BUT HE WASN'T A MAN!
HE WAS A MONSTER!
HE KILLED DADDY...
...AND YOU FEEL JUST LIKE HIM.
YOU'RE JUST LIKE HIM!!!
HE SENT YOU HERE TO KILL ME TOO DIDN'T HE?!
'WHITE-HAIRED MAN'?
'MONSTER'?
IT COULDN'T BE...
WAIT A SECOND, CALM DOWN!
YEAH! WAIT! WE'RE REALLY NOT HERE TO HURT YOU! HE'S NOT A MONSTER AND NEITHER AM I!
WE JUST... *ULP*
FREE?
IYAAAAA!!! HOLMES! HOLMES HELP!!!
GRRRRRRR!!!

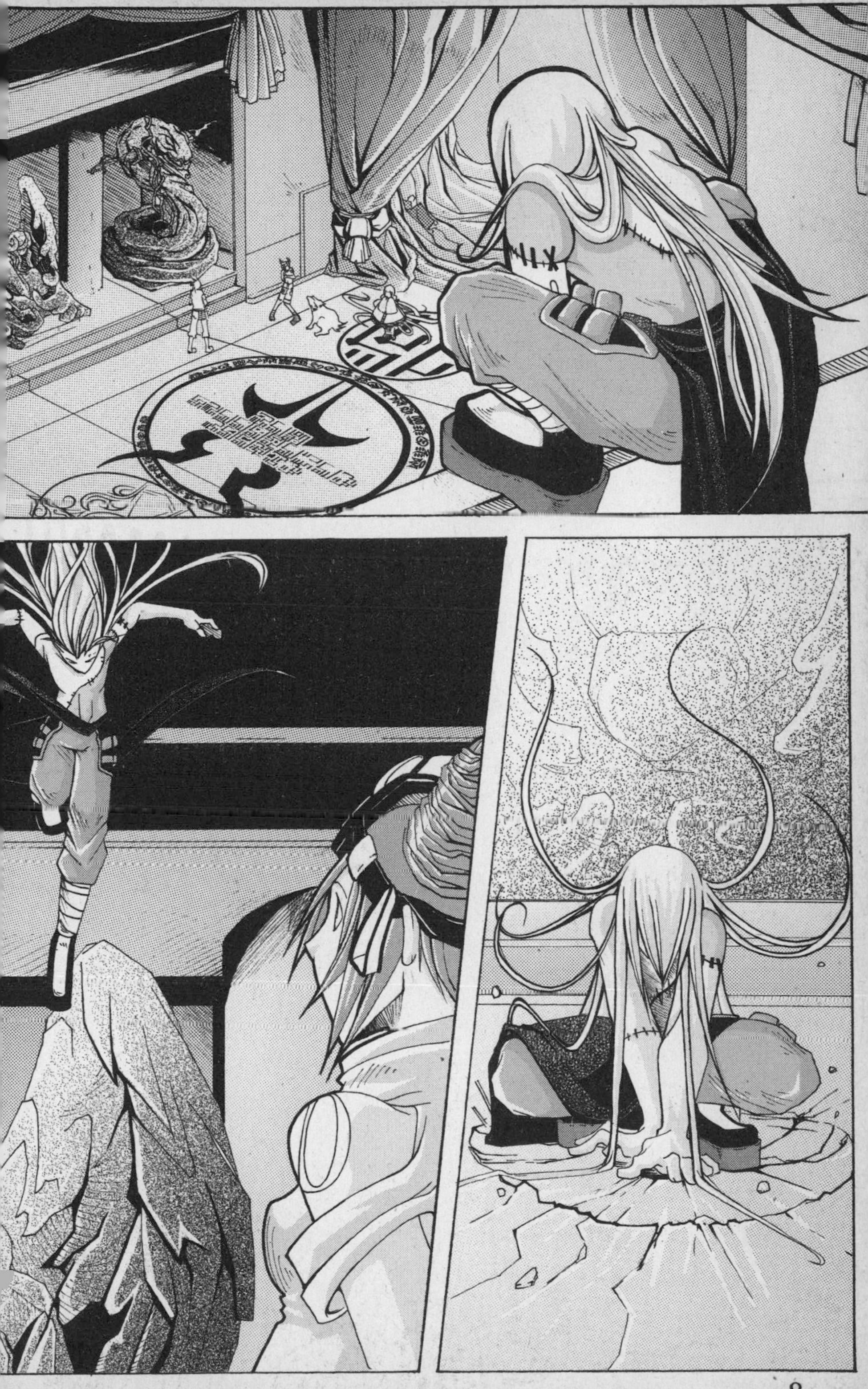

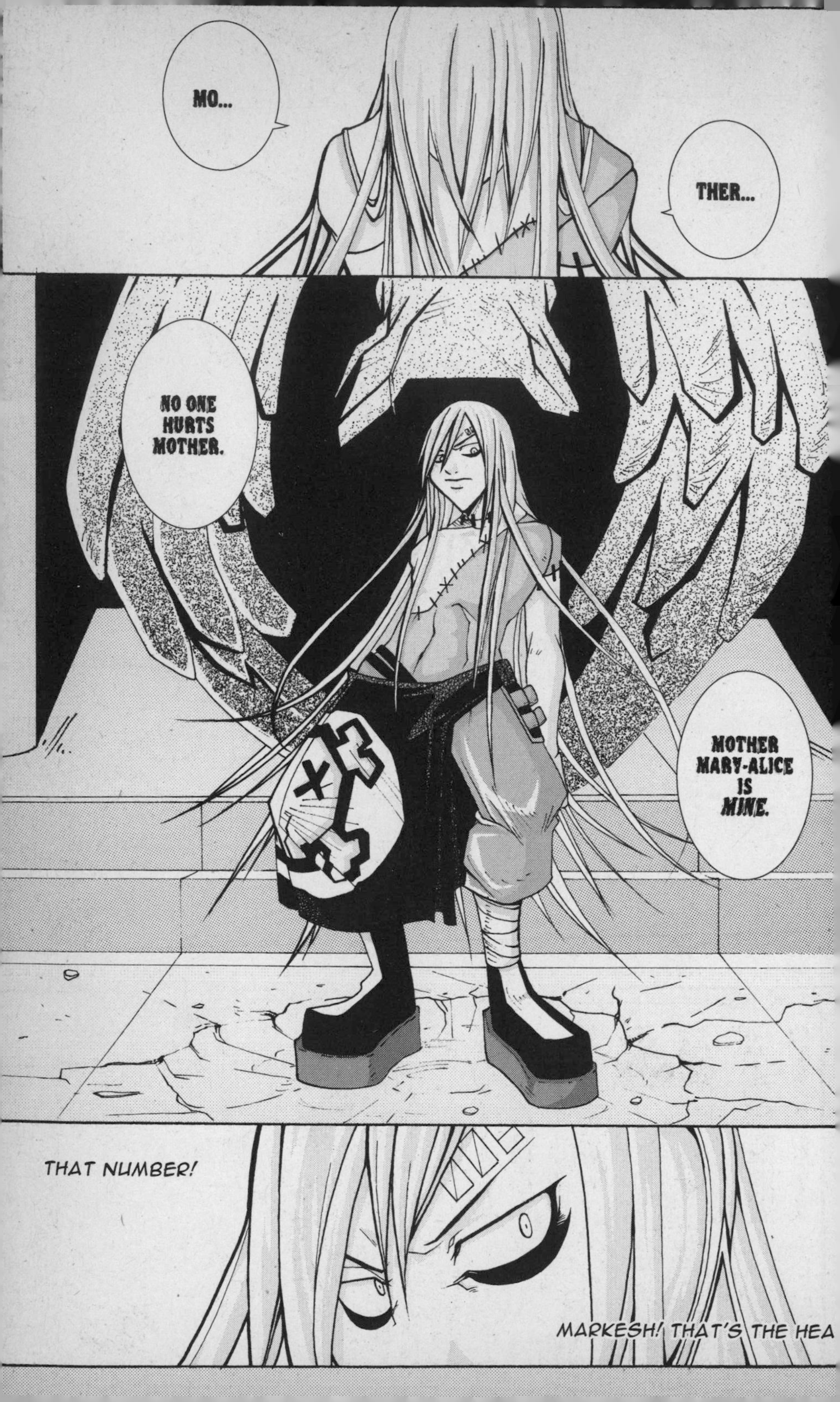
MO...
THER...
NO ONE HURTS MOTHER.
MOTHER MARY-ALICE IS MINE.
THAT NUMBER!
MARKESH! THAT'S THE HEA

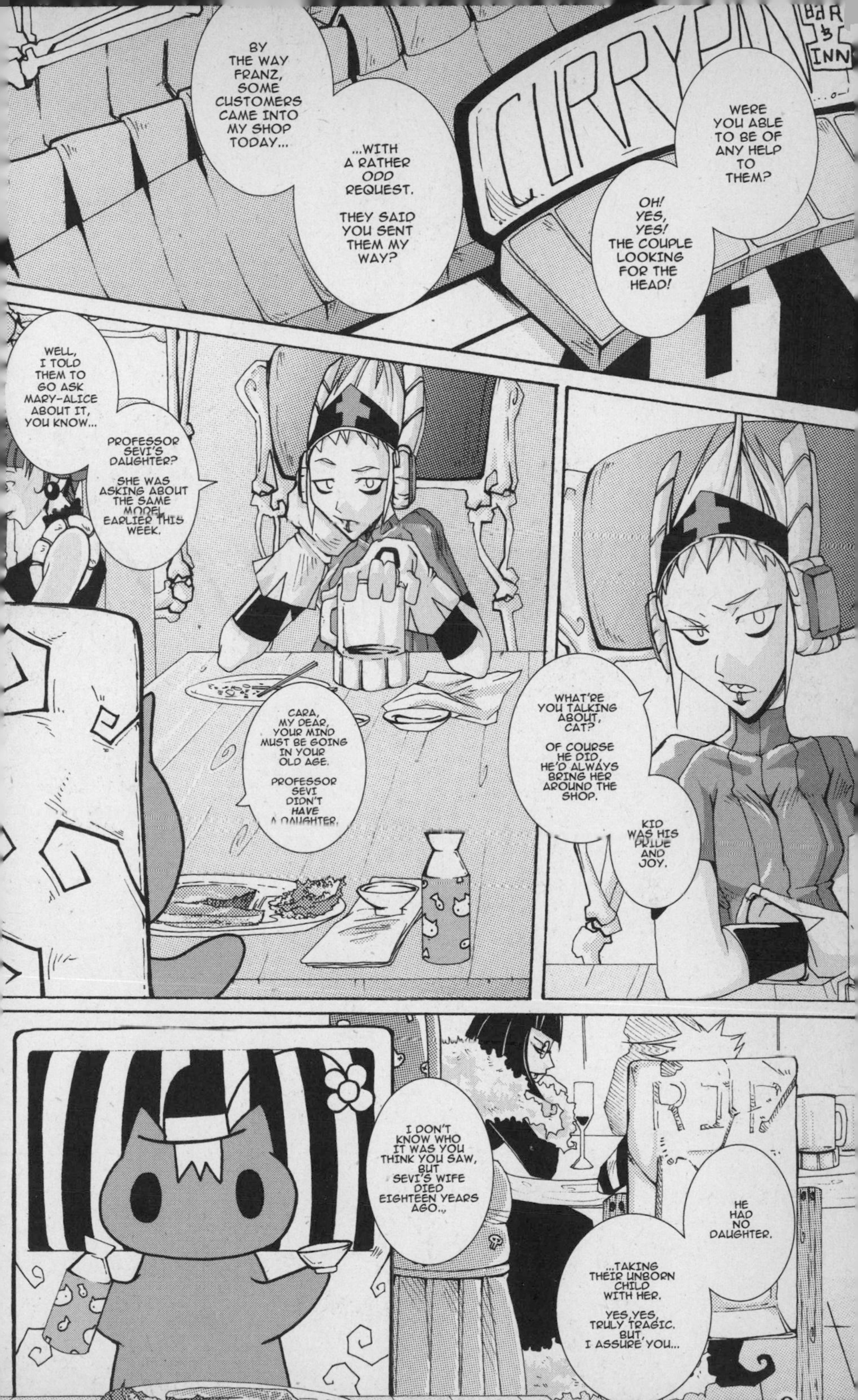
CURRY PAN
BAR & INN
BY THE WAY FRANZ, SOME CUSTOMERS CAME INTO MY SHOP TODAY...
...WITH A RATHER ODD REQUEST.
THEY SAID YOU SENT THEM MY WAY?
WERE YOU ABLE TO BE OF ANY HELP TO THEM?
OH! YES, YES! THE COUPLE LOOKING FOR THE HEAD!
WELL, I TOLD THEM TO GO ASK MARY-ALICE ABOUT IT, YOU KNOW...
PROFESSOR SEVI'S DAUGHTER?
SHE WAS ASKING ABOUT THE SAME MODEL EARLIER THIS WEEK.
CARA, MY DEAR, YOUR MIND MUST BE GOING IN YOUR OLD AGE.
PROFESSOR SEVI DIDN'T HAVE A DAUGHTER.
WHAT'RE YOU TALKING ABOUT, CAT?
OF COURSE HE DID, HE'D ALWAYS BRING HER AROUND THE SHOP.
KID WAS HIS PRIDE AND JOY.
I DON'T KNOW WHO IT WAS YOU THINK YOU SAW, BUT SEVI'S WIFE DIED EIGHTEEN YEARS AGO...
...TAKING THEIR UNBORN CHILD WITH HER.
HE HAD NO DAUGHTER.
YES,YES, TRULY TRAGIC. BUT, I ASSURE YOU...

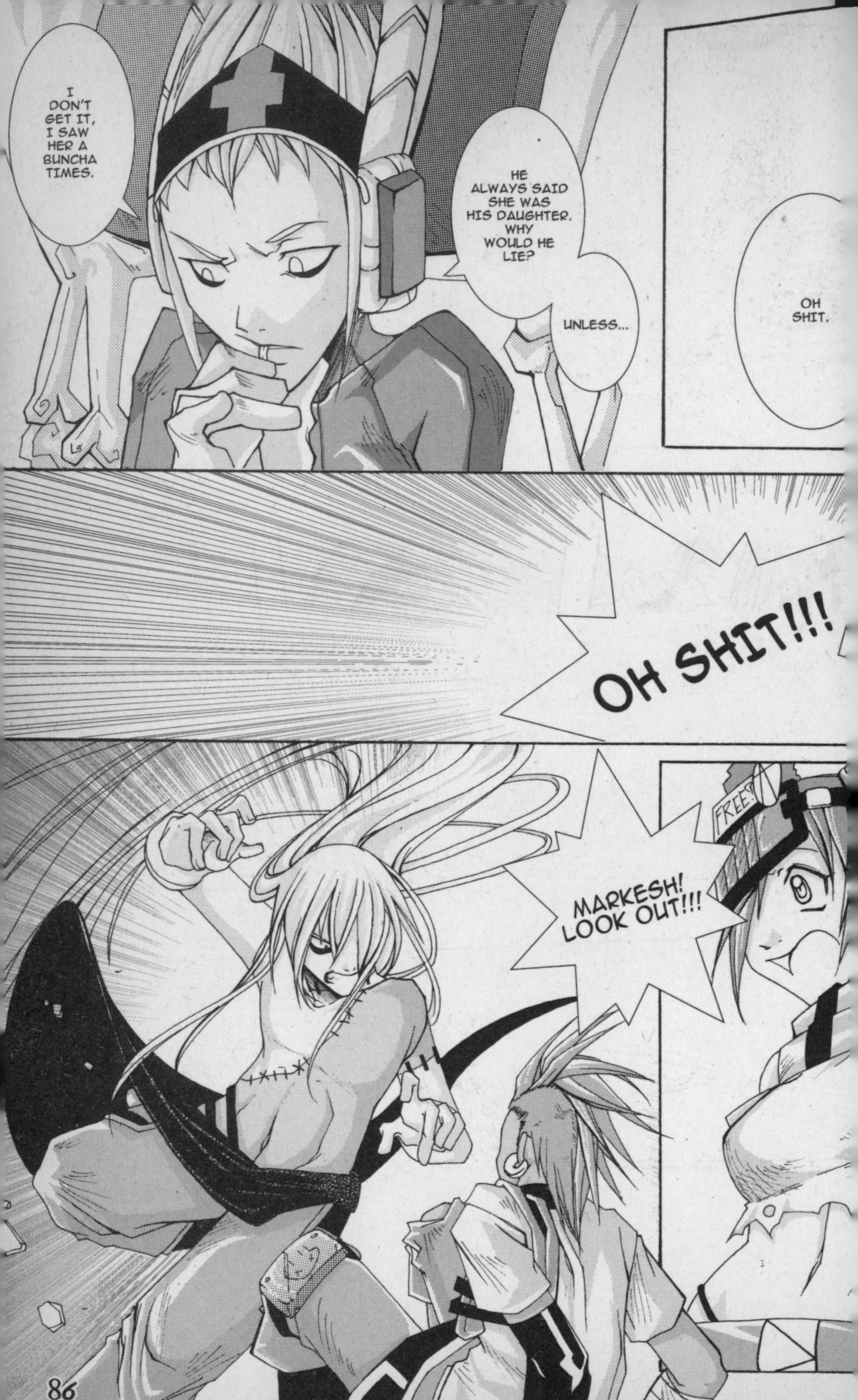
I DON'T GET IT, I SAW HER A BUNCHA TIMES.
HE ALWAYS SAID SHE WAS HIS DAUGHTER. WHY WOULD HE LIE?
UNLESS...
OH SHIT.
OH SHIT!!!
MARKESH! LOOK OUT!!!
FREE

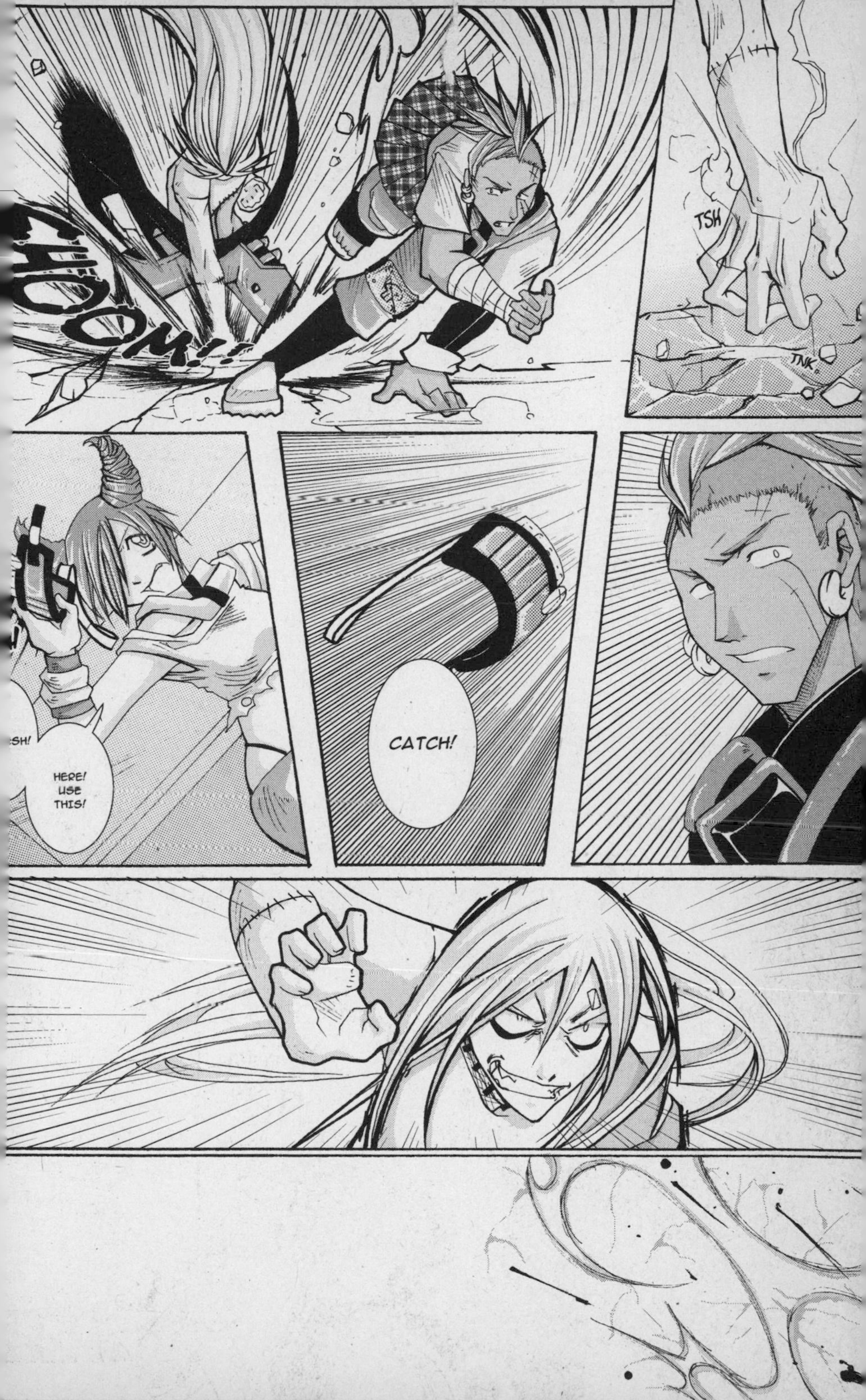
TSH
TNK
CHOOM!!
CATCH!
HERE! USE THIS!

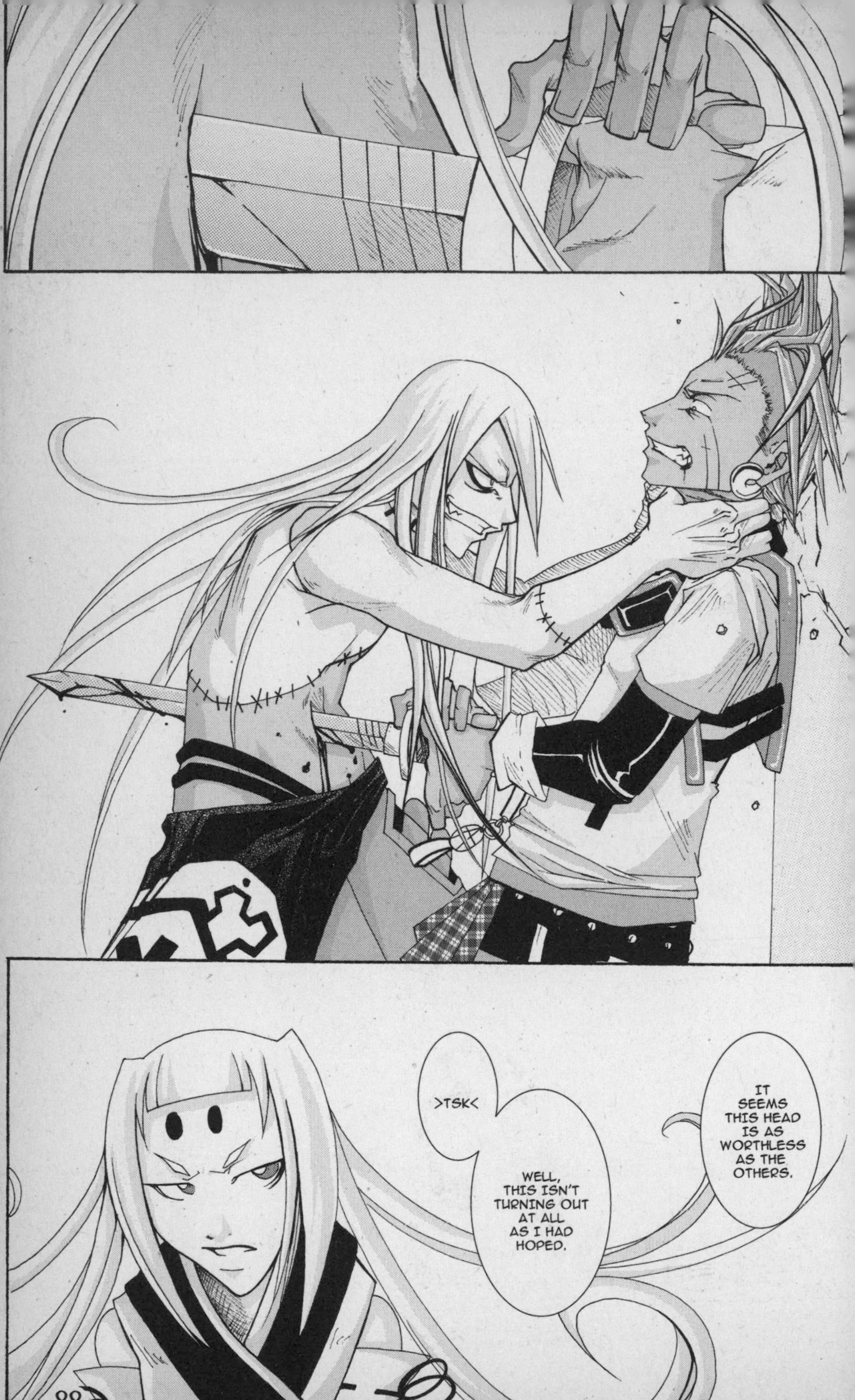
IT SEEMS THIS HEAD IS AS WORTHLESS AS THE OTHERS.
>TSK<
WELL, THIS ISN'T TURNING OUT AT ALL AS I HAD HOPED.

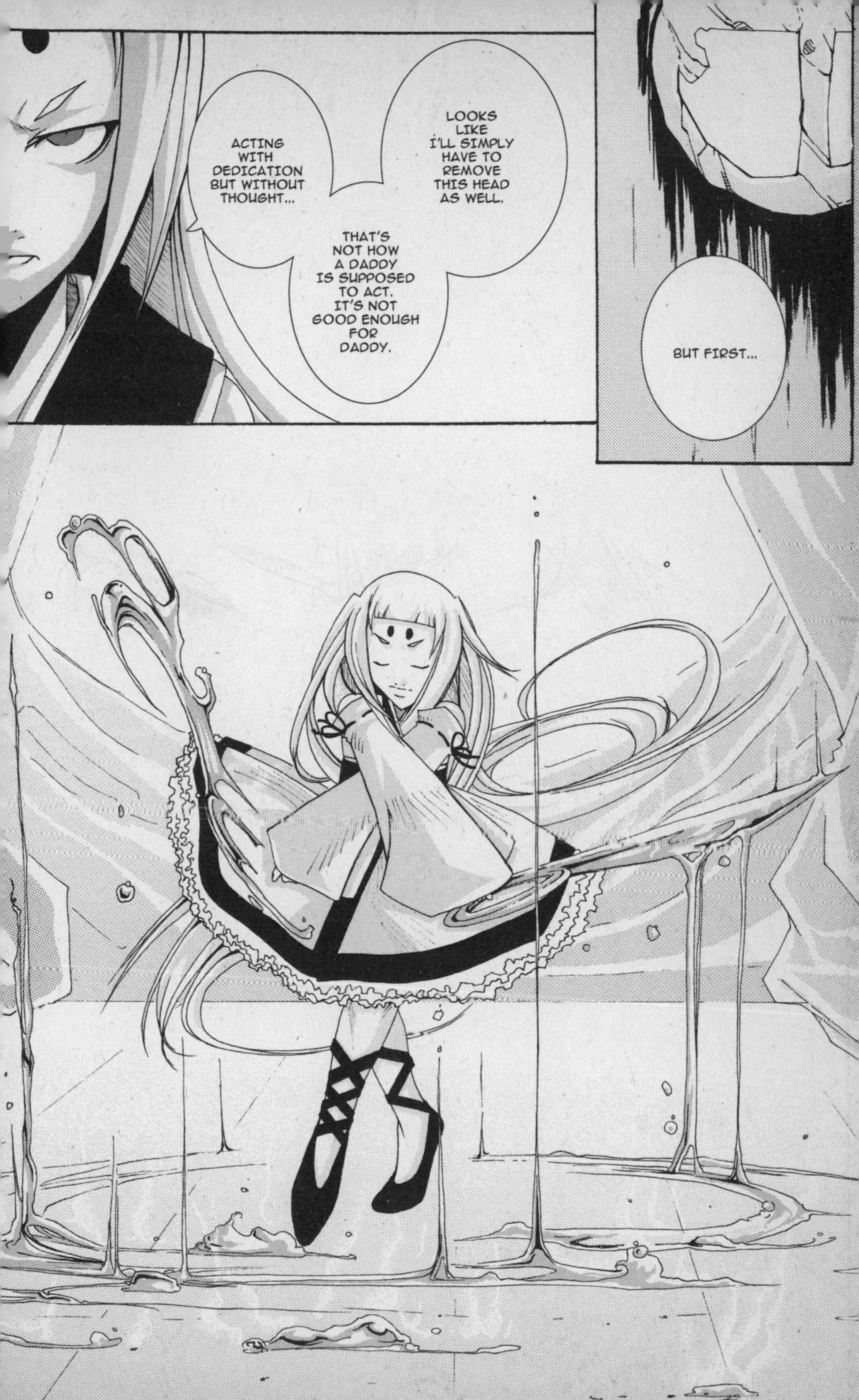
ACTING WITH DEDICATION BUT WITHOUT THOUGHT...
THAT'S NOT HOW A DADDY IS SUPPOSED TO ACT. IT'S NOT GOOD ENOUGH FOR DADDY.
LOOKS LIKE I'LL SIMPLY HAVE TO REMOVE THIS HEAD AS WELL.
BUT FIRST...

SHWNK!

I'LL TAKE CARE OF THIS MONSTER.

YO
MAY L
LIKE
PERS
BUT I
BETT
I WO
BE FO
AGA

'MONSTER'?!

YOU'RE THE MONSTER, YOU LITTLE PSYCHO!

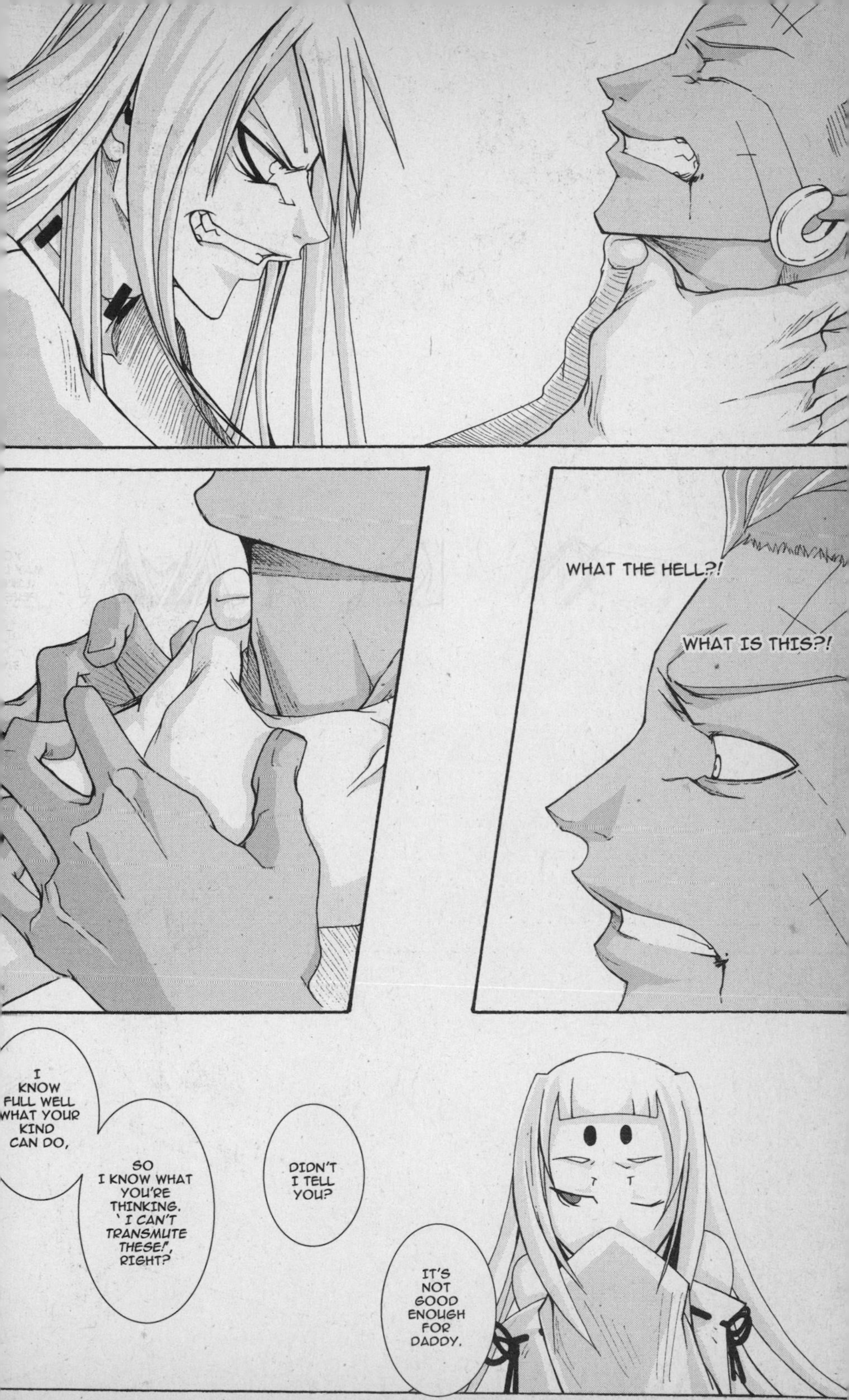
WHAT THE HELL?!
WHAT IS THIS?!
DIDN'T I TELL YOU?
IT'S NOT GOOD ENOUGH FOR DADDY.
I KNOW FULL WELL WHAT YOUR KIND CAN DO,
SO I KNOW WHAT YOU'RE THINKING. 'I CAN'T TRANSMUTE THESE!', RIGHT?

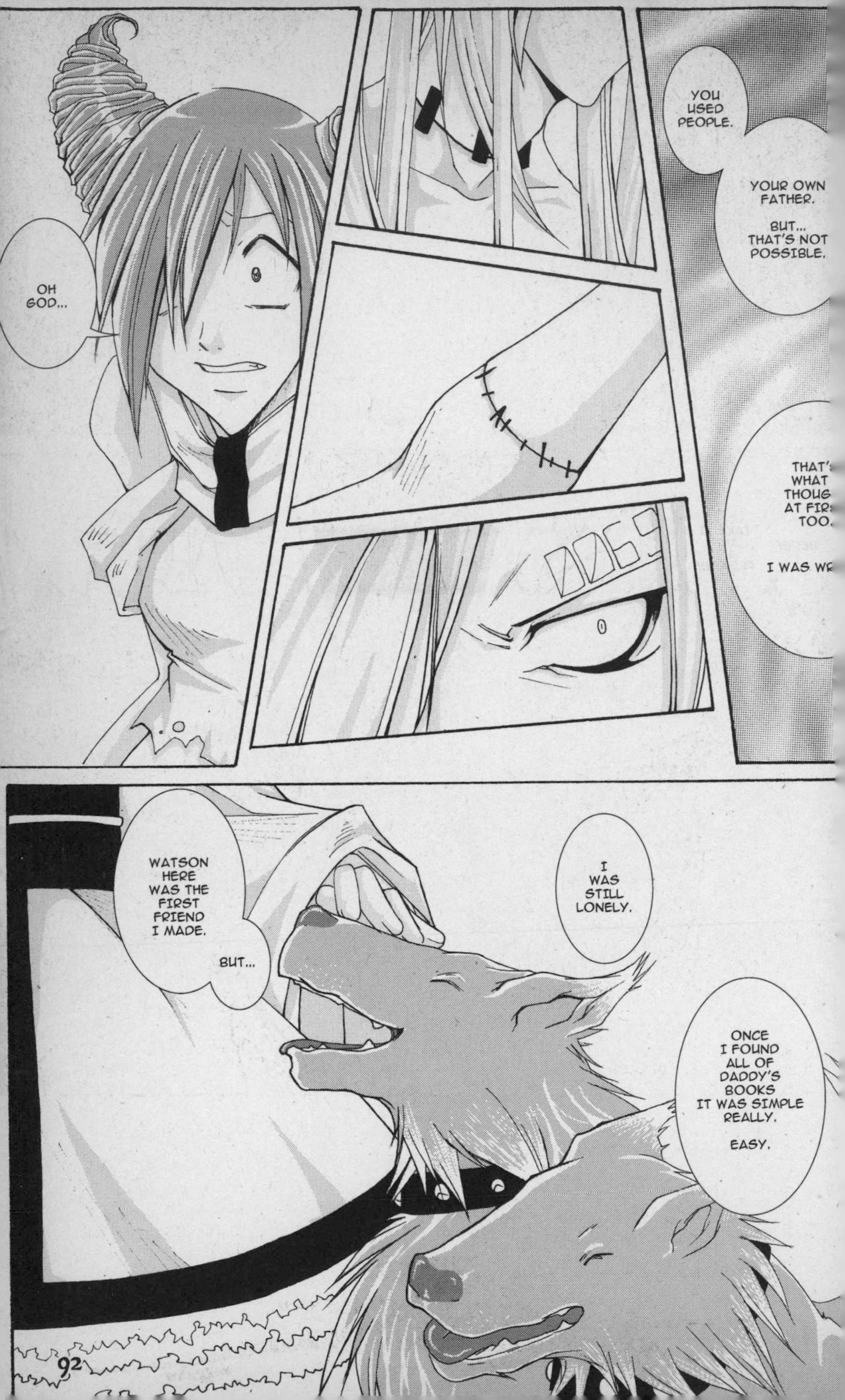
OH GOD...
YOU USED PEOPLE.
YOUR OWN FATHER.
BUT... THAT'S NOT POSSIBLE.
THAT' WHAT THOUG AT FIRS TOO.
I WAS WR
WATSON HERE WAS THE FIRST FRIEND I MADE.
BUT...
I WAS STILL LONELY.
ONCE I FOUND ALL OF DADDY'S BOOKS IT WAS SIMPLE REALLY.
EASY.

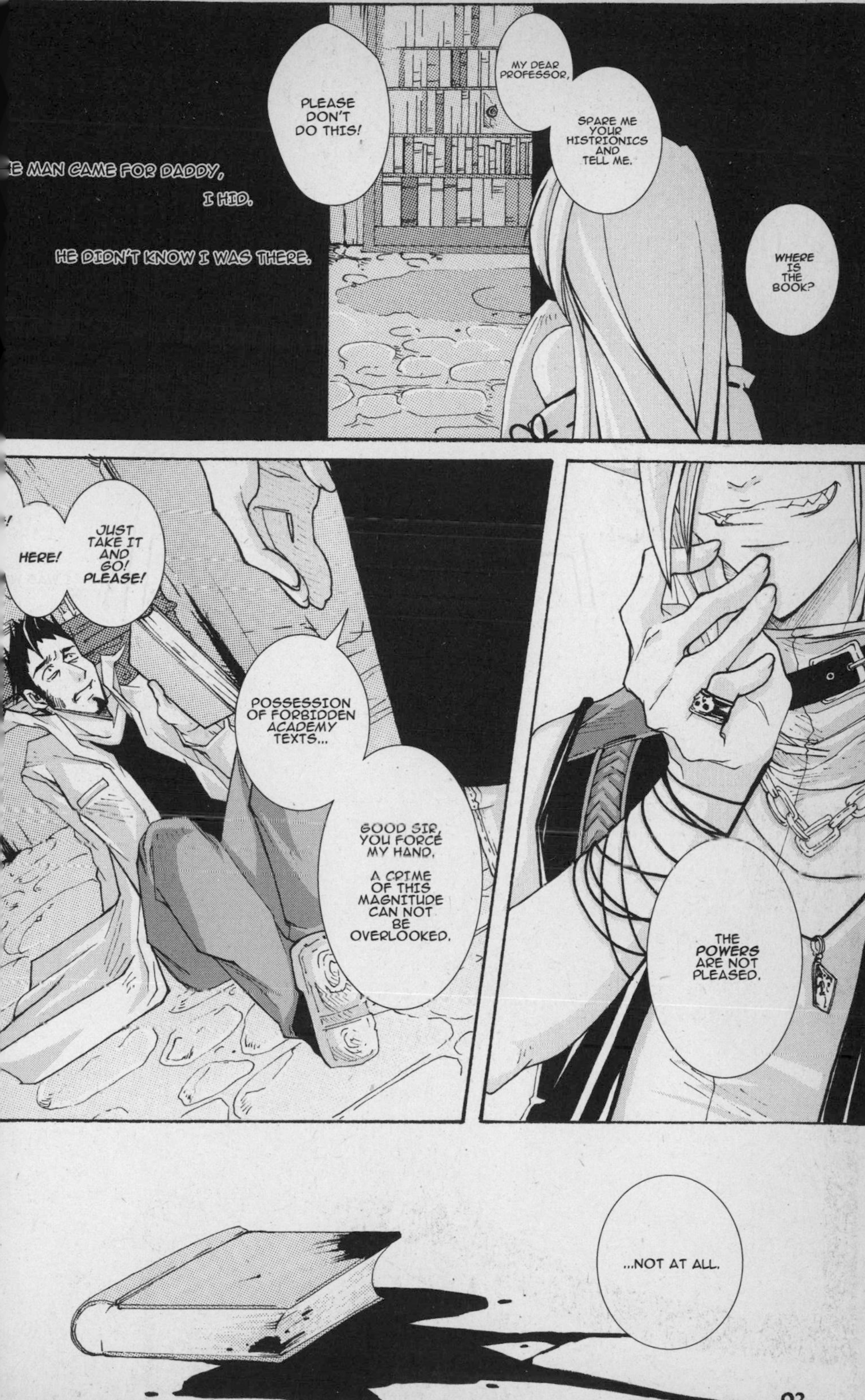
E MAN CAME FOR DADDY,
I HID.
HE DIDN'T KNOW I WAS THERE.
PLEASE DON'T DO THIS!
MY DEAR PROFESSOR,
SPARE ME YOUR HISTRIONICS AND TELL ME.
WHERE IS THE BOOK?
HERE!
JUST TAKE IT AND GO! PLEASE!
POSSESSION OF FORBIDDEN ACADEMY TEXTS...
GOOD SIR, YOU FORCE MY HAND.
A CRIME OF THIS MAGNITUDE CAN NOT BE OVERLOOKED.
THE POWERS ARE NOT PLEASED.
...NOT AT ALL.

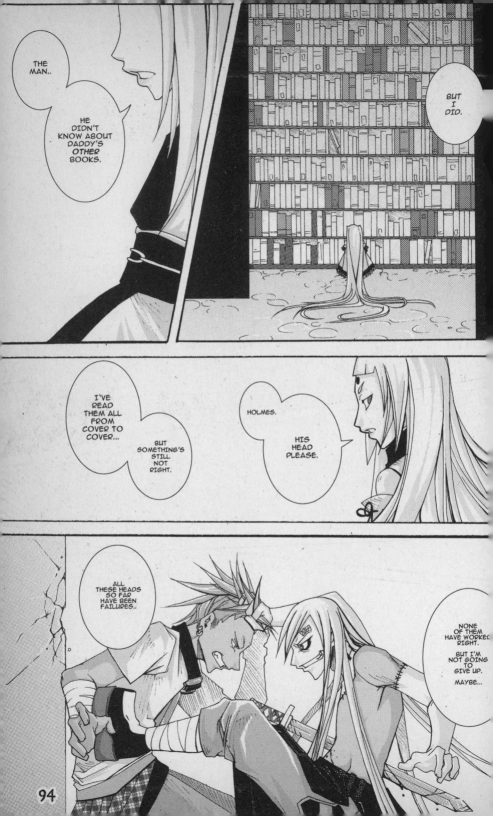

THE MAN..

HE DIDN'T KNOW ABOUT DADDY'S OTHER BOOKS.

BUT I DID.

I'VE READ THEM ALL FROM COVER TO COVER...

BUT SOMETHING'S STILL NOT RIGHT.

HOLMES.

HIS HEAD PLEASE.

ALL THESE HEADS SO FAR HAVE BEEN FAILURES..

NONE OF THEM HAVE WORKED RIGHT.

BUT I'M NOT GOING TO GIVE UP.

MAYBE...

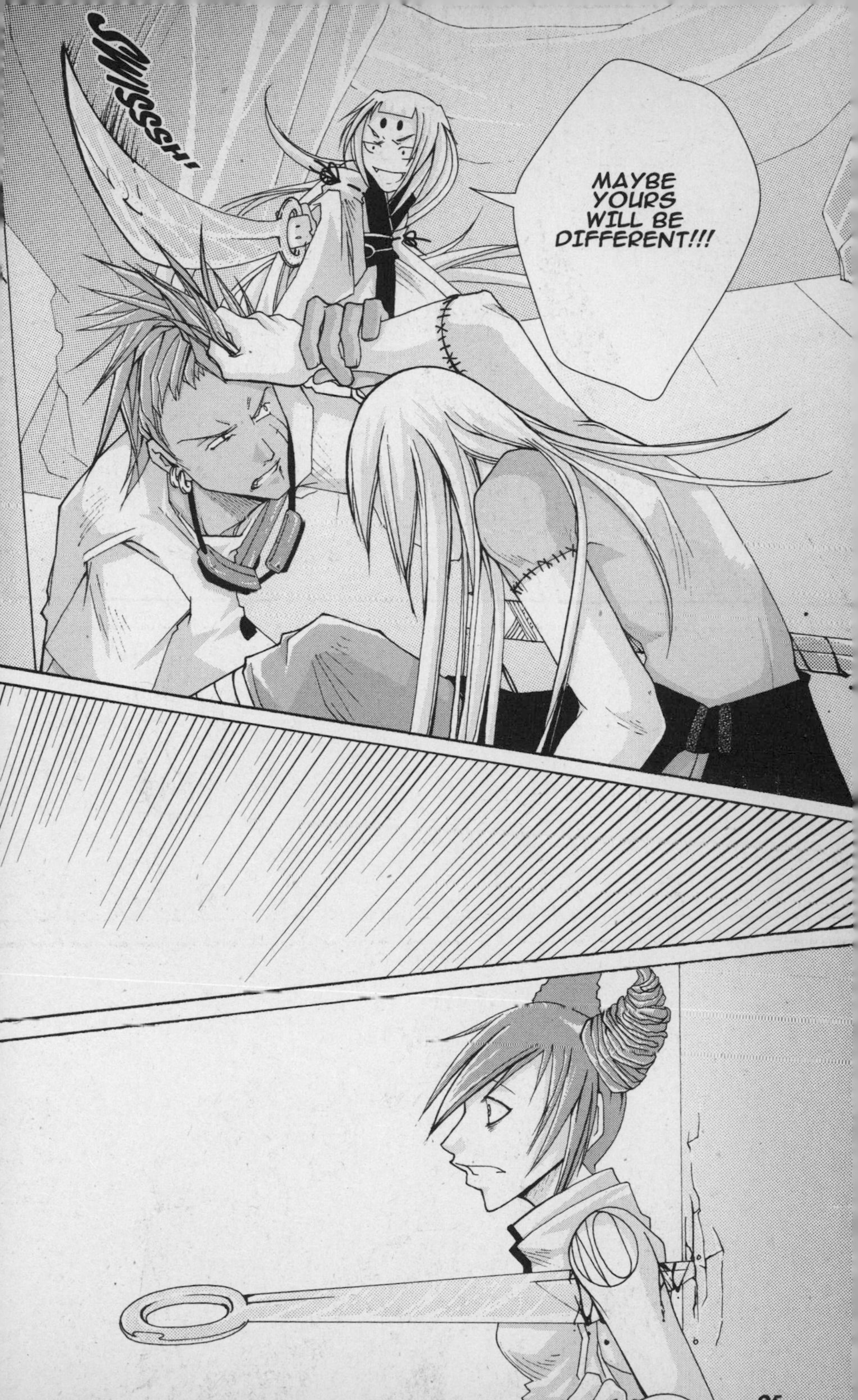
SWISSSH!
MAYBE YOURS WILL BE DIFFERENT!!!

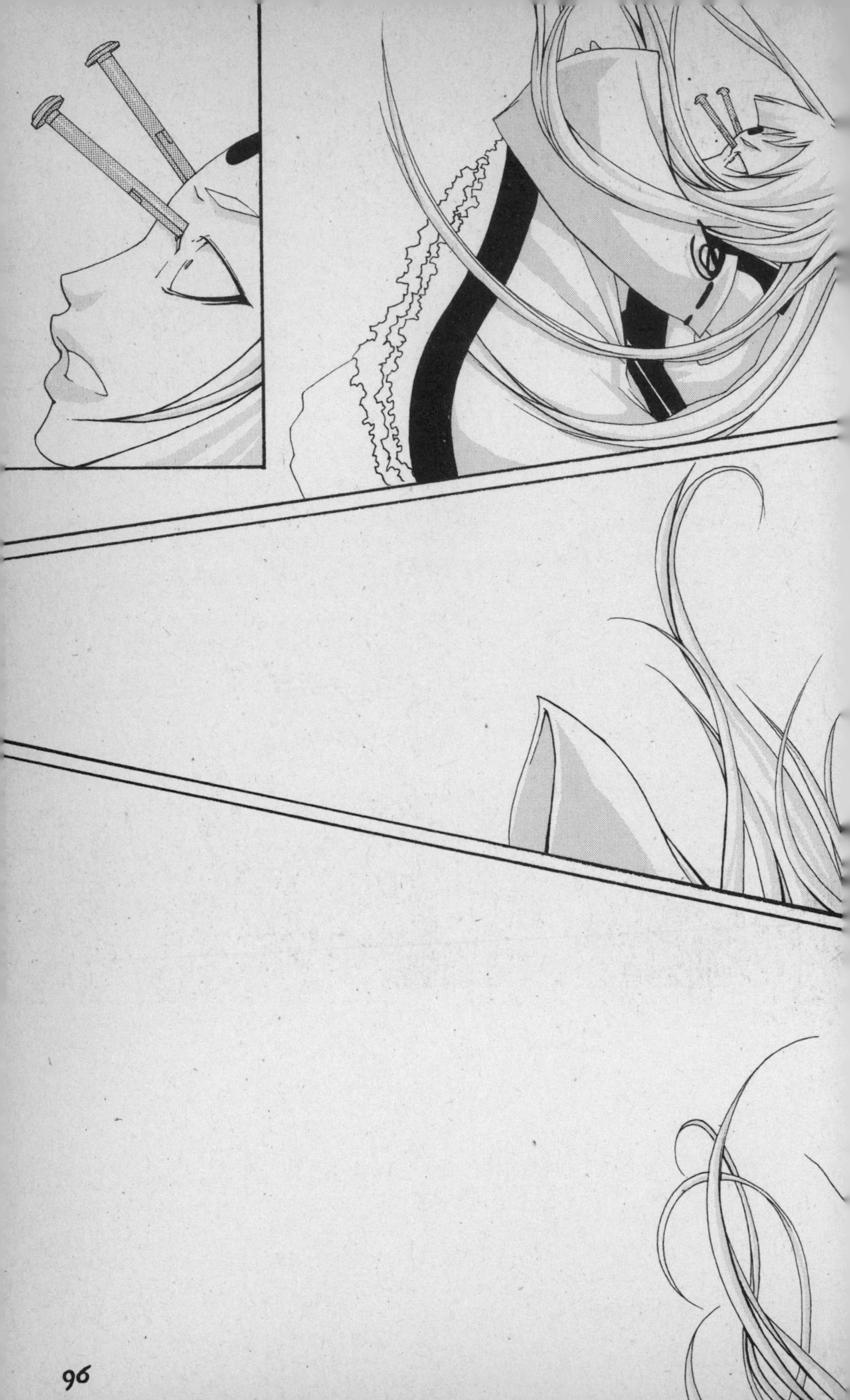

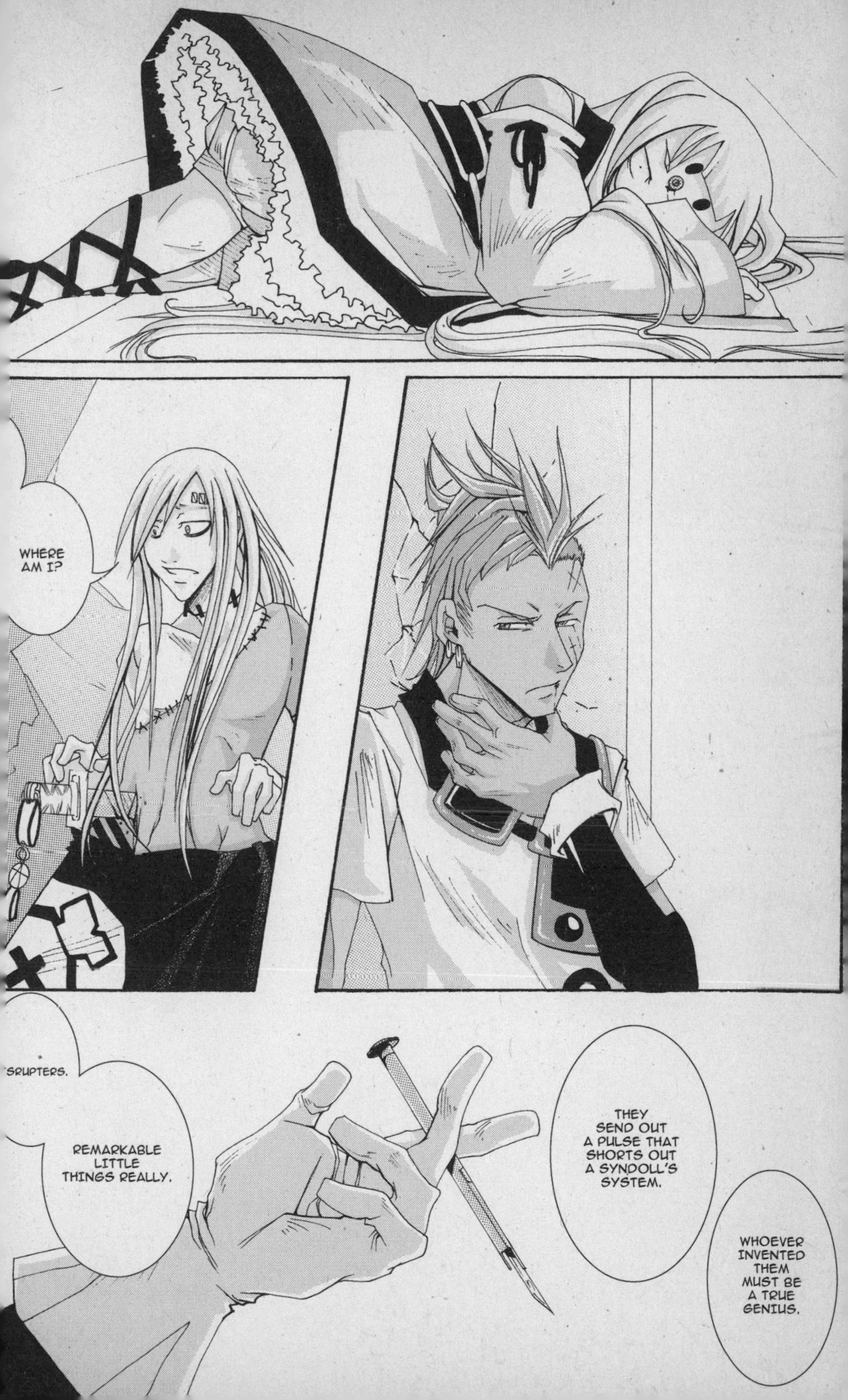
WHERE AM I?
SRUPTERS.
REMARKABLE LITTLE THINGS REALLY.
THEY SEND OUT A PULSE THAT SHORTS OUT A SYNDOLL'S SYSTEM.
WHOEVER INVENTED THEM MUST BE A TRUE GENIUS.

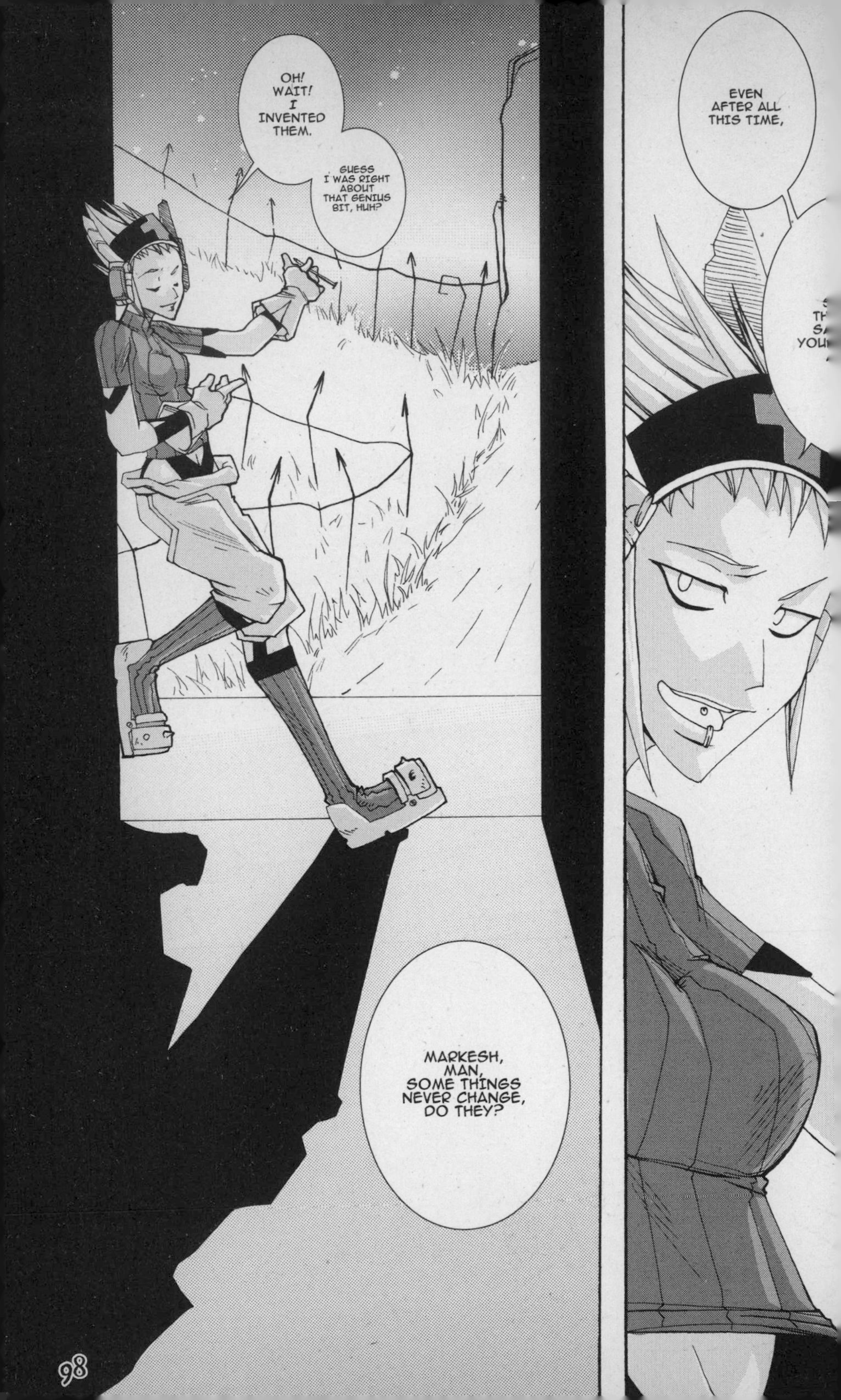
OH! WAIT! I INVENTED THEM.
GUESS I WAS RIGHT ABOUT THAT GENIUS BIT, HUH?
MARKESH, MAN, SOME THINGS NEVER CHANGE, DO THEY?
EVEN AFTER ALL THIS TIME,

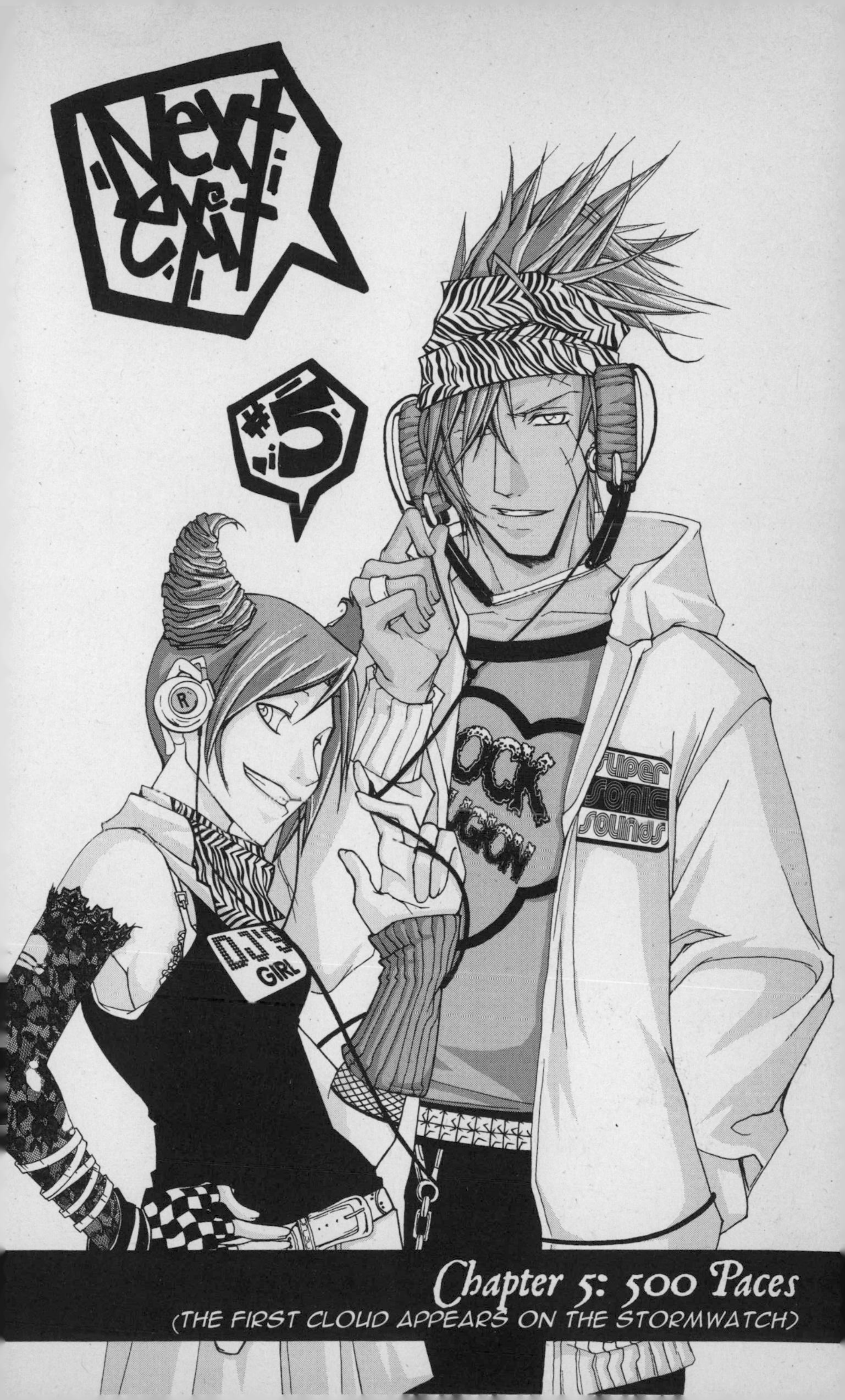
Next
#5
DJ'S GIRL
SUPER SONIC SOUNDS

Chapter 5: 500 Paces

(THE FIRST CLOUD APPEARS ON THE STORMWATCH)

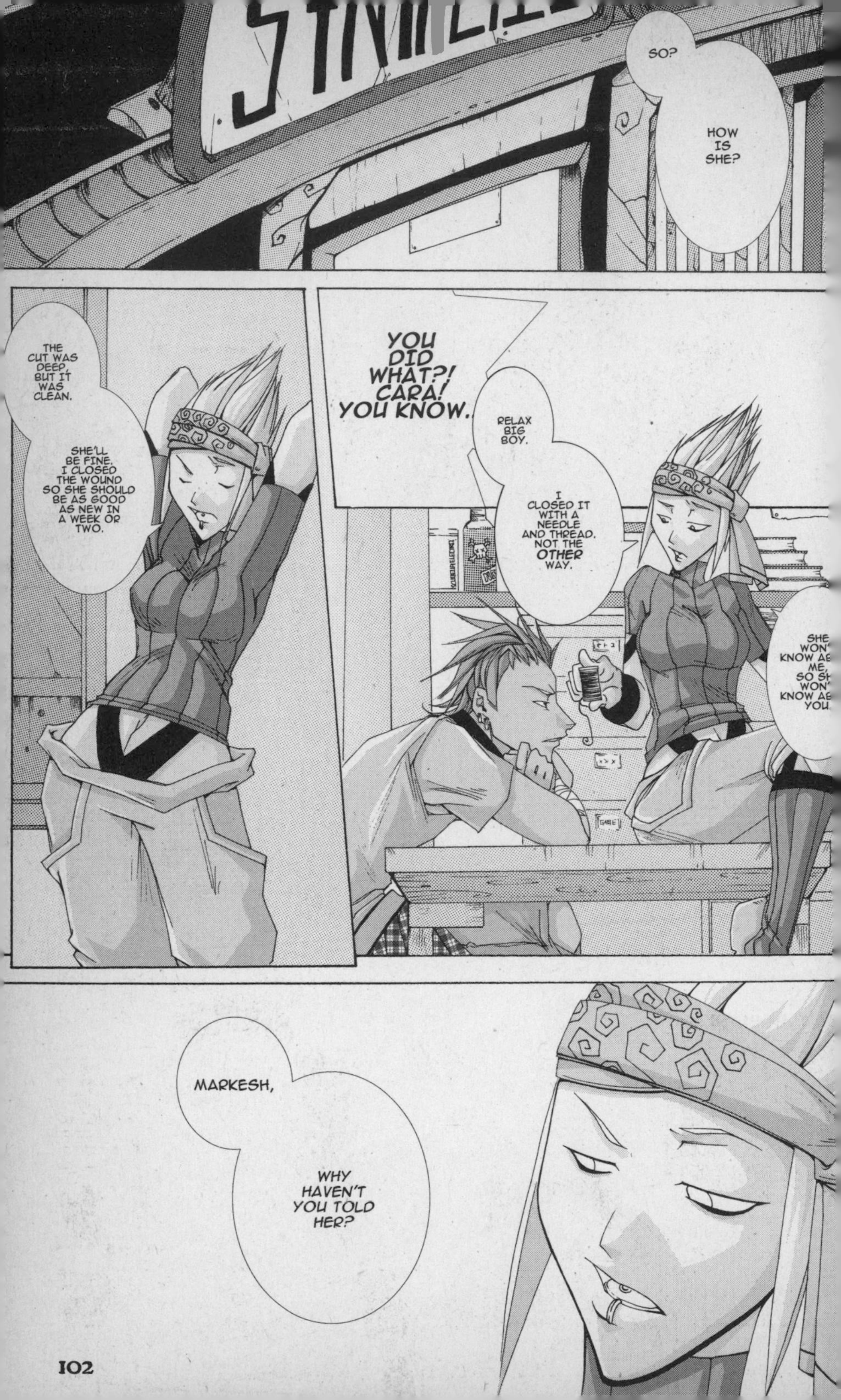
SO?
HOW IS SHE?
THE CUT WAS DEEP, BUT IT WAS CLEAN.
SHE'LL BE FINE. I CLOSED THE WOUND SO SHE SHOULD BE AS GOOD AS NEW IN A WEEK OR TWO.
YOU DID WHAT?! CARA! YOU KNOW...
RELAX BIG BOY.
I CLOSED IT WITH A NEEDLE AND THREAD. NOT THE **OTHER** WAY.
SHE WON' KNOW AB ME, SO SH WON' KNOW AB YOU.
MARKESH,
WHY HAVEN'T YOU TOLD HER?

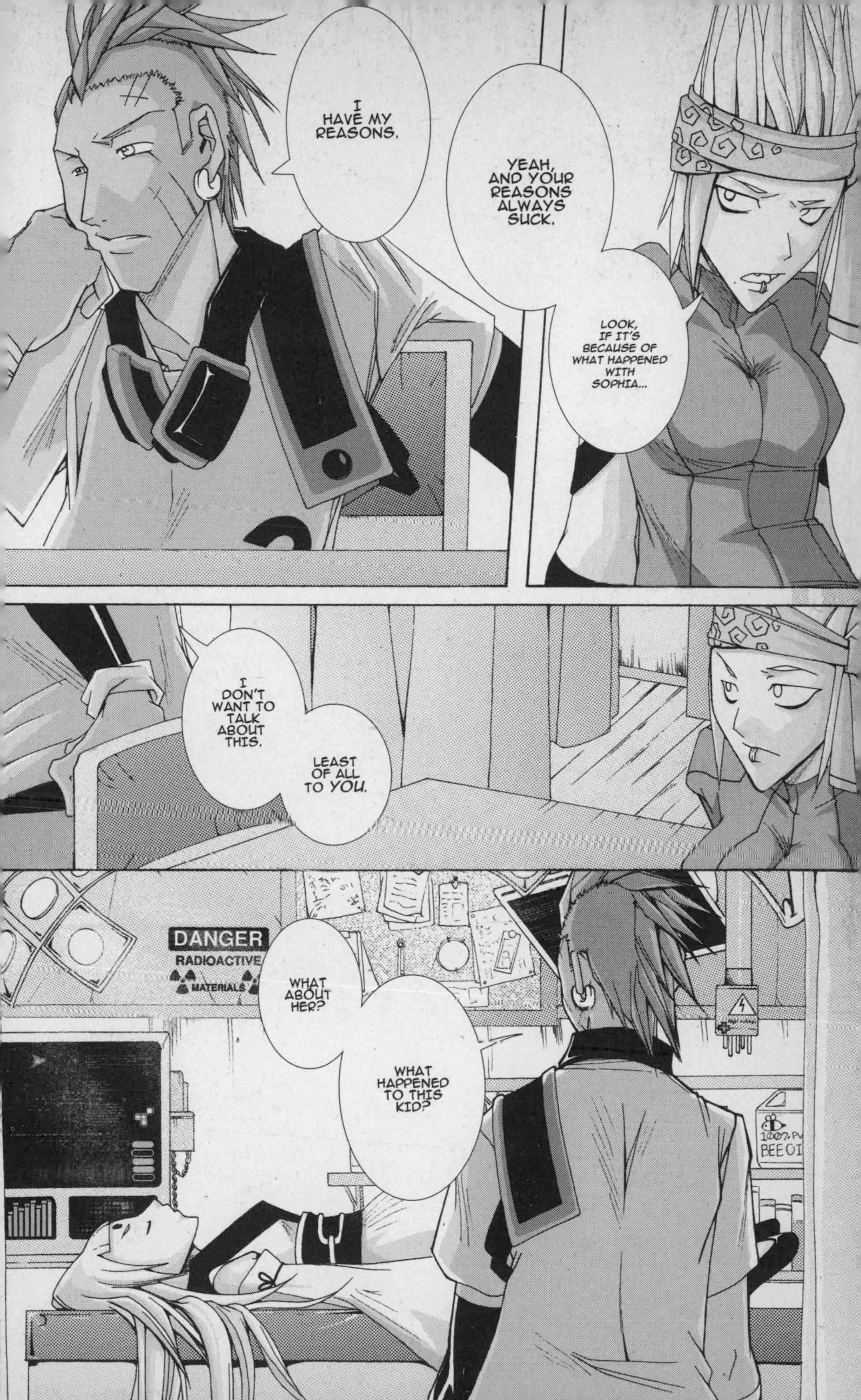
I HAVE MY REASONS.
YEAH, AND YOUR REASONS ALWAYS SUCK.
LOOK, IF IT'S BECAUSE OF WHAT HAPPENED WITH SOPHIA...
I DON'T WANT TO TALK ABOUT THIS.
LEAST OF ALL TO *YOU*.
DANGER
RADIOACTIVE MATERIALS
WHAT ABOUT HER?
WHAT HAPPENED TO THIS KID?

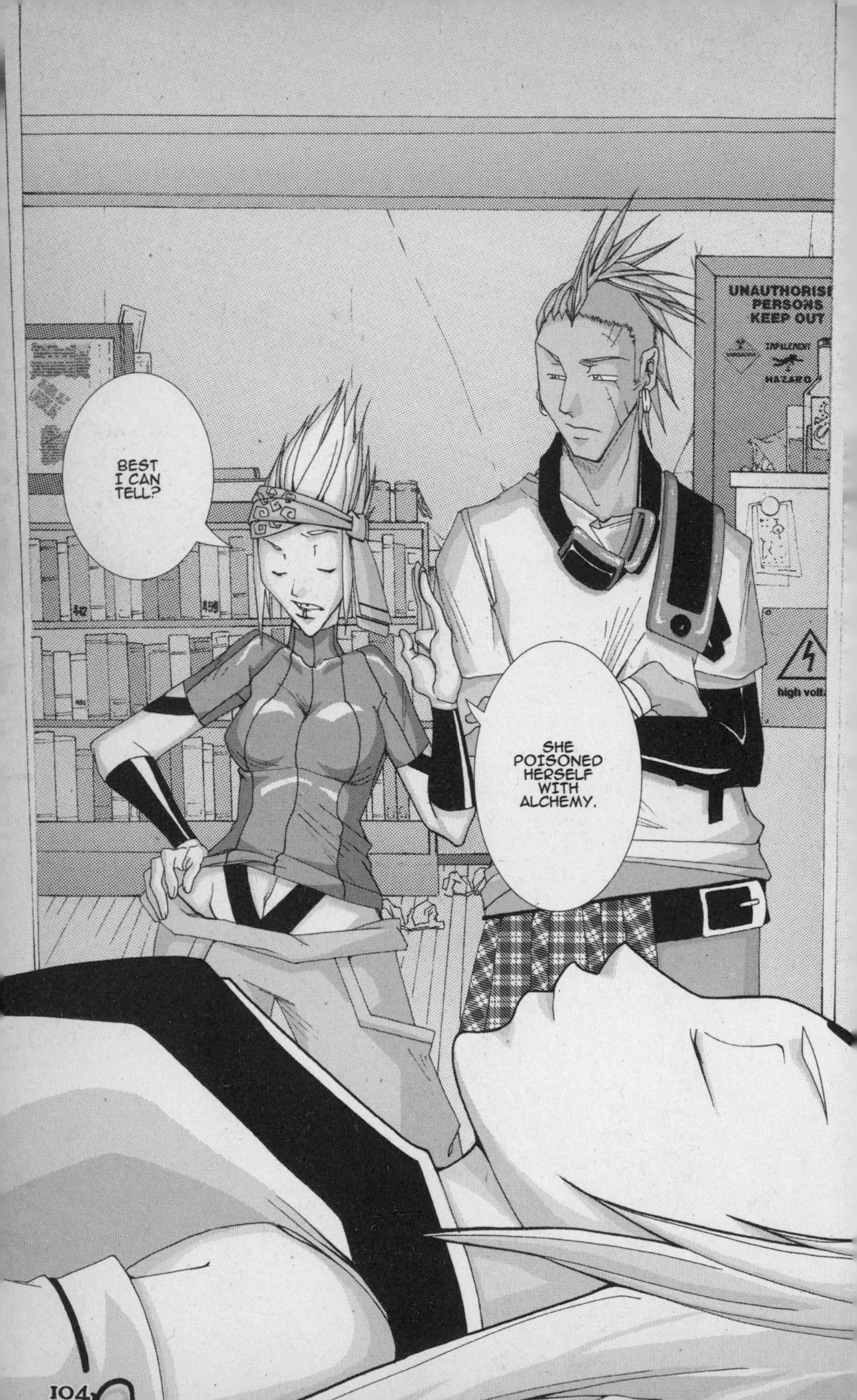
BEST I CAN TELL?
SHE POISONED HERSELF WITH ALCHEMY.
UNAUTHORISE
PERSONS
KEEP OUT
HAZARD
high volta

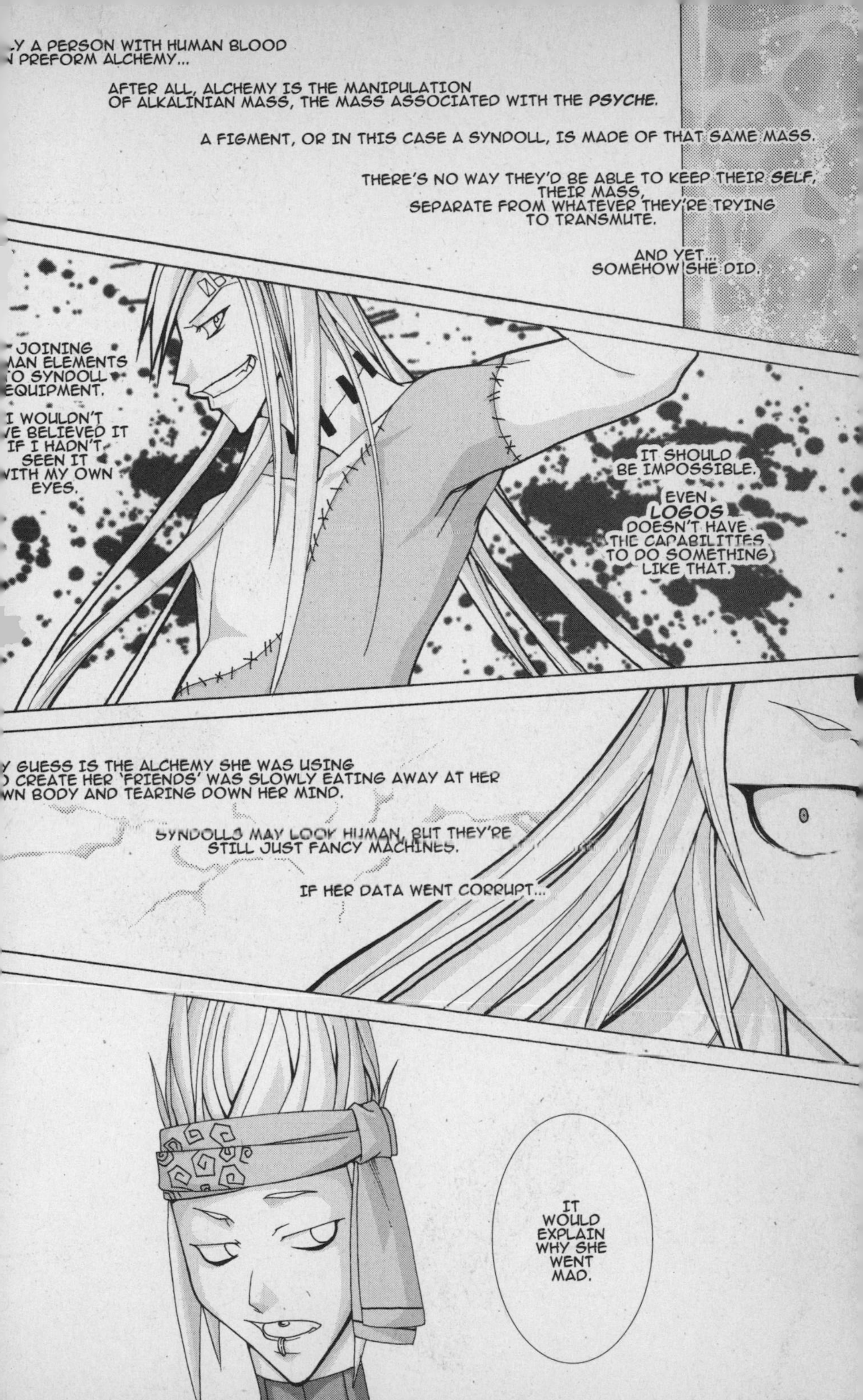

-Y A PERSON WITH HUMAN BLOOD
-N PREFORM ALCHEMY...
AFTER ALL, ALCHEMY IS THE MANIPULATION OF ALKALINIAN MASS, THE MASS ASSOCIATED WITH THE PSYCHE.
A FIGMENT, OR IN THIS CASE A SYNDOLL, IS MADE OF THAT SAME MASS.
THERE'S NO WAY THEY'D BE ABLE TO KEEP THEIR SELF, THEIR MASS, SEPARATE FROM WHATEVER THEY'RE TRYING TO TRANSMUTE.
AND YET... SOMEHOW SHE DID.
-Y JOINING -MAN ELEMENTS -TO SYNDOLL -EQUIPMENT.
I WOULDN'T -VE BELIEVED IT IF I HADN'T SEEN IT -WITH MY OWN EYES.
IT SHOULD BE IMPOSSIBLE.
EVEN LOGOS DOESN'T HAVE THE CAPABILITTES TO DO SOMETHING LIKE THAT.
-Y GUESS IS THE ALCHEMY SHE WAS USING -O CREATE HER 'FRIENDS' WAS SLOWLY EATING AWAY AT HER -WN BODY AND TEARING DOWN HER MIND.
SYNDOLLS MAY LOOK HUMAN, BUT THEY'RE STILL JUST FANCY MACHINES.
IF HER DATA WENT CORRUPT...
IT WOULD EXPLAIN WHY SHE WENT MAD.

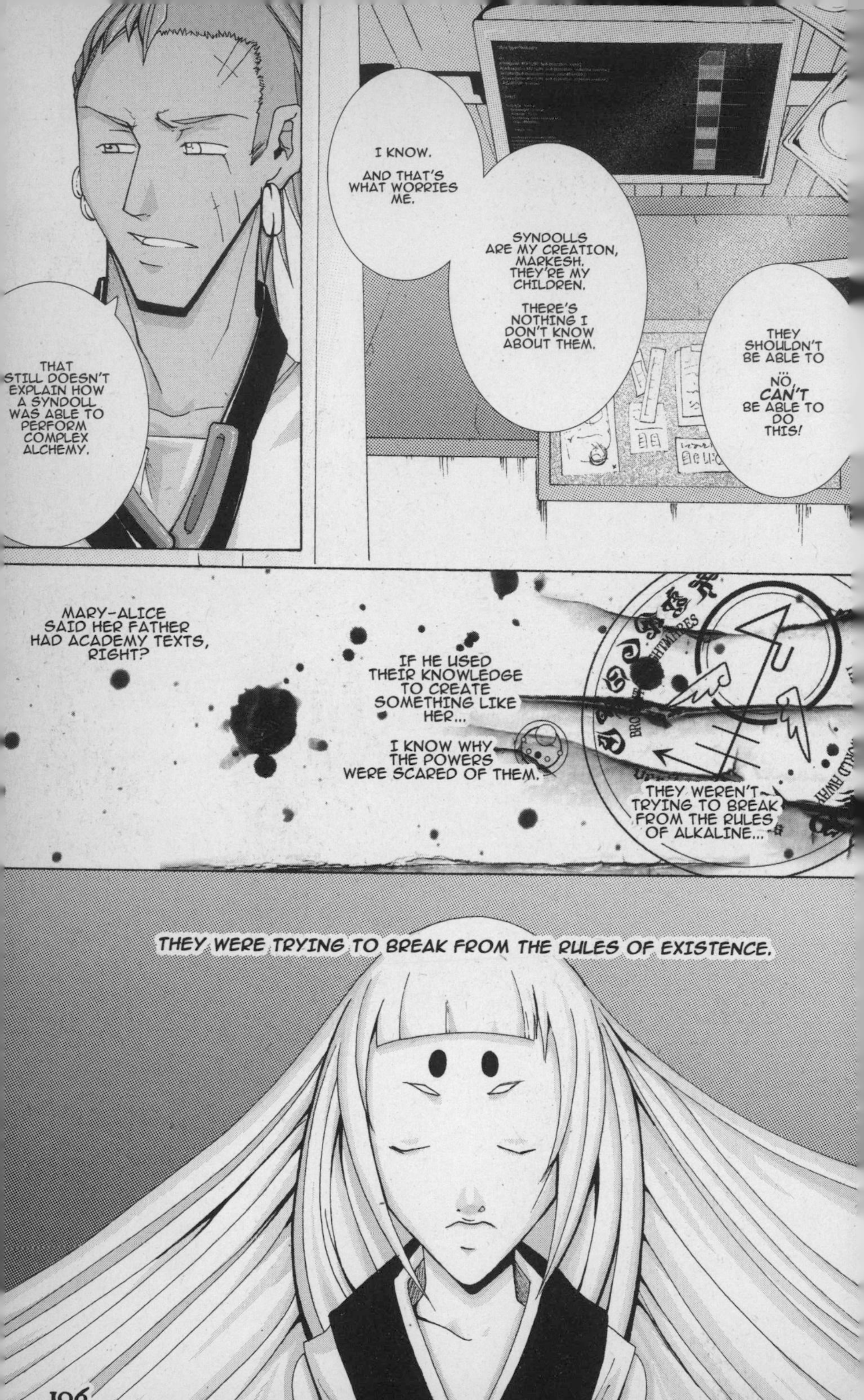
I KNOW.
AND THAT'S WHAT WORRIES ME.
THAT STILL DOESN'T EXPLAIN HOW A SYNDOLL WAS ABLE TO PERFORM COMPLEX ALCHEMY.
THEY SHOULDN'T BE ABLE TO ... NO, CAN'T BE ABLE TO DO THIS!
SYNDOLLS ARE MY CREATION, MARKESH. THEY'RE MY CHILDREN.
THERE'S NOTHING I DON'T KNOW ABOUT THEM.
MARY-ALICE SAID HER FATHER HAD ACADEMY TEXTS, RIGHT?
IF HE USED THEIR KNOWLEDGE TO CREATE SOMETHING LIKE HER...
I KNOW WHY THE POWERS WERE SCARED OF THEM.
THEY WEREN'T TRYING TO BREAK FROM THE RULES OF ALKALINE...
THEY WERE TRYING TO BREAK FROM THE RULES OF EXISTENCE.

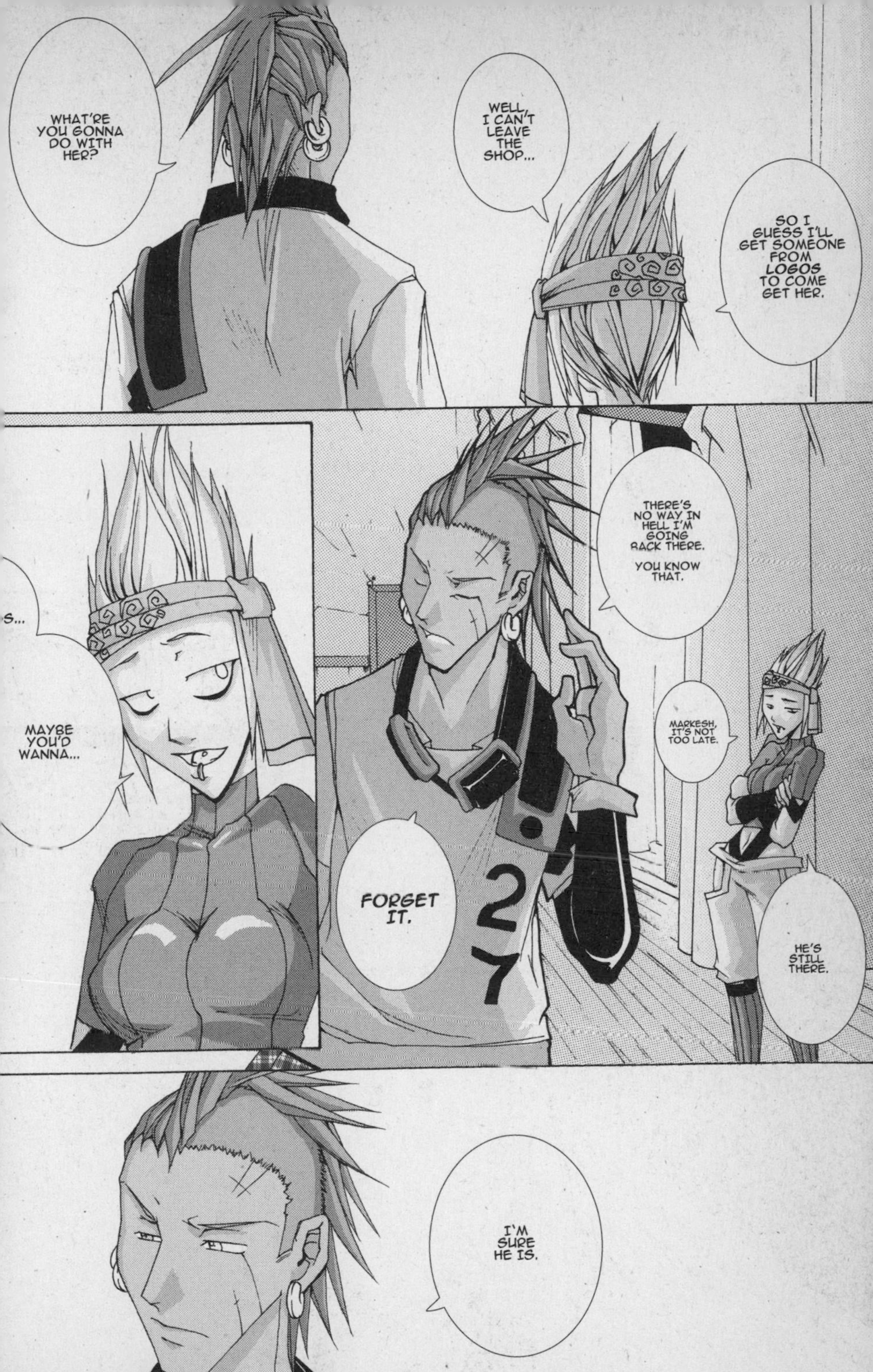
WHAT'RE YOU GONNA DO WITH HER?
WELL, I CAN'T LEAVE THE SHOP...
SO I GUESS I'LL GET SOMEONE FROM LOGOS TO COME GET HER.
THERE'S NO WAY IN HELL I'M GOING BACK THERE.
YOU KNOW THAT.
S...
MAYBE YOU'D WANNA...
FORGET IT.
MARKESH, IT'S NOT TOO LATE.
HE'S STILL THERE.
I'M SURE HE IS.

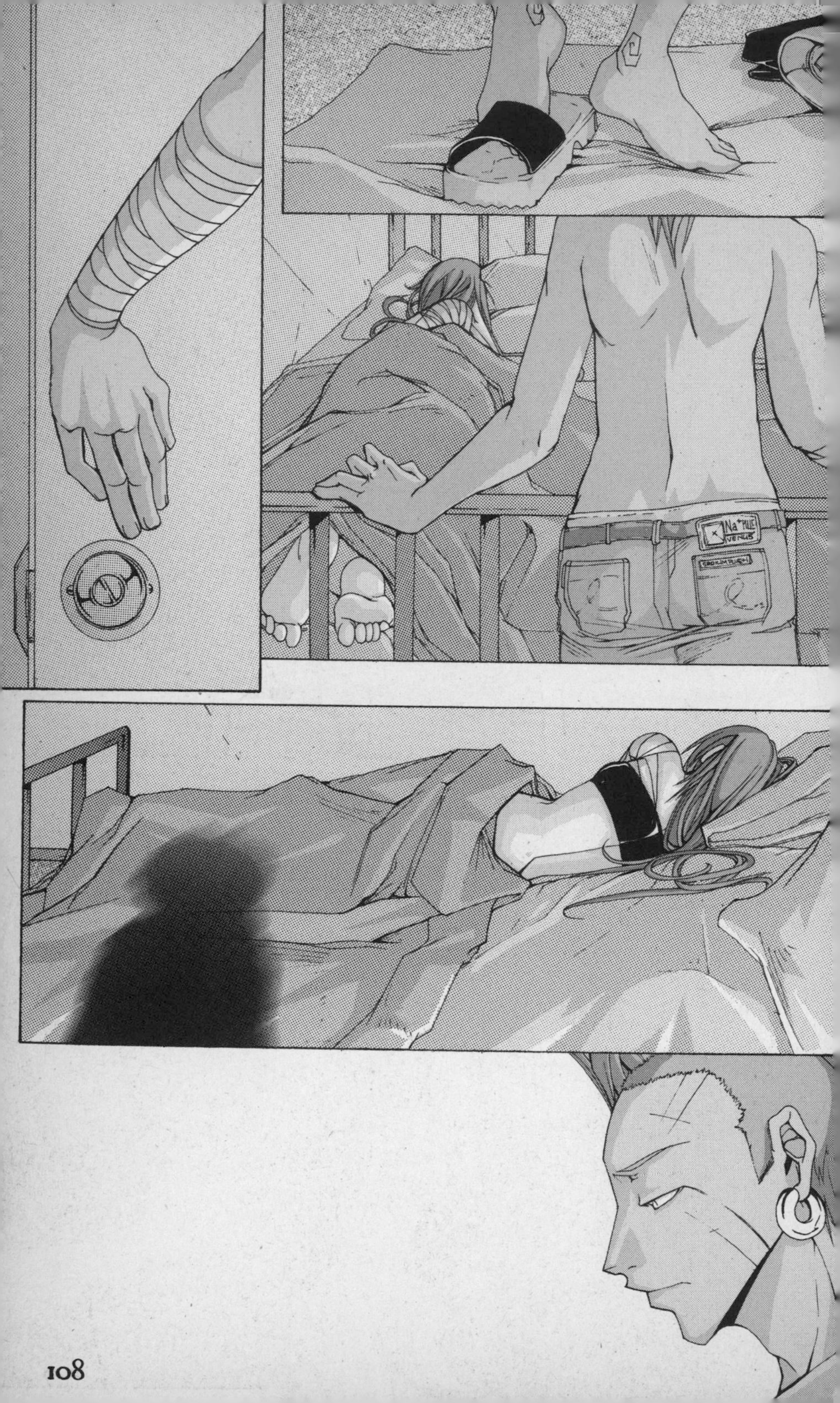

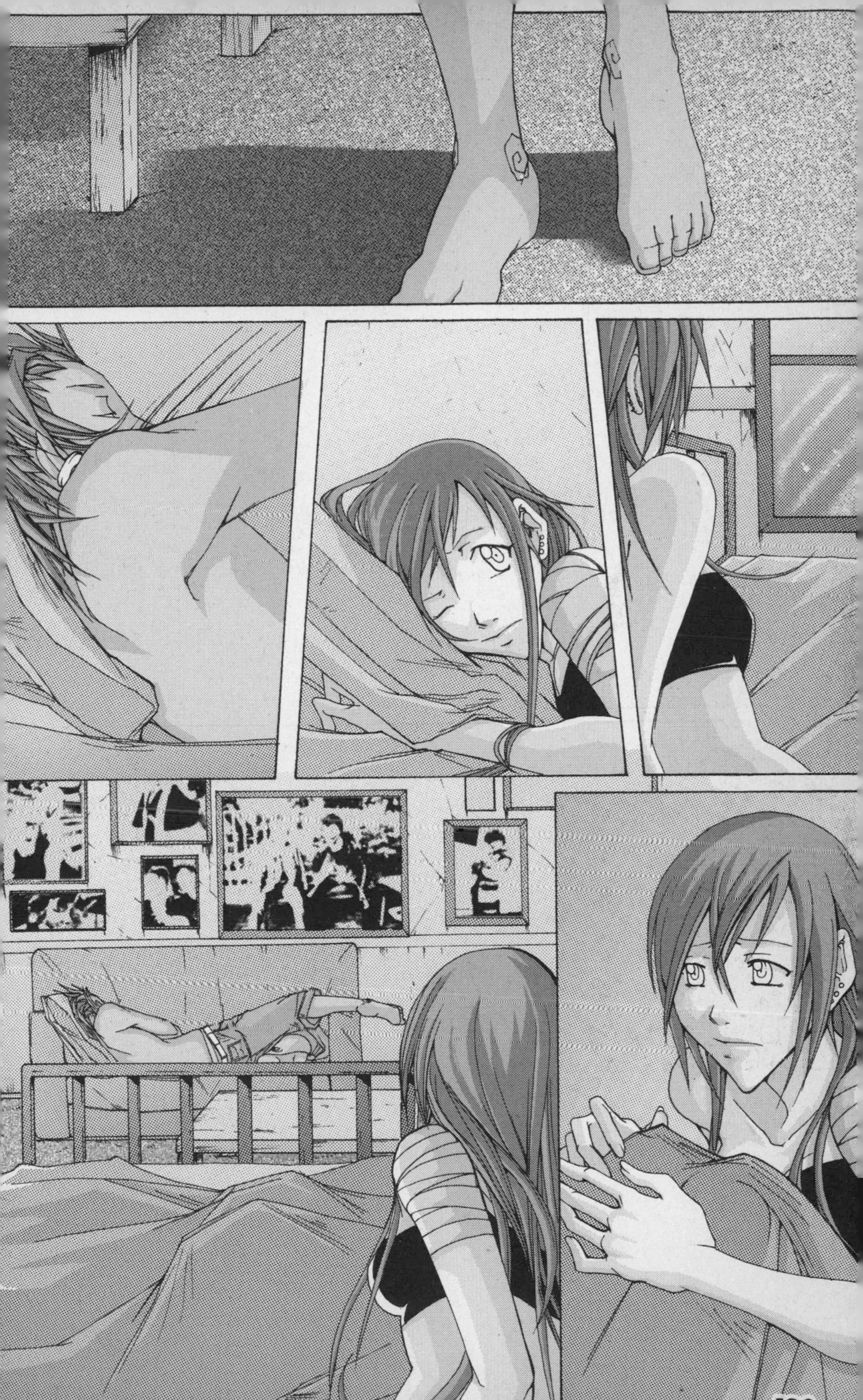

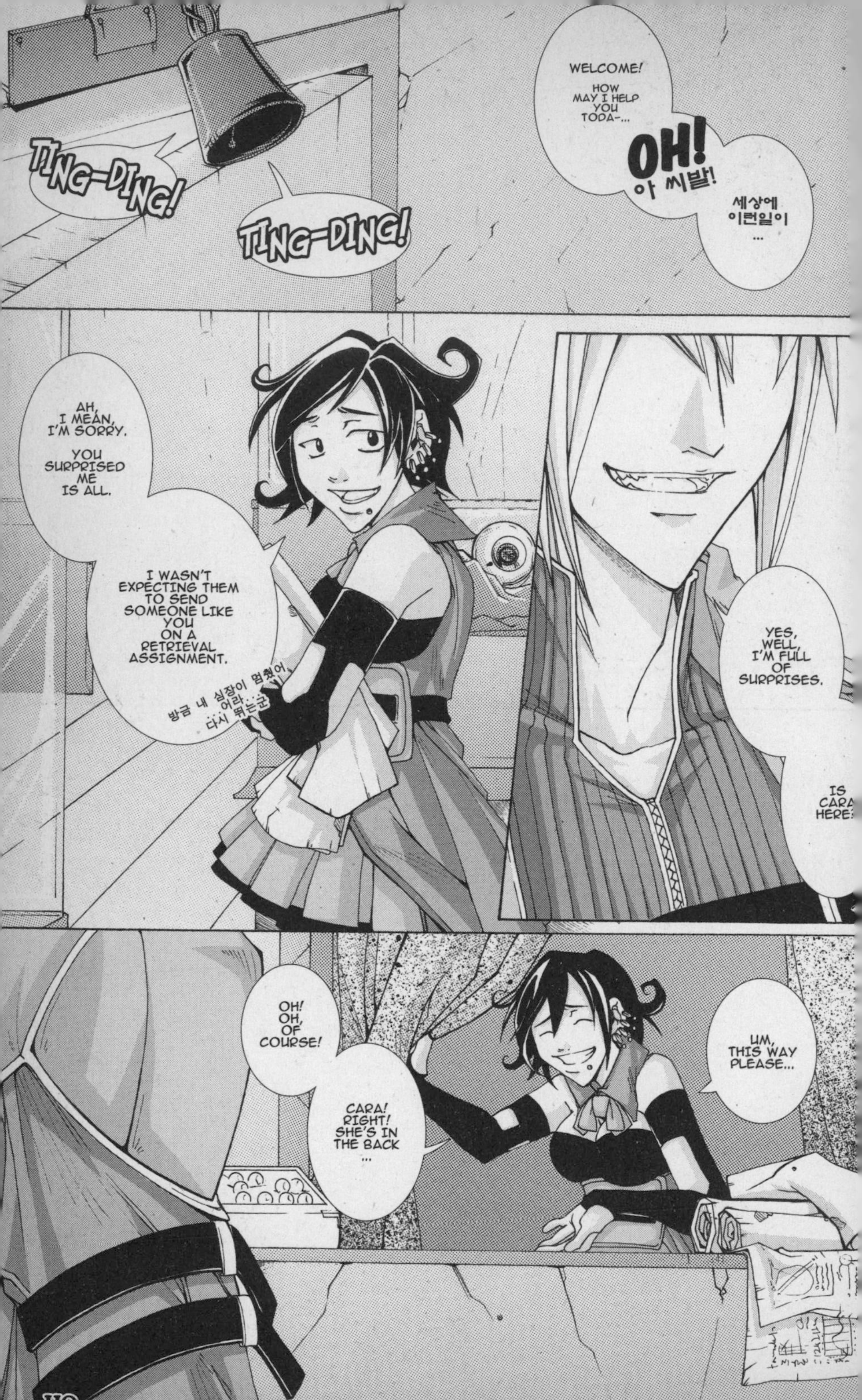
TING-DING!
TING-DING!
WELCOME! HOW MAY I HELP YOU TODA-...
OH! 아 씨발!
세상에 이런일이 ...
AH, I MEAN, I'M SORRY. YOU SURPRISED ME IS ALL.
I WASN'T EXPECTING THEM TO SEND SOMEONE LIKE YOU ON A RETRIEVAL ASSIGNMENT.
방금 내 심장이 멈췄어 어라... 다시 뛰는군
YES, WELL, I'M FULL OF SURPRISES.
IS CARA HERE?
OH! OH, OF COURSE!
CARA! RIGHT! SHE'S IN THE BACK ...
UM, THIS WAY PLEASE...

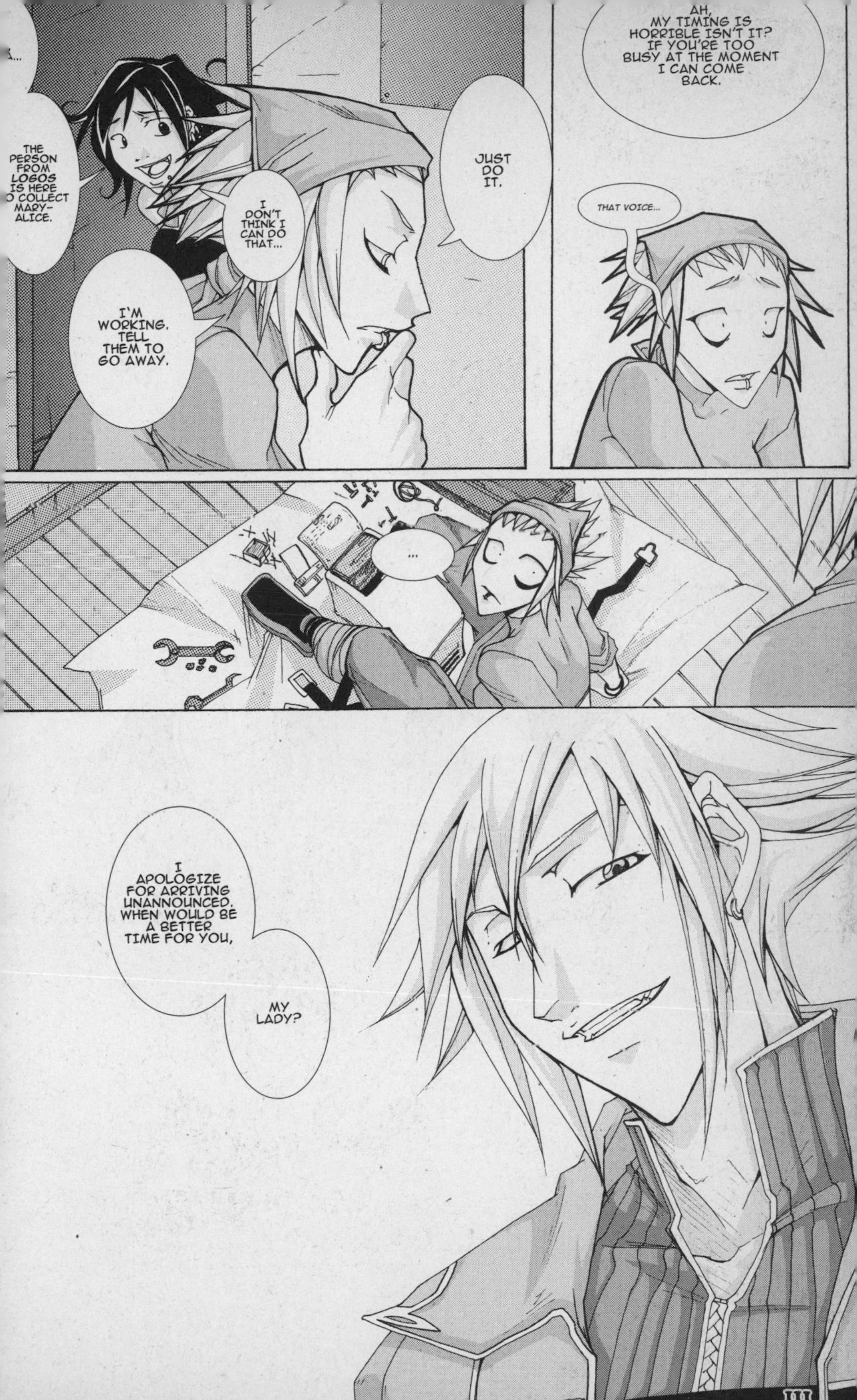
THE PERSON FROM LOGOS IS HERE O COLLECT MARY-ALICE.
I'M WORKING. TELL THEM TO GO AWAY.
I DON'T THINK I CAN DO THAT...
JUST DO IT.
AH, MY TIMING IS HORRIBLE ISN'T IT? IF YOU'RE TOO BUSY AT THE MOMENT I CAN COME BACK.
THAT VOICE...
...
I APOLOGIZE FOR ARRIVING UNANNOUNCED. WHEN WOULD BE A BETTER TIME FOR YOU,
MY LADY?

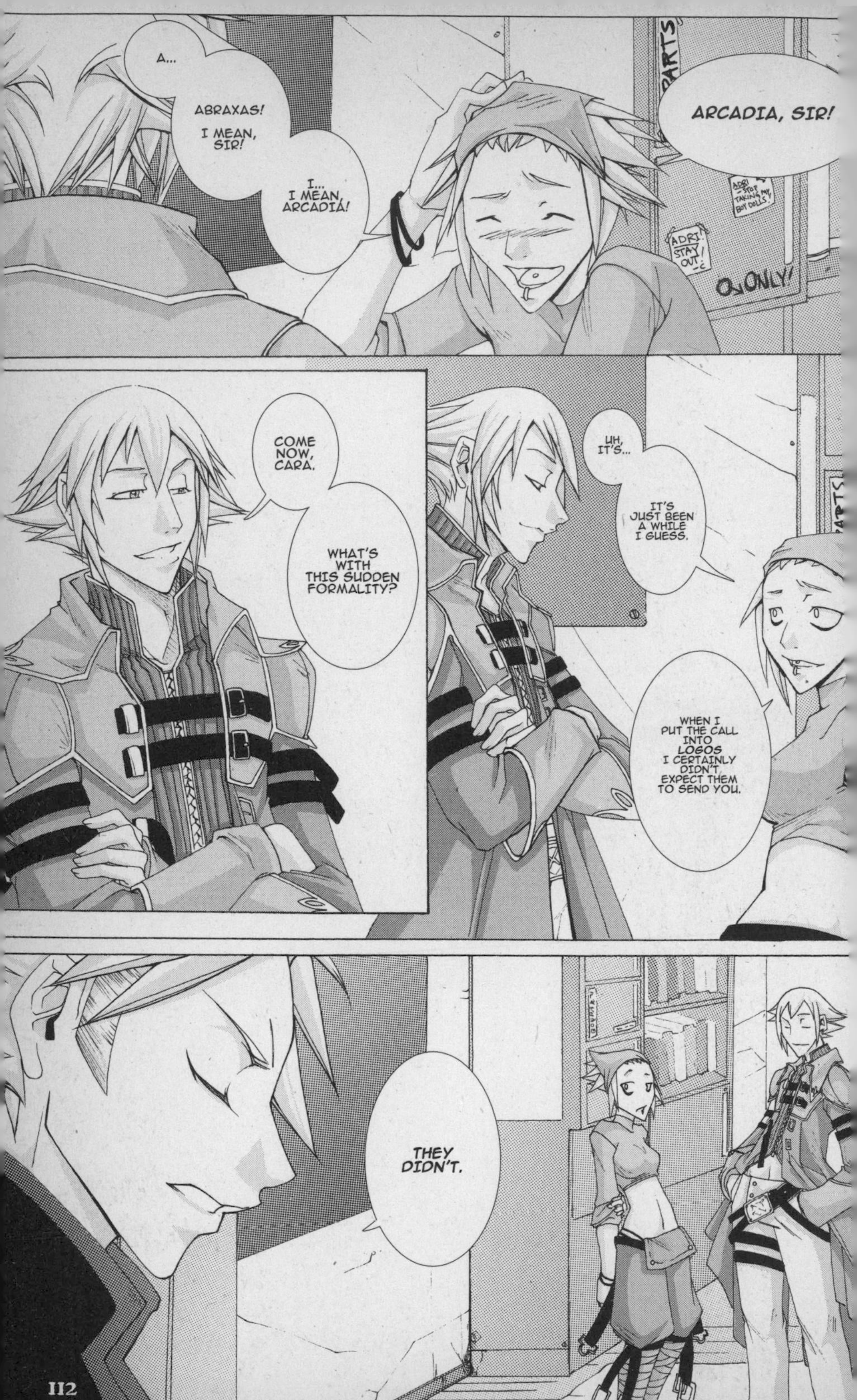
A...
ABRAXAS!
I MEAN, SIR!
I... I MEAN, ARCADIA!
ARCADIA, SIR!
ADRI - STOP TAKING MY BOY DOLLS
ADRI STAY OUT! -C
ONLY!
COME NOW, CARA.
WHAT'S WITH THIS SUDDEN FORMALITY?
UH, IT'S...
IT'S JUST BEEN A WHILE I GUESS.
WHEN I PUT THE CALL INTO LOGOS I CERTAINLY DIDN'T EXPECT THEM TO SEND YOU.
THEY DIDN'T.

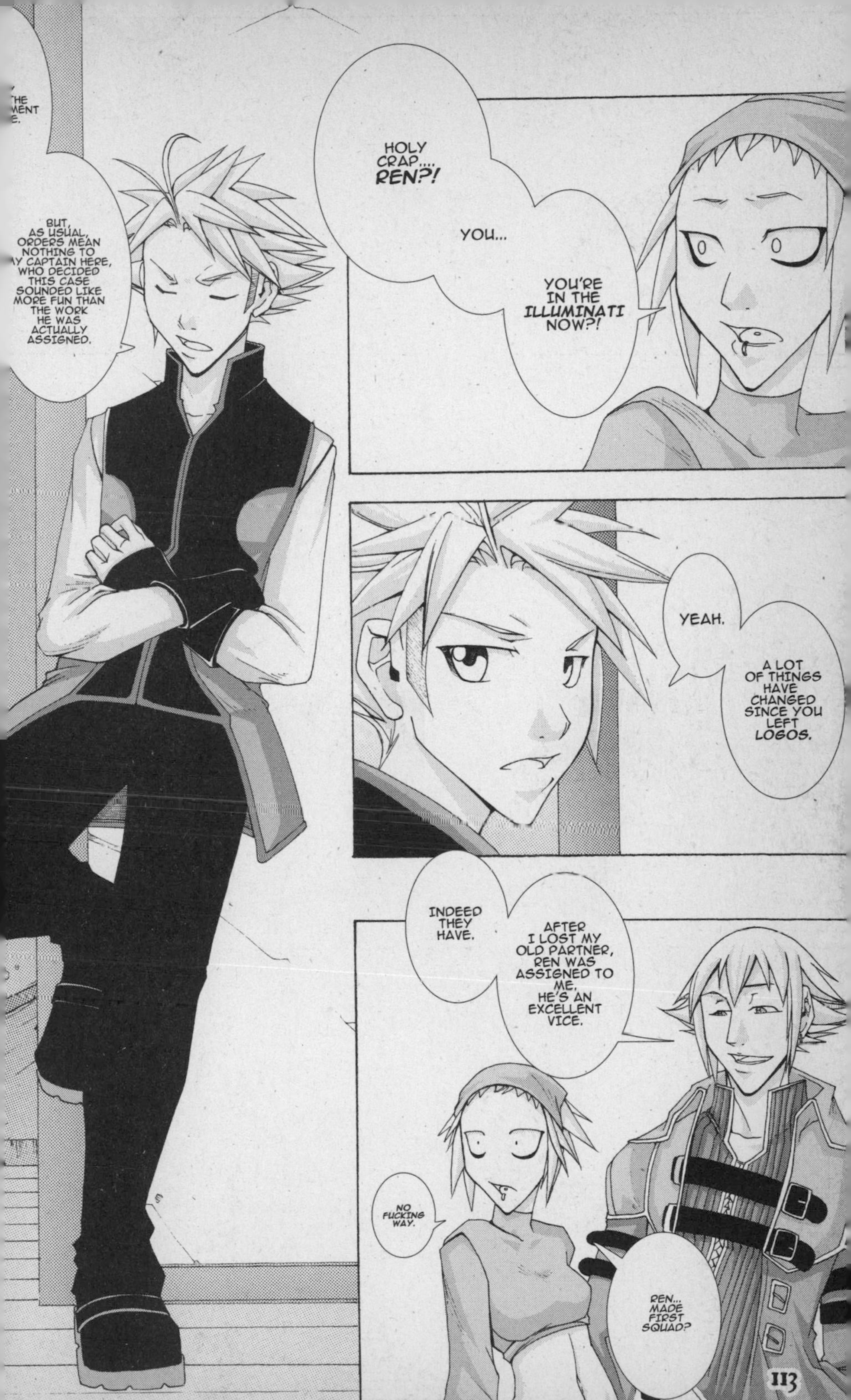
BUT, AS USUAL, ORDERS MEAN NOTHING TO MY CAPTAIN HERE, WHO DECIDED THIS CASE SOUNDED LIKE MORE FUN THAN THE WORK HE WAS ACTUALLY ASSIGNED.
HOLY CRAP.... REN?!
YOU...
YOU'RE IN THE ILLUMINATI NOW?!
YEAH.
A LOT OF THINGS HAVE CHANGED SINCE YOU LEFT LOGOS.
INDEED THEY HAVE.
AFTER I LOST MY OLD PARTNER, REN WAS ASSIGNED TO ME. HE'S AN EXCELLENT VICE.
NO FUCKING WAY.
REN... MADE FIRST SQUAD?

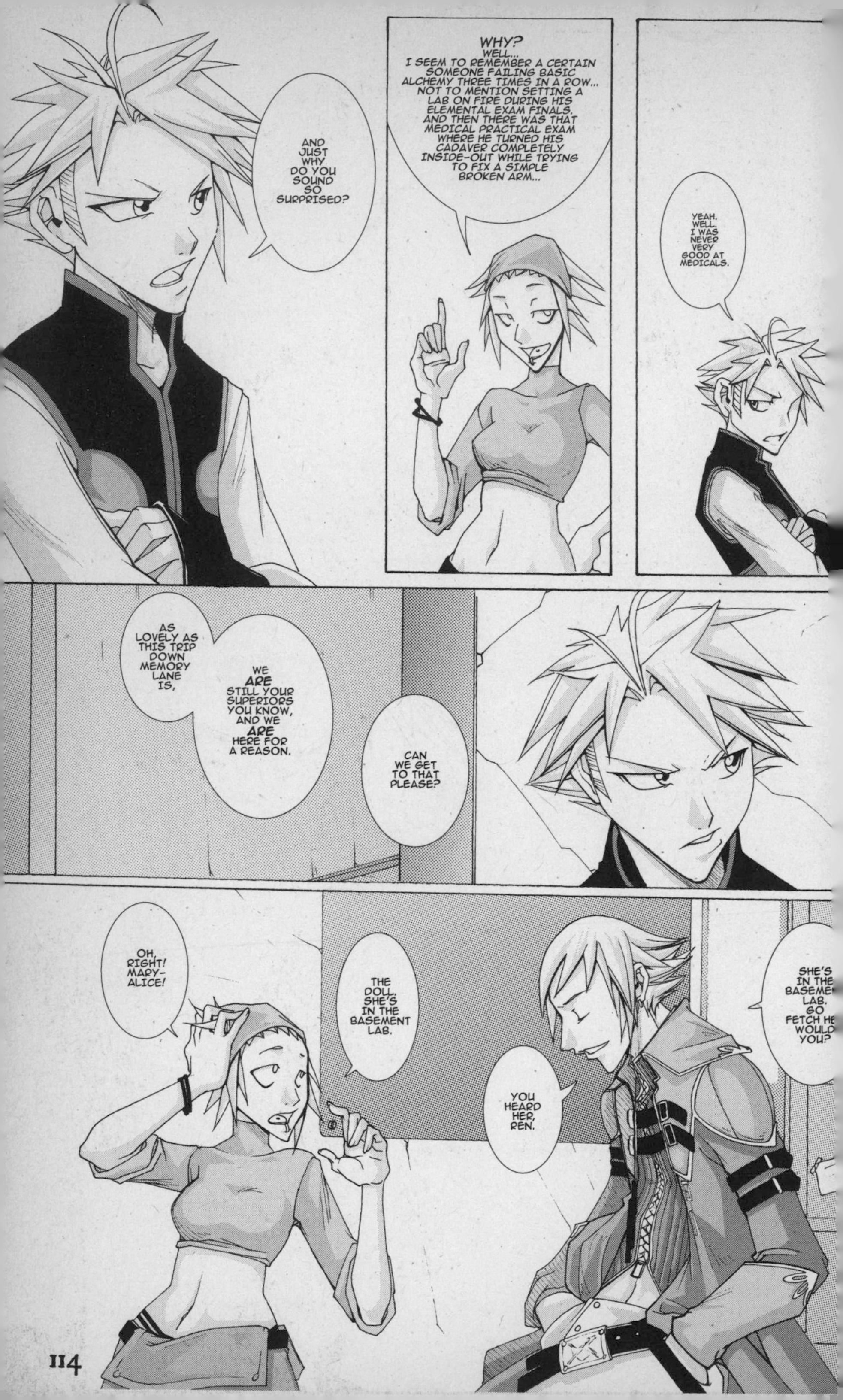
AND JUST WHY DO YOU SOUND SO SURPRISED?
WHY? WELL... I SEEM TO REMEMBER A CERTAIN SOMEONE FAILING BASIC ALCHEMY THREE TIMES IN A ROW... NOT TO MENTION SETTING A LAB ON FIRE DURING HIS ELEMENTAL EXAM FINALS. AND THEN THERE WAS THAT MEDICAL PRACTICAL EXAM WHERE HE TURNED HIS CADAVER COMPLETELY INSIDE-OUT WHILE TRYING TO FIX A SIMPLE BROKEN ARM...
YEAH. WELL. I WAS NEVER VERY GOOD AT MEDICALS.
AS LOVELY AS THIS TRIP DOWN MEMORY LANE IS,
WE **ARE** STILL YOUR SUPERIORS YOU KNOW, AND WE **ARE** HERE FOR A REASON.
CAN WE GET TO THAT PLEASE?
OH, RIGHT! MARY-ALICE!
THE DOLL, SHE'S IN THE BASEMENT LAB.
SHE'S IN THE BASEME LAB. GO FETCH HE WOULD YOU?
YOU HEARD HER, REN.

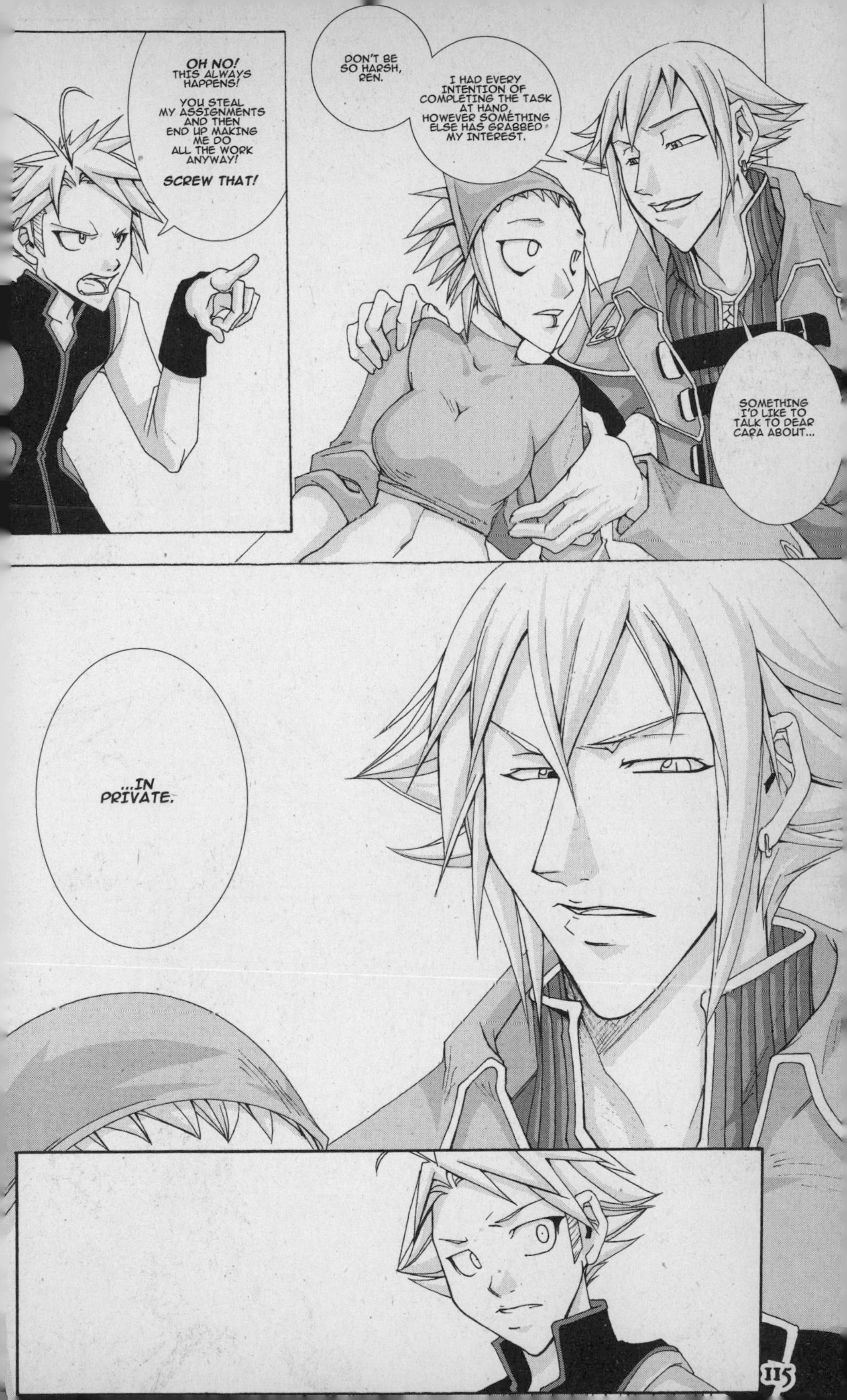
OH NO! THIS ALWAYS HAPPENS!
YOU STEAL MY ASSIGNMENTS AND THEN END UP MAKING ME DO ALL THE WORK ANYWAY!
SCREW THAT!
DON'T BE SO HARSH, REN.
I HAD EVERY INTENTION OF COMPLETING THE TASK AT HAND, HOWEVER SOMETHING ELSE HAS GRABBED MY INTEREST.
SOMETHING I'D LIKE TO TALK TO DEAR CARA ABOUT...
...IN PRIVATE.

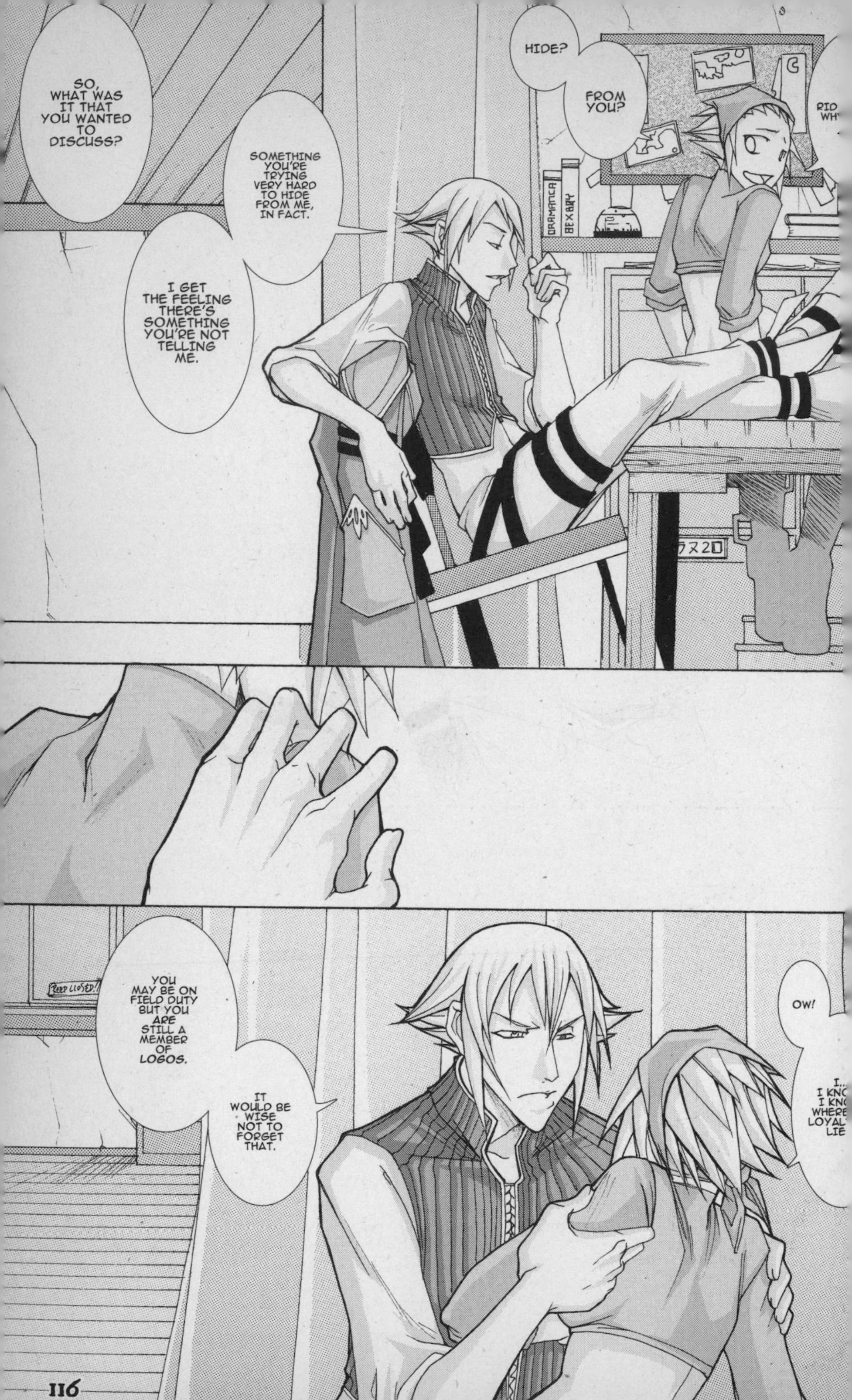
SO, WHAT WAS IT THAT YOU WANTED TO DISCUSS?
SOMETHING YOU'RE TRYING VERY HARD TO HIDE FROM ME, IN FACT.
I GET THE FEELING THERE'S SOMETHING YOU'RE NOT TELLING ME.
HIDE?
FROM YOU?
RID
WHY
YOU MAY BE ON FIELD DUTY BUT YOU ARE STILL A MEMBER OF LOGOS.
IT WOULD BE WISE NOT TO FORGET THAT.
OW!
I... I KNO I KNO WHERE LOYAL LIE

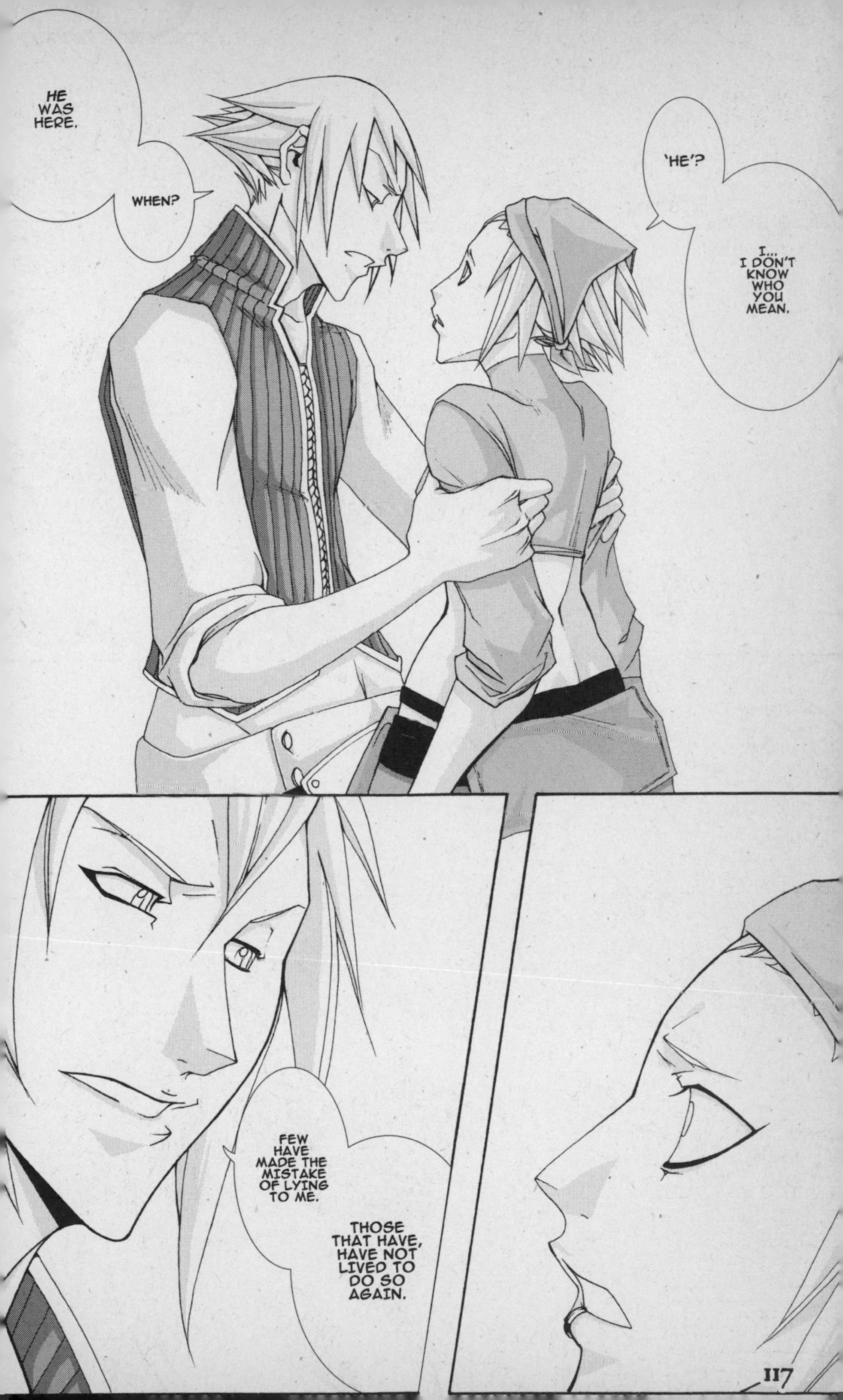
HE WAS HERE.
WHEN?
'HE'?
I... I DON'T KNOW WHO YOU MEAN.
FEW HAVE MADE THE MISTAKE OF LYING TO ME.
THOSE THAT HAVE, HAVE NOT LIVED TO DO SO AGAIN.

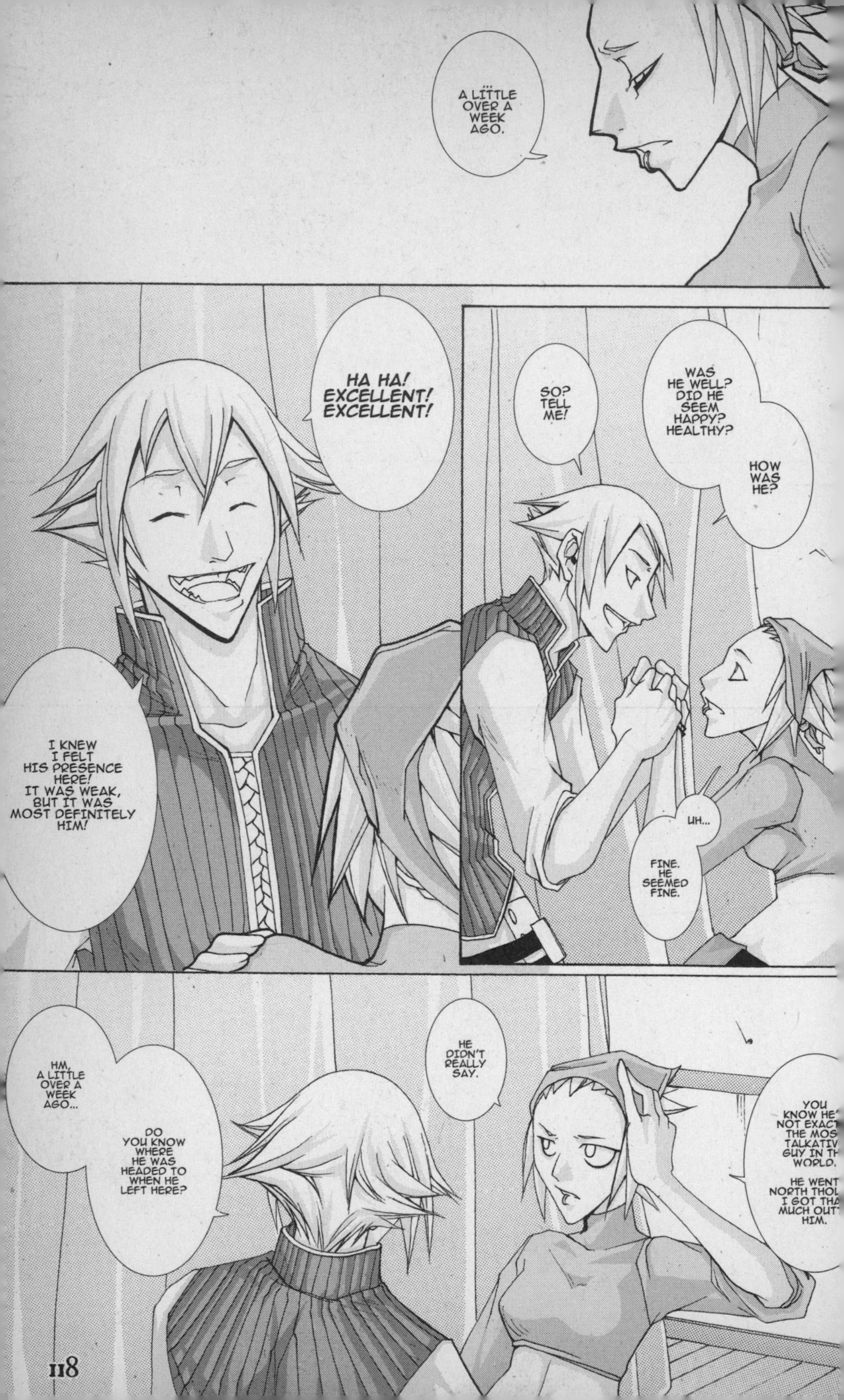

... A LITTLE OVER A WEEK AGO.
HA HA! EXCELLENT! EXCELLENT!
I KNEW I FELT HIS PRESENCE HERE! IT WAS WEAK, BUT IT WAS MOST DEFINITELY HIM!
SO? TELL ME!
WAS HE WELL? DID HE SEEM HAPPY? HEALTHY?
HOW WAS HE?
UH...
FINE. HE SEEMED FINE.
HM, A LITTLE OVER A WEEK AGO...
DO YOU KNOW WHERE HE WAS HEADED TO WHEN HE LEFT HERE?
HE DIDN'T REALLY SAY.
YOU KNOW HE' NOT EXAC THE MOS TALKATIV GUY IN TH WORLD.
HE WENT NORTH THOU I GOT THA MUCH OUT HIM.

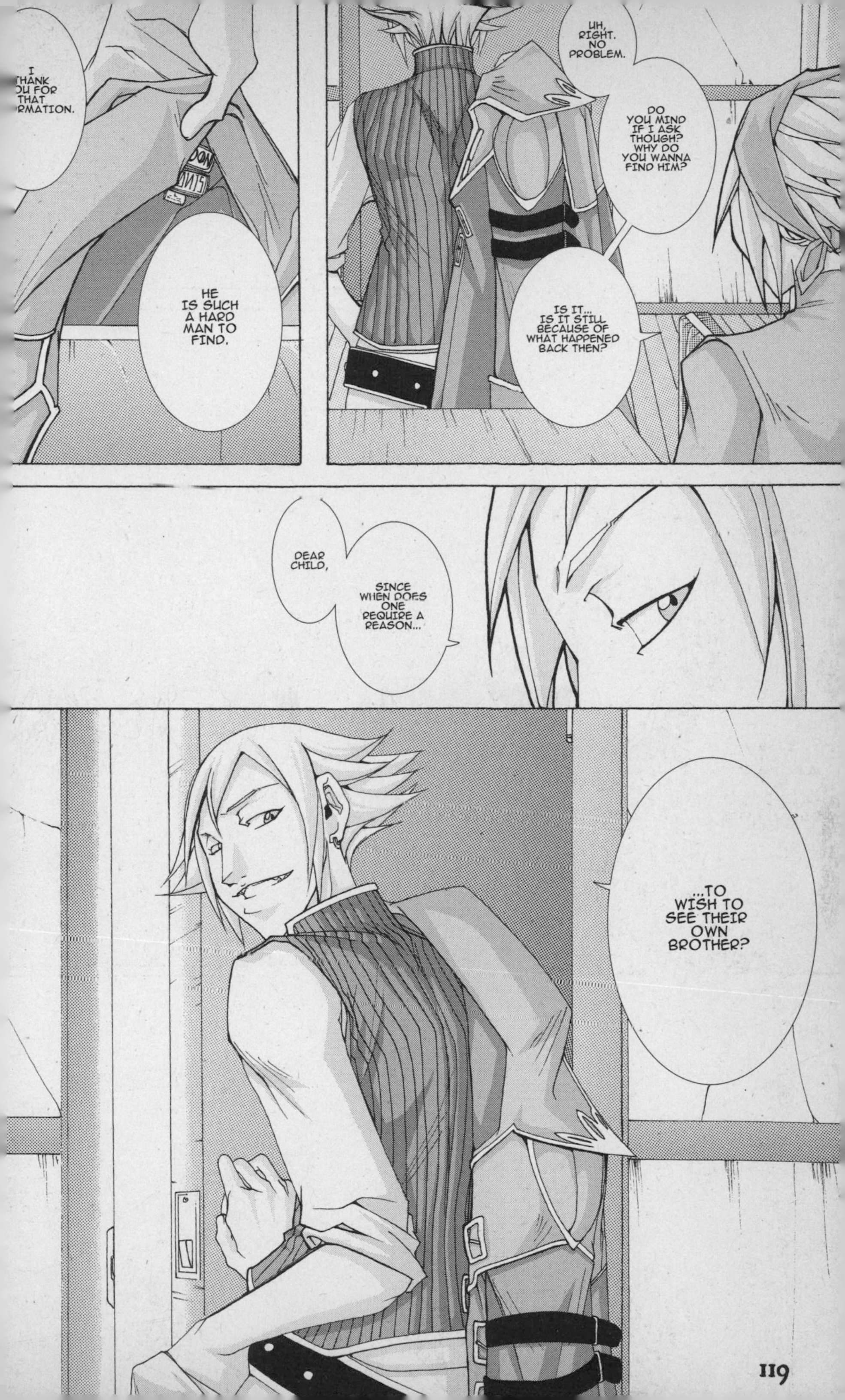
I THANK OU FOR THAT RMATION.
HE IS SUCH A HARD MAN TO FIND.
UH, RIGHT. NO PROBLEM.
DO YOU MIND IF I ASK THOUGH? WHY DO YOU WANNA FIND HIM?
IS IT... IS IT STILL BECAUSE OF WHAT HAPPENED BACK THEN?
DEAR CHILD,
SINCE WHEN DOES ONE REQUIRE A REASON...
...TO WISH TO SEE THEIR OWN BROTHER?

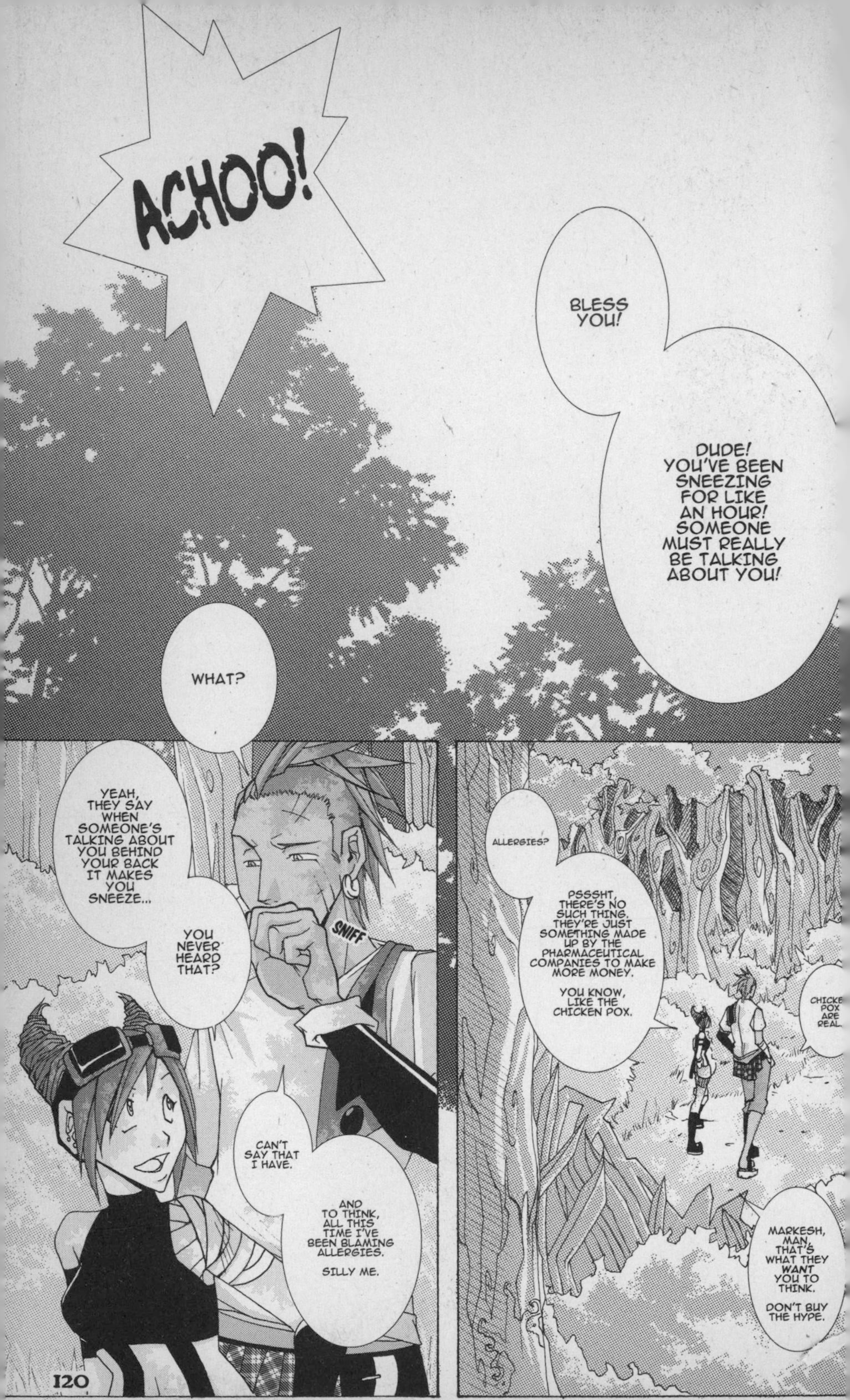

ACHOO!
BLESS YOU!
DUDE! YOU'VE BEEN SNEEZING FOR LIKE AN HOUR! SOMEONE MUST REALLY BE TALKING ABOUT YOU!
WHAT?
YEAH, THEY SAY WHEN SOMEONE'S TALKING ABOUT YOU BEHIND YOUR BACK IT MAKES YOU SNEEZE...
YOU NEVER HEARD THAT?
SNIFF
CAN'T SAY THAT I HAVE.
AND TO THINK, ALL THIS TIME I'VE BEEN BLAMING ALLERGIES.
SILLY ME.
ALLERGIES?
PSSSHT, THERE'S NO SUCH THING. THEY'RE JUST SOMETHING MADE UP BY THE PHARMACEUTICAL COMPANIES TO MAKE MORE MONEY.
YOU KNOW, LIKE THE CHICKEN POX.
MARKESH, MAN, THAT'S WHAT THEY WANT YOU TO THINK.
DON'T BUY THE HYPE.

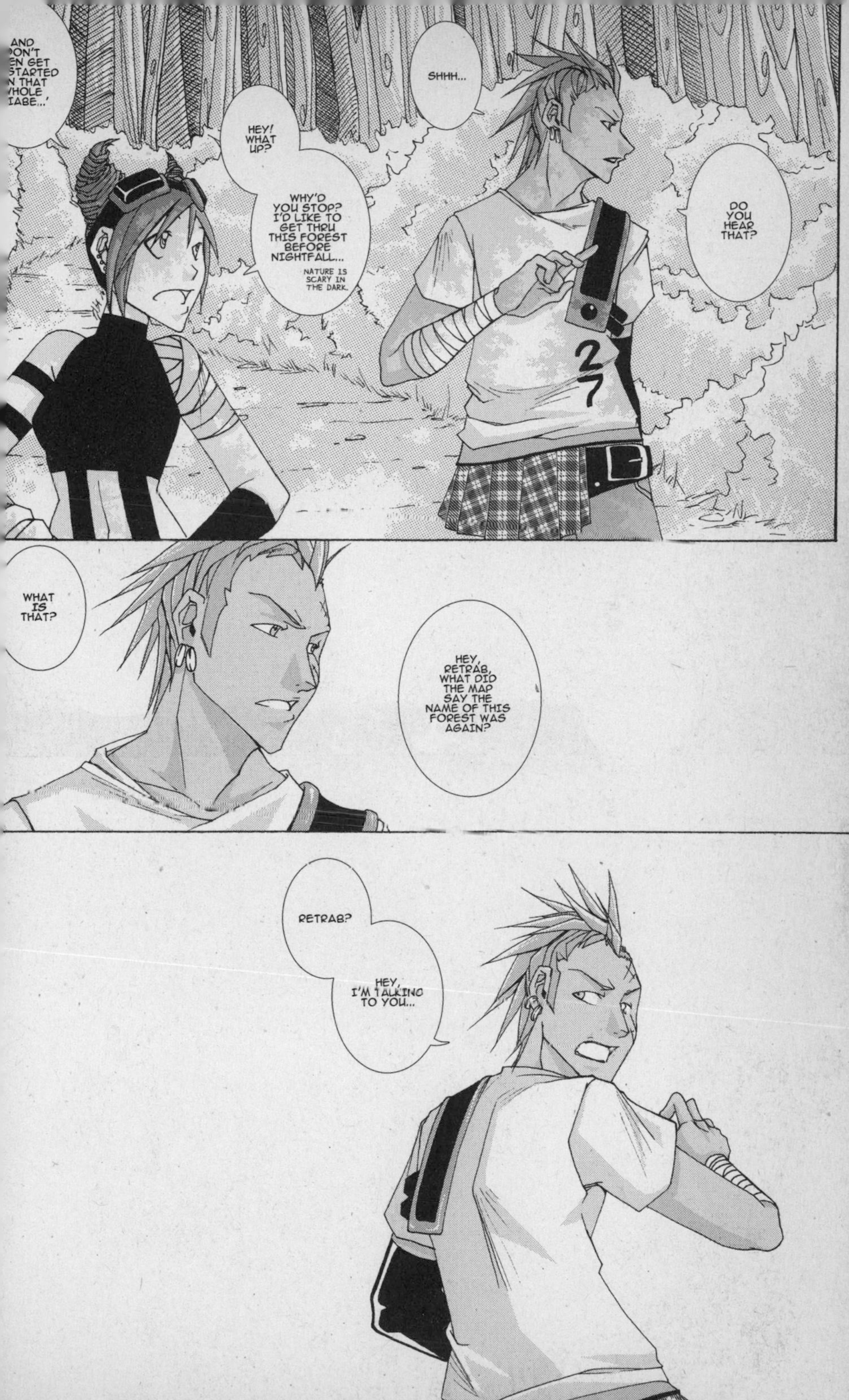
AND ON'T EN GET STARTED N THAT WHOLE IABE...'
HEY! WHAT UP?
WHY'D YOU STOP? I'D LIKE TO GET THRU THIS FOREST BEFORE NIGHTFALL...
NATURE IS SCARY IN THE DARK.
SHHH...
DO YOU HEAR THAT?
WHAT IS THAT?
HEY, RETRAB, WHAT DID THE MAP SAY THE NAME OF THIS FOREST WAS AGAIN?
RETRAB?
HEY, I'M TALKING TO YOU...

WELL.

I DIDN'T
SEE
THAT
COMING.

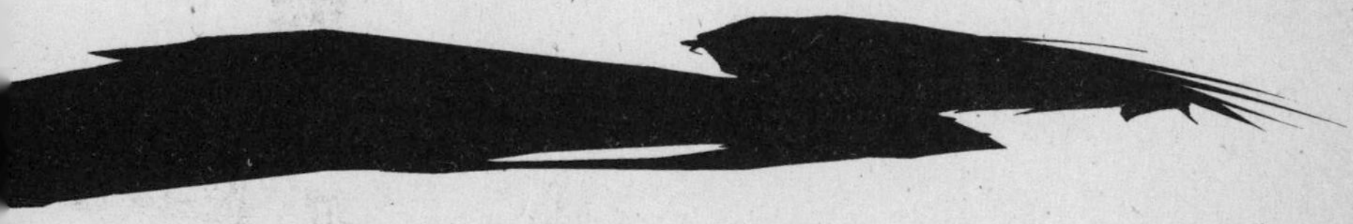

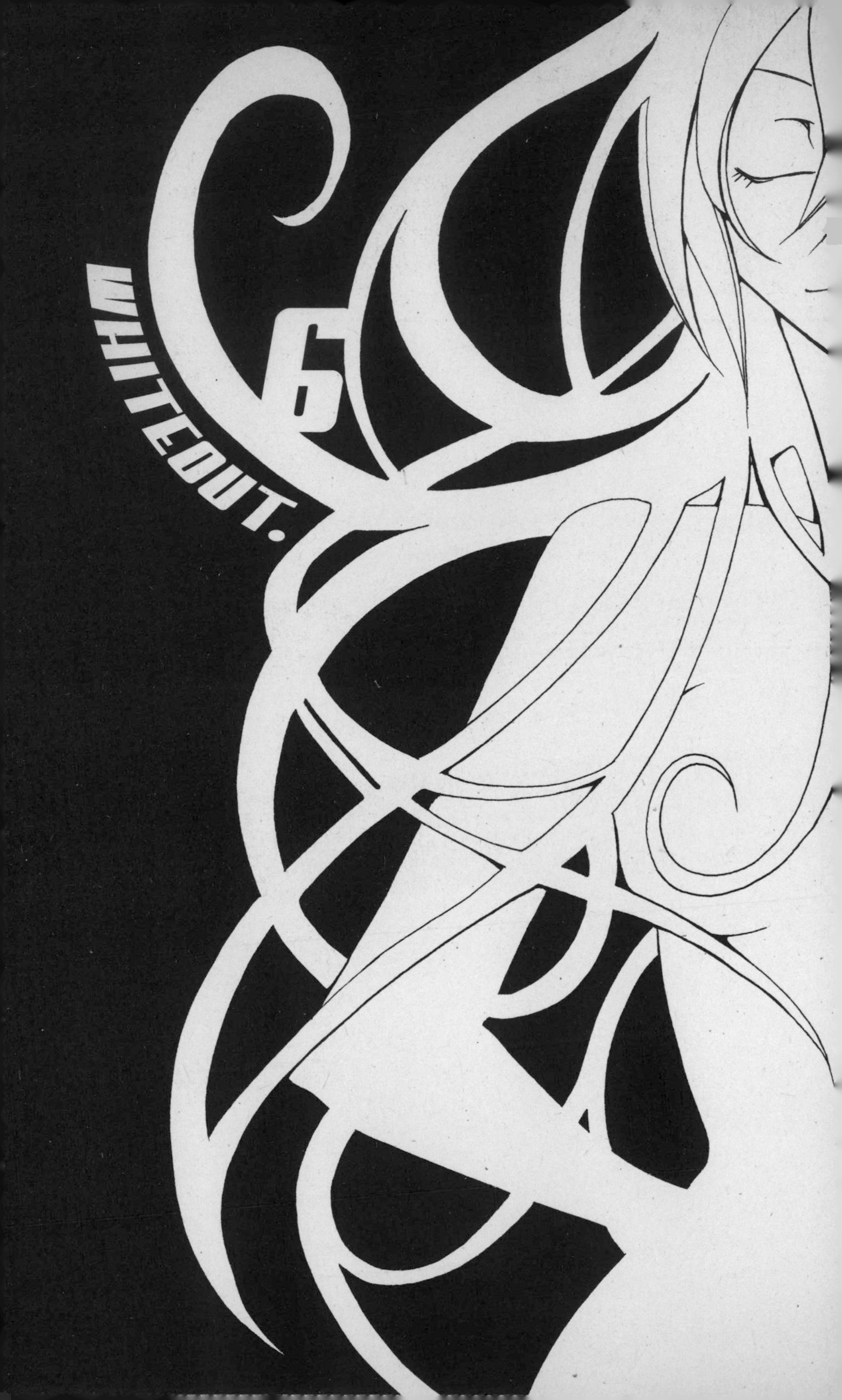
6
WHITEOUT.

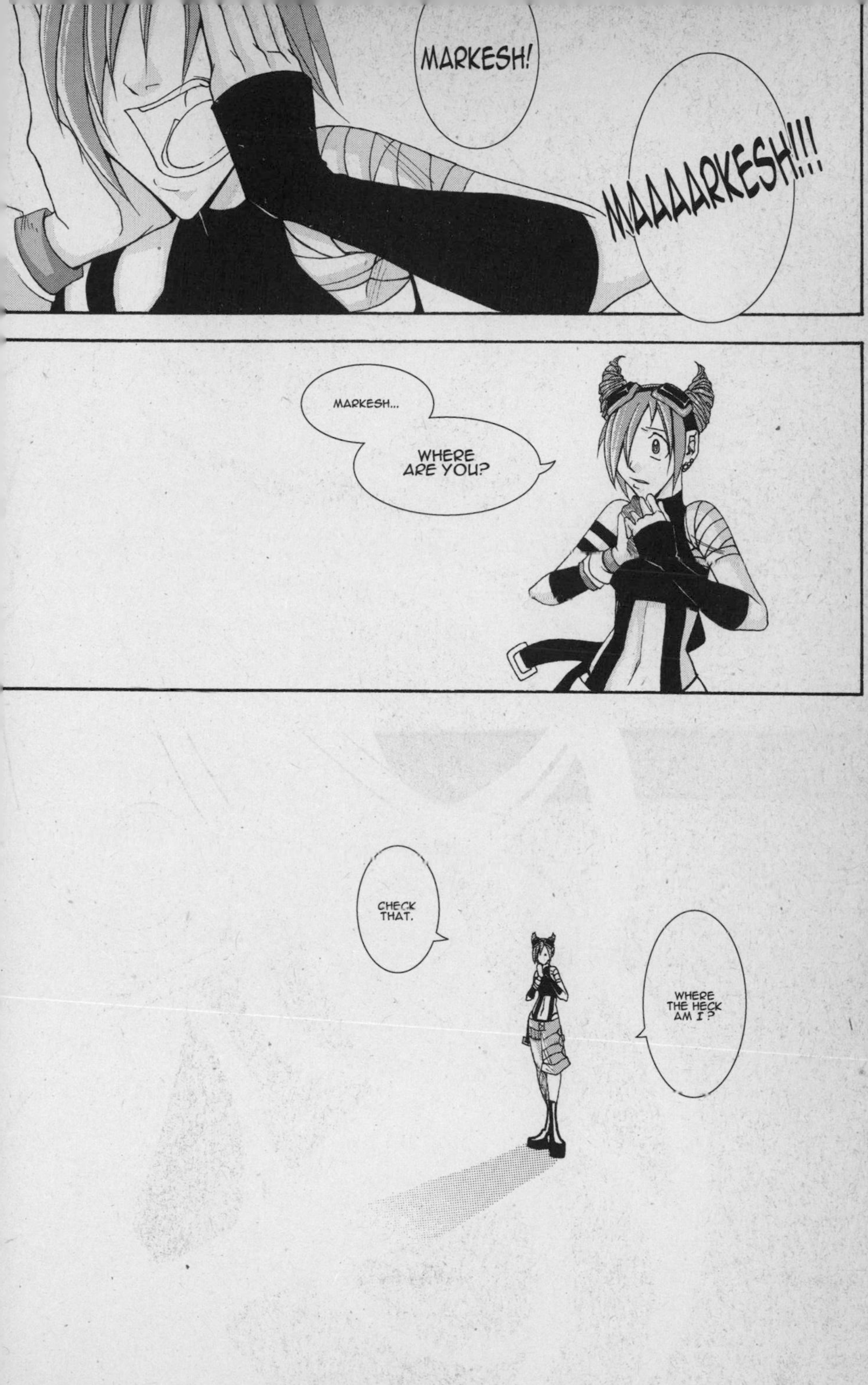
MARKESH!
MAAAARKESH!!!
MARKESH...
WHERE ARE YOU?
CHECK THAT.
WHERE THE HECK AM I?

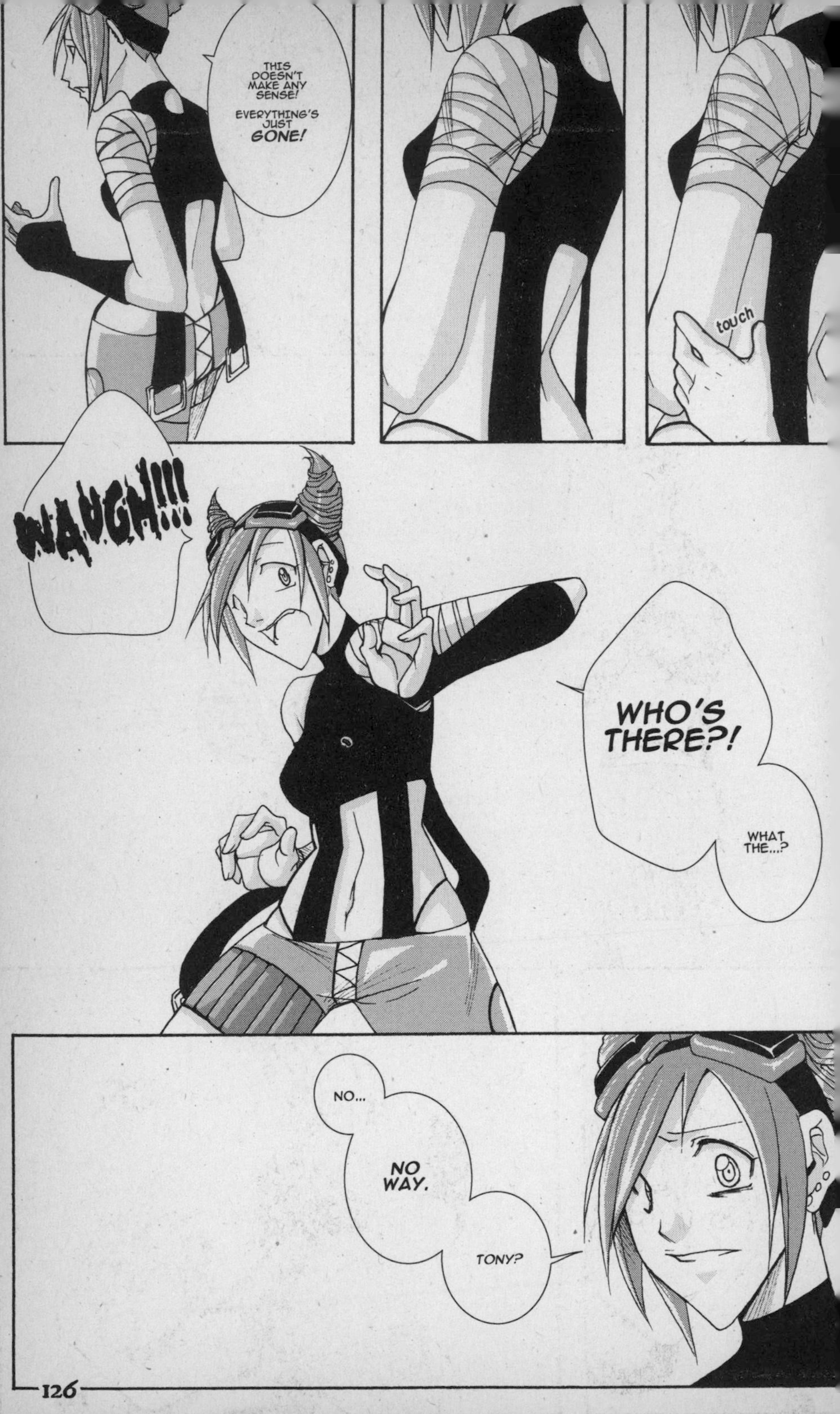
THIS DOESN'T MAKE ANY SENSE!
EVERYTHING'S JUST GONE!
touch
WAUGH!!!
WHO'S THERE?!
WHAT THE...?
NO...
NO WAY.
TONY?

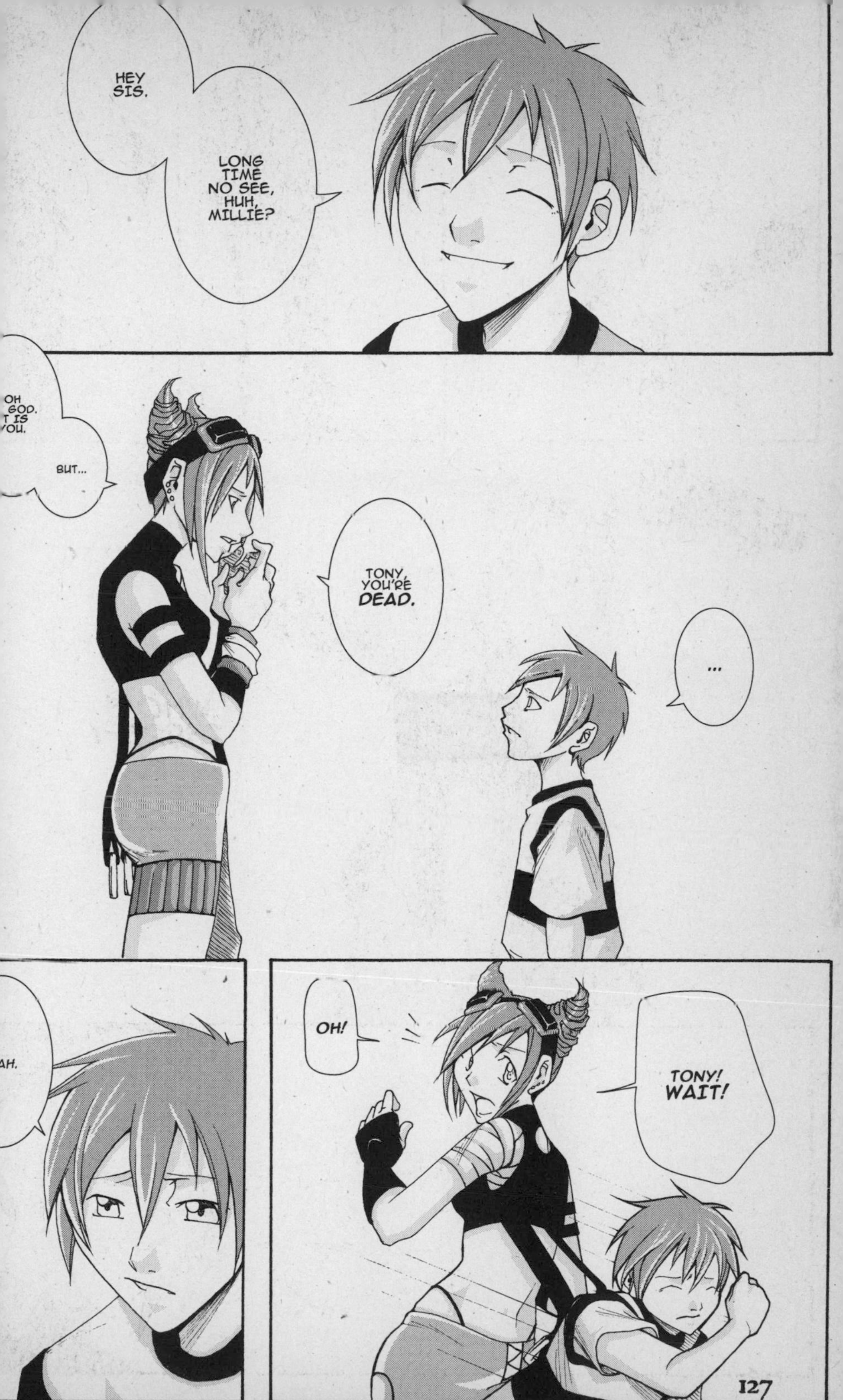
HEY SIS.
LONG TIME NO SEE, HUH, MILLIE?
OH GOD. T IS OU.
BUT...
TONY, YOU'RE DEAD.
...
AH.
OH!
TONY! WAIT!

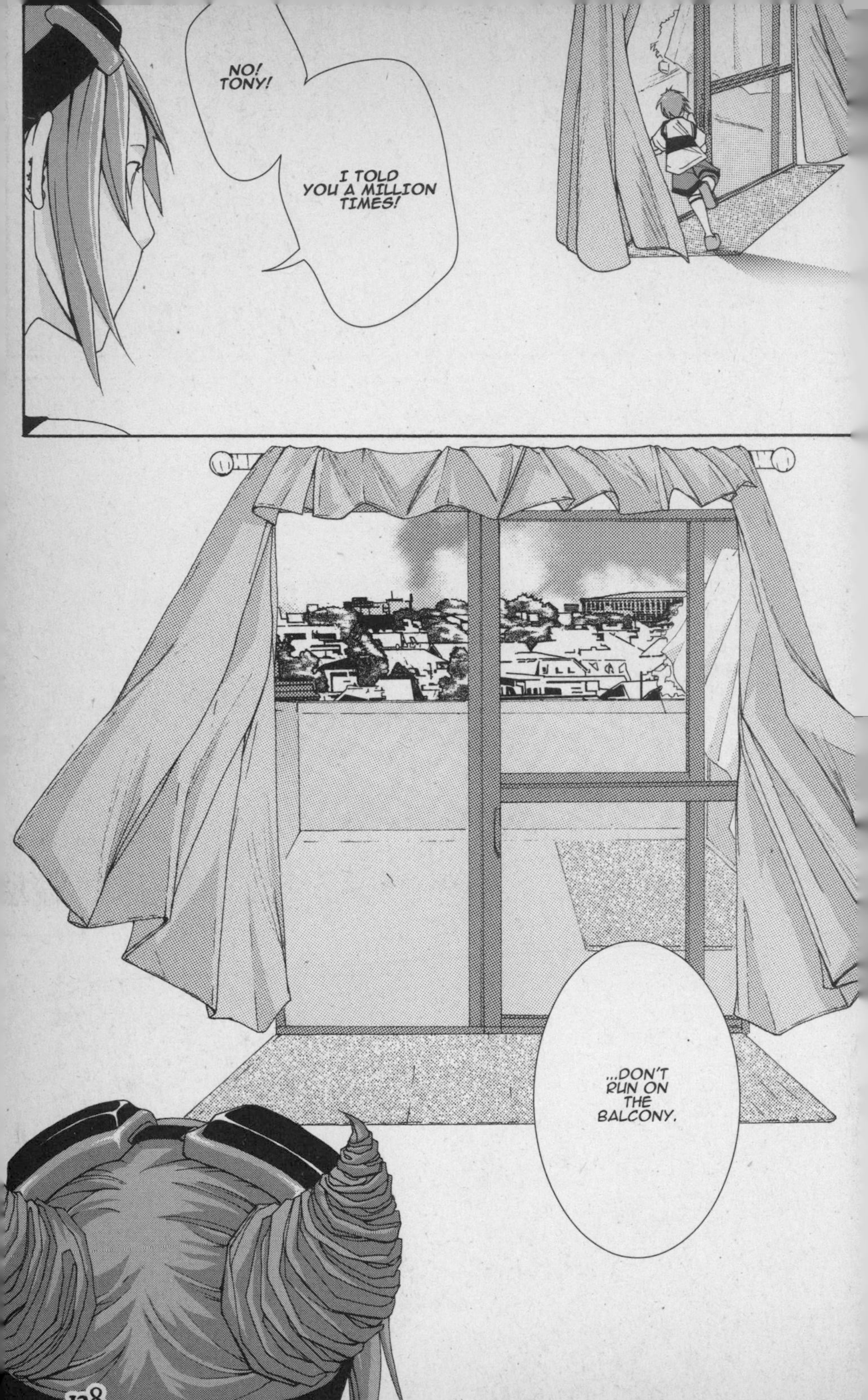
NO! TONY!
I TOLD YOU A MILLION TIMES!
...DON'T RUN ON THE BALCONY.

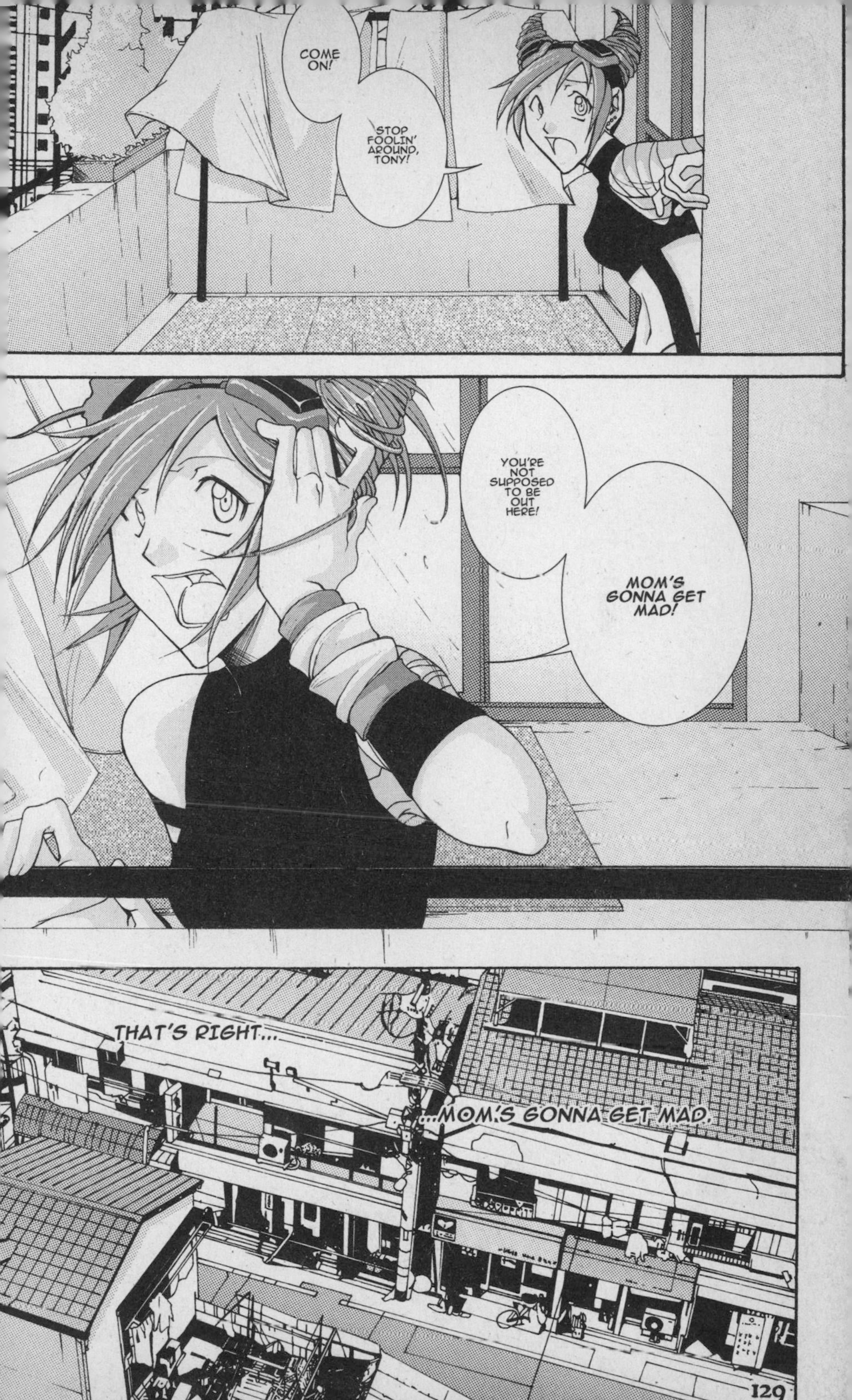
COME ON!
STOP FOOLIN' AROUND, TONY!
YOU'RE NOT SUPPOSED TO BE OUT HERE!
MOM'S GONNA GET MAD!
THAT'S RIGHT...
...MOM'S GONNA GET MAD.

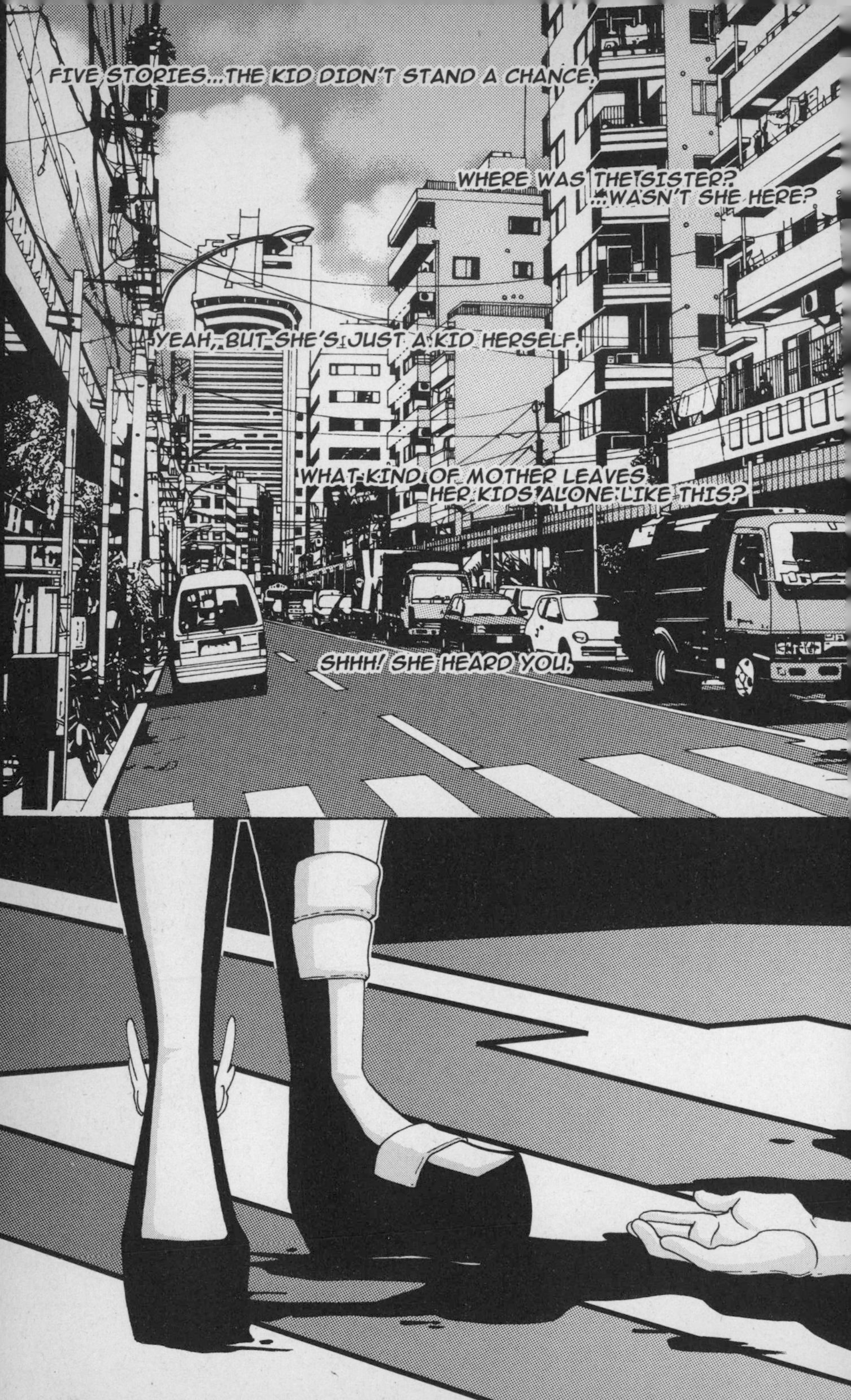
FIVE STORIES...THE KID DIDN'T STAND A CHANCE.
WHERE WAS THE SISTER? ...WASN'T SHE HERE?
YEAH, BUT SHE'S JUST A KID HERSELF.
WHAT KIND OF MOTHER LEAVES HER KIDS ALONE LIKE THIS?
SHHH! SHE HEARD YOU.

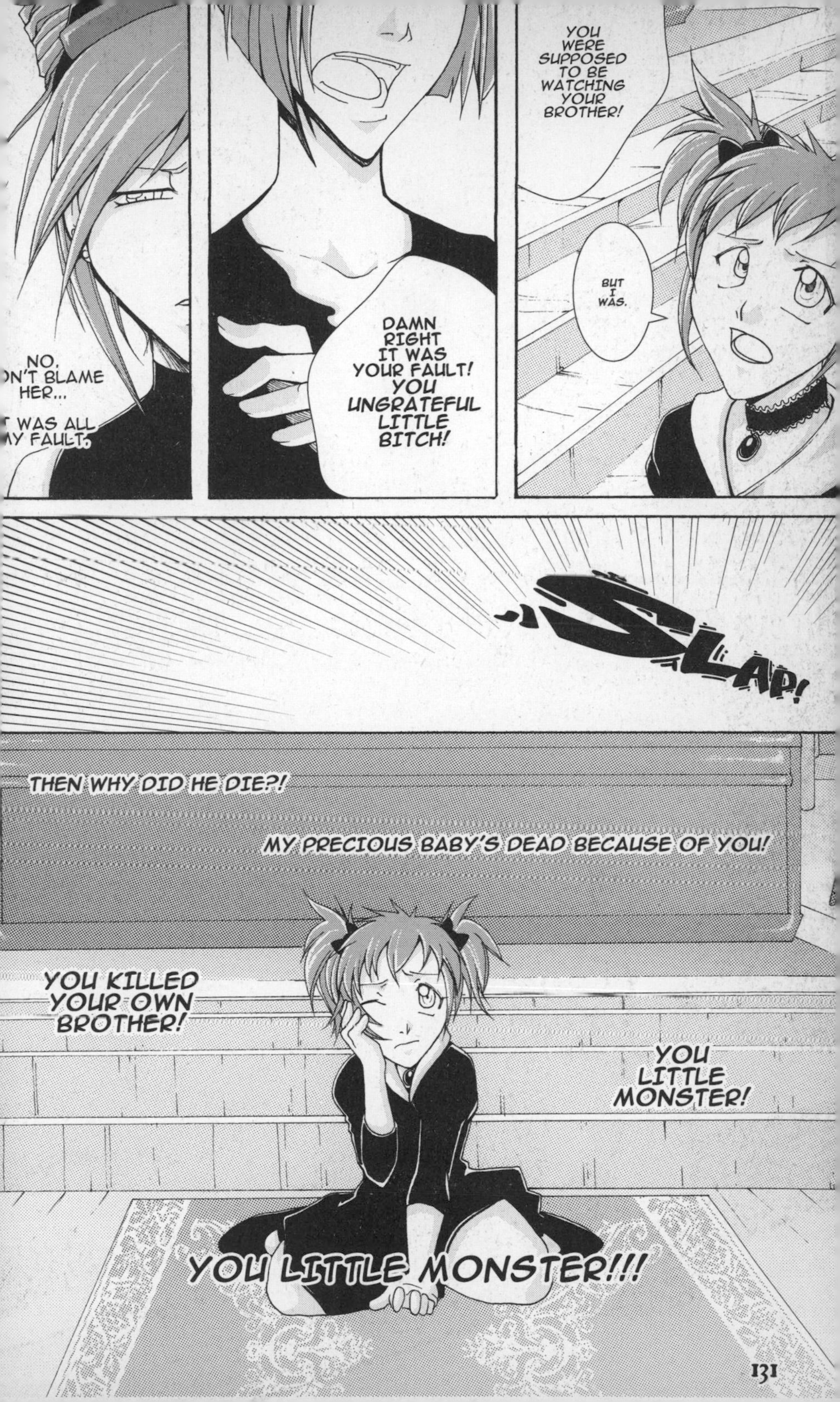
YOU WERE SUPPOSED TO BE WATCHING YOUR BROTHER!
BUT I WAS.
DAMN RIGHT IT WAS YOUR FAULT! YOU UNGRATEFUL LITTLE BITCH!
NO, ...N'T BLAME HER... ...T WAS ALL ...Y FAULT.
SLAP!
THEN WHY DID HE DIE?!
MY PRECIOUS BABY'S DEAD BECAUSE OF YOU!
YOU KILLED YOUR OWN BROTHER!
YOU LITTLE MONSTER!
YOU LITTLE MONSTER!!!

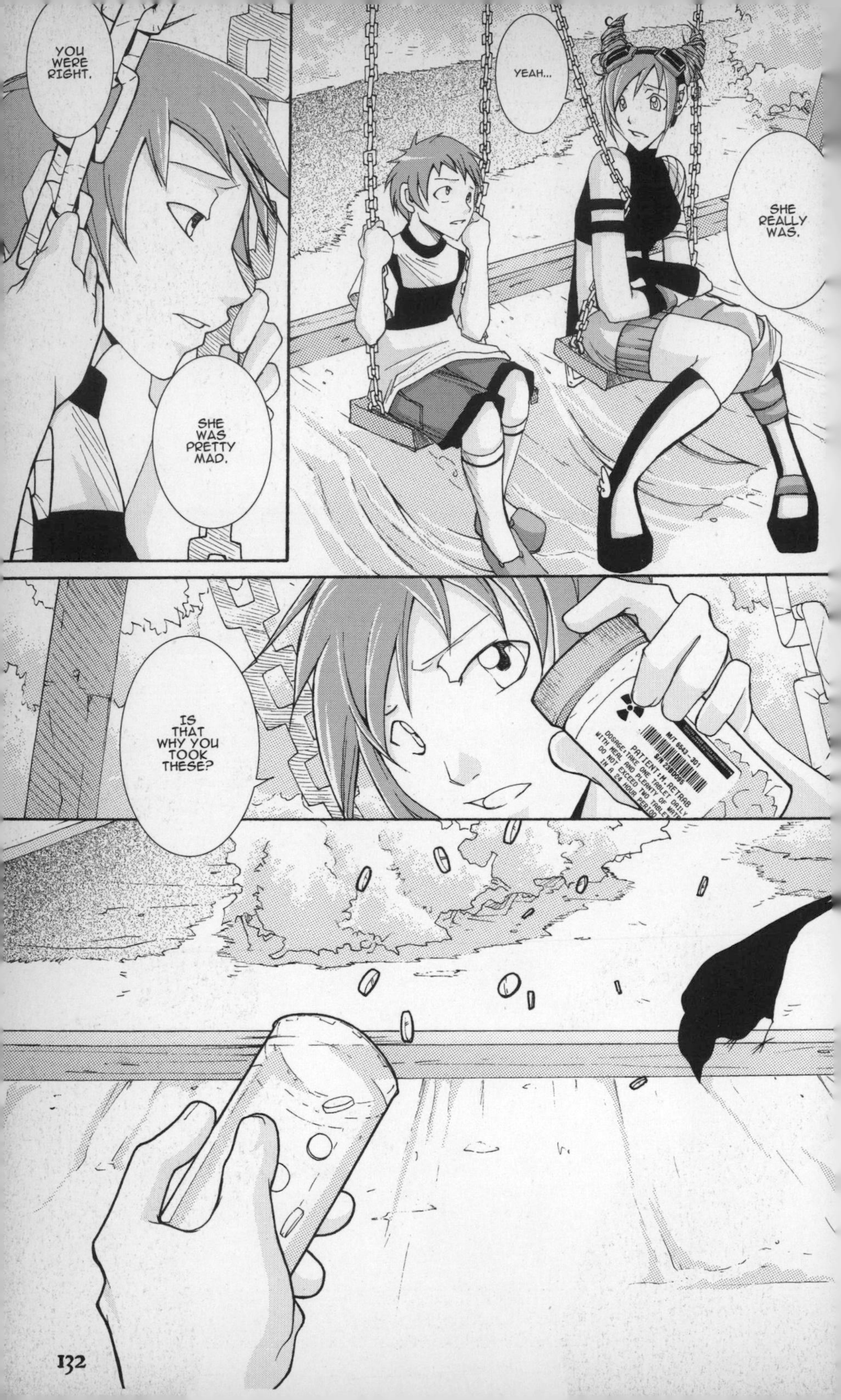
YEAH...
SHE REALLY WAS.
YOU WERE RIGHT.
SHE WAS PRETTY MAD.
IS THAT WHY YOU TOOK THESE?
M/T 6543-301
S/N 2380095
PATIENT:M.RETRAB
DOSAGE:TAKE ONE TABLET DAILY
WITH MEAL AND PLEANTY OF
DO NOT EXCEED TWO
IN A 24 HOUR PERIOD

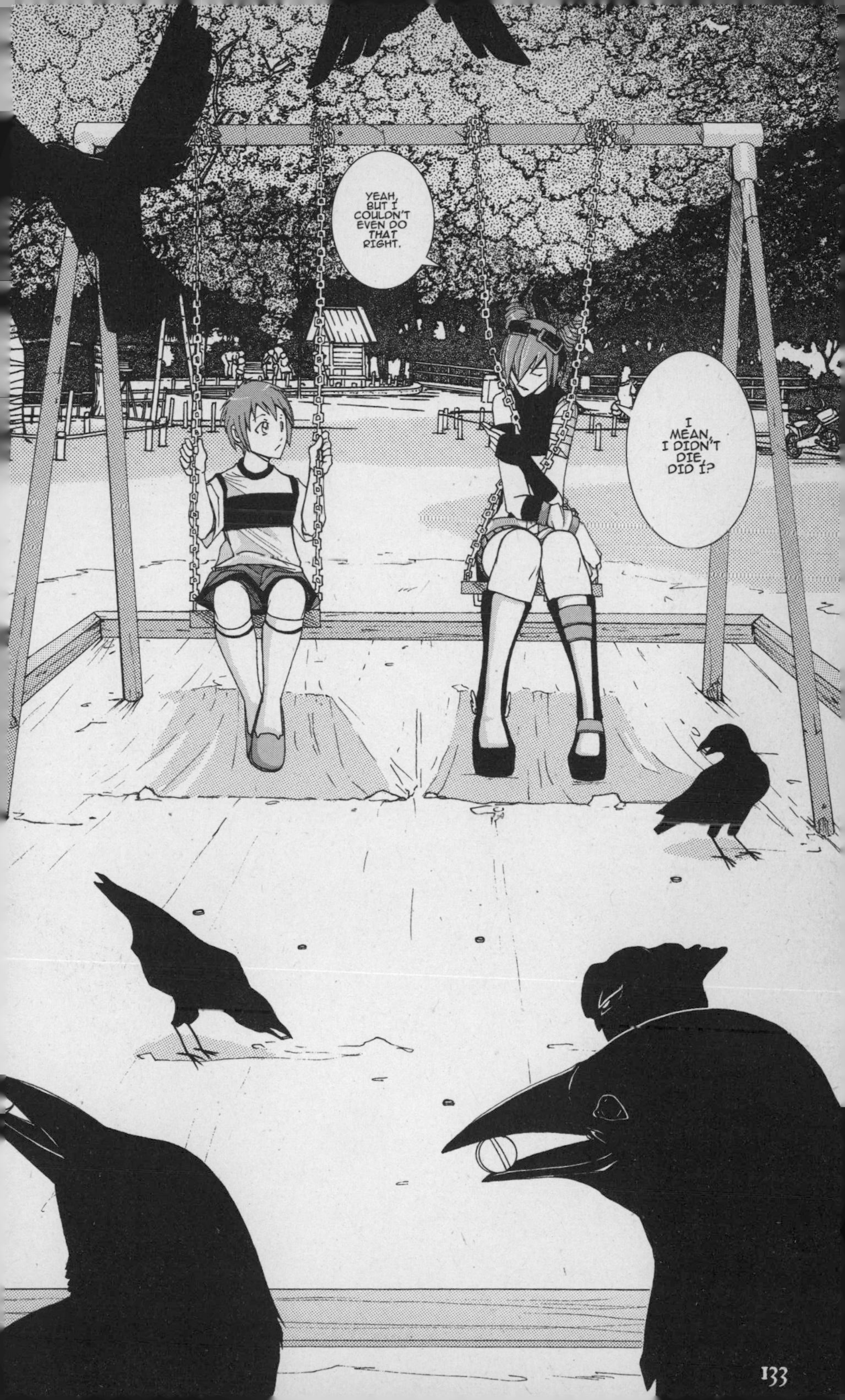
YEAH, BUT I COULDN'T EVEN DO THAT RIGHT.
I MEAN, I DIDN'T DIE, DID I?

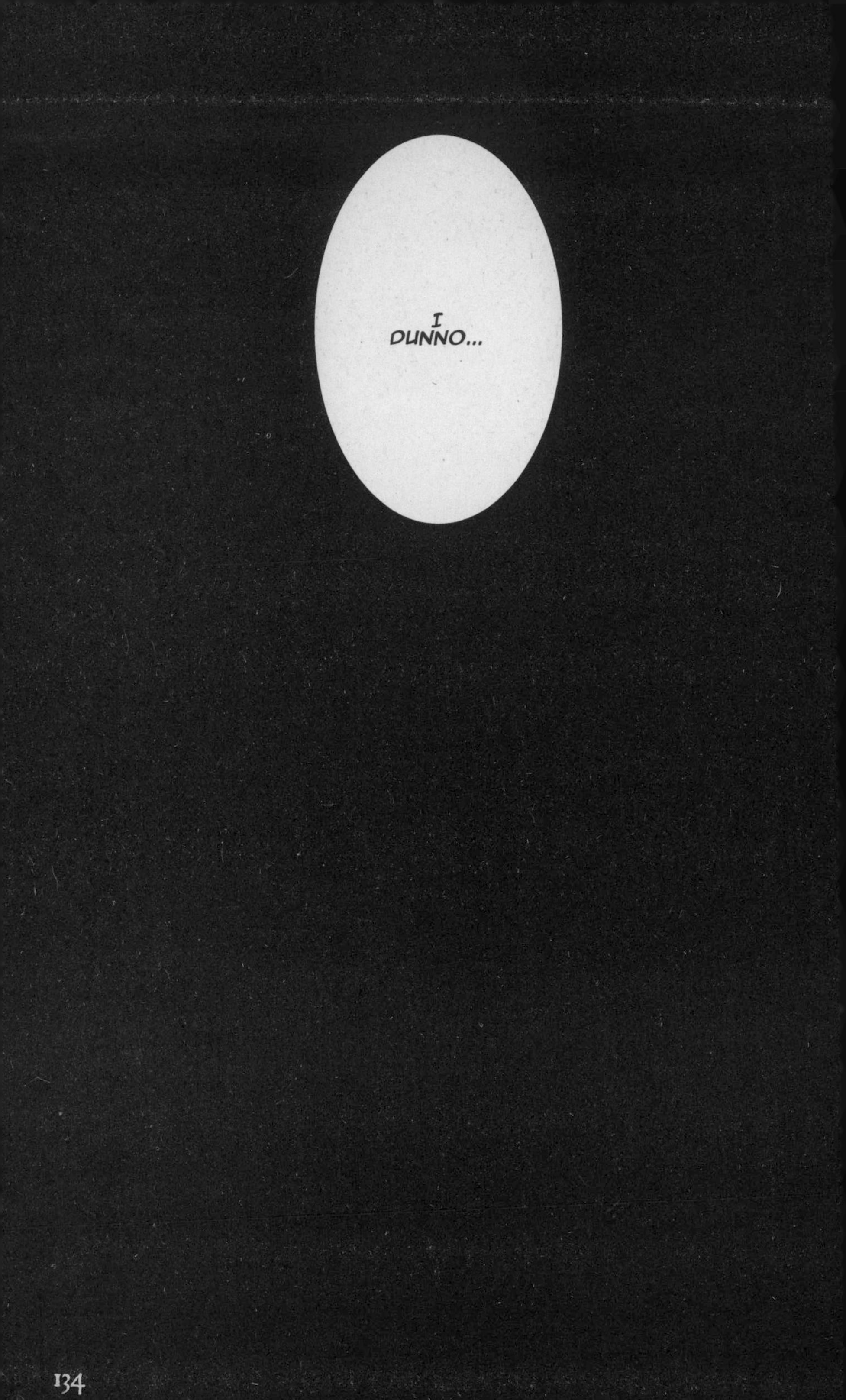
I DUNNO...

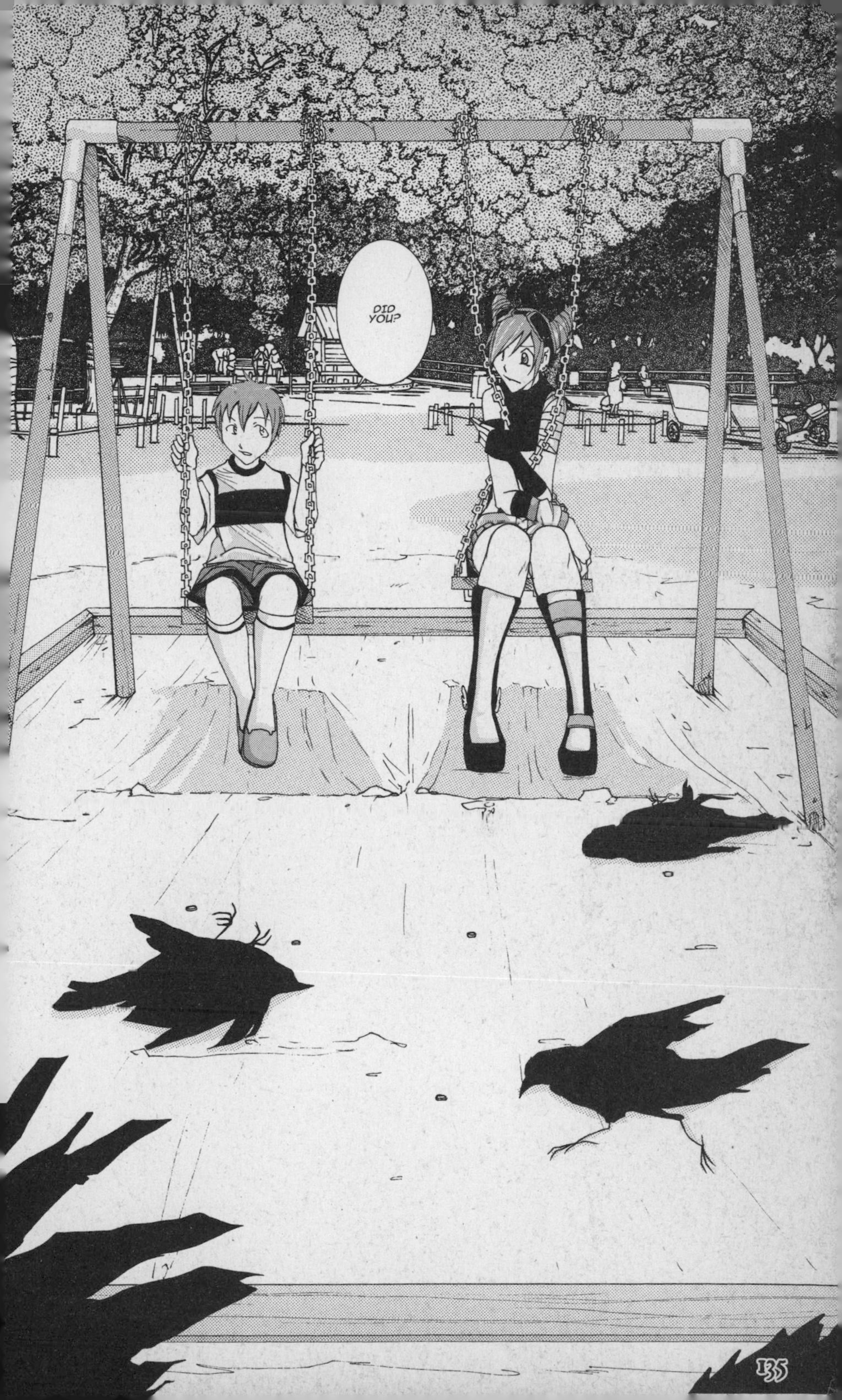
DID YOU?

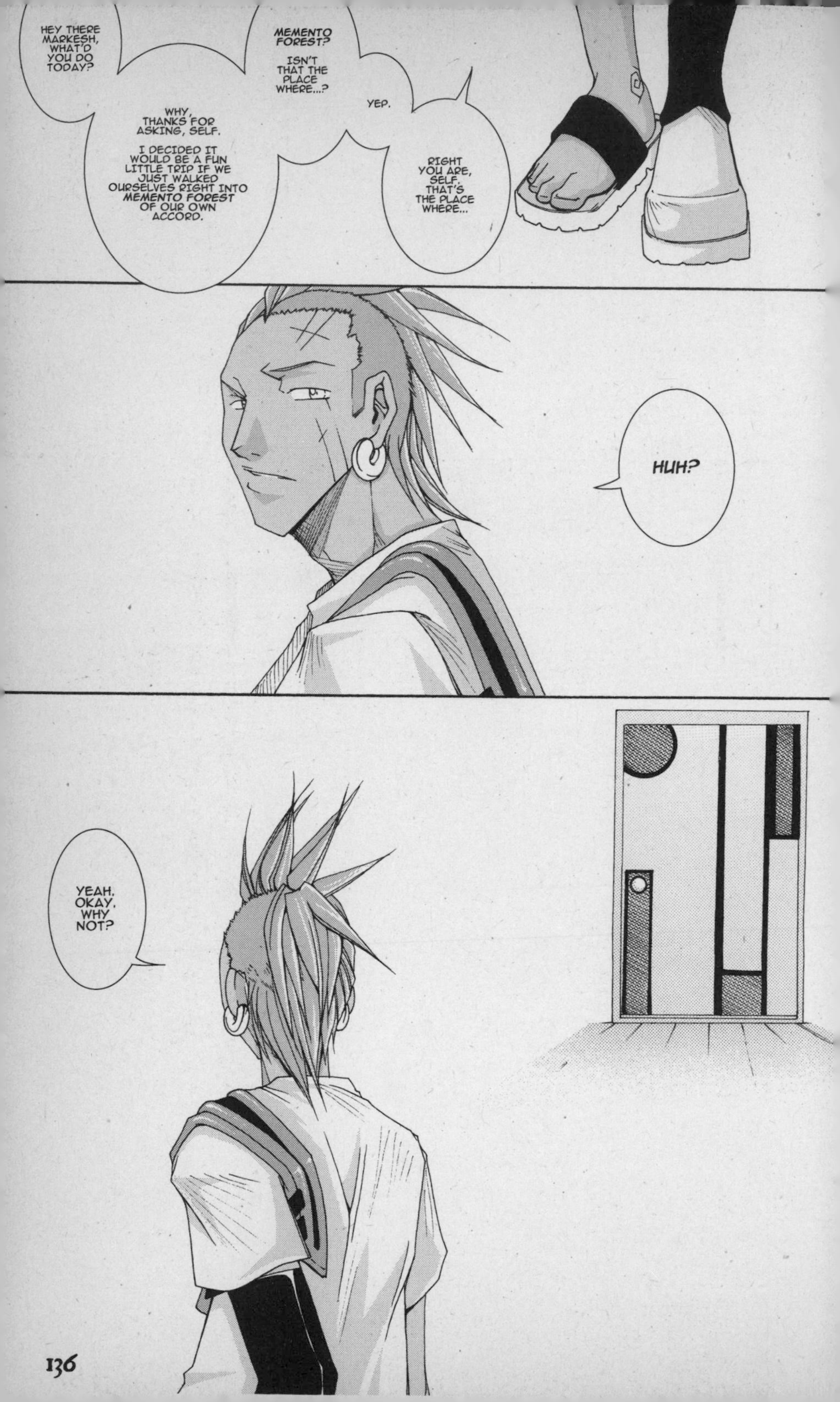
HEY THERE MARKESH, WHAT'D YOU DO TODAY?
WHY, THANKS FOR ASKING, SELF.
I DECIDED IT WOULD BE A FUN LITTLE TRIP IF WE JUST WALKED OURSELVES RIGHT INTO MEMENTO FOREST OF OUR OWN ACCORD.
MEMENTO FOREST?
ISN'T THAT THE PLACE WHERE...?
YEP.
RIGHT YOU ARE, SELF. THAT'S THE PLACE WHERE...
HUH?
YEAH. OKAY. WHY NOT?

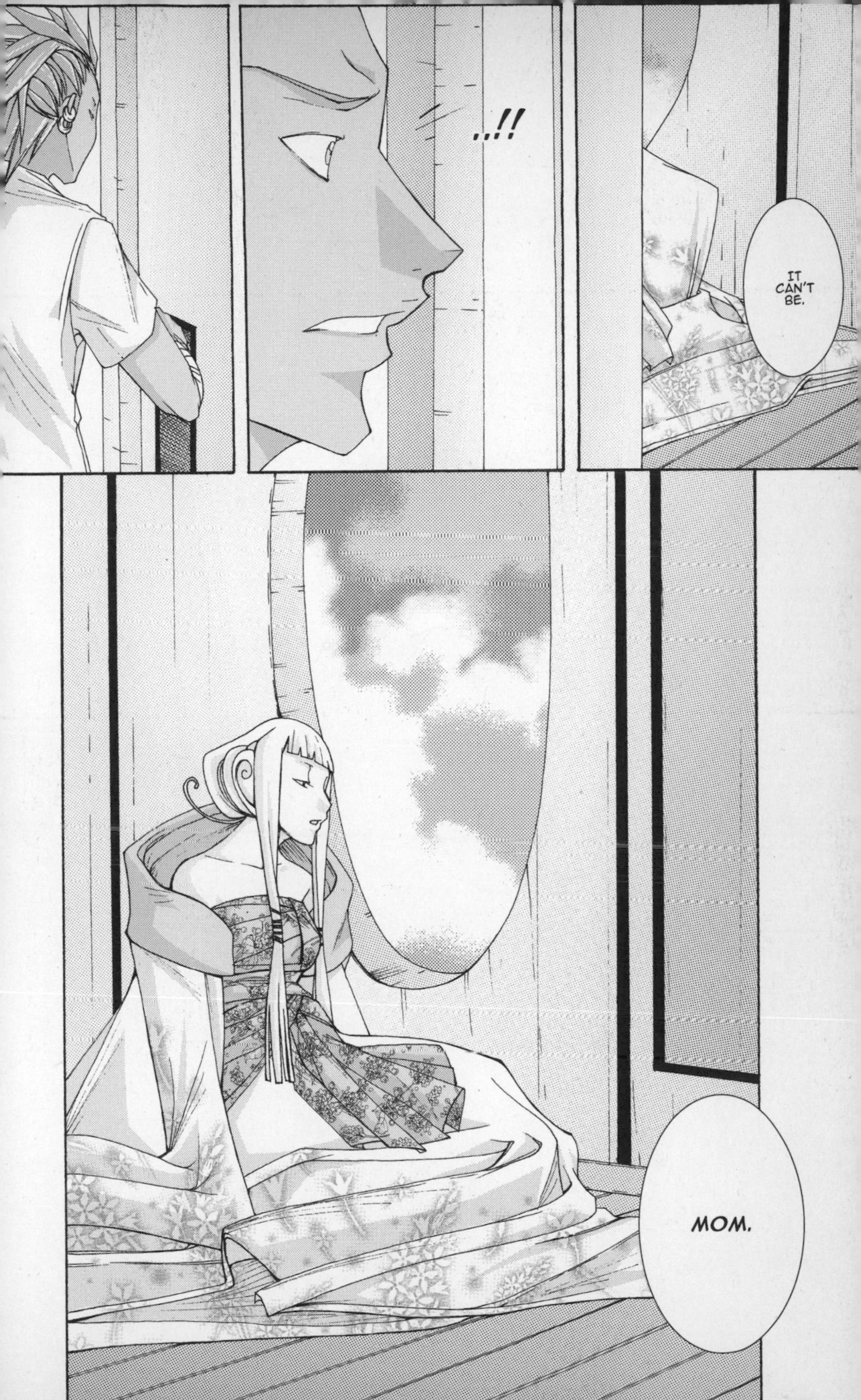
IT CAN'T BE.
..!!
MOM.

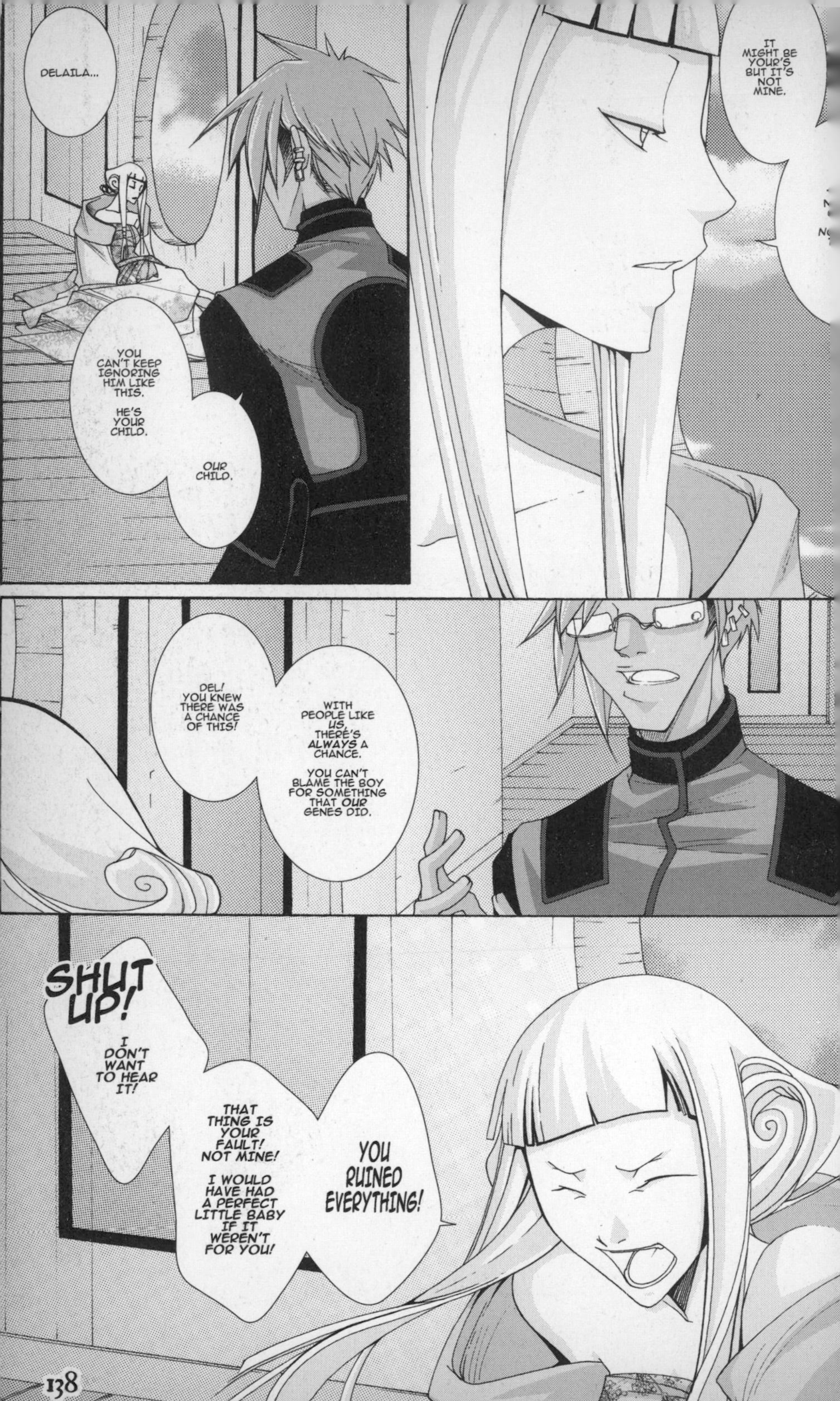
DELAILA...
YOU CAN'T KEEP IGNORING HIM LIKE THIS.
HE'S YOUR CHILD.
OUR CHILD.
IT MIGHT BE YOUR'S BUT IT'S NOT MINE.
DEL! YOU KNEW THERE WAS A CHANCE OF THIS!
WITH PEOPLE LIKE US, THERE'S ALWAYS A CHANCE.
YOU CAN'T BLAME THE BOY FOR SOMETHING THAT OUR GENES DID.
SHUT UP!
I DON'T WANT TO HEAR IT!
THAT THING IS YOUR FAULT! NOT MINE!
I WOULD HAVE HAD A PERFECT LITTLE BABY IF IT WEREN'T FOR YOU!
YOU RUINED EVERYTHING!

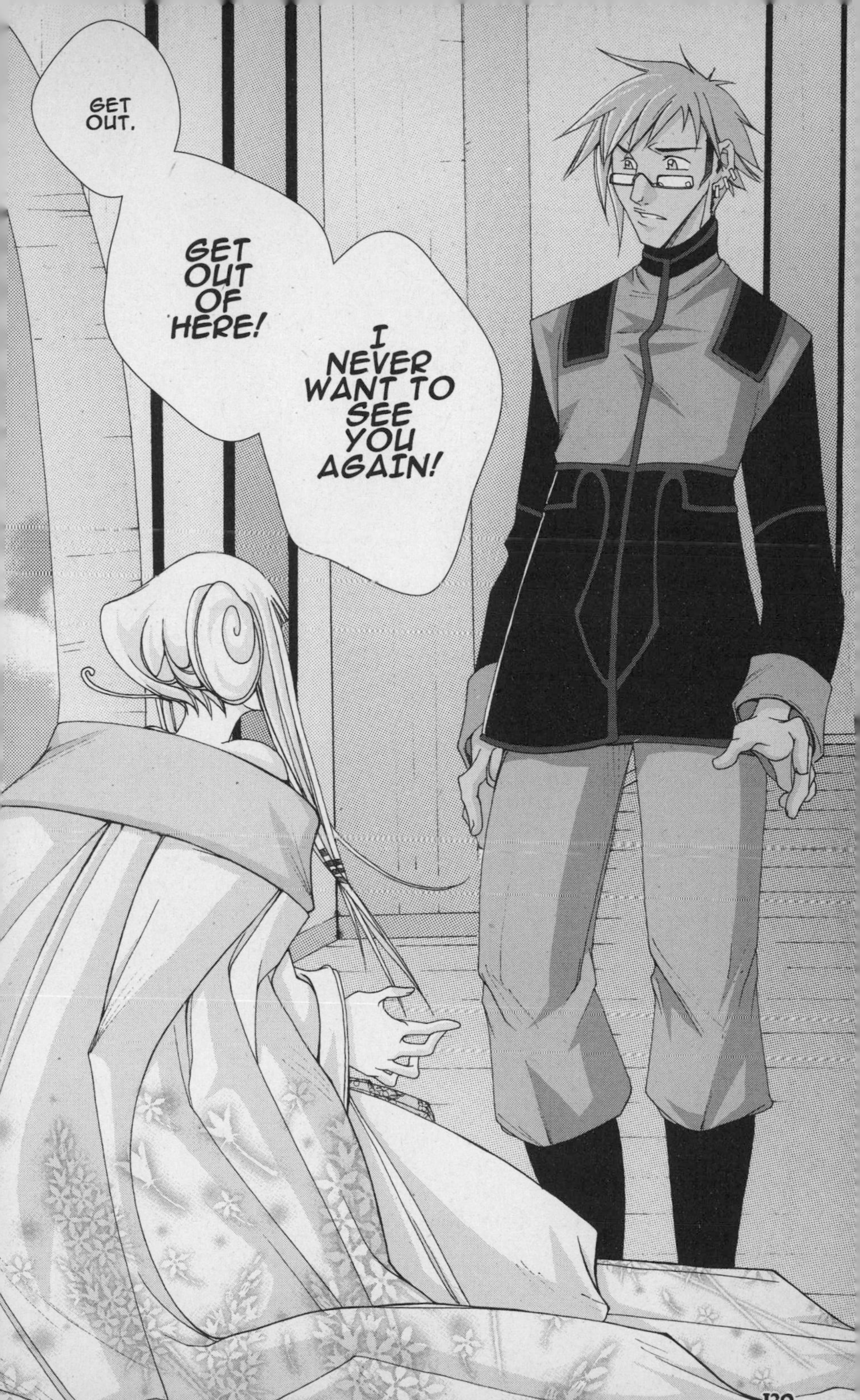
GET OUT.
GET OUT OF HERE!
I NEVER WANT TO SEE YOU AGAIN!

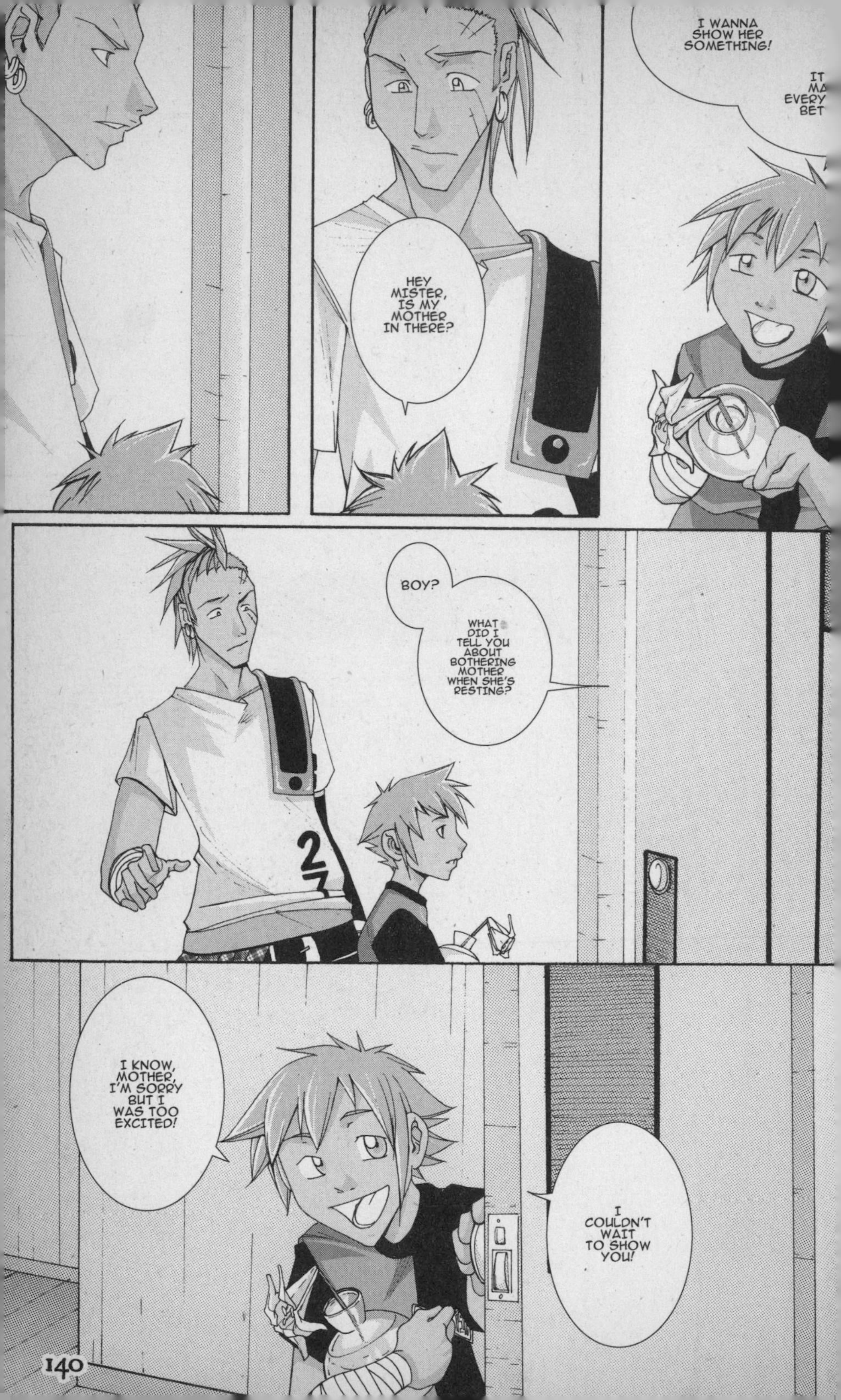
HEY MISTER, IS MY MOTHER IN THERE?
I WANNA SHOW HER SOMETHING!
BOY?
WHAT DID I TELL YOU ABOUT BOTHERING MOTHER WHEN SHE'S RESTING?
I KNOW, MOTHER, I'M SORRY BUT I WAS TOO EXCITED!
I COULDN'T WAIT TO SHOW YOU!

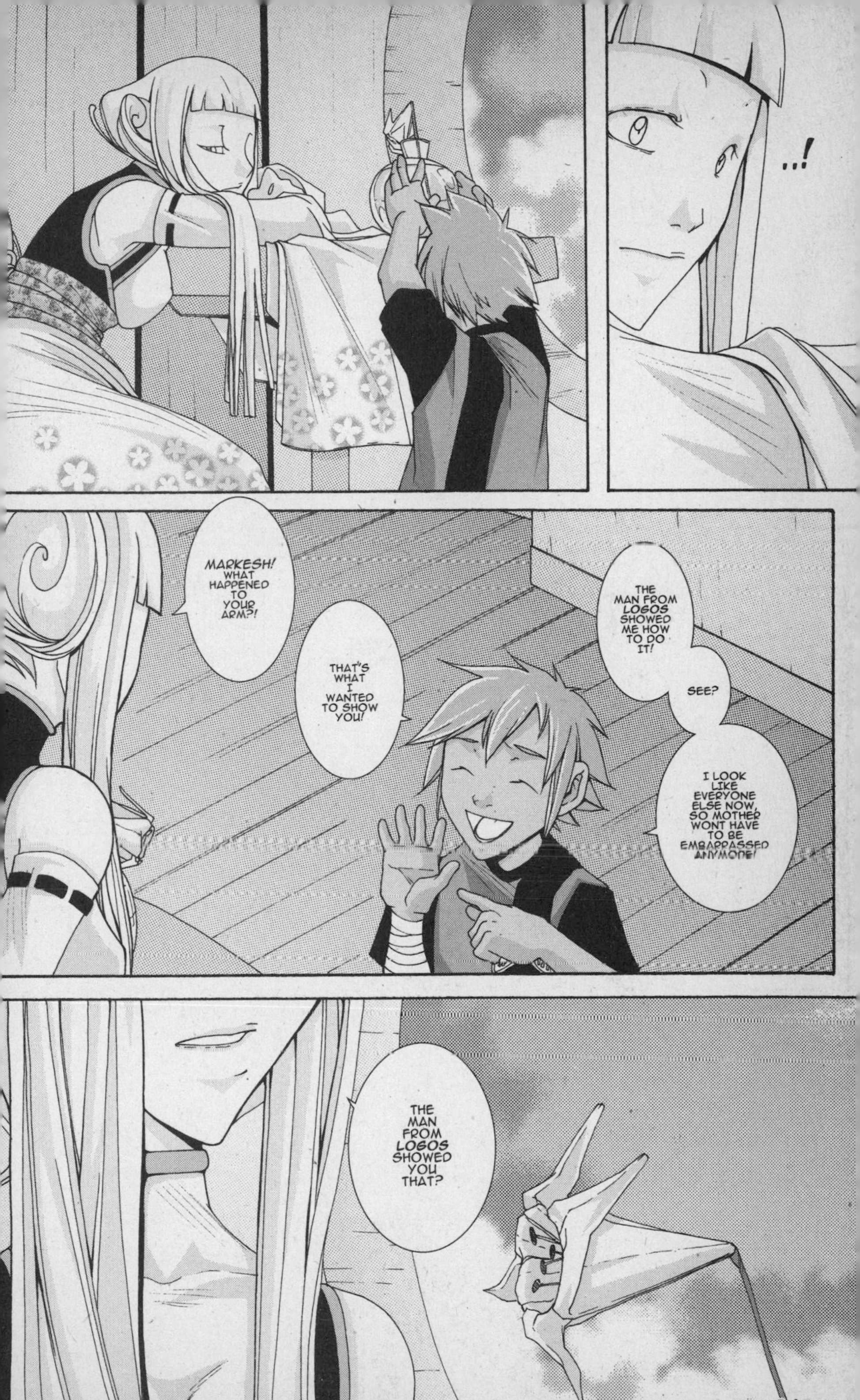
..!
MARKESH! WHAT HAPPENED TO YOUR ARM?!
THAT'S WHAT I WANTED TO SHOW YOU!
THE MAN FROM LOGOS SHOWED ME HOW TO DO IT!
SEE?
I LOOK LIKE EVERYONE ELSE NOW, SO MOTHER WONT HAVE TO BE EMBARRASSED ANYMORE!
THE MAN FROM LOGOS SHOWED YOU THAT?

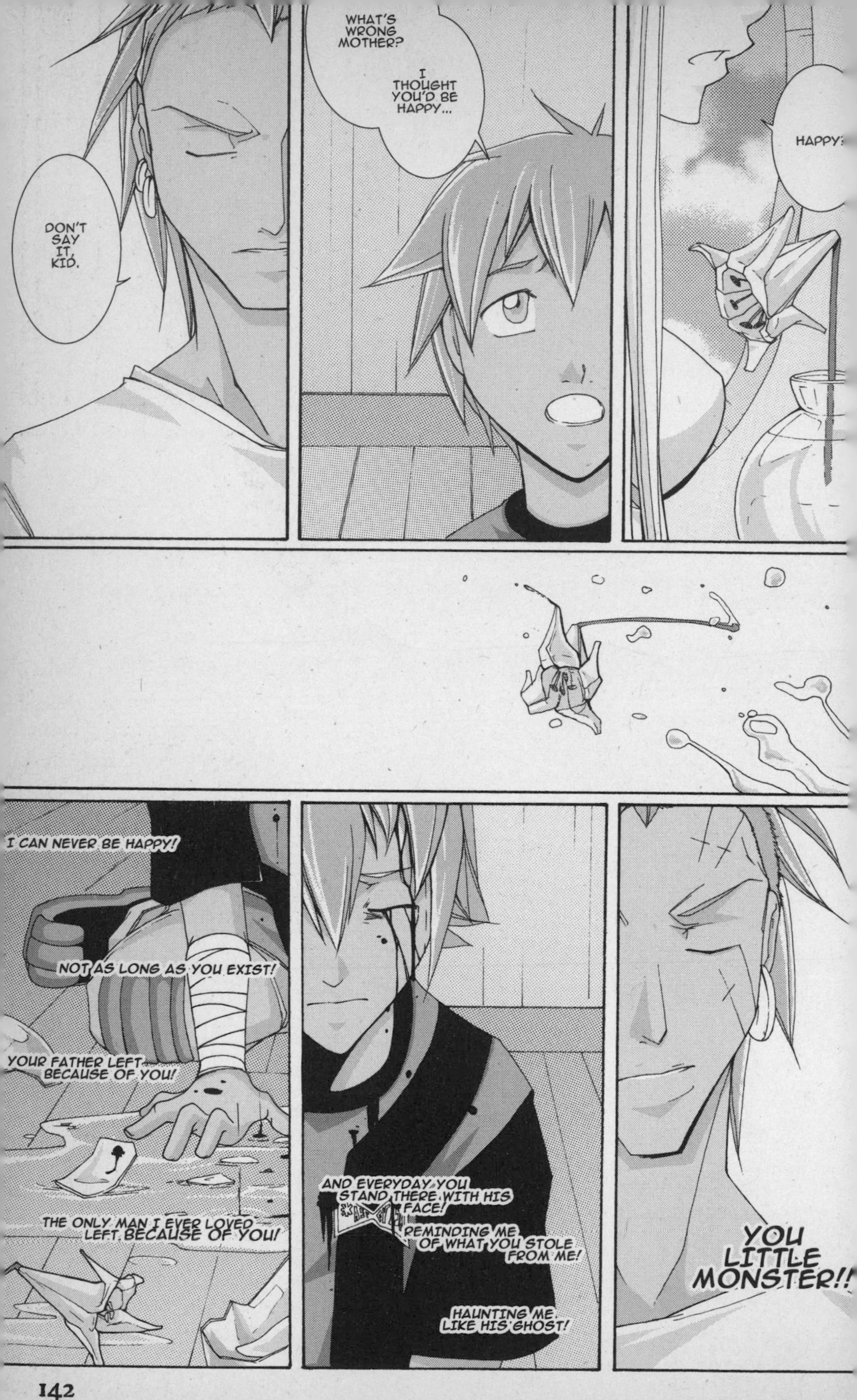

WHAT'S WRONG MOTHER?
I THOUGHT YOU'D BE HAPPY...
DON'T SAY IT, KID.
HAPPY?
I CAN NEVER BE HAPPY!
NOT AS LONG AS YOU EXIST!
YOUR FATHER LEFT BECAUSE OF YOU!
THE ONLY MAN I EVER LOVED LEFT BECAUSE OF YOU!
AND EVERYDAY YOU STAND THERE WITH HIS FACE!
REMINDING ME OF WHAT YOU STOLE FROM ME!
HAUNTING ME LIKE HIS GHOST!
YOU LITTLE MONSTER!!

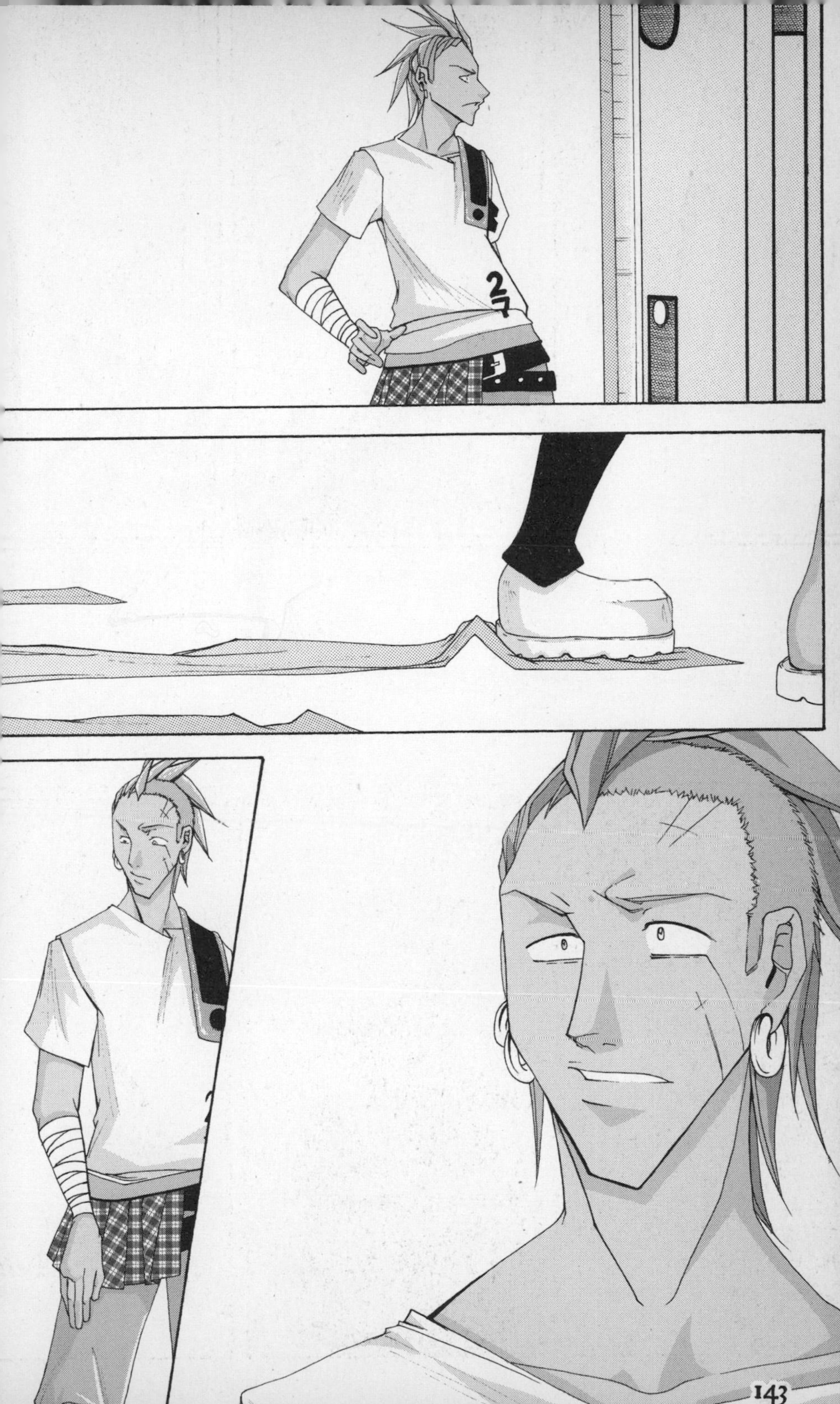

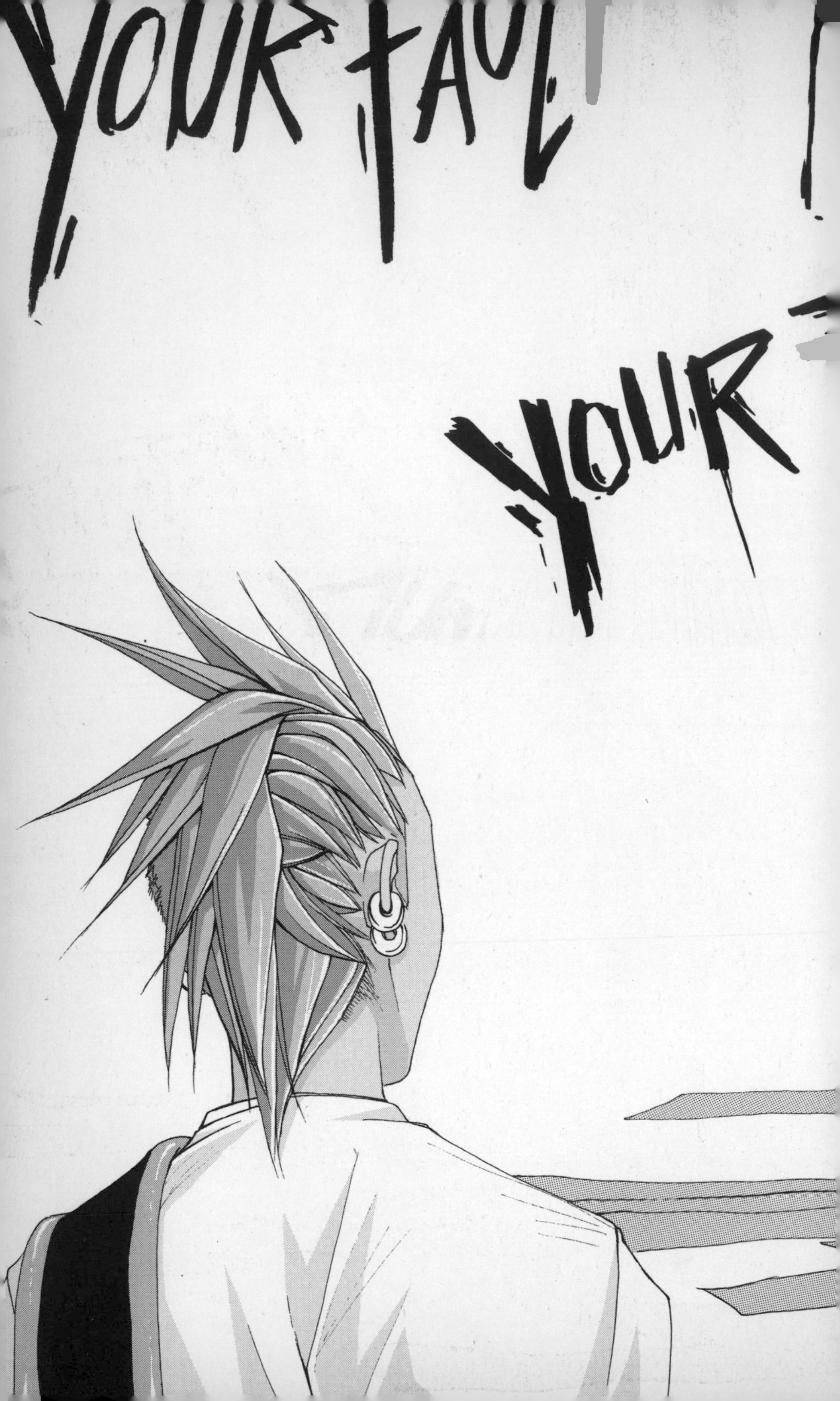

YOUR FAUL
YOUR

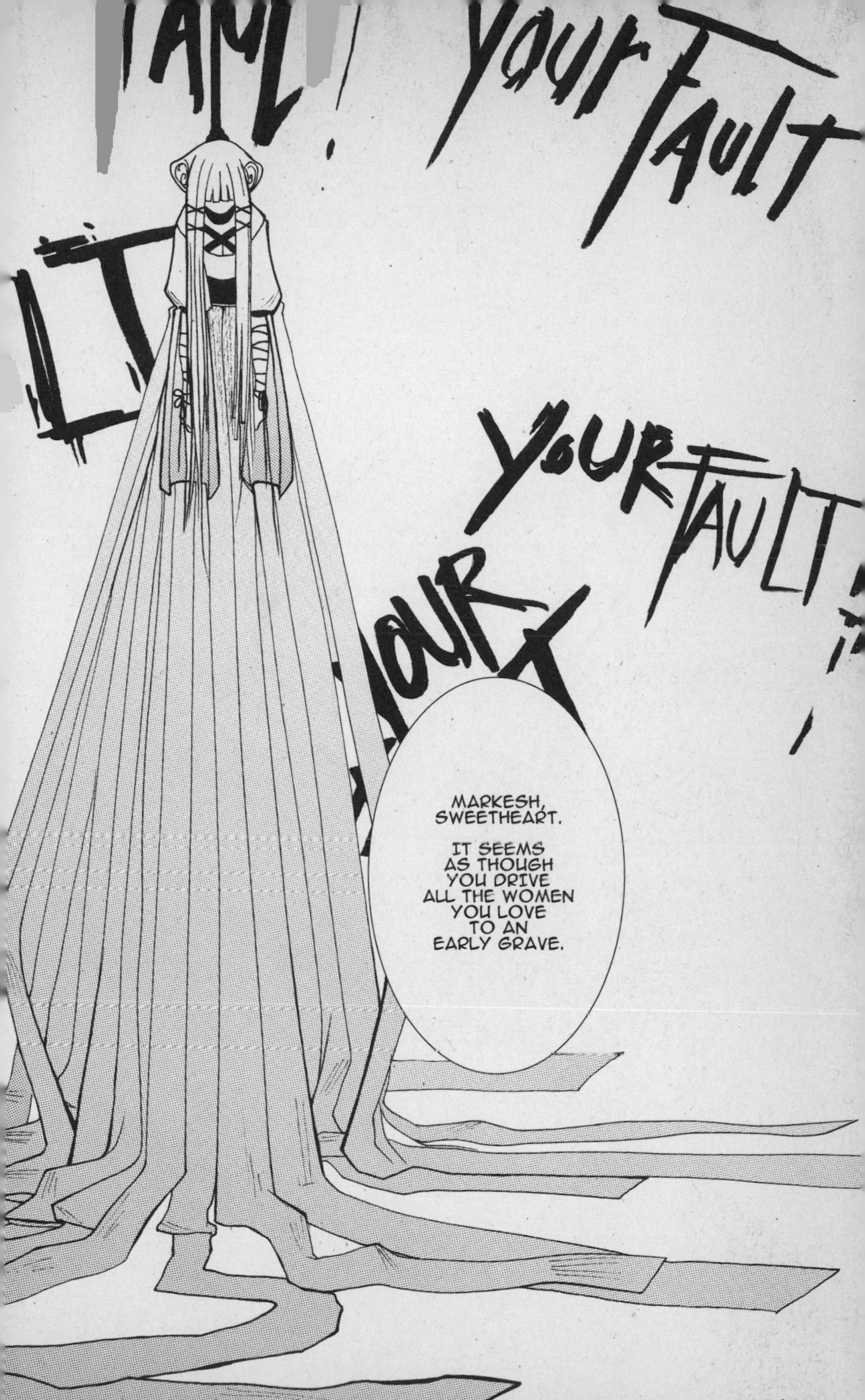
YOUR FAULT
YOUR FAULT!
MARKESH, SWEETHEART.
IT SEEMS AS THOUGH YOU DRIVE ALL THE WOMEN YOU LOVE TO AN EARLY GRAVE.

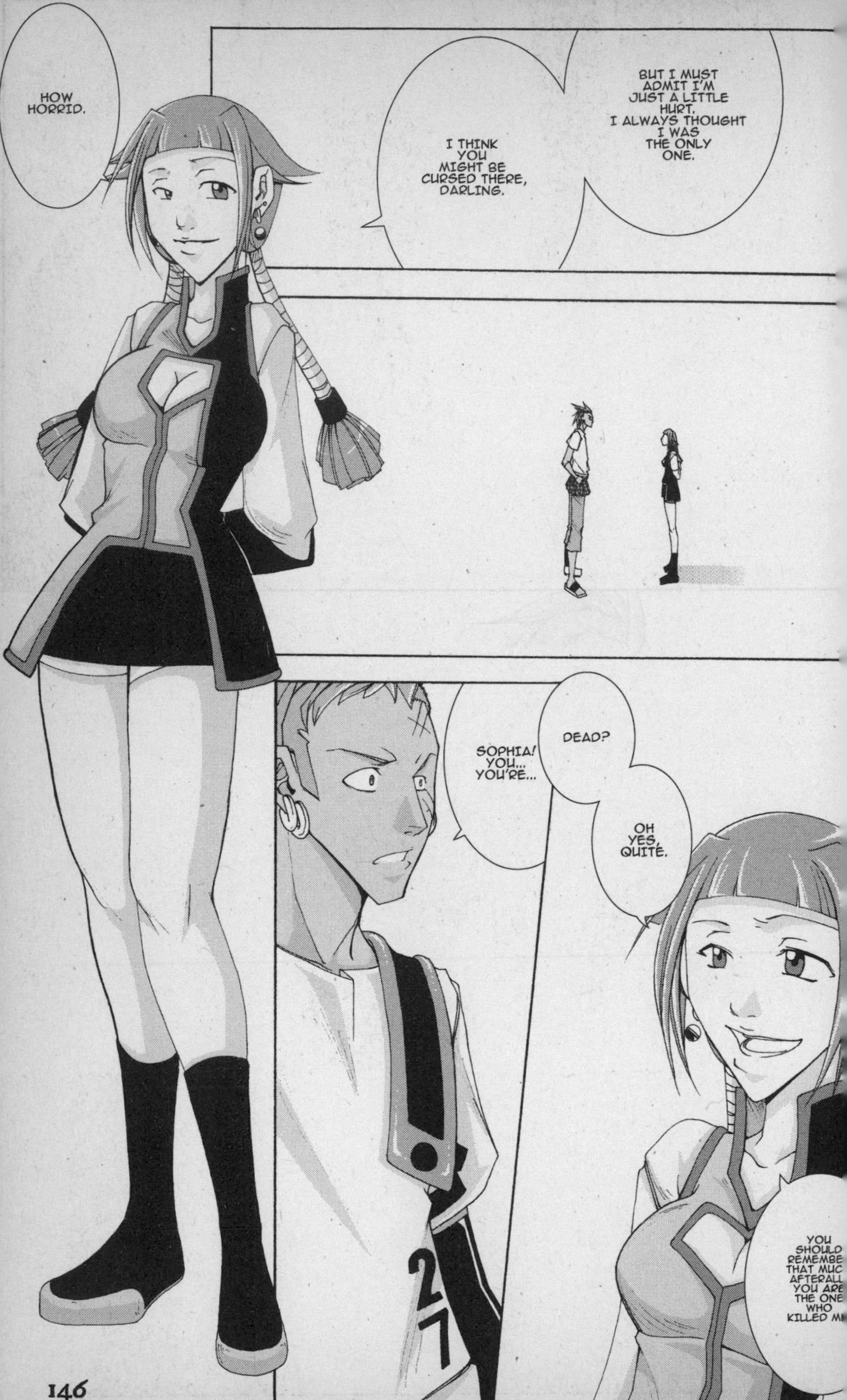

HOW HORRID.
I THINK YOU MIGHT BE CURSED THERE, DARLING.
BUT I MUST ADMIT I'M JUST A LITTLE HURT. I ALWAYS THOUGHT I WAS THE ONLY ONE.
SOPHIA! YOU... YOU'RE...
DEAD?
OH YES, QUITE.
YOU SHOULD REMEMBE THAT MUC AFTERALL YOU ARE THE ONE WHO KILLED M

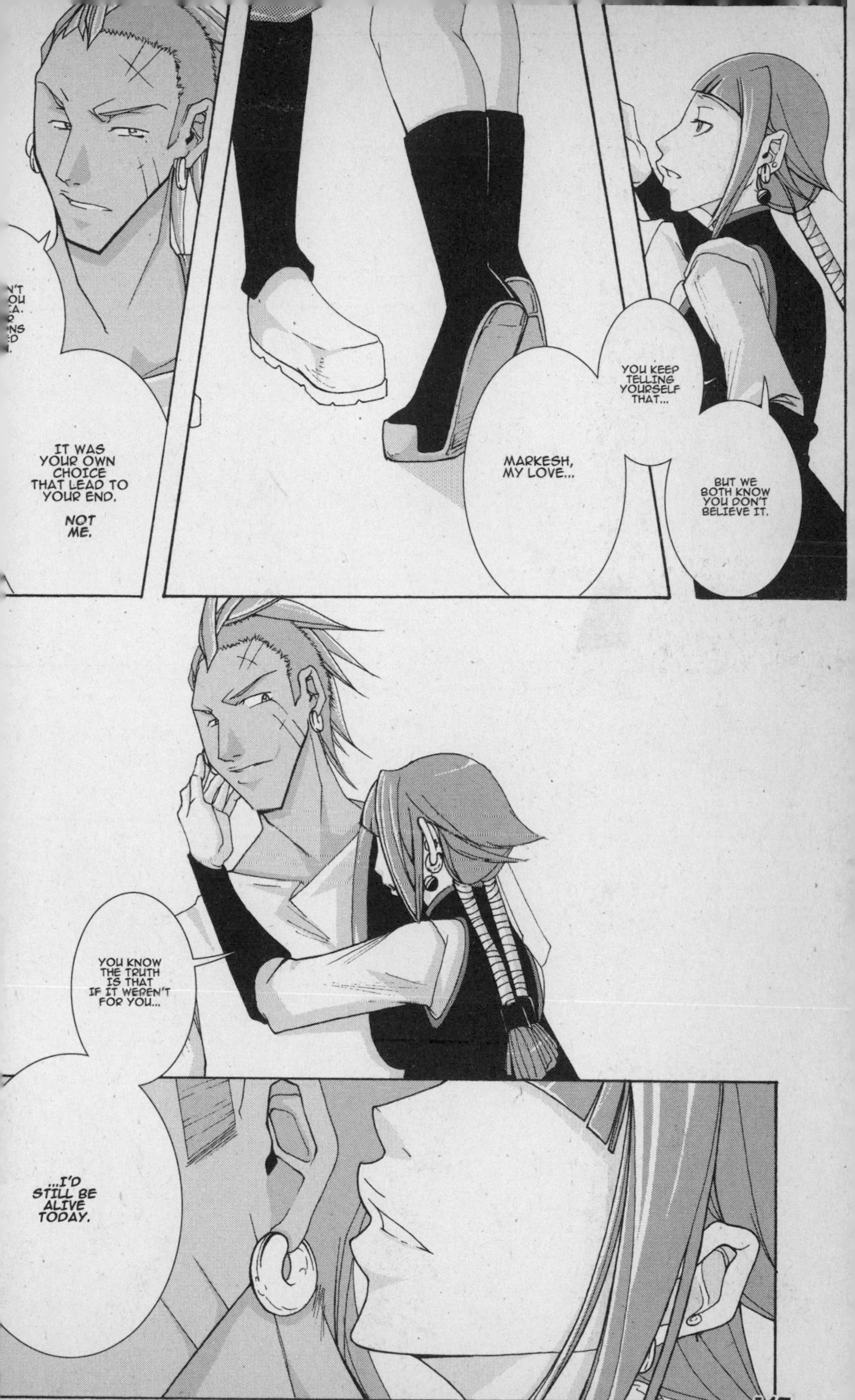
IT WAS YOUR OWN CHOICE THAT LEAD TO YOUR END.
NOT ME.
MARKESH, MY LOVE...
YOU KEEP TELLING YOURSELF THAT...
BUT WE BOTH KNOW YOU DON'T BELIEVE IT.
YOU KNOW THE TRUTH IS THAT IF IT WEREN'T FOR YOU...
...I'D STILL BE ALIVE TODAY.

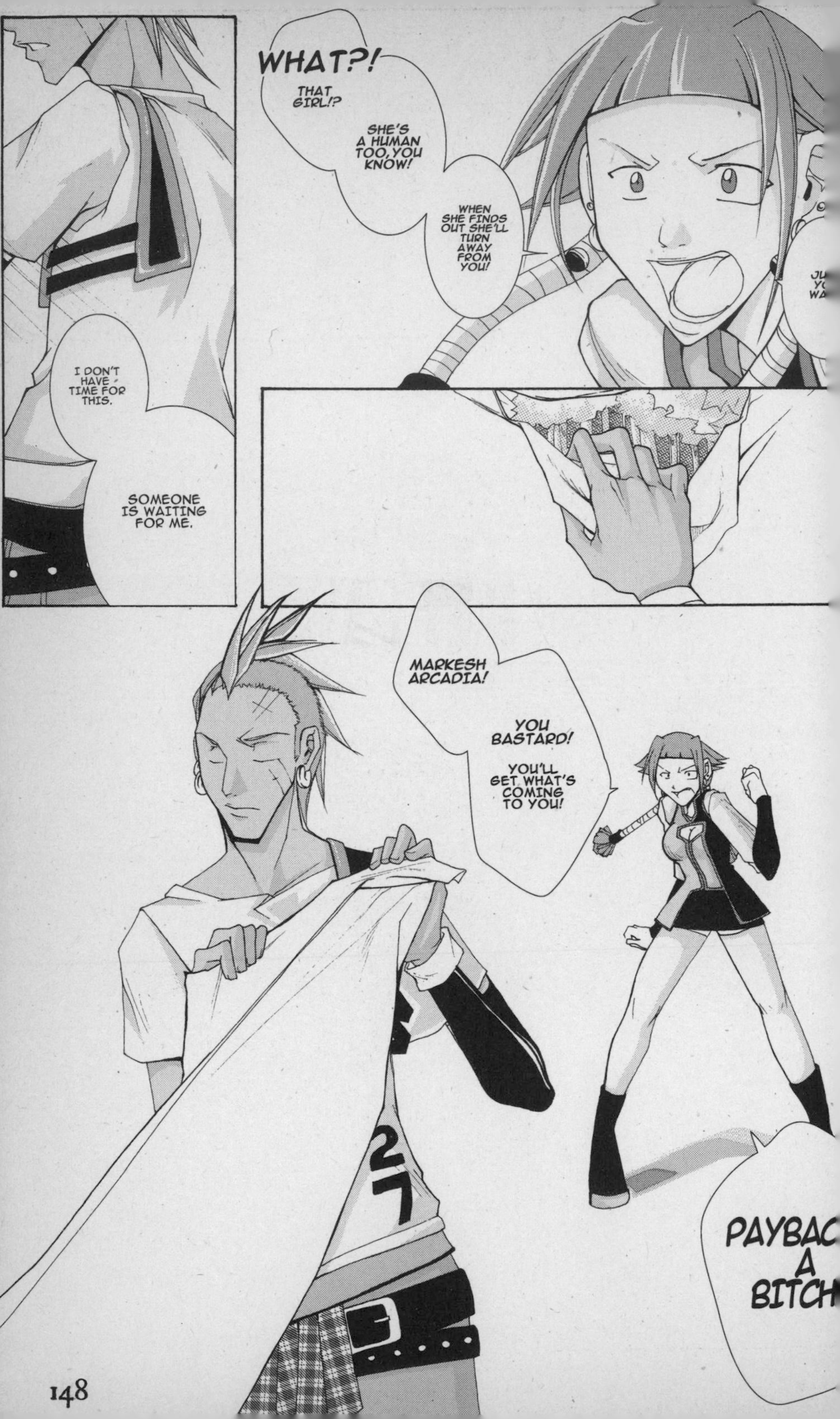

I DON'T HAVE TIME FOR THIS.
SOMEONE IS WAITING FOR ME.
WHAT?!
THAT GIRL!?
SHE'S A HUMAN TOO, YOU KNOW!
WHEN SHE FINDS OUT SHE'LL TURN AWAY FROM YOU!
MARKESH ARCADIA!
YOU BASTARD!
YOU'LL GET WHAT'S COMING TO YOU!
PAYBAC A BITCH

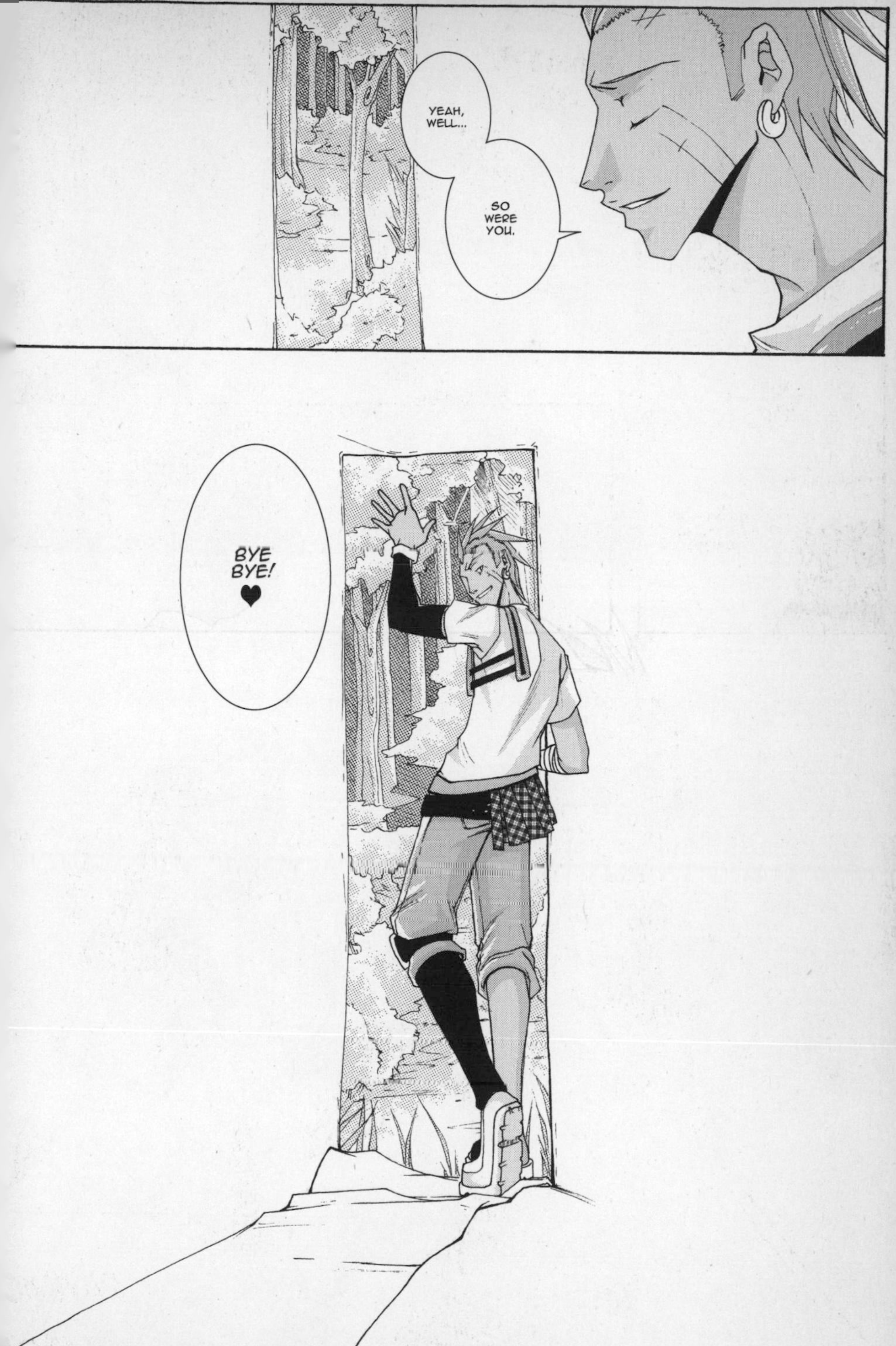
YEAH, WELL...
SO WERE YOU.
BYE BYE! ♥

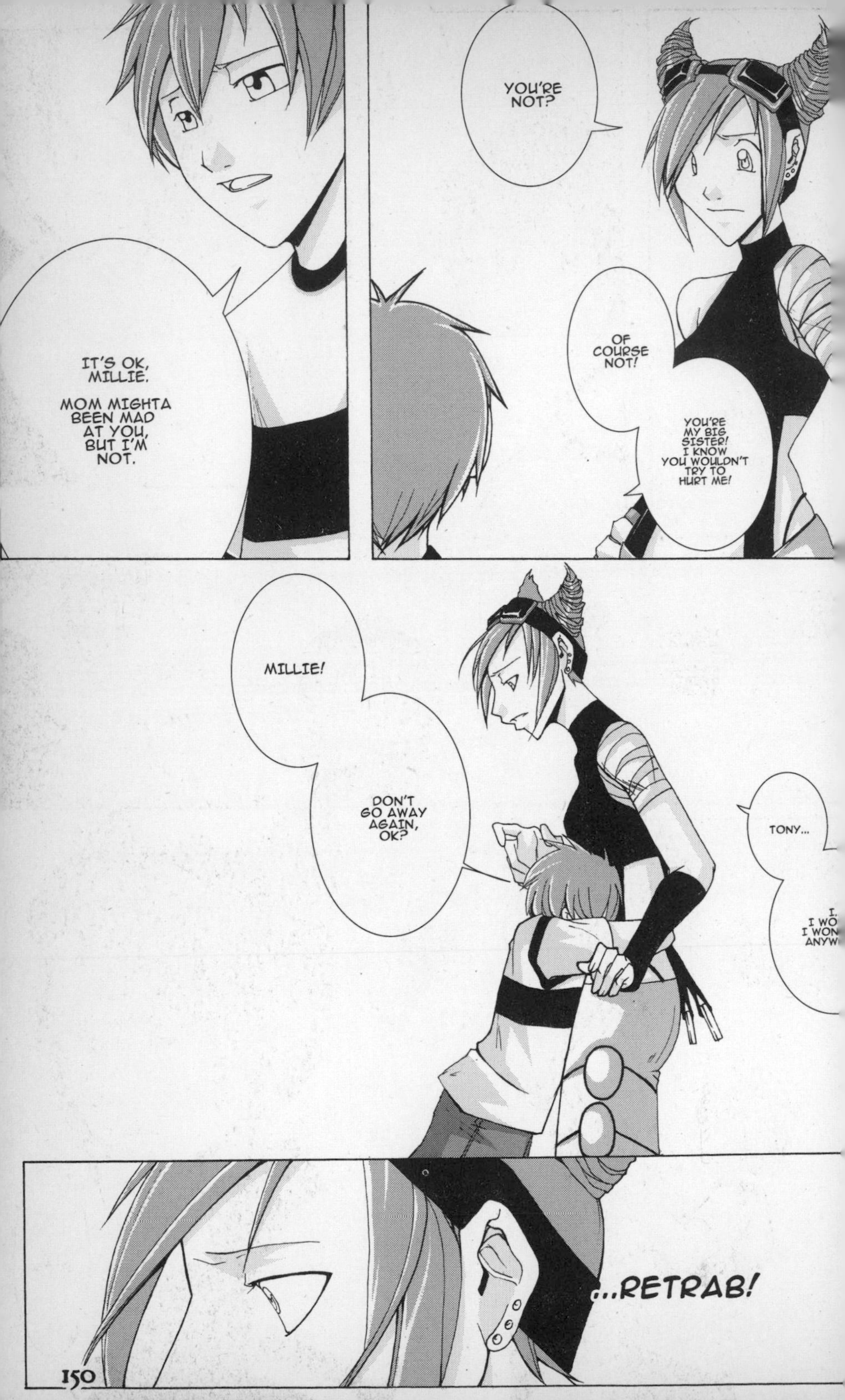
IT'S OK, MILLIE.
MOM MIGHTA BEEN MAD AT YOU, BUT I'M NOT.
YOU'RE NOT?
OF COURSE NOT!
YOU'RE MY BIG SISTER! I KNOW YOU WOULDN'T TRY TO HURT ME!
MILLIE!
DON'T GO AWAY AGAIN, OK?
TONY...
...RETRAB!

TONY, WHAT DID YOU JUST CALL ME?

UH... WHY WOULD I CALL YOU BY OUR LAST NAME?

HUH? MILLIE'... WHAT ELSE WOULD I CALL YOU?

YOU WOULDN'T. BUT I KNOW SOMEONE WHO WOULD.

'RETRAB'... I THOUGHT YOU CALLED ME RETRAB...

WHAT? NO... NO!

YOU'RE GOING TO LEAVE AGAIN, AREN'T YOU?!

AREN'T YOU?!

TONY, I...

YOU CAN'T GO!

PLEASE MILLIE! IT'S SO LONELY! I NEED YOU!

THERE'S SOMEONE ELSE WHO NEEDS ME RIGHT NOW...

I'M SORRY.

151

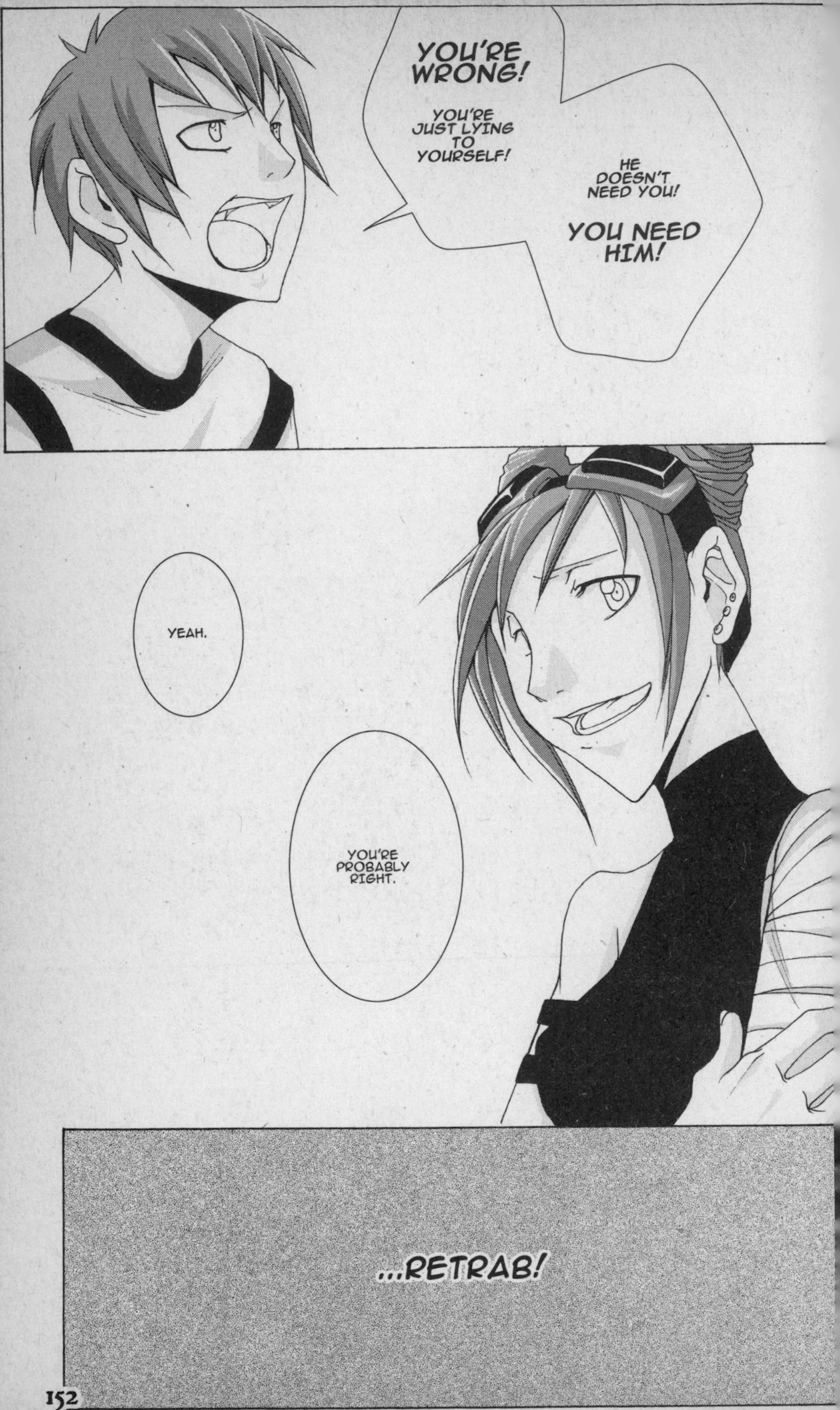
YOU'RE WRONG!
YOU'RE JUST LYING TO YOURSELF!
HE DOESN'T NEED YOU!
YOU NEED HIM!
YEAH.
YOU'RE PROBABLY RIGHT.
...RETRAB!

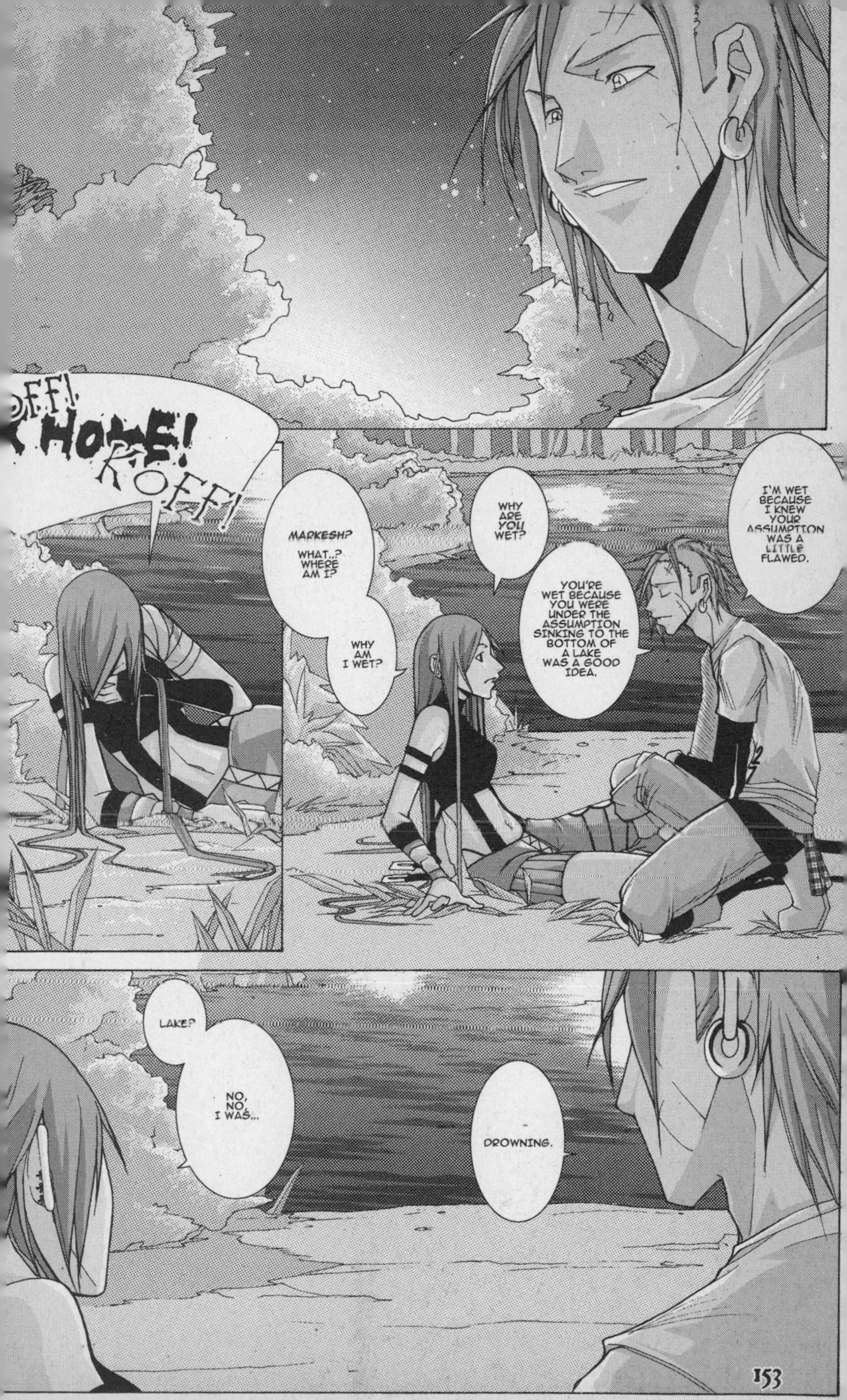

OFF! HOME! KROFF!
MARKESH?
WHAT..? WHERE AM I?
WHY AM I WET?
WHY ARE YOU WET?
YOU'RE WET BECAUSE YOU WERE UNDER THE ASSUMPTION SINKING TO THE BOTTOM OF A LAKE WAS A GOOD IDEA.
I'M WET BECAUSE I KNEW YOUR ASSUMPTION WAS A LITTLE FLAWED.
LAKE?
NO, NO, I WAS...
DROWNING.

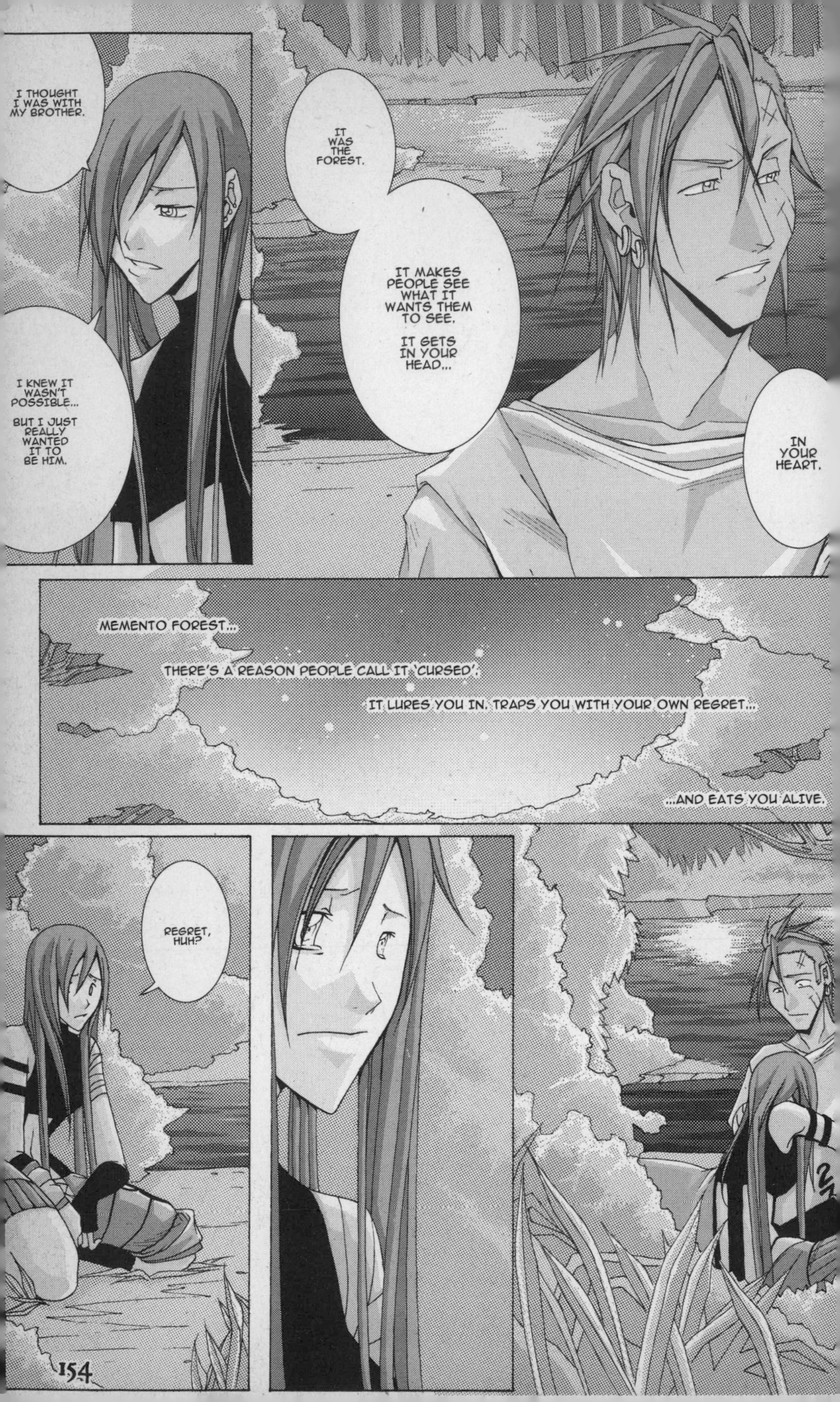

I THOUGHT I WAS WITH MY BROTHER.
I KNEW IT WASN'T POSSIBLE... BUT I JUST REALLY WANTED IT TO BE HIM.
IT WAS THE FOREST.
IT MAKES PEOPLE SEE WHAT IT WANTS THEM TO SEE. IT GETS IN YOUR HEAD...
IN YOUR HEART.
MEMENTO FOREST...
THERE'S A REASON PEOPLE CALL IT 'CURSED'.
IT LURES YOU IN. TRAPS YOU WITH YOUR OWN REGRET...
...AND EATS YOU ALIVE.
REGRET, HUH?

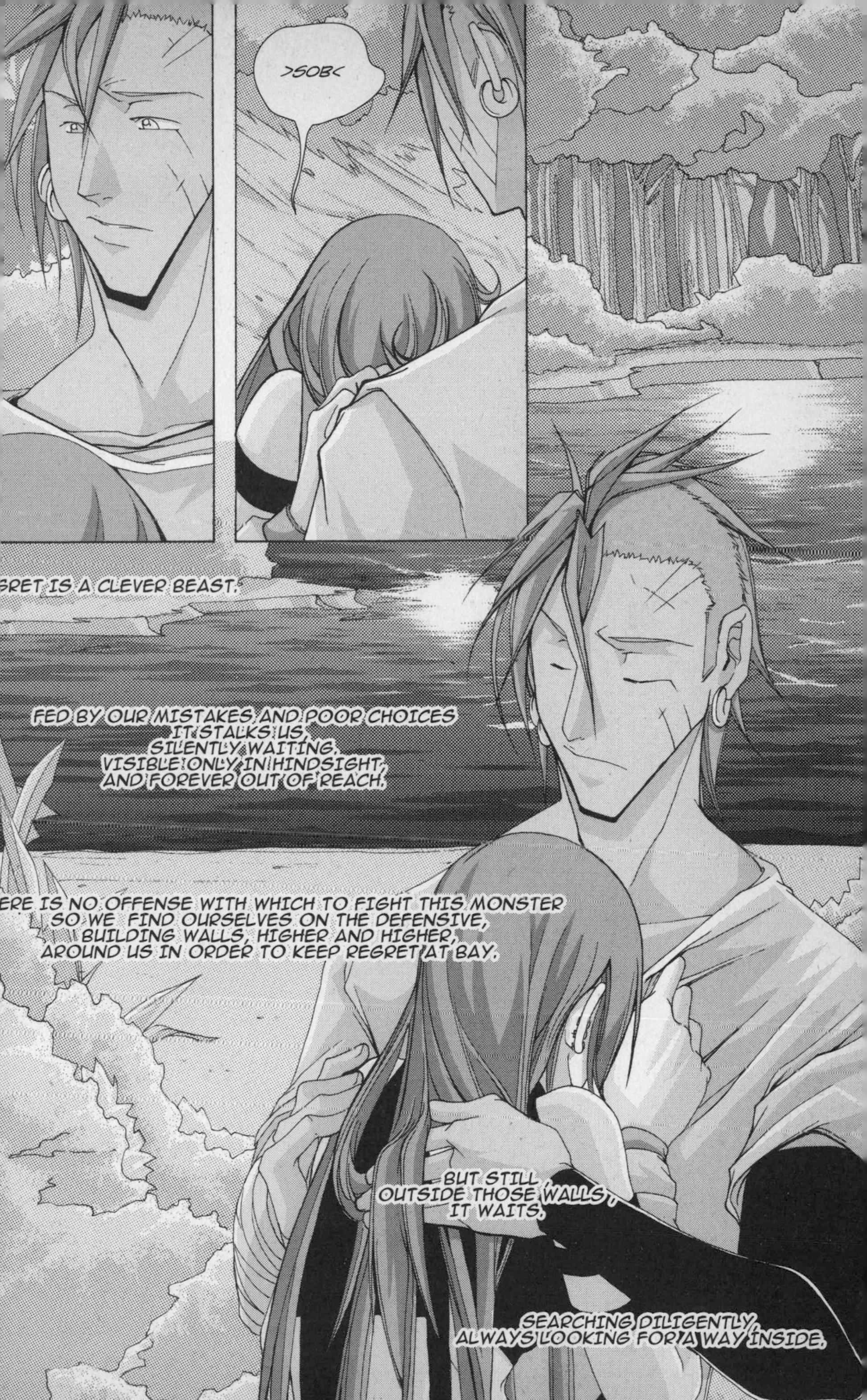
>SOB<
GRET IS A CLEVER BEAST.
FED BY OUR MISTAKES AND POOR CHOICES
IT STALKS US,
SILENTLY WAITING.
VISIBLE ONLY IN HINDSIGHT,
AND FOREVER OUT OF REACH.
ERE IS NO OFFENSE WITH WHICH TO FIGHT THIS MONSTER
SO WE FIND OURSELVES ON THE DEFENSIVE,
BUILDING WALLS, HIGHER AND HIGHER,
AROUND US IN ORDER TO KEEP REGRET AT BAY.
BUT STILL
OUTSIDE THOSE WALLS,
IT WAITS.
SEARCHING DILIGENTLY,
ALWAYS LOOKING FOR A WAY INSIDE.

END VOLUME ONE

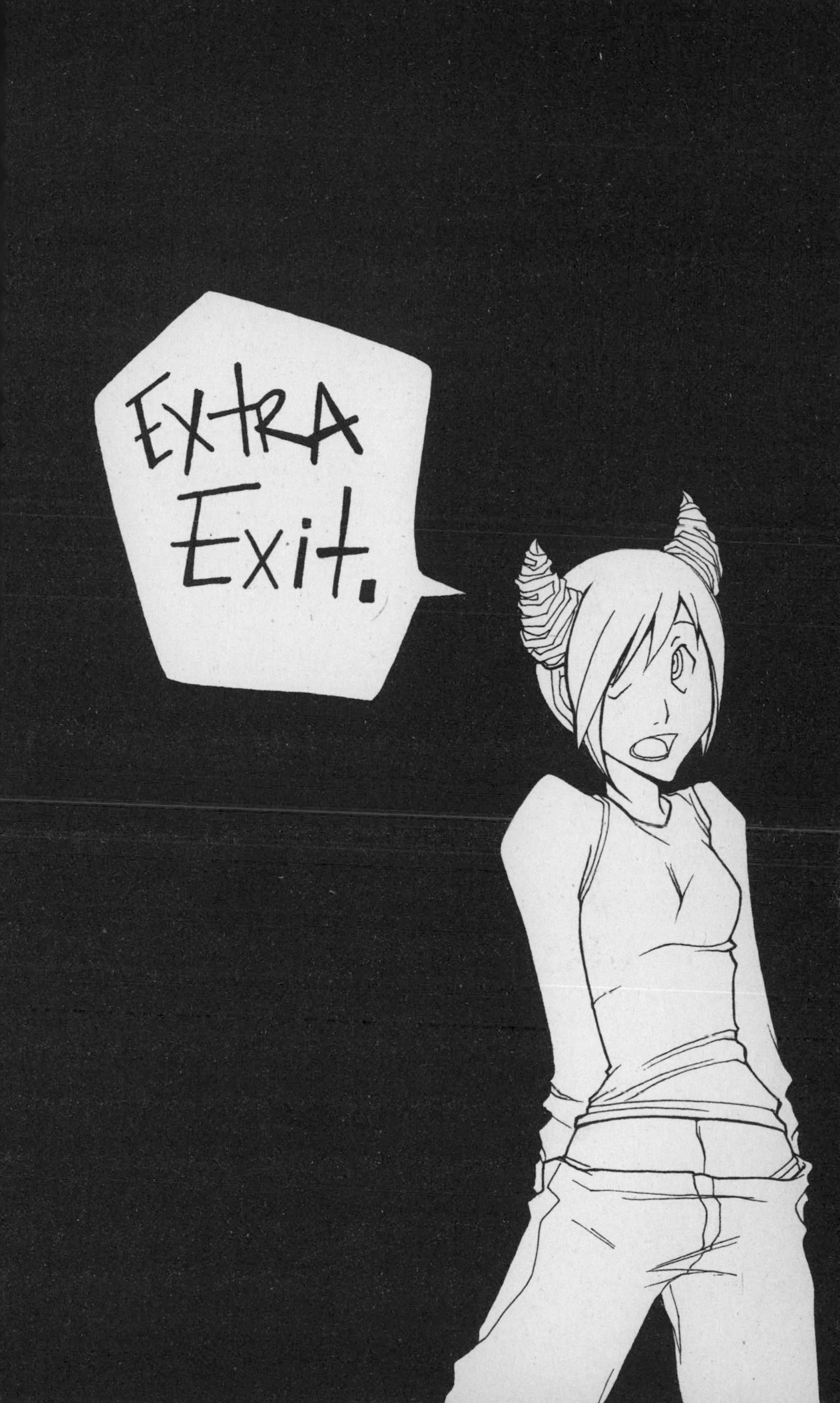
Extra Exit.

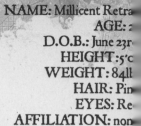

Retrab

NAME: Millicent Retra

AGE: 2

D.O.B.: June 23r

HEIGHT: 5'c

WEIGHT: 84lb

HAIR: Pin

EYES: Re

AFFILIATION: non

FAVORITE FOOD:
Blueberry Crepes
LEAST FAVORITE FOOD:
Vegetables of any kind
LIKES:
Cats, junk food, card games, Markesh
DISLIKES:
Being alone, lies, unimaginative peopl
bugs, rainy days

IMAGE SONGs
'Little Wing' - Lindberg
(from the album 'Lindberg III'

'Extraordinary Girl' - Green Day
(from the album 'American Idiot'

Markesh

NAME: Markesh Arcadia
AGE: 18
D.O.B.: April 2nd
HEIGHT: 6′4″
WEIGHT: 152lbs
HAIR: Orange
EYES: Blue (right) & Yellow (left)
AFFILIATION: none

FAVORITE FOOD:
Anything spicy
LEAST FAVORITE FOOD:
Anything sweet
LIKES:
Sleeping, being outside, warm weather
DISLIKES:
Crowded places, bright lights, being corrected by others

IMAGE SONGs:
'In the Shadows' - The Rasmus
(from the album 'Dead Letters')

静かの海 - Scudelia Electro
(from the album '5er')

Abraxas

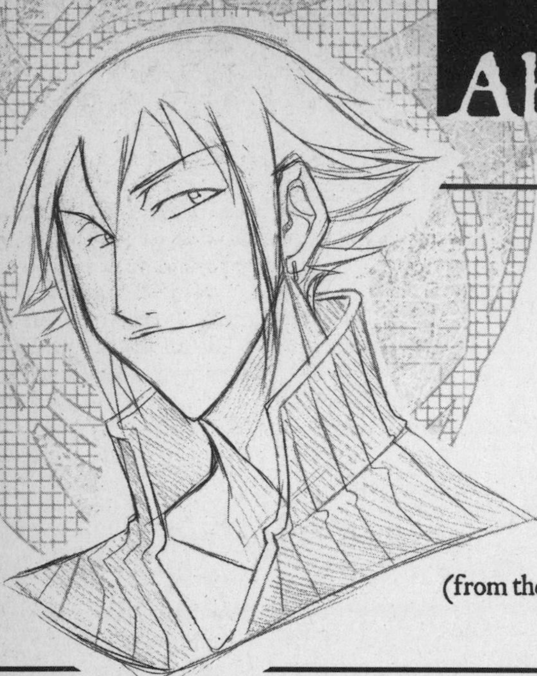

NAME: Abraxas Arcadia
AGE: 21
D.O.B.: January 1st
HEIGHT: 6'1"
WEIGHT: 141lbs
HAIR: Milky White
EYES: Blue
AFFILIATION: LOGOS

IMAGE SONG:
'The Mahout'- Yoko Kanno
(from the album 'Uncharted Waters II SE')

Ren

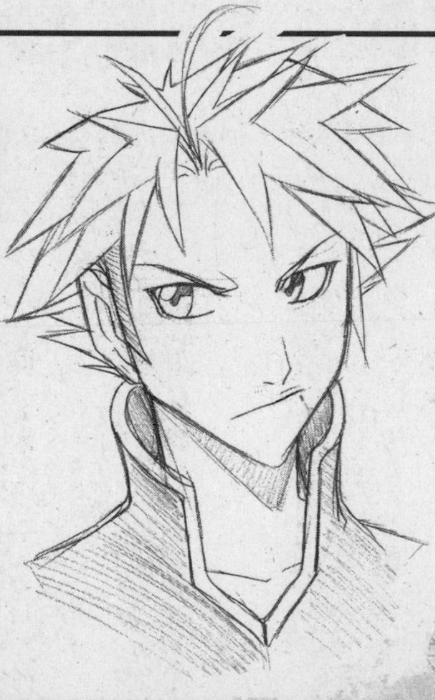

NAME: Ren Cobalt
AGE: 14
D.O.B.: April 13th
HEIGHT: 4'8"
WEIGHT: 69lbs
HAIR: Pale Silver
EYES: Blue
AFFILIATION: LOGOS

IMAGE SONG:
'Endless Loop'- Saiga Mitsuki
(from the album 'Luster')

LOGOS
uniform design

In designing costumes for this comic I went though the most designs while working on the basic design of the LOGOS uniforms. They were something I was going to have to draw frequently so I wanted to make sure I stuck with a design I really liked. Out of all the designs I worked on I narrowed it down to these three and ended up settling on the one you've seen in the comic. So far Ren's been the only one in uniform to show up but I promise you'll be seeing a lot more of LOGOS in future issues.

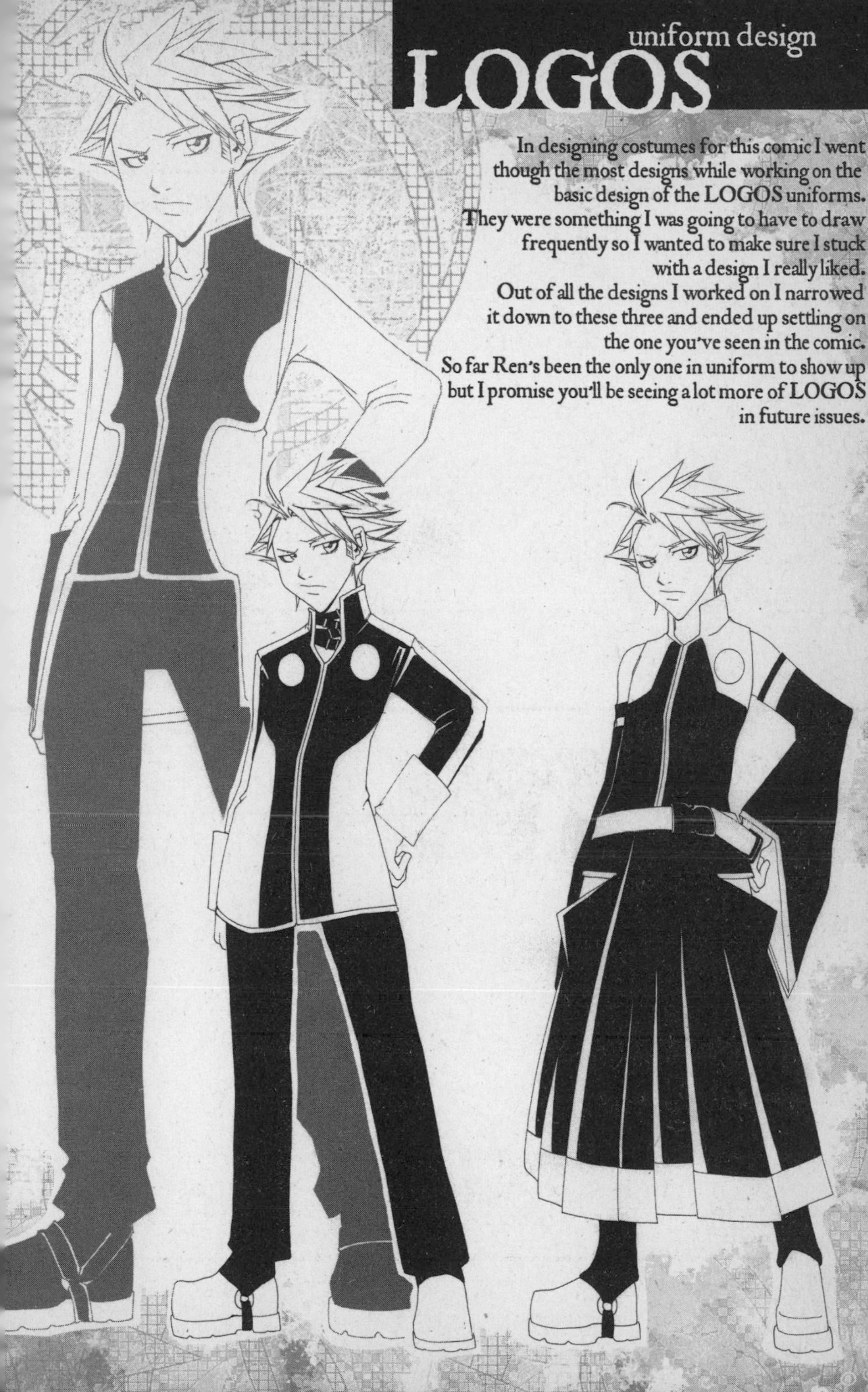

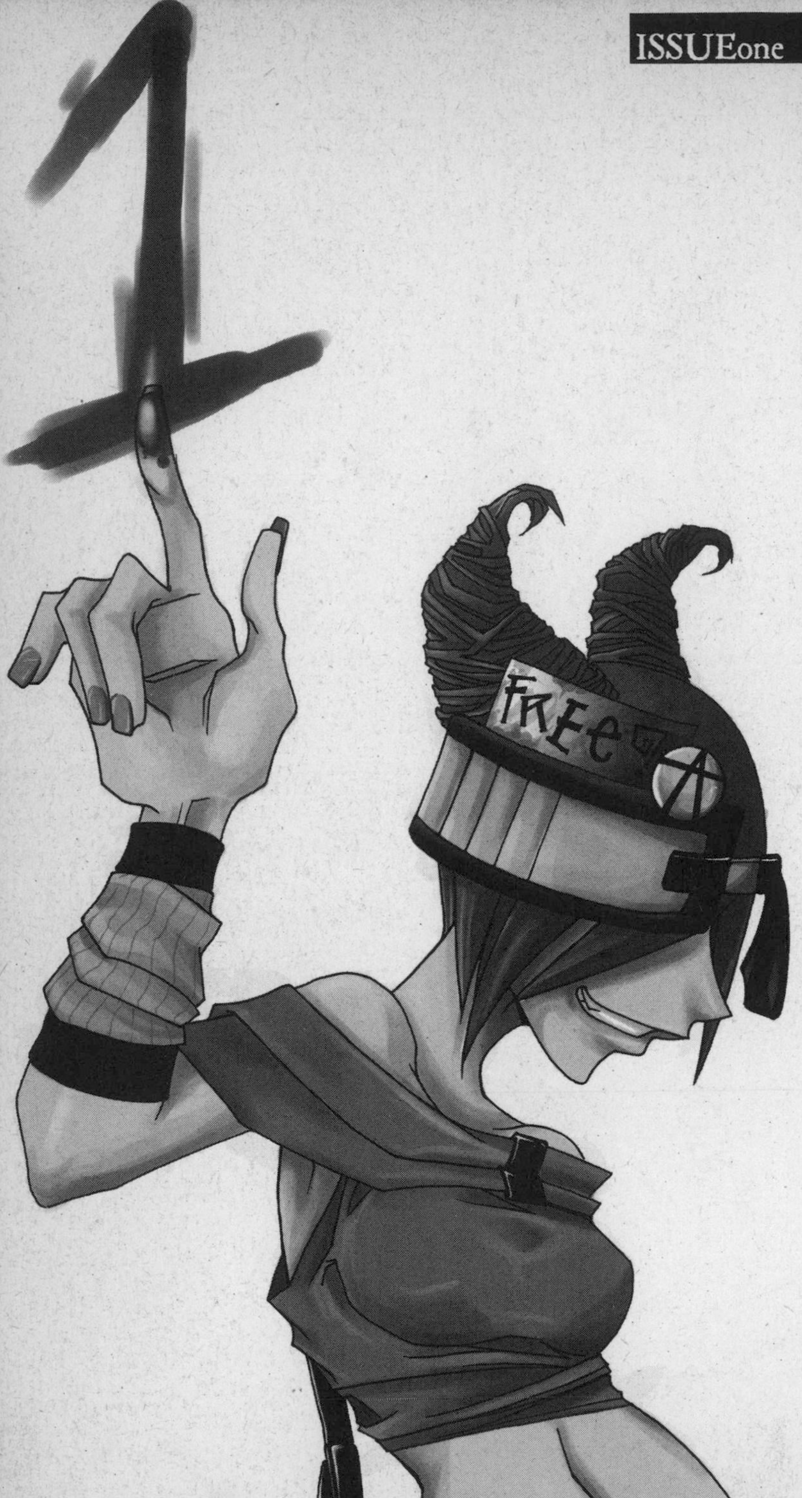
1
FREE

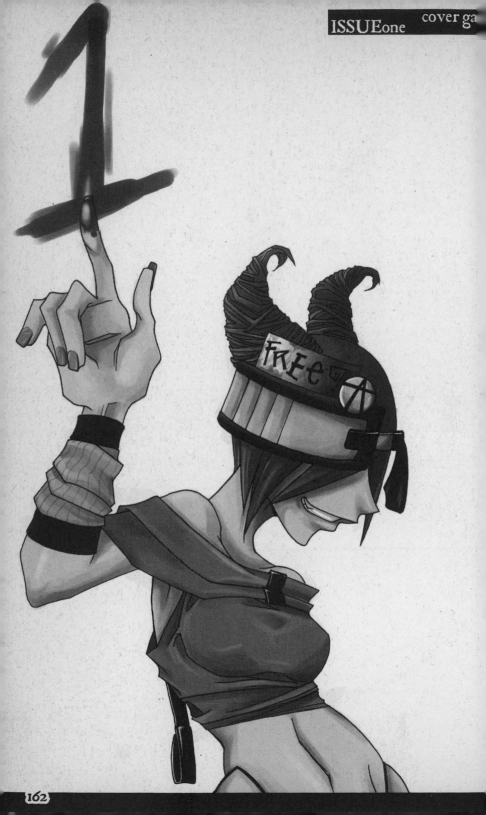

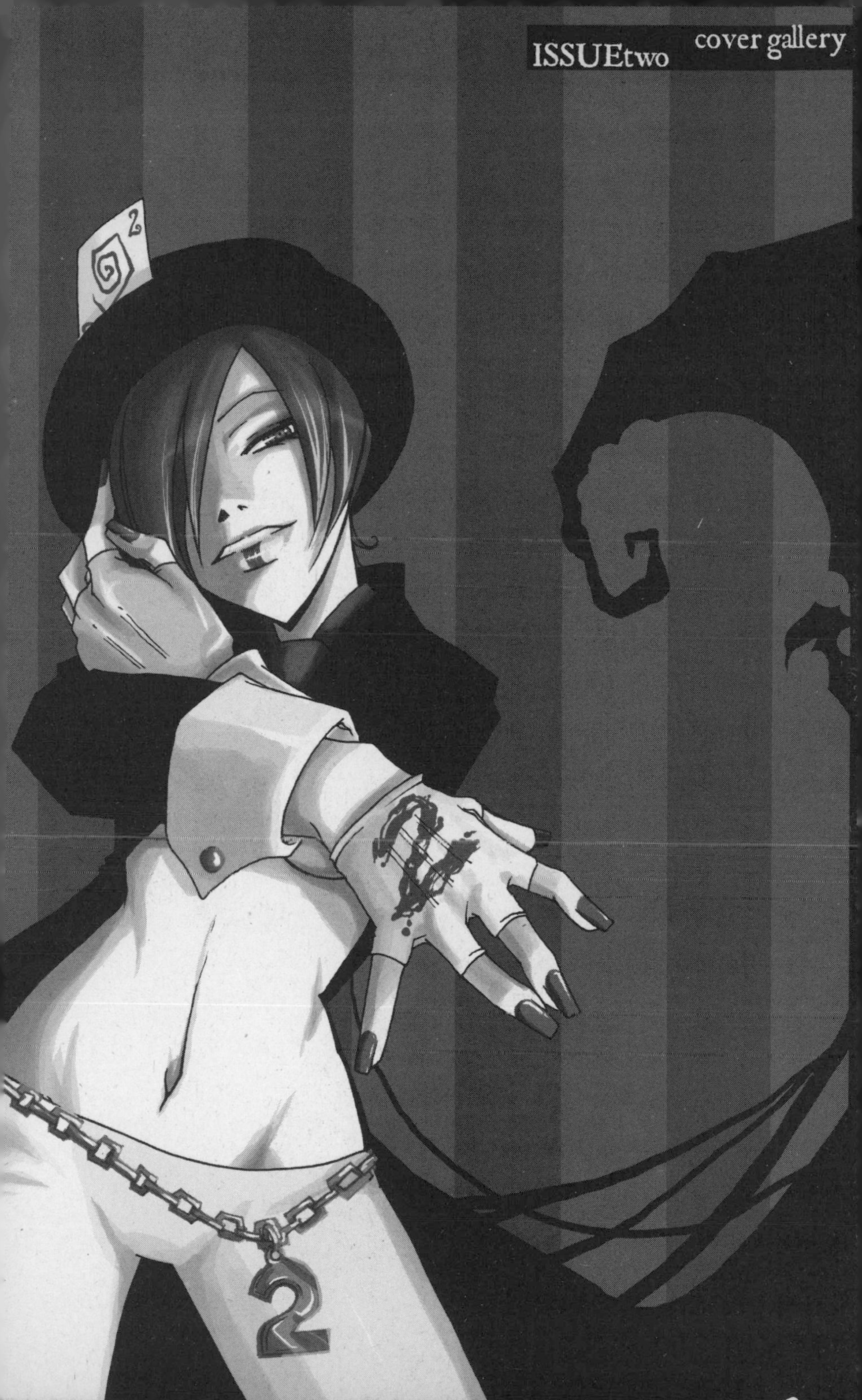
2
2

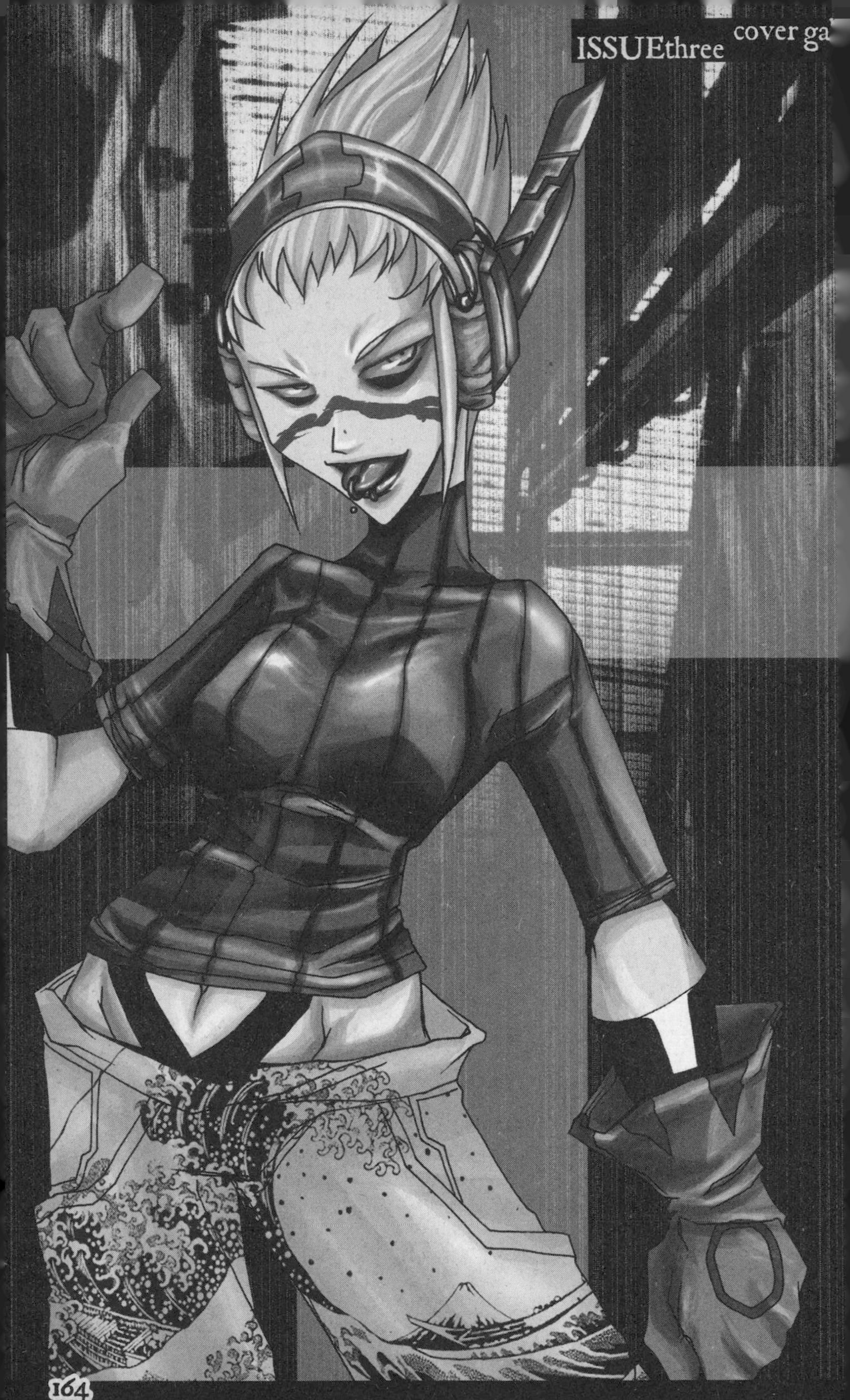

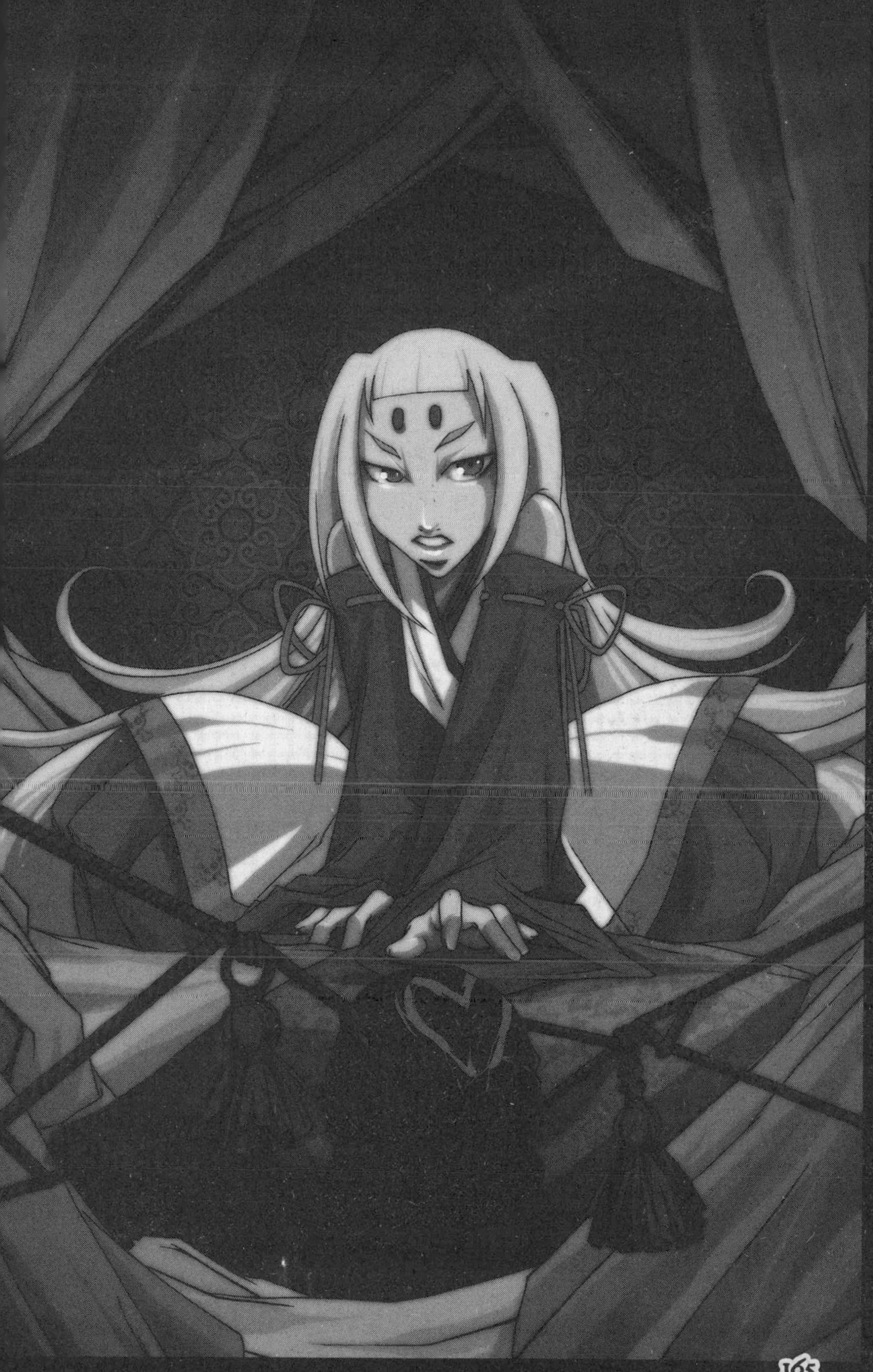

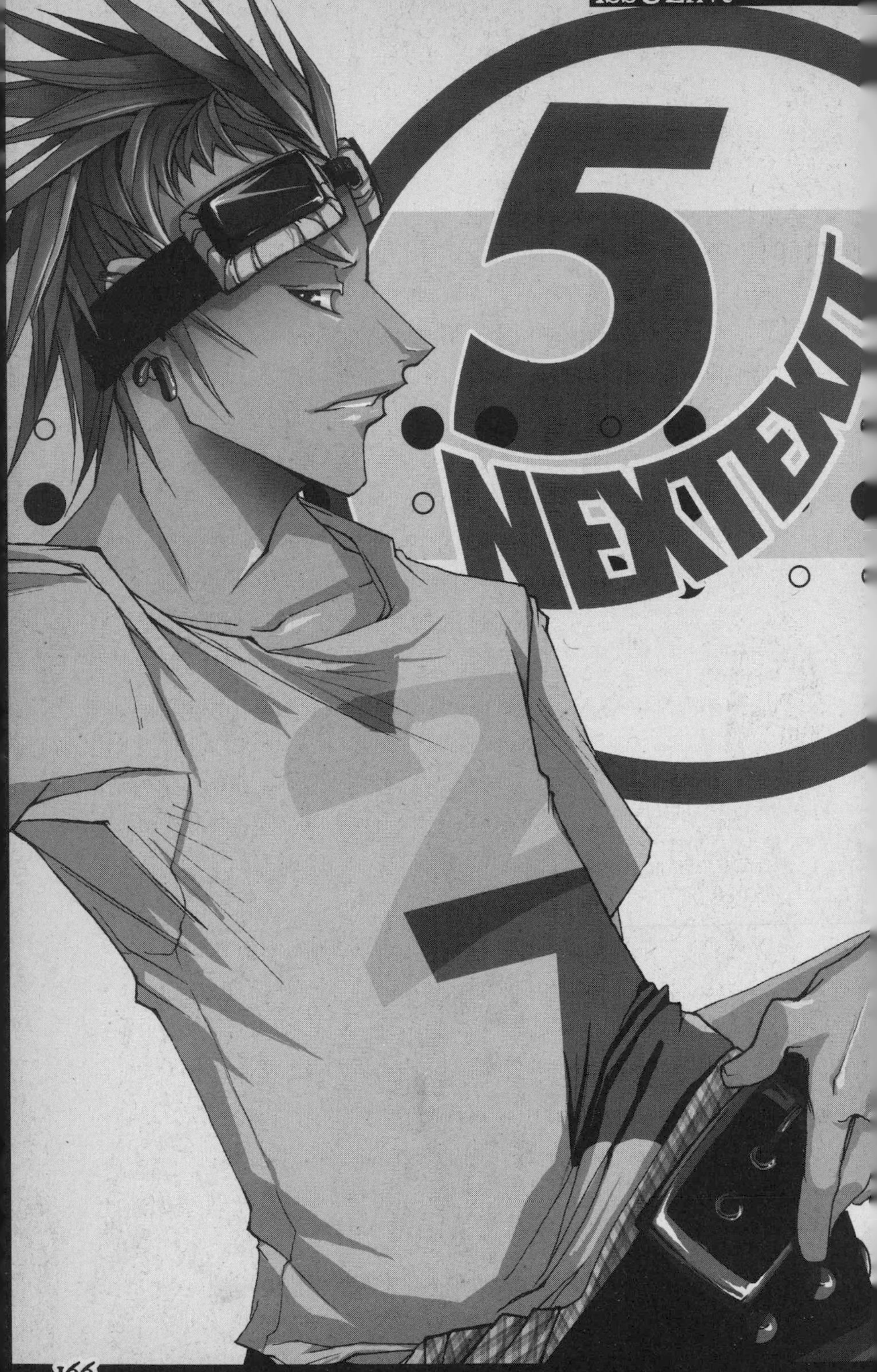

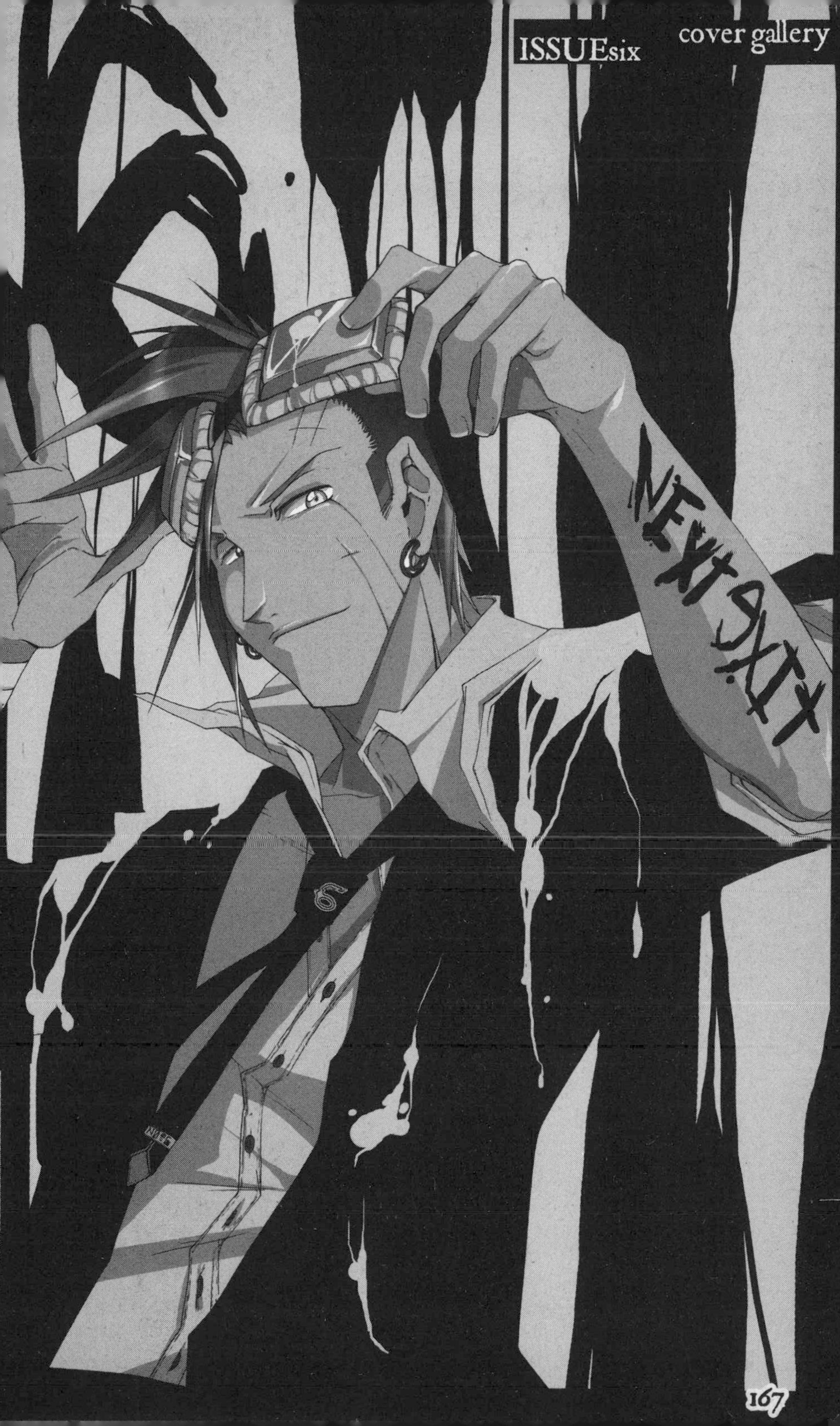
NEXT EXIT

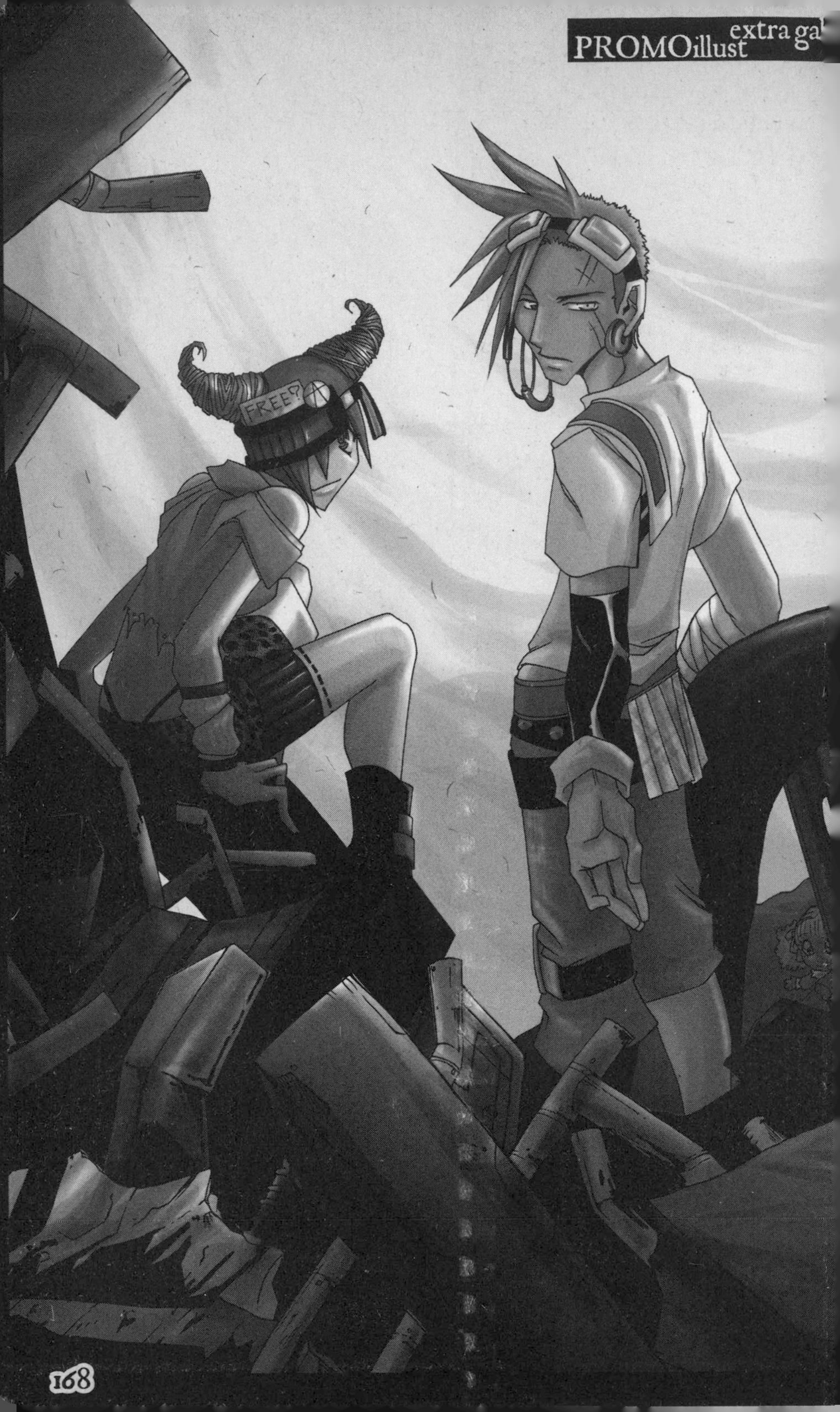
FREE?